MW00986145

MEN AND MASCULINITY IN THE HEBREW BIBLE AND BEYOND

The Bible in the Modern World, 33

MEN AND MASCULINITY IN THE HEBREW BIBLE AND BEYOND

edited by

Ovidiu Creangă

SHEFFIELD PHOENIX PRESS

2010

Copyright © 2010 Sheffield Phoenix Press

Published by Sheffield Phoenix Press
Department of Biblical Studies, University of Sheffield,
45 Victoria Street, Sheffield S3 7QB
UK

www.sheffieldphoenix.com

A CIP catalogue record for this book
is available from the British Library

BWHEBB [Hebrew] and BWGRKL [Greek] PostScript© Type 1
and TrueType™ fonts Copyright© 1994–2002 BibleWorks, LLC.
All rights reserved. These Biblical Greek and Hebrew fonts
are used with permission and are from BibleWorks,
software for Biblical exegesis and research.

Typeset by ISB Typesetting
Printed on acid-free paper by Lightning Source UK Ltd, Milton Keynes

ISBN 978-1-907534-09-6

ISSN 1747-9630

CONTENTS

PREFACE

The beginnings of this book go back to a late-afternoon conversation I had with David J.A. Clines near the Sheffield Phoenix Press book-stand at the Annual Meeting of the Society of Biblical Literature in 2008, held that year in Boston. Wanting to relax after an intense session on Warfare in Ancient Israel, where I had just given a paper, I made it for the book-hall. As I was rambling around stalls and making small conversations with other publishers and scholars—some genuinely interested in buying or selling books, others, like me, desperately needing a respite from academic sessions—I bumped into David Clines. Casually, and knowing that David had written a number of studies on biblical masculinity, I mentioned that I could not find anywhere in the book-hall one volume devoted specifically to masculinity in the Hebrew Bible. That comment was enough to make David pull out a small notebook from his pocket and sketch down a few ideas for such a book. I had no idea that he intended me to edit the book. But he did, apparently. Thus began our collaboration on the present volume—a walk, a talk, a notebook, and an invitation to gather together a group of scholars and submit a book proposal, to which I happily agreed.

As all editors know, one's labour can be tremendously aided by the quality of people contributing. Here, again, I was privileged to have found wonderful colleagues, some of whom I had known, and others whose work I had read but had not yet met in person, but all enthusiastic about the project. A few of us have 'tested the waters' of biblical masculinity during a session at the 2009 SBL International Meeting at the Gregorian University in Rome, Italy, where I was fortunate enough to chair a new program on masculinity in the Hebrew Bible. I was searching for an audience and a new platform to exchange ideas on this newly emerging topic. The response was encouraging, both in terms of numbers of people attending and the quality of discussions that followed. Indeed, I want to thank the attending members for their questions that prompted very useful discussions. I also wish to thank the other two members of the panel, Ela Lazarewicz-Wyrzykowska and Marcel V. Măcelaru, for their papers. In the audience we found more senior colleagues, like Nili Wazana and, of course, David Clines, both of whose questions and comments benefited all those attending.

Small research grants were received from various sources to enable the participation of all panellists in the SBL Rome session. In particular, I want to thank the ever generous Raţiu Family Charitable Foundation for their repeated financial support. I am also grateful to the editors of the *Journal of Men, Masculinity and Spirituality* for granting permission to reprint Roland Boer's article (*JMMS* 4/1 [2010]: 19-31). In addition, I wish to thank the board of editors at Sheffield Phoenix Press, and especially David Clines, for publishing the studies on biblical men and masculinities collected in this volume. And of course, my special thanks go to those who have really made this book at all possible—its contributors. I thank each one of them for getting onboard with the tight schedule of this volume and for trusting me, junior to some of them, with their work.

Ovidiu Creangă
March 2010

LIST OF CONTRIBUTORS

ROLAND BOER (PhD McGill University) is research professor at the University of Newcastle, Australia. Among numerous works, he has recently completed a five-volume work called *The Criticism of Heaven and Earth*. The first two volumes, *Criticism of Heaven* (Brill and Haymarket 2007) and *Criticism of Religion* (Brill 2009) have been published, while the remaining three will be published in 2010–2011.

DAVID J.A. CLINES (PhD University of Amsterdam) is Professor Emeritus of Biblical Studies, University of Sheffield. He is editor of the *Dictionary of Classical Hebrew*, and publisher and director of Sheffield Phoenix Press. His main research interests are in the language of the Hebrew Bible and in literary and ideological criticism of its literature.

OVIDIU CREANGĂ (PhD King's College London) has been a postdoctoral researcher and visiting assistant professor at King's College London, Roehampton University in London and St Michael's College in Cardiff, Wales, UK. His research interests are gender studies, methods of biblical interpretation, the literature and religion of Israel before and during the Babylonian exile, all of which inform his forthcoming book on identity, violence and memory in the Book of Joshua.

C.J. PATRICK DAVIS (PhD University of Manchester) teaches in the Department of Religious Studies at Trinity Western University in Langley, BC, Canada, and is Assistant to the Geneva Chair in Worldview and Religious Studies. Research interests include prophetic traditions and the development of Scripture in Second Temple Judaism.

BRIAN DIPALMA is a Ph.D. student in the Hebrew Bible program at Emory University. He maintains a keen interest in gender studies, especially in the relationship between masculinity and violence in the book of Judges, and the ways in which that link might be deconstructed.

MARK K. GEORGE (PhD Princeton Theological Seminary) is Associate Professor of Hebrew Bible at the Iliff School of Theology in Denver, Colorado. His research focuses on critical spatial theory and the Bible, and he has recently published *Israel's Tabernacle as Social Space* (SBL, 2009) and the

Parashat Terumah (Exod. 25.1–27.19) entry in *Torah Queries: Weekly Commentaries on the Hebrew Bible* (NYU Press, 2009).

SUSAN E. HADDOX (PhD Emory University) is Assistant Professor of Religious Studies at University of Mount Union, Alliance, Ohio. She is interested in the portrayal of sex and gender in the biblical texts, and her research has focused primarily on the rhetoric of masculinity in Hosea and Genesis.

MARIA HARALAMBAKIS (PhD University of Manchester) teaches in the subject area of Religions and Theology at the University of Manchester. Her research interests include: codocology (of late antique and mediaeval manuscripts), textual criticism, narratology (applied to narratives of Hebrew Bible, Apocrypha and Pseudepigrapha) and the reception of ancient (Jewish) texts in mediaeval (Byzantine, Slavonic) contexts.

SANDRA JACOBS (PhD University of Manchester) is an honorary research associate in the Department of Hebrew and Jewish Studies at University College London. Her research is focussed upon the body and its disfigurement in biblical law, with particular reference to ANE literary and epigraphic sources.

ELA LAZAREWICZ-WYRZYKOWSKA (PhD University of Manchester) is Assistant Director of the MA Programme in Pastoral Theology at Cambridge Theological Federation. Her research interests include interdisciplinary approaches to the Hebrew Bible, biblical intercession, gender, and (in)fertility and reproductive loss in biblical literature.

STEPHEN D. MOORE (PhD Trinity College Dublin) is Professor of New Testament at Drew Theological School, Madison, New Jersey. His many books include *God's Gym: Divine Male Bodies of the Bible* (Routledge, 1996); *God's Beauty Parlor: And Other Queer Spaces in and around the Bible* (Stanford University Press, 2001); and *New Testament Masculinities* (Society of Biblical Literature, 2003), which he co-edited with Janice Capel Anderson.

CHERYL STRIMPLE is a PhD candidate in Biblical Studies at Southern Methodist University, Dallas, Texas. Her research interests include Deuteronomy and Deuteronomistic studies, narrative-rhetorical criticism, disability studies, biblical law and gender studies in the Hebrew Bible.

ANDREW TODD (PhD Cardiff University) is Director of the Centre for Chaplaincy Studies, St Michael's College, Cardiff, and former President of the Cambridge Theological Federation. A Practical Theologian, his research interests include chaplaincy discourse and practice, biblical interpretation and discourse analysis, especially in relation to the interaction of authoritative and lay discourses.

ABBREVIATIONS

AA	*American Anthropologist*
AB	Anchor Bible
ABD	David Noel Freedman (ed.), *The Anchor Bible Dictionary* (New York: Doubleday, 1992)
AGR	Advances in Gender Research
ATJ	*Ashland Theological Journal*
Bib	*Biblica*
BibInt	*Biblical Interpretation*
BDB	F. Brown, S. Driver, and C. Briggs (eds.), *The Brown-Driver-Briggs Hebrew and English Lexicon* (Peabody, MA: Hendrickson Publishers, 2000)
BIS	Biblical Interpretation series
BL	Bible and Literature
BibRev	*Bible Review*
BKAT	Biblischer Kommentar: Altes Testament
BZAW	Beihefte zur *Zeitschrift für die alttestamentliche Wissenschaft*
CBQ	*Catholic Biblical Quarterly*
CC	Continental Commentaries
CCEPOA	Les cahiers de Centre d'Etude Proche-Orient Ancien
CI	*Critical Inquiry*
CSHJ	Chicago Studies in the History of Judaism
DJD	Discoveries in the Judean Desert
ET	English translation
FOTL	Forms of Old Testament Literature
FT	*Feminist Theory*
GCT	Gender, Culture, Theory
HAR	*Hebrew Annual Review*
HBM	Hebrew Bible Monographs
HBT	*Horizons in Biblical Theology*
HR	*History of Religions*
HSM	Harvard Semitic Monographs
HTR	*Harvard Theological Review*
HUCA	*Harvard Union College Annual*
IBCTP	Interpretation: A Bible Commentary for Teaching and Preaching
IDB	Keith R. Crim and George A. Buttrick (eds.), *The Interpreter's Dictionary of the Bible* (5 vols; Nashville: Abingdon Press, 1962)
ICC	International Critical Commentary
IESBS	Neil J. Smelser and Paul B. Baltes (eds.), *International Encyclopedia of the Social and Behavioral Sciences* (26 vols; Oxford: Elsevier Science, 2001)

IESS	David L. Sills (ed.), *International Encyclopedia of the Social Sciences* (18 vols; New York: Macmillan, 1968)
ILR	*Israel Law Review*
ISBE	Geoffrey W. Bromiley (ed.), *The International Standard Bible Encyclopedia* (4 vols; Grand Rapids, MI: Eerdmans, 1986)
ISBL	Indiana Studies in Biblical Literature
ITC	International Theological Commentary
JANES(CU)	*Journal of the Ancient Near Eastern Society of Columbia University*
JApL	*Journal of Applied Linguistics*
JBL	*Journal of Biblical Literature*
JCS	*Journal of Cuneiform Studies*
JDDS	Jian Dao Dissertation Series
JEnc	Isidore Singer (ed.), *Jewish Encyclopedia* (12 vols; New York and London: Funk and Wagnalls, 1901–1906)
JHistSex	*Journal of the History of Sexuality*
JMMS	*Journal of Men, Masculinity, and Spirituality*
JNES	*Journal of Near Eastern Studies*
JSHRZ	Jüdische Schriften aus hellenistisch-römischer Zeit
JSIJ	*Jewish Studies, an Internet Journal*
JSNTSup	*Journal for the Study of the New Testament*, Supplement Series
JSOT	*Journal for the Study of the Old Testament*
JSOTSup	*Journal for the Study of the Old Testament*, Supplement Series
JSP	*Journal for the Study of Pseudepigrapha*
JSR	*Journal of Sleep Research*
JSS	*Journal of Semitic Studies*
JTS	*Journal of Theological Studies*
KCLSBG	King's College London Studies in the Bible and Gender
KJV	King James Version
LCL	Loeb Classical Library
LHB/OTS	Library of Hebrew Bible/Old Testament Studies
LXX	Septuagint
MT	Masoretic Text
NIDB	Katharine Doob Sakenfeld (ed.), *New Interpreter's Dictionary of the Bible* (5 vols; Nashville: Abingdon, 2006–2009)
NJB	New Jerusalem Bible
NJPS	New Jewish Publication Society translation of the Tanakh
NKJV	New King James Version
NRSV	New Revised Standard Version
ÖBS	Österreichische biblische Studien
OTL	Old Testament Library
PAPS	*Proceedings of the American Philosophical Society*
PC	Papyrologica coloniensia
RB	*Revue biblique*
RevExp	*Review and Expositor*
RSB	*Ricerche storico bibliche*
RSV	Revised Standard Version
QualHealthRes	*Qualitative Health Research*
SAA	State Archives of Assyria
SBLDS	Society of Biblica Literature Dissertation Series
SBLSS	Society of Biblical Literature Semeia Studies

SBLSympS	Society of Biblical Literature Symposium Series
SELVOA	Studi epigrafici e linguistici sul vincino oriente antico
SemeiaSt	Semeia Studies
SNTSMS	Society for New Testament Studies Monograph Series
STL	*Stanford Literature Review*
StudLit	*Studia liturgica*
TAPS	Transactions of the American Philosophical Society
TGN	Theory, Geography, Narrative
TheorSoc	*Theory and Society*
TJ	*Trinity Journal*
TOTC	Tyndale Old Testament Commentaries
TUGAL	Texte und Untersuchungen zur Geschichte der altchristlichen Literatur
TynB	*Tyndale Bulletin*
UF	*Ugarit-Forschungen*
VT	*Vetus Testamentum*
WBC	Word Biblical Commentary
WTJ	*Westminster Theological Journal*
YJC	*Yale Journal of Criticism*
ZAW	*Zeitschrift für die alttestamentliche Wissenschaft*

Part I

SUBORDINATING MEN, DESTABILIZING HEGEMONIES

FAVOURED SONS AND SUBORDINATE MASCULINITIES

Susan E. Haddox

The book of Genesis tells the story of the emergence of the nation of Israel, through its eponymous ancestors. In the course of the book, the lineage of Israel, as well as its relationship to its neighbors, is laid out through family structures. The stories are marked with difficult and unexpected births, sibling rivalries, and intense maternal interest, which emphasize the significance of the designated heir.[1] While these rivalries occur primarily at the human level, God clearly affirms the decisions about which men should be the patriarchs. Many studies have explored various aspects of the relationships and rivalries in Genesis, but few have looked at the way the masculinity of the characters is constructed and the role it plays in the selection of the favored son.[2] In this essay I will first briefly consider Abraham's masculinity, then concentrate on the portrayal of two pairs of brothers, Isaac and Ishmael and Jacob and Esau, applying insights from the field of masculinity studies to assess how each man fits or falls short of aspects of the construction of masculinity in the ancient Near East.[3] While conforming to some elements of the hegemonic standard of masculinity, the man most favored by God often appears less masculine than the rejected brother. Finally, I will examine why the men displaying the subordinate masculinities are chosen.

1. The lineage stories of Isaac (Gen. 21), Jacob (Gen. 25; 27), Joseph (Gen. 30; 37), Perez (Gen. 38), and Ephraim (Gen. 48) all involve conflict around the first and later born sons with respect to who is the true heir to the tradition.

2. Deborah Sawyer (2004) examines Abraham's masculinity (see below), but not the role masculinity plays in selecting subsequent generations. Johanna Stiebert (2002) discusses the way Esau is portrayed as honorable in Genesis, but is shamed and feminized in the prophetic texts, but she does not address how the masculinity of Jacob and Esau compare. Dennis Olson (2006) looks at the role masculinity plays in the story Adam and Eve, as well as Cain and Abel, but does not compare the brothers' masculinity.

3. Masculinity and femininity are social constructions, rather than biological markers, of sex. Marilyn Strathern provides a typical expression of the implications of gender construction: 'By "gender" I mean those categorizations of persons, artifacts, events, sequences, and so on which draw upon sexual imagery—upon the ways in which the distinctiveness of male and female characteristics make concrete people's ideas about the nature of social relationships' (1988: ix).

Hegemonic Masculinity

Anthropological masculinity studies have shown that across many cultures, conceptions of gender relations and gendered language signify complex relations of power, economics, and social status (Carrigan, Connell, and Lee 1987: 92, 94). Masculinity is thus a multifaceted concept in any culture, and it cannot be ascertained simply by studying individual men, because the social construction is more than the sum of the various individual expressions of masculinity (Sedgwick 1995: 12). While all cultures in actuality display multiple masculinities, in most societies, one ideal is dominant, the standard against which all other masculinities are judged. This is known as hegemonic masculinity. Hegemonic masculinity implies two important concepts for studying the construction of gender in a society. One is the promotion of a particular kind of masculinity at the expense of other expressions. This particular form becomes entrenched in the social structure and reproduced, even if it is not an accurate model of how most men live. Tim Carrigan, who introduced the term hegemonic masculinity, observes: '…the culturally exalted form of masculinity, the hegemonic model so to speak, may only correspond to the actual characters of a small number of men… Yet very large numbers of men are complicit in sustaining the hegemonic model' (Carrigan, Connell, and Lee 1987: 92). Thus the way a society talks about what makes a 'Real Man' is restricted, even if there is a wide variation in how actual men act. The imposition on a society of a particular kind of masculinity as the norm leads into the second concept: hegemonic masculinity propagates itself through the institutions and power structures of society. Carrigan observes that hegemonic masculinity emerges out of a power struggle: 'To understand the different kinds of masculinity demands, above all, an examination of the practices in which hegemony is constituted and contested—in short, the political techniques of the patriarchal social order' (Carrigan, Connell, and Lee 1987: 94). Those who have the power dictate the norms of masculinity. Once the elements of a particular hegemonic masculinity become embedded in the power structures, however, they become self-perpetuating.

In addition to hegemonic masculinity, which dominates the power structures of society, various forms of subordinate masculinities exist. Subordinate masculinities are those that embody characteristics excluded from the definition of hegemonic masculinity, and the men associated with those masculinities suffer in terms of social power and prestige (Connell 2005: 78-79). The relationship between hegemonic and subordinate masculinities (and femininities) is not fixed, however, but requires constant negotiation to maintain hegemony (Cornwall and Lindisfarne 1994b: 24-25). The play between the hegemonic and subordinate variants of masculinity is particularly active in the biblical texts.

Characteristics of Masculinity

Those who are in privileged positions of power, or want to become so, are very concerned to present an image that conforms to the norms of hegemonic masculinity. One of these concerns is not to seem feminine. In the social construction of gender, masculinity, at least in public arenas, frequently represents political and social dominance (Strathern 1988: 77; Gilmore 1996: 60). Becoming like women or feminized is a frequent metaphor used by men to represent loss of social prestige or power.[4] Because of this, there is great concern among men with maintaining and building up their masculinity and keeping themselves from becoming feminized, which would lower their status in many aspects of social life. One way to avoid being identified as a woman is to avoid associating with women and women's areas. In cultures with distinctive roles for men and women, men who choose to frequent the private realm, normally the woman's place, rather than engaging other men in public, are viewed with suspicion (Gilmore 1990: 49-55). David Clines observes this detachment from women in ancient Israel in his study of David's masculinity. David had many wives, but does not appear to be emotionally attached to them (Clines 1995: 206). Not only do real men not look and act like women, but they avoid excessive engagement with them outside of the necessity of procreation.

While the avoidance of appearing feminine is important, the ideals of hegemonic masculinity extend into many other areas. Being a real man is at least as important as not being a woman. Part of being a man is displaying sexual potency, which is clearly intertwined with military and political power in ancient Near Eastern models of masculinity. For example, the epithets in Assyrian royal inscriptions often explicitly claim that the king is a man, and the kings are usually portrayed standing erect with full beards and drawn weapons.[5] In Assyrian iconography the battering ram penetrating the city wall is clearly represented as an extension of the king's phallus (Chapman

---

4.　Conversely, Geoffrey P. Miller in his study of the Song of Deborah proposes that claiming that a society's women were acting like men was an insult and associated with uncouth hill people. He argues that as a riposte, the song accepts the truth of part of the insult and turns it around as a virtue. In this way, the manly women dominate not their own men, but Sisera and the Canaanites (1998: 114). Thus it appears that while women acting as men were generally looked down upon, there were occasions on which they could be celebrated. One should note, however, that the insult in Judges was not solely that the women were manly, but that they dominated their men, who were thus feminized.

5.　Cynthia Chapman in her work on gendered language in warfare notes that the titulary of every Assyrian king from Aššurnasirpal II to Aššurbanipal contained at least one epithet with a form of *zikaru* (man, male, manly one, warrior), implying the king's valiant and potent nature, especially on the battlefield (2004: 23-24).

2004: 173, 179). Conversely, David's decline in power at the end of his life is indicated in 1 Kgs 1.1-4 by the fact that the most beautiful virgin in Israel cannot get a rise out of him. He has lost control of his kingdom and his virility. In 1 Sam. 4.9, the Philistine warriors were encouraged to 'be men' and fight (והייתם לאנשים ונלחמתם). Being a warrior and being a man were closely linked, so that skill in warfare increased one's masculinity. Defeat brings feminization, as seen in Assyrian friezes where the conquered warriors have their beards cut off and are forced to prostrate themselves before the king (Chapman 2004: 39, 173). Potency also implies physical strength and power over other people.

A third key component of masculinity is maintaining one's honor. Honor is another multifaceted concept. On the positive side, it includes generosity and hospitality, characteristics particularly important in the nomadic society portrayed in Genesis.[6] Sodom and Gomorrah, the cities notoriously overthrown in Genesis 19, are known for their wickedness. That wickedness is described in Ezekiel as pride, an unjust distribution of wealth, and mistreatment of the poor (Ezek. 16.48-50). In other words, the cities did not honor the ideals of generosity and hospitality. A second significant part of honor is protecting one's family. This involves providing them with food and shelter and defending them from attackers.[7] Many curses in Assyrian treaties relate to these provisioning/protecting features of masculinity (Chapman 2004: 42-43). One common curse stipulates that if a king violates the treaty, cannibalism will result from his inability to provide food for his people. For example, the Treaty of Aššur-nerari V with Mati'-ilu, king of Arpad, curses the violator, saying: 'May Adad, the canal inspector of heaven and earth, put an end to Mati'-ilu's land, and the people of his land through hunger, want, and famine, may they eat the flesh of their sons and daughters, and may it taste as good to them as the flesh of spring lambs' (Parpola and Watanabe 1988: 11). Similar curses occur in Esarhaddon's Succession Treaty, which phrases the predicted cannibalism in more personal terms for the rebellious king. In the most developed example:

> May Adad, the canal inspector of heaven and earth, cut off sea[sonal flooding] from your land and deprive your fields of [grain], may he [submerge] your land with a great flood; may the locust who diminishes the land devour your harvest; may the sound of mill or oven be lacking from your houses, may the grain for grinding disappear from you; instead of grain may your sons and

6.   For more on the importance of honesty and hospitality for honor, including implied dominance and submission, see Gilmore 1987b and Herzfeld 1987.

7.   Such provisions were often stipulated as a part of ancient Near Eastern marriage contracts (Buss 1969: 88). See also Kelle 2005: 67-68; Hendriks 1982: 67. Provisioning and protection is an important part of honor in contemporary cultures of the Circum-Mediterranean as well. See Gilmore 1990: 42-48.

your daughters grind your bones; may not (even) your (first) finger-joint dip in the dough, may the [...] of your bowls eat up the dough. May a mother [bar the door] to her daughter. In your hunger eat the flesh of your sons! In want and famine may one man eat the flesh of another; may one man clothe himself in another's skin (Parpola and Watanabe 1988: 46).

The Assyrian inscriptions describe defeated kings as cowards, fleeing in fear to save their own lives and abandoning their people, showing that bravery in the protection of one's family is important to honor. For example, Tiglath-Pileser III uses the image of a fleeing bird to describe his defeated enemies: '[...over]threw him and like a bird [...] he fled' (Kuan 1995: 177).

In addition to supplying physical needs, the proper patriarch should ensure his women are protected sexually. It is his job to keep his wives faithful and his daughters chaste (Gilmore 1987: 3-4). Allowing another man to have unauthorized access to the women under his control is a direct threat to a man's masculinity, which leads to great dishonor. When Absalom revolted against David and chased him out of the palace, Absalom had sex with ten of David's concubines on the roof, before the eyes of all Israel. This not only displayed his own potency, but showed that David could not protect his own wives. The text notes that this grave dishonor made Absalom odious to David (כִּי־נִבְאַשְׁתָּ אֶת־אָבִיךָ, 2 Sam. 16.21-22).

The final characteristic of masculinity I will consider is wisdom and persuasiveness (Clines 1995: 220). The ability to show good leadership and to persuade others to agree and conform increases a person's power and thus his masculinity. Honesty and keeping one's word add to a man's persuasiveness, as well as to his honor. Links between masculinity and honesty, especially within kin groups, have been found in the sociological literature in various cultures (Uchendu 2008: 8-9; Crossley 2001: 155-56). The value of wisdom and its links to power, particularly in the ideal monarchy are illustrated in the story of Solomon, whose reputation and influenced increased as a direct result of his desire for wisdom (1 Kgs 3–4). Proverbs 8 also links wisdom and honesty to masculine power through the rule of kings.[8] Conversely, Proverbs 6 links lying to adultery, both of which lead to dishonor (v. 33). A man's honor through persuasiveness is also demonstrated by his willingness to stand up to protect and to advocate for his family and kin group (Gilmore 1990: 45).

Based upon the above analysis, I will use these four areas of masculinity to examine the selected men from Genesis: (1) Avoidance of being feminized, especially avoidance of excessive attachment to women, (2) Potency, including strength, virility, and skill as a warrior, (3) Honor, including provision for

---

8.   Wisdom itself is personified as a woman in Proverbs, which may seem counter its associations with masculinity. It is something that men seek out and possess, however, and is represented as the good chaste bride opposed to the adulterous woman folly (Prov. 7).

and protection of one's family, especially the women, and (4) Persuasiveness, wisdom, and honesty in speech.

Masculinity in Genesis

a. *Abraham*

Having established some criteria of masculinity, I will now move on to a consideration of masculinity in Genesis, beginning with Abraham. Abraham clearly meets some of the standards of masculinity. He is a very successful warrior, doing battles with kings and rescuing his nephew Lot (Gen. 14.13-16). He is a successful herdsman, accumulating considerable wealth (Gen. 13.2). He seems to be articulate and persuasive, even haggling successfully with God (Gen. 18.16-33). In that episode, Abraham seeks to protect the lives of the potentially righteous men of Sodom and Gomorrah and to advocate for justice and honor. Yet in other ways Abraham falls short, particularly with respect to his relations with his wives and sons. In the peculiar wife-sister episode in Gen. 12.10-20 (repeated in Gen. 20), Abram shows a lack of protection of his wife. Rather than ensuring her chastity and her well-being, Abram deceives Pharaoh and allows Sarai to be taken into the royal court in order to protect his own life and to gain riches.[9] He lies to Pharaoh, and later Abimelech, out of fear, hiding behind his wife, rather than standing up for her. It is God who takes on the role of protector, sending a plague upon Pharaoh until Sarai is released. In the area of procreation, Abraham shows little initiative and no control. Instead, it is Sarah and God who are the actors, with Abraham obeying meekly (Sawyer 2004: 169). When she hears the messengers announce the upcoming birth of her son (18.12), Sarah even questions Abraham's potency and ability to give her sexual pleasure in his old age (אחרי בלתי היתה־לי עדנה ואדני זקן), when she hears the messengers announce the upcoming birth of her son (18.12).[10]

Measured against the four characteristics above, then, Abraham has a mixed score. He does not appear to be directly feminized, but he does defer to his wife on important decisions regarding reproduction and inheritance. He is strong and skilled in warfare, and though his potency is questioned, he does father two sons. He does successfully protect his nephew Lot, but purposefully puts his wife in danger on two separate occasions. He also sends Hagar and Ishmael out into the wilderness with nothing but a few loaves and a skin of water, despite the fact that he is a wealthy man. Finally, he shows that he can be persuasive in his negotiations with God and men, but he also

---

9. Randall C. Bailey observes that while the story posits sexual deviance on the foreign monarchs, in the course of the story they are absolved and act with righteousness, once the truth is known (1995: 125).

10. The angel omits the implied insult in the next verse when questioning Abraham.

deceives two different kings, who take offense at the deception (Gen. 12.18-20; 20.9-10). So despite the fact that Abraham is established as a faithful man and the father of great nations, he does not uniformly display the characteristics of hegemonic masculinity.

b. *Isaac and Ishmael*

Next I will turn to Abraham's sons, Isaac and Ishmael. Ishmael is Abraham's firstborn. While birth order is not inherently a part of masculinity, in the patriarchal culture of the time, the firstborn may be expected to receive the greater part of the inheritance and blessing, which bestowed the power and prestige that did add to manliness.[11] The catch in the case of Ishmael is that his mother was Hagar, Sarah's slave. According to the terms of the surrogacy, Ishmael might be expected to be claimed as Sarah's son, but this does not happen in the text.[12] Ishmael remains Hagar's son and therefore has subordinate status. Nonetheless, Abraham favors him, petitioning God in Genesis 17 to look favorably on Ishmael, rather than fulfilling the rather preposterous proposal of granting a son to the aged Sarah. Isaac is the second born, but he is the son of the primary wife. Sarah's claim that he should thus be the primary inheritor is fully supported by God (Gen. 21.12). So in this case, the birth status of the sons is not definitive. Each could conceivably have claims to the inheritance rights and their power.

More pertinent for the issue of masculinity are the blessings each receives from God. In Genesis 16 and 17 God promises both Hagar and Abraham that, although Ishmael is not to be Abraham's primary heir, he will be blessed with being the father of a great nation. In the oracle to Hagar in Gen. 16.12, Ishmael is prophesied to become a wild ass of a man (פֶּרֶא אָדָם) at odds with others. The wild ass is seen in the biblical text as a symbol of sexual virility (Hos. 8.9) and untamed power (Job 39.5-8). The prophecy that he will contend with his fellows sets him up as a warrior. This image of Ishmael is further supported by the description of him in Gen. 21.20 as an expert with the bow (קַשָּׁת). The bow was a common metonym for masculinity in the ancient Near East, representing potency in its many senses, especially in linking prowess in warfare and sexual virility (Haddox 2006: 196-99). Though he is not the chosen son, Ishmael is shown as a virile warrior and the father of

---

11. The case for primogeniture is not clearly established in biblical texts or ancient near eastern practice, as noted by Frederick E. Greenspahn (1996: 69-79), though Abraham and Sarah seem to assume he will inherit (Gen. 17.18; 21.10) and the elder twin Esau was entitled to a birthright (21.31).

12. Sarah claims that she will be built up through Hagar (Gen. 16.2), but it is Abram who is attributed the son (Gen. 16.15) who remains in Hagar's custody. Sarah is left out, as noted by Trible (2006: 42). See Exum 1985: 76; Speiser 1964: 120-21.

twelve sons (Gen. 25.12-18), a fine example of the masculine. The text makes no mention one way or the other about Ishmael's honor or persuasiveness.

The blessings God bestows on Isaac seem at first glance much more positive than those given to Ishmael, renewing the promise of countless descendents and the land of Canaan (Gen. 26.2-5, 23-24). Upon closer inspection, however, it is notable that the blessings are stated as fulfillment of the promise to Abraham and based on Abraham's worth. Isaac is merely the tool through which it will be accomplished.

Isaac's masculinity is ambiguous throughout the text. Isaac's first major scene is Genesis 22, where he is nearly sacrificed by his father. In this story, he appears as a passive figure, questioning his father once as to the missing ram, but otherwise submitting wordlessly to his potential death. Ishmael had also faced a death scene in the desert after being cast out by Abraham, but it was his cries that brought God's attention to his plight and prompted his subsequent salvation (Gen. 21.17). Isaac did not cry out, and the focus of the story is on Abraham.

In his adulthood, Isaac continues to be a relatively passive figure. His father finds a wife for him, and the text notes that he took her into his mother Sarah's tent and thus was 'comforted after the death of his mother' (Gen. 24.67). He is shown here as having a long mourning period, being attached to his mother rather than his father, who had, admittedly, nearly killed him. He loves Rebekah, and when she is found to be barren, he prays to God for offspring for her. In general, Isaac appears more attached to the world of women than to that of men.[13]

Isaac follows his father's footsteps in passing off Rebekah as his sister in Abimelech's kingdom in Genesis 26, but in Isaac's version of this thrice-repeated story, there is little tension. Rebekah has already borne sons, so the patriarchal lineage is not in jeopardy. No man from Gerar takes her as his wife, and the king finds out Isaac's deception by seeing him 'sporting' (מצחק) with Rebekah. Abimelech chastises Isaac and does not give him any gifts, as had the Pharaoh and Abimelech when Sarah had been placed in a similar position by Abraham. In comparison, Isaac's episode looks almost pathetic. His lie does not bring him benefit, but dishonors him in the king's eyes.

After this episode, Isaac gets into an argument with the Philistines over wells that his men have dug, but he puts up no resistance, choosing to move on and avoid conflict (Gen. 26.14-17). He is also chased away from his second set of wells (Gen. 26.18-21). After digging the third set of wells, God finally appears to him and tells him not to be afraid (Gen. 26.24). He is wealthy, but does not seem particularly powerful. He avoids warfare, rather

---

13. Seeman observes that the interior space of the tent is not only representative of women's sphere of influence, but also symbolizes fertility, intimacy, and the covenant community, as opposed to outsiders (1998: 117-18).

than excelling in it. His potency and control of his family come under question as well. He has only two sons Jacob and Esau, who were twins. He shows little authority over these sons. While Abraham arranged Isaac's marriage to Rebekah without consulting him, Isaac's son Esau seems to arrange his own marriages to Hittite women who make Isaac and Rebekah's lives bitter (מרת רוח, Gen. 26.34-35). Jacob's marital arrangements also seem largely out of Isaac's hands. In the J narrative (27.42-45), Isaac is not involved at all, as Rebekah sends Jacob away out of fear for his life. Although the P version (28.46–29.5) has Isaac sending Jacob to Laban to seek an approved wife, Rebekah still initiated the action by complaining about Esau's Hittite wives (Speiser 1964: 215-216; von Rad 1961: 276-77).

Isaac becomes old and enfeebled before his time, becoming blind and easily deceived. Though he expects his death to come soon in Genesis 27, which prompts him to bestow his blessings on his sons, he does not actually die until some 20 years later (Gen. 35.28-29). The text paints a picture of a man who is associated with women, passive, not in control of his own family, blind, and waiting to die. He hardly speaks in the text and when he does, it is to deceive Abimelech or to bestow his blessing on the wrong son. This is not a vision of robust masculinity. God chose Isaac over Ishmael, the wimp over the manly man, but it does not seem to be for any merit of Isaac.

c. *Jacob and Esau*
I will now turn to a consideration of Isaac's sons. Their cases are more complex. Like Ishmael, Esau is the first born, but in this case the first of twins, and his brother Jacob emerges grasping his heel (וידו אחזת בעקב עשו, Gen. 25.25-26). Esau is described as red and hairy from the moment of birth (אדמוני כלו כאדרת). Hairiness, as seen with Absalom and Samson, is associated with virility and strength in the biblical texts (Stiebert 2002: 34). He is an outdoorsman and a skillful hunter, thus becoming his father's favorite (Gen. 25.28). Isaac's own masculinity does not get a boost from this favoritism, however. He prefers his elder son, not seemingly for his robust strength, but rather because he likes the taste of game (Gen. 25.28). Esau apparently inherits this love of food from his father, as he is willing to trade his birthright for a bowl of lentils (Gen. 25.29-34). The image of Esau is a physically strong and powerful man, skilled with the bow, but a bit weak on the intellectual side. His warrior status is confirmed by the secondary blessing he receives from Isaac after Jacob cheats him out of the primary blessing. It sounds similar to God's promise to Ishmael: he will live by the sword. Isaac tells him he will serve his brother, which initially puts him in a subordinate position, but he will later break free of his yoke (ופרקת עלו מעל צוארך, Gen. 27.40). Despite the ominous words of the blessing, when the two brothers reconcile after many years, Esau comes across as the more dominant

figure. Jacob prostrates himself before Esau, giving him many gifts (Gen. 33). Esau shows himself wealthy and generous in his forgiveness. Though he was the wronged party, and has the strength to retaliate, he chooses to be beneficent and show mercy, and thus displays great honor.

Esau also shows control of his own family life, unlike his father. He apparently does not consult with his parents in choosing his initial Hittite brides, but when he sees that these women displease his parents, he tries to make amends and honor their wishes by taking an additional wife from his father's lineage, a daughter of Ishmael (Gen. 28.8-9). In sum, Esau is portrayed as conforming to most of the expectations of masculinity: he is strong in body, hunting, and warfare. He identifies with his father rather than his mother. He is an agent in procuring his marriages. He shows mercy from a position of strength. He is wealthy and has many offspring. He honors his father, though he has mixed reviews in this category, because of the Hittite wives. He falls short of expectations in not showing much intelligence or persuasiveness, at least as a young man.[14]

Jacob's character is quite complex. In contrast with Esau, he is described as smooth, a homebody who prefers to stay near the tents, and a favorite of his mother (Gen. 25.27-28; 27.11). He is a trickster, refusing his brother food until he sells his birthright. He heeds his mother's plan to deceive his father and steal Esau's blessing. While intelligence and persuasiveness is associated with masculinity in the biblical texts, the cunning of a trickster is a different matter.

Examples of tricksters from Genesis include Lot's daughters, who get him drunk to get children by him (Gen. 19.30-38), Rebekah, who connives to get her favored son Jacob blessed (Gen. 27), Rachel, who steals her father's household gods and hides them in her camel saddle during her period (Gen. 31.25-42), Tamar, who dresses like a prostitute and sleeps with her father-in-law to get an heir for her dead husband (Gen. 38), and Potiphar's wife, who gets Joseph thrown into prison when he refuses to sleep with her (Gen. 39.7-20). The role of the trickster is normally taken on by a person who is not in a position of power, as a way to get something accomplished (Niditch 1998: 21-22). A person of power and authority does not need to be a trickster: he can get what he wants without subterfuge. I use the pronoun 'he' purposely here. The woman is normally the trickster, because the woman was in a position of subordination. Thus when Jacob is portrayed as a trickster, it points out his position of subordination. In his early life, Jacob appears feminized. He chooses to associate with the women's space, hanging around the tents,

---

14. This masculine portrayal of Esau is restricted to Genesis. As Johanna Stiebert points out, in the prophetic texts, the masculinity of Esau and the Edomites is repeatedly undermined (2002: 38-39).

rather than the masculine realms of the field, and he takes on the feminine role of trickster (Niditch 1998: 19).[15]

Esau has the claim to greater power and honor as the firstborn favored by the father. Jacob uses trickery to gain that position for himself in collusion with his mother. Because he uses trickery, however, that power is tainted and his masculinity suffers. He has, after all, lied to his own father, as well as defrauded his brother. He is dishonorable, because a man should respect his father and show loyalty to his brothers. In addition, after he succeeds in stealing his brother's blessing through deception, he has to flee for his life. His trickery does not immediately grant him a position of dominance, but makes him appear a coward.

Once he leaves the influence of his mother, however, his masculinity starts to increase, though it remains complicated. First, he shows considerable physical strength. When he arrives at Laban's household and sees Rachel, he single-handedly moves the stone from the mouth of the well, a task normally accomplished by several shepherds working together (Gen. 29.7-10). After leaving Laban's household, he wrestles with the angel of God by the river Jabbok (Gen. 32.23-33 [Eng. 22-32]) and loses only when his opponent hits below the belt (ויגע בכף־ירכו) , so to speak, which has its own implications for virility.[16]

Second, he shows intelligence and wisdom with regard to his task. Jacob shows knowledge of the breeding and robustness of sheep and goats and achieves prosperity in business. While he does not forgo the role of trickster, in Laban's household he is pitted against an even greater trickster. When his actions are contrasted to wily Laban, rather than honest, if dense, Esau, Jacob's cunning comes across much more favorably. The text further assures us that God is with Jacob, which increases his righteousness and honor, despite some devious tactics. When Jacob set out toward Laban, he has a theophany in a dream, in which God renews the promise made to Abraham. Unlike in the promise to Isaac, God blesses Jacob directly (Gen. 28.13-15).

Third, Jacob proves himself virile. He has four wives and thirteen children, twelve of them sons. Jacob's interactions with his wives, however, mark a diminishment of his masculinity. He shows an inordinate love of Rachel. It causes him to lift the heavy well-stone and to strike an unfavorable bargain for the bride-price. Seven years labor is a steep price. According to the laws

15. For private vs. public spaces as gendered, see Strathern 1988: 77. Seeman discusses the feminine portrayal of Jacob in comparison with Esau in terms of their symbolism as nations. Jacob seems weaker than Esau, but is favored and prevails (1998: 119-20).

16. Smith (1990) argues that 'hip' and 'thigh' in the wrestling story are euphemisms for the male genitalia. Thus Jacob suffers a genital injury, which symbolizes the subordination of his masculinity to God. Only after he has submitted his procreative force can he be renamed Israel and made the symbolic father of the nation.

of Hebrew slaves in Exodus 21 and Deuteronomy 15, six years was the maximum length of time a person could hold a fellow Israelite in bondage. They were to be freed in the sabbatical year. Jacob effectively became Laban's slave for seven years, receiving no other wage than a wife.[17] Slaves have significantly impaired masculinity because they are under the power of another (Larson 2004: 86). When Laban tricks him, by marrying him off to Leah instead of Rachel, he manages to extract a second seven year period of service (Gen. 29.25-30). Jacob shows great attachment and favoritism toward Rachel, yet does not pray for her fertility as Isaac had prayed for Rebekah, when she had been childless (Gen. 30.1-2). His bedtime services are bargained among his wives: he goes where they tell him (Gen. 30.14-16). When Rachel takes Laban's teraphim, Jacob is also deceived (Gen. 31.30-32). Jacob's control of himself and his family is impeded by his attachment to Rachel.

When Jacob leaves Laban, his encounter with Esau again brings his manliness into question. He gives Esau extensive gifts, not out of benevolent generosity, but because he is afraid of Esau's power and wants to appease his anger (Gen. 32.9-21). When the two meet, he calls himself Esau's servant and prostrates himself before him (Gen. 33.3). This position of submission, bowing seven times, is the action a vassal would take in front of a suzerain.[18] He showers Esau with honor, as an inferior does to a superior.[19] With these actions, Jacob effectively reverses the blessing and birthright that he had taken from Esau years before (Walters 1992: 605).

From that moment, Jacob's masculinity starts to slip away again. He still receives visions from God, but he loses control over his own family. His daughter Dinah goes to the city alone in Genesis 34. By itself, this action brings Jacob's masculinity into question.[20] While she is in the city, she is seduced by Shechem. Jacob fails to protect his daughter's chastity and is thereby greatly dishonored (Matthews 1998: 104; Giovannini 1987: 67). He does not initially pursue the matter, but lets the offenders come to him. Shechem's father Hamor wants to arrange a bride price to marry Dinah to his son Shechem, which conforms to the required actions listed in Deuteronomy

17. While most commentators do not view Jacob as a slave and the term is not used, he does obligate himself to serve Laban in a form of debt bondage in lieu of a bride price. Lev. 25.39-41 specifies that a Hebrew who sells himself into slavery for debt should have a legal status as a freeman and should be able to return to his family in the sabbatical year. See Dandamayev 1992: 63.

18. See, for example, the Black Obelisk (British Museum), which shows Jehu prostrating himself before Shalmaneser III (Hayes and Miller 2006: 330).

19. For discussion of the direction of honor, see Olyan 1996: 204.

20. Nancy Lindisfarne has observed that Durrani men in Afghanistan whose daughters elope or who are cuckolded are often labeled as dishonorable or feminized as 'soft' or 'weak' (1994: 85).

22 and Exodus 22, where a rapist must marry the daughter and pay the bride price for virgins. Jacob, who should be vigorously defending his honor, removes himself from the action and lets his sons Simeon and Levi decide the matter. They deceive Hamor and Shechem, requiring all the men of the city to be circumcised in order for Shechem to marry Dinah, to which they agree. While they are still recovering from their wounds, however, Levi and Simeon slaughter all the men of the town, and loot it. While Jacob is angry about the matter, he does nothing to punish the sons. Jacob's honor is thus triply tarnished in this story. First, he is unable to control his daughter and protect her chastity. Second, he takes no initiative in defending his honor, and third, through his inaction, he tacitly condones the deception and murder of an entire city and is forced to leave the region (Gen. 34.30).

Later, Jacob himself is deceived by his sons when they kidnap his favorite Joseph and sell him into slavery (Gen. 37.25-35). This event seems to break Jacob, for in the Joseph cycle, Jacob is portrayed as a whiny old man, who clings desperately to his youngest son Benjamin, ignoring the contributions of his other sons. His own son Reuben cuckolds him with his secondary wife Bilhah (Gen. 35.22). He knows about it, but does nothing.[21] Again, he loses honor by being unable either to preserve the chastity of the women under his control or to have authority over his sons.

Like his father Isaac, Jacob becomes blind in his old age (Gen. 48.10). His last act is to bless his sons, through which blessings his is able to mete out some of the punishments and rewards he refrained from administering at the time of the initial offenses. He takes out his first three sons Reuben, Simeon, and Levi as his primary inheritors, and instead bestows that privilege on Judah, his fourth born (Gen. 49.1-12). He blesses the two sons of Joseph, but continues the theme of Genesis by granting the younger son the favored blessing (Gen. 48.13-20).

Jacob's legacy is to father the twelve tribes of Israel, but his character is not consistently masculine. Jacob displays some of the characteristics: strength, virility, persuasiveness, intelligence, but falls short in the area of honor. He also frequently cedes his authority and initiative to other people: his mother, his wives, Laban, and Esau. He is attached to women. Esau more consistently meets the masculine norms, yet he is not the one chosen by God.[22]

---

21. For a man to know that he has been cuckolded and to do nothing can be much more shameful than the fact of the unfaithfulness of the wife itself. See Brandes 1980: 88; Galambush 1992: 34.

22. Niditch also notes the more 'womanish' son Jacob is chosen by God (1998: 23).

Conclusion

The complex portrayal of masculinity in Genesis raises some questions about why God favors the less masculine. The answers may be as multifaceted as the masculinities presented. I will consider two aspects of significance: the significance of subordinate masculinities for a relationship with God, and the way these subordinate masculinities reflect political and social realities in the history of Israel.

First, the subordinate masculinities critique hegemonic masculinity as the way to approach God. The biblical texts on several occasions stress the difference between God's judgment and human judgment (2 Sam. 16.7; Hos. 11.9). Humans set up hegemonic masculinity as the epitome of power and control. Those characteristics can interfere with a faithful relationship with God, however, because the human covenant partner should cede authority and honour to the divine. The covenantal relationship described in the Hebrew Bible requires submission to a higher authority (Sawyer 2004: 170; Landy 1995: 155). The prophetic literature, which is generally aimed at the elite men in charge of the country, critiques the leadership for making decisions and taking action independent of God's will. The remedy is to submit to God. Submission to anyone, even a deity, is not part of the standard construction of masculinity, thus the prophetic word generally goes unheeded.[23]

The patriarchs in Genesis, while flawed individuals, model a proper relationship with God. The patriarchs chosen are explicitly the less masculine of the pair, the one more likely to submit to God's will. Despite the many faults the patriarchs have in their dealings with humans, they do show themselves willing to worship and submit to God, at the cost of their masculine honour and even their lives. Abraham, the father of the nations, submits to God in the area of paternity, obeying the command to listen to his wife, cast out one son, and sacrifice the other son (Sawyer 2004: 170). Isaac allows himself to be nearly sacrificed, then later on literally turns a blind eye to the fact that he was duped by his son, who is later blessed by God. Jacob, perhaps the most complicated and resistant, yields to God when hit below the belt (Smith 1990: 473). He remains faithful to God despite his many flaws. While the biblical text in many ways reflects and supports the categories of hegemonic masculinity, in the realm of the relation with God, these norms are frequently subverted, because no human can assume the position of ultimate power. That position is left to God.

---

23. This is not to say that leaders claim equality to or independence from a deity. When the deity is invoked, however, it is often to show the divine favor and battle prowess of the leader, to buttress his own authority and masculinity, rather than showing the leader's submission to the deity.

Second, the subordinate masculinities of the patriarchs in many ways reflect the position of Israel among the nations. The stories in Genesis show that different masculinities are appropriate in different situations, so, for example, Jacob is feminized with respect to Esau, but masculine with respect to his wives, representing exterior and interior identities (Seeman 1998: 119-120). Israel is a small nation, which, despite the stories of Solomon's glory, even at the height of its power historically wielded little international influence. It was largely at the mercy of the various superpowers: Egypt, Assyrian, Babylonia, Persia, who were interested in the area because of its strategic location. In order to survive as a nation in that situation, Israel had to take positions symbolized by subordinate masculinities. When the nation acted according to the norms of hegemonic masculinity, thinking it was powerful, it was crushed by nations in a position of real strength, such as Assyria, as described, for example, in Hosea (Haddox 2006). The stories of the patriarchs offer a number of alternatives. Abraham acts according to the norms of hegemonic masculinity in his battles with the kings of the valley (Gen. 14), but when faced with the superior powers of the Egyptians or the Philistines, assumes a subordinate position (Gen. 12; 20). Isaac likewise backs away from conflicts with the Philistines (Gen. 26) and concentrates on the interior space of begetting nations (Gen. 24-25). Jacob's very complex masculinity, especially with respect to Esau, reflects the complex relationship between those nations, neither of which was clearly dominant. Joseph, though not discussed in this paper, offers a way for a subordinate people to succeed in a more powerful country, as also seen in Daniel and Esther. These subordinate masculinities offer the nation of Israel strategies for survival.

The masculinities portrayed in the book of Genesis, like the men themselves, have multiple significations. While men may strive toward performing the norms of hegemonic masculinity, these are constantly in tension with various subordinate masculinities. These tensions help define the emerging identity of Israel. Israel is, on the one hand, a nation chosen by God, who is powerful and blesses the chosen patriarchs with wealth and descendents, and leads them in victory in battles (see Josh. 1–12), all attributes of hegemonic masculinity. On the other hand, the biblical text repeatedly emphasizes that Israel is not chosen on the basis of merit (Deut. 7.7; 9.4-5) and needs to obey God or be rejected and destroyed. The nation's identity is negotiated within a complex framework symbolized in part through gender. Genesis favors those patriarchs expressing subordinate masculinities as the best choice for the emerging nation of Israel, both as a political entity and as a people in relationship to God.

Bibliography

Bailey, Randall C.

1995 'They're Nothing but Incestuous Bastards: The Polemical Use of Sex and Sexuality in Hebrew Canon Narratives', in Fernando F. Segovia and Mary Ann Tolbert (eds.), *Reading from this Place*. I. *Social Location and Biblical Interpretation in the United States* (Minneapolis: Fortress Press): 121-38.

Brandes, Stanley

1980 *Metaphors of Masculinity: Sex and Status in Andalusian Folklore* (Publications of the American Folklore Society New Series, 1; Philadelphia: University of Pennsylvania Press).

Buss, Martin J.

1969 *The Prophetic Word of Hosea* (BZAW, 111; Berlin: Alfred Töpelmann).

Carrigan, Tim, Bob Connell, and John Lee

1987 'Toward a New Sociology of Masculinity', in Harry Brod (ed.), *The Making of Masculinities: The New Men's Studies* (Boston: Allen & Unwin): 63-100.

Chapman, Cynthia R.

2004 *The Gendered Language of Warfare in the Israelite–Assyrian Encounter* (HSM, 62; Winona Lake, IN: Eisenbrauns).

Clines, David J.A.

1995 *Interested Parties: The Ideology of Writers and Readers of the Hebrew Bible* (JSOTSup, 205; Sheffield: Sheffield Academic Press).

Connell, R. W.

2005 *Masculinities* (2nd edn; Berkeley: University of California Press).

Cornwall, Andrea, and Nancy Lindisfarne

1994b 'Dislocating Masculinities: Gender, Power, and Anthropology', in Cornwall and Lindisfarne 1994: 11-47.

Cornwall, Andrea, and Nancy Lindisfarne (eds.)

1994a *Dislocating Masculinities: Comparative Ethnographies* (London, New York: Routledge).

Crossley, Nick

2001 *The Social Body: Habitat, Identity, and Desire* (London: Sage Publications).

Dandamayev, Muhammad A.

1992 'Slavery (OT)', in *ABD*, VI: 62-65.

Exum, J. Cheryl

1985 '"Mother in Israel"': A Familiar Story Reconsidered', in Letty M. Russell (ed.), *Feminist Interpretation of the Bible* (Louisville: Westminster John Knox, 1985): 73-85.

Galambush, Julie

1992 *Jerusalem in the Book of Ezekiel: The City as Yahweh's Wife* (SBLDS, 130; Atlanta: Scholars Press).

Gilmore, David D. (ed.)

1987a *Honor and Shame and the Unity of the Mediterranean* (Special Publication of the American Anthropological Association, 22; Washington, DC: American Anthropological Association).

Gilmore, David D.
  1987b   'Honor, Honesty, Shame: Male Status in Contemporary Andalusia', in
           Gilmore 1987a: 90-103.
  1990   *Manhood in the Making: Cultural Concepts of Masculinity* (New Haven,
           CT: Yale University Press).
  1996   'Above and Below: Toward a Social Geometry of Gender', *AA* 98: 54-66.
Giovannini, Maureen J.
  1987   'Female Chastity Codes in the Circum-Mediterranean: Comparative
           Perspectives', in Gilmore 1987a: 61-74.
Greenspahn, Frederick E.
  1996   'Primogeniture in Ancient Israel', in Joseph Coleman and Victor Matthews
           (eds.), *Go to the Land I Will Show You* (Winona Lake, IN: Eisenbrauns):
           69-79.
Haddox, Susan E.
  2006   '(E)Masculinity in Hosea's Political Rhetoric', in Brad E. Kelle and Megan
           Bishop Moore (eds.), *Israel's Prophets and Israel's Past* (New York: T. &
           T. Clark): 174-200.
Hayes, John H., and J. Maxwell Miller
  2006   *A History of Ancient Israel and Judah* (Louisville: Westminster John
           Knox).
Hendriks, Hans Jurgens
  1982   *Juridical Aspects of the Marriage Metaphor in Hosea and Jeremiah* (PhD
           dissertation, University of Stellenbosch).
Herzfeld, Michael
  1987   '"As in your Own House": Hospitality, Ethnography, and the Stereotype
           of Mediterranean Society', in Gilmore 1987a: 75-89.
Kelle, Brad E.
  2005   *Hosea 2: Metaphor and Rhetoric in Historical Perspective* (Academia bib-
           lica, 20; Atlanta: Society of Biblical Literature).
Kuan, Jeffrey Kah-jin
  1995   *Neo-Assyrian Historical Inscriptions and Syria–Palestine: Israelite/
           Judean–Tyrian–Damascene Political and Commercial Relations in the
           Ninth–Eighth Centuries BCE* (JDDS, 1; BL, 1; Hong Kong: Alliance Bible
           Seminary).
Landy, Francis
  1995   'Fantasy and the Displacement of Pleasure: Hosea 2.4-17', in Athalya
           Brenner (ed.), *A Feminist Companion to the Latter Prophets* (Feminist
           Companion to the Bible, 8; Sheffield: Sheffield Academic Press): 146-60.
Larson, Jennifer
  2004   'Paul's Masculinity', *JBL* 123: 85-97.
Lindisfarne, Nancy
  1994   'Variant Masculinities, Variant Virginities: Rethinking Honor and Shame',
           in Cornwall and Lindisfarne 1994a: 82-96.
Matthews, Victor H.
  1998   'Honor and Shame in Gender-Related Legal Situations in the Hebrew
           Bible', in Matthews, Levinson, and Frymer-Kensky 1998: 97-112.
Matthews, Victor H., Bernard M. Levinson, and Tikva Frymer-Kensky (eds.)
  1998   *Gender and Law in the Hebrew Bible and the Ancient Near East* (JSOTSup,
           262; Sheffield: Sheffield Academic Press).

Miller, Geoffrey P.
　1998　'A Riposte Form in the Song of Deborah', in Matthews, Levinson and Frymer-Kensky 1998: 113-27.
Niditch, Susan
　1998　'Genesis', in Carol A. Newsom and Sharon H. Ringe (eds.), *Women's Bible Commentary* (exp. edn; Louisville: Westminster John Knox): 13-29.
Olson, Dennis T.
　2006　'Untying the Knot? Masculinity, Violence, and the Creation–Fall Story of Genesis 2–4', in Linda Day and Carolyn Pressler (eds.), *Engaging the Bible in a Gendered World* (Louisville: Westminster John Knox): 73-86.
Olyan, Saul M.
　1996　'Honor, Shame, and Covenant Relations in Ancient Israel and its Environment', *JBL* 115: 201-218.
Parpola, Simo, and Kazuko Watanabe
　1988　*Neo-Assyrian Treaties and Loyalty Oaths* (SAA, 2; Helsinki: Helsinki University Press).
Rad, Gerhard, von
　1961　*Genesis* (OTL; trans. John Marks; Philadelphia: Westminster).
Sawyer, Deborah F.
　2004　'Biblical Gender Strategies: The Case of Abraham's Masculinity', in Ursula King and Tina Beattie (eds.), *Gender, Religion, and Diversity: Cross-Cultural Perspectives* (New York: Continuum): 162-71.
Sedgwick, Eve Kosofsky
　1995　'"Gosh, Boy George, You Must Be Awfully Secure in your Masculinity"', in Maurice Berger, Brian Wallis, and Simon Watson (eds.), *Constructing Masculinity* (New York: Routledge): 11-20.
Seeman, Don
　1998　'"Where is Sarah your Wife?" Cultural Poetics of Gender and Nationhood in the Hebrew Bible', *HTR* 91: 103-25.
Smith, S.H.
　1990　'"Heel" and "Thigh": The Concepts of Sexuality in the Jacob–Esau Narratives', *VT* 40: 464-73.
Speiser, E.A.
　1964　*Genesis* (AB; Garden City, NY: Doubleday).
Stiebert, Johanna
　2002　'The Maligned Patriarch: Prophetic Ideology and the "Bad Press" of Esau', in Alastair G. Hunter and Phillip R. Davies (eds.), *Sense and Sensitivity* (JSOTSup, 348; Sheffield: Sheffield Academic Press): 33-48.
Strathern, Marilyn
　1988　*The Gender of the Gift: Problems with Women and Problems with Society in Melanesia* (Studies in Melanesian Anthropology, 6; Berkeley: University of California Press).
Trible, Phyllis
　2006　'Ominous Beginnings for a Promise of Blessing', in Phyllis Trible and Letty M. Russell (eds.), *Hagar, Sarah, and their Children* (Louisville: Westminster John Knox): 33-70.
Walters, Stanley D.
　1992　'Jacob Narrative', in *ABD*, III: 599-608.

OF FINE WINE, INCENSE AND SPICES: THE UNSTABLE MASCULINE HEGEMONY OF THE BOOKS OF CHRONICLES

Roland Boer

The two books of Chronicles are forbidding territory for all but the hardiest of readers. As a world full of men, priests, kings, battles, and a vengeful God, only a small band of biblical scholars dare to make Chronicles their home.[1] Rarely if ever does a feminist, gay, lesbian, postcolonial, poststructuralist or even a Marxist critic dare to enter this forbidding text that begins with nine gruelling chapters of genealogies. Fortunately, that closed world has begun to open up in the last few years, with utopian studies by Schweitzer (2007a), who builds on my earlier work (Boer 1997, 1999), and the feminist study by Kelso (2007). This refreshing opening also enables the study and critique of masculinity in Chronicles, not despite but because it is a work devoted to the world of men.

In what follows, I begin with some theoretical concerns, drawn from Antonio Gramsci, Louis Althusser and Antonio Negri, which deal with the unstable nature of hegemonies, the internal conflicts of ideologies and the constitutive power of resistance. From there I introduce two features of Chronicles: its nature as a literary utopia (for whom?) and its central motif of the rigid phallic temple. Yet this phallic world is not as firm as it seems, for the stories in Chronicles continually soften one's initial impression: the overt machismo is a little too camp to be taken seriously; David and Solomon turn out to be expert interior designers; and the crucial sign of one's faithfulness to God is through the correct observance of the temple cult[2]—in terms of cutlery, cooking, spices, oils, incense, fine wine, and singing. What sort of masculinity is this? Let us see.

---

1. Needless to say, the reading offered here differs from anything the reader will find in the standard commentaries on Chronicles. See, for example, Curtis (1910), Ackroyd (1973), Japhet (1993), McKenzie (2004), and Knoppers (2004a; 2004b). Even Jarick's mildly different commentary (2007a; 2007b) does not come close.

2. I am actually falling in line here with the standard scholarly position on Chronicles and the cult, but see Schweitzer 2007b, who argues that in a text like 2 Chronicles 30, with its repentance and unworthiness for keeping the cult the way they have, the people seek forgiveness.

Masculinity, Hegemony and Ideology

It has become a standard if somewhat banal point that masculinity is by no means an eternal, static, and singular quality inherent to men, but that it is constructed, performed, multiple, fluid and subject to historical change (see, for example, Connell 2005; Hooper 2001: 17-76). Masculinities may be constructed discursively, socially or economically, they may be constituted through performance, they may be fluid and constantly shifting, the multiplicity of masculinities is a feature of any historical period, and masculinities change over time, are created, die and are recreated again and again. Apart from the obligatory theoretical touchstones of Foucault, Butler, Haraway, and a host of lesser lights, another who makes a regular appearance in studies of gender and masculinity is Antonio Gramsci. Or rather, a bowdlerized version of Gramsci's theory of hegemony that owes much to Edward Said's misreading usually turns up. According to this perception of hegemony, it designates the dominant position, the one of the ruling class or race or gender (e.g. Connell 2005: 77-78; Hooper 2001: 40). It is reinforced by force (police, both secret and not so secret, law courts and army) and persuasion (propaganda in the media, education and argument).

There is some limited truth in this perception. However, a careful reading of the many treatments of hegemony in Gramsci's notebooks (1971; 1992; 1996; 2007) reveals that such an interpretation is superficial (see especially Boer 2007: 215-74; Fontana 1993). Instead, Gramsci's purpose in developing the theory of hegemony (a reworking of the Marxist theory of ideology) was to find a way to overthrow those in power, to explore how a new, liberating, hegemony might develop. A corollary to this purpose is the argument that the ruling hegemony is inherently uncertain and shaky. So also with the Bible: despite the effort in the Bible to present a series of overlapping ruling and dominating perspectives, all the way from social organization to sexuality, not to mention religion, they are very shaky indeed. Or to put it even more forcefully, the very act of asserting dominance is inherently unstable. Subversion lurks in every murky doorway and under every bed. In fact, hegemony is continually undermined from within and without. A major reason that the dominant hegemony is unstable is that it must constantly deal with insurrection—in politics, social movements, ideas, personal beliefs and so on. After all, the reason Antonio Gramsci, the communist, developed the notion of hegemony was to find a way to overcome the dominance of the fascist state under Mussolini and capitalism more generally.

To this account of Gramsci's theory I would like to add two brief points that are relevant for the analysis of Chronicles that follows. The first comes from Louis Althusser's argument concerning what he calls 'Ideological State Apparatuses'—a term that adds some economic and social depth to what are usually called institutions (Althusser 1971: 121-73). For Althusser, Ideological State Apparatuses include education, religion, family, politics, the legal system, and culture. But the important point for my analysis is that while these apparatuses are zones where the ruling ideas seek to be inculcated, they are also *sites of ideological struggle*.³ And these struggles take place *within* the apparatuses. Although the ruling class attempts to dominate and control the Ideological State Apparatuses, their hold is unstable and contested—a point Althusser owes to Gramsci's notion of hegemony. Ideological struggles take place in precisely these institutions. Thus, in our own day we can witness in the debates over media representation (is it biased or balanced?), education (public versus private, and the drive to render universities subject to the vagaries of the market), religious institutions (orthodoxy versus social justice), culture (funding for the arts), the continued attacks on trade unions as part of a neo-liberal agenda and so on.

The second point comes from Antonio Negri, whose work is simply absent from studies of masculinity. One of Negri's major arguments, coming out of the workerism (*operaismo*) of Italy in the 1960s and 1970s, is that a dominant power is not a given against which one resists.⁴ Rather, resistance itself is constitutive, and power must constantly adapt and reshape itself in response to such resistance. For Negri this creative resistance is embodied in the trade union movements, in the global anti-capitalist protests, in anti-colonialism, and in the green and feminist movements. I would suggest it also applies very well to studies of masculinity, for what are assumed to be dominant masculinities do not occupy centre stage, givens against which resistance must struggle. No, those dominant forms must constantly change and respond to what resists them.

Obviously Negri's position is a step beyond those of Gramsci and Althusser, but let us see how all of them apply to my reading of masculinity in the biblical book of Chronicles. In this text we find a wholesale construction of an exclusively male world of priests, but it is an unstable hegemony, one that must constantly be reasserted in the face of a constant resistance. In this ideal world religion, politics and gender are the dominant Ideological State

---

3.   'Ideology' Althusser famously defines as the representation of the imaginary relationship of individuals to their real conditions of existence, thereby revolutionizing Marxist approaches to ideology (it is not simply false consciousness). It is not the *imaginary relationship* itself that is ideology—for instance, an illusion such as belief in justice, or God, or the honesty of one's rulers. It is not, in other words, a deliberate concealment of the truth by a conspiracy of priests and the powerful. Rather, ideology is the way this imaginary relation is *represented*. It operates at a second remove from reality.

4.   This position runs through Negri's works (Negri, 1991a, 1991b, 2003, 2004, 2006, 2008b; Negri and Casarino 2008; Negri and Defourmantelle 2004; Negri and Scelsi 2008), but has made its largest impact through *Empire* (Hardt and Negri 2000; Negri 2008a) and *Multitude* (Hardt and Negri 2004). See also Boer (in press).

Apparatuses, woven together through the temple in a way that suggests their separation is artificial. However, the instability of that artificial world is due to its own inconsistencies and conflicts, to internal ideological struggle, rather than any external threat. In fact, that resistance will turn out to be the constitutive feature of Chronicles, a resistance to which the dominant masculine ideology must try to assert itself. So let us see how all this works in my reading of Chronicles.[5]

Utopia and Phallic Temples

I begin my reading of Chronicles with two positions, one concerning utopia and the other dealing with the centrality of the temple. To begin with, Chronicles may be read as a utopia, an effort to represent an ideal world that resists the world as it is (see Boer 1997: 136-68; Boer 1999; Schweitzer 2007a). I should point out that such a reading is a radical break in itself with the bulk of Chronicles' scholarship, which obsesses over matters of historical reliability, textual production and transmission, manuscript variations and theology.[6] It is a text that creates a different memory of the past in order to construct the picture of a different present and hope for future. It challenges, erases, and rewrites the established patterns, providing an appeal to alternative collective memories—embodied particularly in the genealogies—for the hope of the future. More correctly, Chronicles may be read as uchronian fiction. It tells a different story of the past in order to open up the possibility of a different and better present and future—the basic definition of uchronian literature. Chronicles presents a picture of an ideal or utopian Israel in opposition to the strongly dystopian lines of the story in the Deuteronomistic History, especially Samuel and Kings. By contrast with the Deuteronomist History, which presents an increasingly apostate people and leadership, or as Steven Schweitzer puts it (2007a), a fatalistic determinism, Chronicles has a much more positive picture of both people and kingship.[7] In presenting an ideal past, with the (dis)obedience or disobedience of king and people acting as a trigger for immediate divine favour or disfavour, with the priests as the actual rulers, Chronicles also generates a hope for a future in which such an ideal state will be realized.

But now we need to ask a further question: for whom is this utopia? Chronicles is a document that expresses the ideas and hope of a distinct class,

---

5. In contrast to ancient Greece and Rome, there is still relatively little on this subject in biblical studies. See especially the work of Stephen Moore (1996; 2003), David Clines (1995) and Howard Eilberg-Schwartz (1993), who make far greater use of deconstructive strategies which soon run up against their limits.

6. See the references in note 1.

7. In traditional historical critical scholarship such a perspective has been described as eschatology or messianism (Braun 1979: 59-61; Williamson 1977: 135; 1982: 24-26).

or rather sub-class. And that sub-class is none other than the Levites. Particularly in the sections that describe an ideal organization of the temple and its worship, the Levites, who are usually relegated to a second-class status, are granted a much greater role than in other pieces from the Hebrew Bible. Not only do they have a role in the cult, but they are entrusted with matters of defence as well. Although they are a sub-class within the ruling class, they are disenfranchised on two counts: Levites were usually placed in secondary roles to the priests; the ruling class itself was a class without much power, since Judah (or Yehud) was a province of the Persian Empire when Chronicles was penned. Without a king, with a Persian appointed governor, the clerics and scribes had to find another avenue to express their wishes. So they redirected their efforts towards the only other area they knew best: religious observance. Yet this Levitical utopia is clearly one for men. Women are few and far between in this text, especially when its central concern is the temple and its worship—an exclusively male zone.[8] It may be utopia for them, but it is a dystopia for women, and indeed anyone who is not a Levite—especially the different lineages of regular priests and Zadokite priests as well as high priest.[9] In short, this utopia is one that belongs to the interwoven Ideological Apparatuses of religion, politics and gender in which the religious dominates.

Further, at the centre of the masculine utopia of Chronicles is the temple, a distinctly phallic temple. The narrative itself leads us to the building and organization of the temple. David passes on the task to Solomon without a hitch (in contrast to Samuel and Kings where David is not permitted to build the temple) and then we come across no less than six chapters (2 Chron. 2–7) devoted to the construction and organization of the temple. Even in the lead-up to these chapters, David plays a massive role in preparing for the temple. But this is a literary and ideological temple, never built.[10] I would suggest that the temple is a figure for the books of Chronicles as a whole, an image that represents the phallic economy of this ideal world.

I do not make this assertion without textual ground, for in 2 Chron. 3.3-4 the following measurements appear:

> These are Solomon's foundations for building the house of God: the length, in cubits of the old standard, was sixty cubits and the width twenty cubits. The vestibule (*ha 'ulam*) that was in front of the length, across the breadth of the

---

8.   The desperate effort by Knoppers (2001) and Labahn and Ben Zvi (2003) to salvage some role for women in Chronicles only reinforces this point.

9.   So Kelso 2007, but see the argument by Schweitzer (2003 and 2007b) that this disenfranchising of priests, Zadokites and the high priest has an implicit democratizing tendency, since it breaks the stranglehold on power by the traditional priesthood as well as moving the focus away from the monarchy.

10.   A standard point in Chronicles' scholarship; see the references in note 1.

house, was twenty cubits, and *the height one hundred and twenty*' (emphasis added).

Compare this text with the other description in 1 Kgs 6.2-3:

> The house that King Solomon built for Yahweh was sixty cubits long, twenty wide and thirty cubits high. The vestibule in front of the temple of the house was twenty cubits long, across the width of the house. Ten cubits was its width in front of the house.

Note the difference: in the Kings text no height is given for the vestibule at all; it is 10 by 20 cubits on the ground plan. By contrast, in Chronicles height is included: the vestibule is 20 cubits across and *120 high*. Given that the main section of the temple is only 60 cubits long, that makes the vestibule twice as high as the length of the whole temple! It is a massive phallic tower, a high-rise temple for Solomon, like some angular cock raised to the heavens with its balls on the ground. Commentators on Chronicles are keen to cut down this phallus: the unanimous agreement is that 2 Chron. 3.4a is—of course!—corrupt. It could not possibly mean a massive tower of 120 cubits. However, I suggest that this text is a telltale sign of the text's masculine economy, for it is the image par excellence of the overwhelming if desperate effort to assert a male-only world.[11] The text of both books of Chronicles leads to this climax, this high point, this massive effort to assert a distinct hegemony.

With this image of the priapic temple at the centre of Chronicles a number of other texts begin to make sense. Let me deal with one example, which necessitates a dip into Hebrew terminology, namely, the genealogies in 1 Chronicles 1–9 and their formulae.[12] The dominant formula for the genealogies makes use of *holidh*, translated variously as 'was the father of' or, in a still classic translation, 'begat'. So we get 'A *holidh* B, C, D….' As in 'Abraham begat Isaac' (1 Chron. 1.34). Semantically there is nothing exceptional about the formula, partly because we are so used to the statement that such-and-such 'begat' a child, or became the father of a child. The problem with all of this is that at a basic level the *holidh* formula leaves the mother entirely out of the process. Where the mother's name does appear, we find *yaledhah*, 'she bore', the form of the verb (qal) in which the mother is the direct subject, the son the object and the father the indirect object. And so we get, 'X bore Y for A' (see 1 Chron. 2.19, 21 and so on), or just 'X bore Y' (see 1 Chron. 2.17; 7.14). However, with *holidh* we have a different form of the verb (hiphil), which means strictly, 'A caused to bear B'—for instance, 'Abraham caused to bear Isaac'. The question then becomes: whom did he cause to

---

11. For a comparable assessment of the role of the temple in Ben Sira, see Camp 2002. See, however, Kelso's study (2007), where she argues that the temple also contains within itself a womb, appropriating the productive capacity of women into a male-only world.

12. On what follows, see especially Kelso (2007), whom I follow quite closely here.

bear? The mother is the obvious answer, but the formula itself effaces her presence, attributing the verb for giving birth to the man. Thus, what we have in the genealogies is an endless list of men producing men, with the occasional exception, such as Keturah, Abraham's 'concubine' in 1 Chron. 1.32, or Tamar in 1 Chron. 2.4, or Ephrathah in 1 Chron. 2.24, or Caleb's concubines in 1 Chron. 2.46-49.[13]

Let us estrange[14] the genealogies for a moment, asking what it means for men to 'beget' men without women. The image that keeps coming back to me is of the whole human tradition from Adam onwards with men giving birth to men. How did Abraham manage his pregnancy? Did he worry about how he was going to give birth? How did he deal with the hormonal changes? Did he produce the child all on his own, coming in his own mouth perhaps? The genealogies become a huge story from the beginning of time of pregnant men, waddling about, belly-buttons popped out, waiting for the birth of yet another son from their own bodies. In the very effort of Chronicles to restrict the ideal world to men, they have to become pregnant, carrying a child and giving birth if the line was going to continue. The masculine hegemony of Chronicles has already started to come unstuck, if indeed there was any uniformity in the first place.

Machismo

This phallic world is not as rigid as it might be, the temple less than solid and somewhat flaccid, the apparent masculinity showing signs that it is not quite what it at first seemed to be. A series of texts indicate that this masculinity is queerer than we might expect. Indeed, a distinct campiness pervades the books of Chronicles.[15] On top of the auto-generation of the genealogies, three other items of this increasingly strange masculinity emerge from Chronicles: excessive if somewhat comical machismo; an extraordinary concern with interior design; and an intense emphasis on those crucial cultic items such as utensils, incense, spices and freshly baked bread.

13. In fact, when the mother's name does appear in the formula, the syntax breaks down. It seems as though that masculine world cannot handle the presence of women even in the structure of its sentences. For example, in 1 Chron. 2.18 there is the strange sentence: 'Caleb the son of Hezron begat (*holid*) Azubah, his wife, and Jerioth'. Or is that 'Caleb the son of Hezron begat by means of ('*et*) his wife, Azubah and with Jerioth'? It is unclear here whether the '*et* is a marker of the direct object—in which case Caleb begets his wives—or the preposition 'with'.

14. The estrangement effect, or *Verfremdungseffekt*, owes itself famously to both Bertolt Brecht and the Russian Formalists (*ostranenie*).

15. On camp, see Sontag (1994: 275-92), Robertson (1996), LaValley (1995), Meyer (1994), Michasiw (1994), Babuscio (1977), Cleto (1999) and Tinkom (2002).

Testosterone seems to be overabundant in the 'mighty men' (*hagibborim*) of David, who flex their muscles all the way through Chronicles, wielding swords and massive spears as though they were prosthetic penises (see 1 Chron. 11.10-47). They slaughter hundreds of enemies at a blow (Jashobeam and Abishai), dispense with gigantic enemies bare-handed (Benaiah and the Egyptian), and leap into snow-filled pits to wrestle lions (Benaiah again)— enough to shame even those mad dog Viking berserkers. Yet the mightiest act of all is not some feat that would outdo even these astounding achievements; instead it is nothing less than King David's glass of water. Out in the field of battle, David looks wistfully out over the troops, licks his lips and croaks, 'O that some one would give me water to drink from the well of Bethlehem which is by the gate' (1 Chron. 11.17). A heartrending wish, is it not a small thing to ask these great men? But there is one small problem: that well with its sweet, fresh water, lies a good distance away, behind Philistine lines. Dumbly obedient to their king and his wish for a drink, Jashobeam, Eleazer and third unnamed man, crash through enemy lines, draw out the water from the well as masses of Philistines run towards them, faces contorted in anger and swords at the ready, and carefully carry the mug of water back to David— presumably without spilling a drop.

Given that these men are David's bodyguard, one would expect them to be well organized, just like the temple and its furnishings (see below). Sadly, it is not so, for they can hardly count at all, let alone get themselves into any sense of order. Do these three brave souls who fetch David a drink belong to the two, the three or the thirty? An extraordinary and bewildering passage from 1 Chronicles 11 leaves everyone confused. Is Jashobeam at the head of the thirty (1 Chron. 11.11) or of the three (2 Sam. 23.8)? For his part, Eleazar believes he is just behind Jashobeam among the 'three mighty men' (1 Chron. 11.12). But then another mighty man, Abishai, feels that he is chief of the three, except that he 'had no name among the three' (1 Chron.11.20). What is going on here? Perhaps the next verse will help us: 'Among the two was he more renowned than the three, and he became their leader, but unto the three he did not come' (1 Chron. 11.21). If we are confused, then spare a thought for poor Abishai. To add to the confusion, Benaiah turns out to 'have a name among the three mighty men' (1 Chron. 11.24). Then again, perhaps he didn't; he certainly was better known than the thirty, but he wasn't actually part of the three (1 Chron. 11.25). One can only assume that David feared for his own life at the hands of these dolts who mill about in numerical confusion, especially when Benaiah was appointed over David's bodyguard (1 Chron. 11.25). Reading this passage, I can't help thinking of the oxymoron 'military intelligence'.

However, the real answer to organization for battle lies elsewhere—in the temple choir. Later, towards the end of the second book of Chronicles we meet King Jehoshaphat, face to face with the marauding army of the Ammonites, Moabites and men of Mount Seir. Unfazed, Jehoshaphat asks God what he should do (2 Chron. 20.1-17). The answer: sing! Forget complex manoeuvres like ambushes, pincers or disciplined advances under cover of the archers. No, faced with the enemy, Jehoshaphat 'appointed those who were to sing to Yahweh and praise him in holy array' (2 Chron. 20. 21). They were to beat back the enemy with the refrain, 'Give thanks to Yahweh, for his steadfast love endures forever' (2 Chron. 20. 21). The result: God takes control of the battle and enemy ends up slaughtering itself through 'friendly fire'. Battle as a musical: all that is left for the victors is gather the spoil and head for home, still singing (2 Chron. 20.24-28).

Masculine hegemony? If so, it is not what we would expect. In fact, I would suggest that here a resistant masculinity is emerging that makes mockery of the phallic rigidity of the temple. What appears in this battle account is perhaps the central theme of Chronicles, namely correct observance of the cult. Follow the minute rules for organizing the temple and for worship and God's blessings will smile on you. If not, then a curse soon follows.[16] Incense mixed incorrectly, a golden basin out of place, a false note sung—these unforgivable sins among many others would bring God's immediate wrath, usually in terms of marauding foreigners, strange diseases, loss of those valuable sons the men laboured so valiantly to produce, and gruesome early deaths.

Cult Matters: The Finer Things of Life

All this campy machismo is in the end a sideshow for Chronicles (which is a shame in many respects). After all, the temple is the main concern of these two books of the Bible, which brings us to the matters of interior design, organization, crockery and other masculine matters of cultic correctness. Here at least, the men can organize themselves.

And what an organization it is! It begins with David, who is no hack when it comes to interior design, and then that organizational skill passes (genetically?) on to Solomon. David leaves Solomon a detailed shopping list for an exclusive home furnishings store (see 1 Chron. 28.15-18; 29.3): gold and silver lamp-stands, tables and bowls, forks and basins and cups of pure gold, a golden altar of incense, precious stones throughout the temple, and even the

16. This is the well-known 'immediate divine retribution', first identified by Julius Wellhausen (1994 [1885]: 203-10). To spell it out: the divine response to obedience or disobedience is immediate blessing or punishment, particularly by the kings and often exhibited in terms of cultic correctness (see, for example, 2 Chron. 29–31). The inevitable punishment that follows disobedience may be averted by repentance after a warning. However, this immediate retribution may not be as smooth or as immediate as many have assumed. See especially Dillard (1984) and Dillard (2003).

pièce de résistance, a golden chariot for those cherubim on the ark of the covenant. Anything David can do, Solomon can do better: he ensures that every corner of the temple is adorned with gold, decorates the tops of each pillar with necklaces of pomegranate and gold, and above all pays special attention to the curtain concealing the most sacred place, the Holy of Holies. That, stipulates Solomon, must be woven 'of blue and purple and crimson fabrics and fine linen' (2 Chron. 3.14), and it must be embroidered with cherubim. The list is endless, as is Solomon's delight with these vital matters of state: forks, tongs, snuffers, fire-pans, lamp-stands, pots, shovels, finely wrought and carved wash basins, not to forget the all important flowers (see 2 Chron. 4.1-22). Solomon, it seems, had a soft spot for the finer things in life.

How did one care for such an elaborate interior? The forward thinking David has it in hand, for he appoints no less than 38,000 Levites in the thirty-plus age group (1 Chron. 23.3). Even they were not enough, so David drops the age barrier to twenty (1 Chron. 23.24). What were they to do? Lead the odd worship service? Pray? Meditate? No, they were to clean, cook the breads and wafers and baked offerings, mix the various oils and…sing at every opportunity (1 Chron. 23.28-31). To accompany them others were to strum lyres and harps and ring cymbals. So involved were these tasks that they were rostered on a monthly basis; even the mighty men we met above came in on the act (see 1 Chron. 25–27).

Perhaps the best summary of these vital tasks appears towards the beginning of the first book of Chronicles:

> Some of them had charge of the utensils of service, for they were required to count them when they were brought in and taken out. Others of them were appointed over the furniture, and over all the holy utensils, also over the fine flour, the wine, the oil, the incense, and the spices. Others, of the sons of the priests, prepared the mixing of the spices, and Mattithiah, one of the Levites, the first-born of Shallum the Korahite, was in charge of making the flat cakes. Also some of their kinsmen of the Kohathites had charge of the showbread, to prepare it every sabbath (1 Chron. 9.28-32).

What do real men do in Chronicles? They concern themselves with crockery and cutlery, furniture, fine flour, wine, oil, incense, spices, flat cakes and showbread. Everywhere we find the singers; released from any other service, they were rostered on to sing day and night (1 Chron. 9.33). Picture the scene: the men in the temple, finely dressed and perfumed, mix the spices, cook the flat cakes, arrange the furniture, ensure that the holy crockery and cutlery are correctly ordered; as they go about their tasks, they are surrounded by groups of singers and choristers who launch into song 24/7. A musical? An early version of piped music? Masculine?

In case we might think that these foppish dandies were engaged in peripheral matters, like some high church Anglicans, then we need to think again.

Cultic correctness is, for Chronicles at least, a matter of life or death—in short, God's favour or disfavour. Perhaps the best example of its importance appears in some words uttered by King Abijah, soon after the breakup of the united kingdom after Solomon's reign. After the breakup the two kingdoms— faithful Judah and rebel Israel—face each other. Abijah begins by pointing out the cultic errors of the wayward Israelites, and then he says:

> But as for us, the Lord is our God, and we have not forsaken him. We have priests ministering to the Lord who are sons of Aaron, and Levites for their service. They offer to the Lord every morning and every evening burnt offerings and incense of sweet spices, set out the showbread on the table of pure gold, and care for the golden lamp-stand that its lamps may burn every evening; for we keep the charge of the Lord our God, but you have forsaken him. Behold, God is with us at our head, and his priests with their battle trumpets to sound the call to battle against you (2 Chron. 13.10-12a).

Are the signs of faithfulness an upright heart, a prayerful and moral life, justice for the poor, a humble walking with your God? Or does it require the offering of sweet spices at the right times, setting out the showbread on the gold table and making sure that the golden lamp stand keeps burning? No and yes would be Abijah's answer to these questions, berating the Israelites as he did so for their failure to live up to these standards. Yet even here there is ambivalence. Abijah's confidence may well be covering a deeper uncertainty. Standing there in his carefully washed linen robe with its jiggling tassels and tinkling bells, his beard trimmed and carefully oiled, Abijah has yet to realize that even his preferred approach does not live up to what Yahweh wants, for in 2 Chronicles 30 his successor, Hezekiah, would lead all the people to become aware of how inadequate their cultic observance had been. Yahweh was obviously a difficult god to please.

Conclusion

Chronicles consistently undermines the masculine hegemony it so desperately seeks to establish; it is a very unstable hegemony, an Ideological State Apparatus that is deeply conflicted within itself. It is a text full of queers doing their thing, whether in the genealogies of men begetting men, in the comic machismo of the 'mighty men', in the interior design of the temple, or in the attention to the finest detail of temple organization and decoration. Or, given that it is an utopian representation that was never realized, is it a very different masculinity, an alternative hegemony from what we might have expected, a resistant masculinity that must be thwarted by more conventional phallic models?

Bibliography

Ackroyd, Peter R.
1973   *I and II Chronicles, Ezra, Nehemiah* (London: SCM Press).
Althusser, Louis
1971   *Lenin and Philosophy and Other Essays* (trans. B. Brewster; London: New Left Books).
Babuscio, Jack
1977   'Camp and the Gay Sensibility', in R. Dyer (ed.), *Gays and Film* (London: British Film Institute): 40-57.
Boer, Roland
1997   *Novel Histories: The Fiction of Biblical Criticism* (Sheffield: Sheffield Academic Press).
1999   'Utopian Politics in 2 Chronicles 10–13', in M.P. Graham and S.L. McKenzie (eds.), *The Chronicler as Author: Studies in Text and Texture* (Sheffield: Sheffield Academic Press): 360-94.
2007   *Criticism of Heaven: On Marxism and Theology* (Leiden: Brill).
in press *Criticism of Theology: On Marxism and Theology III* (Leiden: Brill).
Braun, R.
1979   'Chronicles, Ezra and Nehemiah: Theology and Literary History', in J.A. Emerton (ed.), *Studies in the Historical Books of the Old Testament* (Leiden: Brill): 52-64.
Camp, Claudia V.
2002   'Storied Space, or, Ben Sira "Tells" a Temple', in David M. Gunn and Paula M. McNutt (eds.), *'Imagining' Biblical Worlds: Studies in Spatial, Social and Historical Construction in Honor of James W. Flanagan* (JSOTSup, 359; Sheffield: Sheffield Academic): 64-80.
Cleto, Fabio (ed.)
1999   *Camp: Queer Aesthetics and the Performing Subject—A Reader* (Ann Arbor, MI: University of Michigan Press).
Clines, David J.A.
1995   *Interested Parties: The Ideology of Writers and Readers of the Hebrew Bible* (JSOTSup, 266; GCT, 7; Sheffield: Sheffield Academic Press).
Connell, R.W.
2005   *Masculinities* (Berkeley, CA: University of California Press).
Curtis, E.L.
1910   *A Critical and Exegetical Commentary on the Books of Chronicles* (Edinburgh: T. & T. Clark).
Dillard, Raymond
1984   'Reward and Punishment in Chronicles: The Theology of Immediate Retribution', *WTJ* 46: 164-72.
Eilberg-Schwartz, H.
1993   *God's Phallus* (New York: Beacon).
Fontana, B.
1993   *Hegemony and Power: On the Relation Between Gramsci and Machiavelli* (Minneapolis: University of Minnesota Press).

Gramsci, Antonio
    1971   *Selections from the Prison Notebooks* (trans. Q. Hoare and Geoffrey
              Nowell Smith; London: Lawrence & Wishart).
    1992   *Prison Notebooks*, I (trans. J.A. Buttigieg and Antonio Callari; New York:
              Columbia University Press).
    1996   *Prison Notebooks*, II (trans. J.A. Buttigieg; New York: Columbia Univer-
              sity Press).
    2007   *Prison Notebooks*, III (trans. J.A. Buttigieg; New York: Columbia Univer-
              sity Press).
Hardt, Michael, and Antonio Negri
    2000   *Empire* (Cambridge, MA: Harvard University Press).
    2004   *Multitude: War and Democracy in the Age of Empire* (New York: Penguin).
Hooper, Charlotte
    2001   *Manly States: Masculinities, International Relations, and Gender Politics*
              (New York: Columbia University Press).
Japhet, Sara
    1993   *I and II Chronicles: A Commentary* (Louisville: Westminster John Knox).
Jarick, John
    2007a   *1 Chronicles* (Sheffield: Sheffield Phoenix Press).
    2007b   *2 Chronicles* (Sheffield: Sheffield Phoenix Press).
Kelly, Brian
    2003   '"Retribution" Revisited: Covenant, Grace and Restoration', in M. Patrick
              Graham, Steven L. McKenzie, and Gary N. Knoppers (eds.), *The Chroni-
              cler as Theologian: Essays in Honor of Ralph W. Klein* (JSOTSup, 371;
              London: T. & T. Clark): 206-27.
Kelso, Julie
    2007   *O Mother, Where Art Thou? An Irigarayan Reading of the Book of Chroni-
              cles* (London: Equinox).
Knoppers, Gary N.
    2001   'Intermarriage, Social Complexity and Ethnic Diversity in the Genealogy
              of Judah', *JBL* 120.15-30.
    2004a   *1 Chronicles 1–9* (New Haven: Yale University Press).
    2004b   *1 Chronicles 10–29* (New Haven: Yale University Press).
Labahn, A., and Ehud Ben Zvi
    2003   'Observations on Women in the Genealogies of 1 Chronicles 1–9', *Bib* 84:
              457-478.
LaValley, Al
    1995   'The Great Escape', in C.K. Creekmur and A. Doty (eds.), *Out in Culture:
              Gay, Lesbian, and Queer Essays in Popular Culture* (Durham, NC: Duke
              University Press): 60-70.
McKenzie, Steve L.
    2004   *1–2 Chronicles* (Nashville, TN: Abingdon).
Meyer, Moe (ed.).
    1994   *The Politics and Poetics of Camp* (London: Routledge).
Michasiw, Kim
    1994   'Camp, Masculinity, Masquerade', *Differences: A Journal of Feminist
              Cultural Studies* 6.146-73.

Moore, Stephen D.

1996   *God's Gym: Divine Male Bodies of the Bible* (New York: Routledge).

Moore, Stephen D., and J. C. Anderson (eds.)

2003   *New Testament Masculinities* (Atlanta, GA: SBL Publications).

Negri, Antonio

1991a   *Marx beyond Marx: Lessons on the Grundrisse* (trans. H. Cleaver, M. Ryan and M. Viano; Brooklyn: Autonomedia).

1991b   *The Savage Anomaly: The Power of Spinoza's Metaphysics and Politics* (trans. M. Hardt; Minneapolis: University of Minnesota Press).

2003   *Time for Revolution* (trans. M. Mandarini; London: Continuum).

2004   *Subversive Spinoza: (Un)contemporary Variations* (trans. T.S. Murphy, M. Hardt, T. Stolze and C.T. Wolfe; Manchester: Manchester University Press).

2006   *The Political Descartes: Reason, Ideology and the Bourgeois Project* (trans. M. Mandarini and A. Toscano; London: Verso).

2008a   *Empire and Beyond* (trans. E. Emery; Cambridge: Polity Press).

2008b   *The Porcelain Workshop: For a New Grammar of Politics* (trans. N. Wedell; Los Angeles: Semiotext(e)).

Negri, A, and C. Casarino

2008   *In Praise of the Common: A Conversation on Philosophy and Politics* (Minneapolis: University of Minnesota Press).

Negri, A., and A. Defourmantelle

2004   *Negri on Negri* (trans. M.B. DeBevoise; New York: Routledge).

Negri, A., and Raf V. Scelsi

2008   *Goodbye Mr Socialism* (trans. P. Thomas; New York: Seven Stories Press).

Robertson, Pamela

1996   *Guilty Pleasures: Feminist Camp from Mae West to Madonna* (Durham, NC: Duke University Press).

Schweitzer, Steven J.

2003   'The High Priest in Chronicles: An Anomaly in a Detailed Description of the Temple Cult', *Bib* 84: 388-40.

2007a   *Reading Utopia in Chronicles* (New York: T. & T. Clark).

2007b   'Exploring the Utopian Space of Chronicles: Some Spatial Anomalies', in J.L. Berquist and C.V. Camp (eds.), *Constructions of Space*. I. *Theory, Geography, and Narrative* (LHB/OTS; TGN, 1; London: T. & T. Clark International): 141-56.

Sontag, Susan

1994   *Against Interpretation* (London: Vintage).

Tinkcom, Matthew

2002   *Working like a Homosexual: Camp, Capital, Cinema* (Durham, NC: Duke University Press).

Wellhausen, J.

1994 [1885] *Prolegomena to the History of Israel* (Atlanta: Scholars Press).

Williamson, H.G.M.

1977   *Israel in the Books of Chronicles* (Cambridge: Cambridge University Press).

1982   *1 and 2 Chronicles* (Grand Rapids, MI: Eerdmans).

Part II

Fantasies of (Male) Governance

DE/CONSTRUCTING MASCULINITY IN EXODUS 1–4[*]

Brian Charles DiPalma

Although masculinity as a distinct area of inquiry in the Hebrew Bible is still emerging, the topic is already broad. In order to narrow the scope to a viable size, I will focus on three aspects of masculinity in Exodus 1–4 that other scholars have identified elsewhere in the Hebrew Bible: (1) violence, especially as expressed through killing, (2) wisdom in administrative affairs, which is closely associated with persuasive speech, and (3) detachment from women.[1] At this point, these aspects are only noted, but will be commented on more extensively below. In terms of method, I offer a close literary analysis of these chapters, especially by paying attention to the subtle uses of language throughout. Focusing narrowly on masculinity in Exodus 1–4 unavoidably draws attention away from the women in these chapters, which have been extensively discussed by feminist scholars.[2] This intentional focus on men and masculinity in these chapters is not to subvert the important work of feminist scholars, but only a corollary of intentionally exploring masculinity. I argue that in the characterization of Pharaoh, the narrator utilizes these assumptions about masculinity to depict him as a failed man. These assumptions are

[*]   I am indebted to Dennis T. Olson for constructive feedback on an earlier draft of this paper, which greatly helped clarify my ideas, especially in the section on persuasive speech. The editor, Ovidiu Creangă, graciously invited me to submit this essay and provided insightful comments to refine and improve my nascent ideas. David J.A. Clines kindly granted permission to cite his previously unpublished work. A colleague, Paul M. Kurtz, also provided suggestions to help polish this paper. Finally, my wife, Audrey Hindes DiPalma, meticulously reviewed this paper and provided engaging conversations throughout its various phases. I am immensely grateful to all for their assistance. None of them can be faulted for any errors or deficiencies that remain, for which I am solely responsible.

1.   The primary scholarly literature on this topic discussed more thoroughly below includes: Clines 1995a; 1995b; 1996; 1997; 2002; Goldingay 1995: 37-44; Hoffner 1966: 326-334; Olson 2006: 73-86; Washington 1997: 324-63. Their work has focused on a variety of texts in the Hebrew Bible including Genesis, Exodus, the Deuteronomic Law codes, Samuel, Kings, Job, and the Prophetic corpus.

2.   Some important feminist scholarship that has influenced my own thinking about these texts at various points include: Lapsley 2005: 69-88; Frymer-Kensky 2002: 24-33; Pardes 1992: 79-97; Weems 1992: 25-34; Exum 1994a: 37-61; 1994b 75-87.

utilized to deconstruct the power of Pharaoh, so they are initially reinscribed, but as the narrative focuses on Moses, a critical evaluation of the same assumtions emerges. The result, this paper contends, is a deconstruction of the values themselves that ultimately resists their reinscription.

Some Assumptions about Masculinity in the Hebrew Bible

The link between violence and masculinity in the Hebrew Bible is well noted. John Goldingay suggests that the Bible's first murder, Cain's killing of Abel (Genesis 4.1-16), reveals violence is a feature of masculinity in Genesis 1–4 (1995: 39). David J.A. Clines argues that violence is 'the essential male characteristic in the David story' (1995: 216). In Clines's online articles, verbal or physical violence is an aspect of masculinity for Moses, the speaker in the Psalms, Job, and the Prophets (1995b, 1996, 1997, 2002). Harold Washington argues that in the Deuteronomic law-codes and the prophets 'a capacity for violence is synonymous with manliness' (1997: 326). Dennis T. Olson shows that while some stories in Genesis, such as the reconciliation of Jacob with Esau (Gen. 33.1-17) and of Joseph with his brothers (Gen. 45.1-14), subvert the link between masculinity and violence, other stories, such as Cain's killing of Abel (Gen. 4.1-16), make this association for some masculinities (2006: 78ff.). In the ancient Near East, Harry Hoffner cites 'prowess in battle' as indicative of masculinity in magic rituals (1966: 327).

The association of masculinity with persuasive speech and detachment from women is more complicated. While exploring 1 Samuel 16 to 1 Kings 2, Clines argues that the need for wisdom in administrative affairs, which is closely linked with persuasive speech, and detachment from women are important aspects of David's masculinity (1995: 219-11, 225-27). Both traits reappear in Clines's unpublished work on masculinity in the book of Job and the character of Moses (1996, 1997). But Goldingay and Olson suggest that connectedness with women is an important part of masculinity in Genesis 1–4 (1995: 38-39; 2006: 80). Moreover, Linda Day notes that there are many wise women in the Hebrew Bible such as Deborah (Judges 4), Abigail (1 Sam. 25.2-42), and Huldah (2 Kgs 22.14-20), and that the wisdom tradition more broadly is closely associated with the feminine (2006). Similarly, Jacqueline Lapsley points to the role of women's persuasive speech in texts, such as the story about Rachel in Genesis 31 or of the midwives in Exod. 1.15-21, that reflect 'women's values' (2005: 27-34, 73-75). Clines demonstrates awareness of this difficulty by citing the example of Abigail but he still shows that persuasive speech remains a masculine trait in the stories about David (1995: 220-21). The tensions that arise by the portrayal of the same features in notably different manners are meaningfully illumined by insights from contemporary research on masculinity, which help nuance how these aspects of masculinity that occur elsewhere in the Hebrew Bible are understood in this paper.

R.W. Connell, an important contributor to contemporary masculinity studies, suggests more is needed when articulating the relationship between male bodies and masculinity than biologically deterministic schemes or social construction models or even some compromise between the two (2005: 45-52). Connell proposes masculinity 'is simultaneously a place in gender relations, the practices through which men and women engage that place in gender, and the effects of these practices on bodily experience, personality, and culture' (71). As gender becomes an important part of ordering social practice, it is both influenced by and influences other socio-cultural factors, such as race and class (76). This amalgamation of diverse socio-cultural features produces 'multiple masculinities' (76). Amidst the diversity of masculinities, Connell suggests that a hegemonic form of masculinity emerges that successfully 'embodies a "currently accepted" strategy' for legitimating claims to authority, power, and domination (77). But because few men are capable of impeccably embodying the hegemonic form of masculinity, subordinated, complicit, and marginalized masculinities emerge (76-81). Complicit masculinities do not meet the current hegemonic standards, but also do not actively subvert those ideals, thereby passively reaping a 'patriarchal dividend' of the general privileging of men over women (79). While subordinated and marginalized masculinities are similar because they are both demoted by the hegemonic expression, subordinate masculinities remain located within the hegemonic hierarchy whereas marginalized masculinities are pushed outside this framework (78-81). This observation adds further complexity to the multiple and competing images of masculinity. Moreover, there are not only many kinds of masculinities within any given society, but because they are shaped by history and help shape history, they change over time and across cultures (185-203). A collection of essays describing the place of the duel in modern Europe helps illustrate this point (Spierenburg 1998a: 1-26). For example, Ute Frevert argues that while the duel is consistently associated with masculinity in Central Europe from the sixteenth to the nineteenth century, it began among the aristocracy with an elaborate set of rituals, which included an initial provocation associated with lost honor, a formal challenge, and a third party arranging the actual details of the duel, but eventually it lost some of this formalism as it transferred to the middle-class (1998: 39-51). In a more synchronic approach, Pieter Spierenburg argues that court cases in Amsterdam around the eighteenth century reveal that knives were the weapon of choice for the lower classes, while lower middle class people found this distasteful, instead preferring to use sticks as their weapon of choice (1998b: 109-111).

The idea that gender assumptions change over time is not entirely a modern phenomenon. A recent collection of essays documents how assumptions about gender in the ancient Near East changed over the life of an individual and over extended periods of time (Bolger 2008). For example, in exploring the remains found at Domuztepe in southeastern Anatolia from around 5500 BCE, Karina Croucher notes that while there are some gendered differences in figurines, as evidenced by comparing a phallus made of stone to a figurine of a complete female body fashioned of clay into a vessel, mortuary practices, which reveal male and female remains scattered together, suggest that gender differences decline in importance upon death (2008: 39-40). She also cautions that modern binary understandings of gender, which employ a rigid dichotomization of male/female as polar opposites, are not able to adequately account for the sexual ambiguities of figurines found elsewhere (26-30). Unfortunately, the specific details of the other papers in Bolger's collection of essays do not illumine the features of masculinity investigated in this paper beyond the more general point that gender assumptions were liable to change in the ancient Near East as well.

Given these insights regarding the pliable nature of gender configurations, it is not surprising for some authors in the Hebrew Bible to uphold detachment from women as a masculine ideal and others to suggest attachment to women is a masculine ideal. The same is true regarding speaking persuasively when dealing wisely. And even violence, while associated with some masculinities, is not consistently associated with all masculinities. Therefore, I assume that violence, persuasive speech when dealing wisely, and detachment from women, are *some assumptions* about *some masculinities* in the Hebrew Bible. What kinds of masculinities these characteristics should be associated with in relation to various time periods, places in social hierarchies, and ethnicities needs far more theorizing than the narrow constraints of this paper allow. This study only intends to examine how these characteristics function in Exodus 1–4.

Masculinity in the Characterization of Pharaoh: Is He Wise, Persuasive, Womanless, or a Killer? (Exodus 1.8–2.10)

Exod. 1.8–2.10 can be divided into three distinct scenes, each of which begins with Pharaoh ordering a course of action that is followed by responses to that command. When Pharaoh dictates his will, he also sets the parameters for his own masculine evaluation. In the first scene, 1.8-14, the characteristic for evaluation is wisdom. After noticing the Israelite population boom, in 1.10 Pharaoh says, 'Let us *be seen as wise* (נתחכמה) in relation to them so that they will not *become more numerous* (רבה)'.[3] The verb נתחכמה is a hithpael from the root חכם (to be wise, act wisely). According to H.W.F. Gesenius, a

---

3. Unless otherwise noted, all translations are my own.

function of the hithpael is to express a desire to show oneself in a certain state (54.3). Pharaoh is expressing not only a desire 'to deal shrewdly', as in the NRSV, but also to be seen as wise. The narrator depicts Pharaoh as trying to behave in accordance with a feature of masculinity that occurs elsewhere in the Hebrew Bible. The condition under which Pharaoh will be seen as wise is signaled by the particle פֶּן, 'so that they will not become more numerous'. To curtail the population growth, he implements a scheme of afflicting forced labor (Exod. 1.11). While Pharaoh's afflicting plan is enacted, the Hebrews not only 'become more numerous', but are 'bursting forth' (פָּרַץ) (1.12). The addition of this phrase not found in the narrator's description in Exod. 1.7, reveals an even greater fecundity from the Israelites. Pharaoh's wise dealing backfires and makes the situation worse. In response, Pharaoh increases the forced labor, with the root עָבַד (to serve, enslave) deployed five times in two verses (Exod. 1.13-14). The repetition achieves the effect of 'pounding into the reader the severity of the oppression' (Lapsley 2005: 72). But Pharaoh's instructions to the midwives reveals that the increased forced labor also fails to achieve his goal. While Pharaoh again implements his afflicting plan, he fails to achieve what he proposed. Pharaoh is obviously failing. Within an assumption that equates masculinity with wisdom, he is a failing man. He achieves some success with violence, but fails completely in wisdom. His capacity for violence is evaluated in the following section.

In the second scene, Exod. 1.15-21, Pharaoh's capacity for violence, persuasive speech, and detachment from women are tested. As before, Pharaoh proposes the characteristics for evaluation. Pharaoh tells the midwives to let every Hebrew daughter live and to kill every Hebrew son born (1.15). Pharaoh tries to persuade others to kill. In two important areas, persuasive speech and violence, the narrator depicts Pharaoh trying to act within some assumptions about masculinity. But Pharaoh transgresses in the third aspect of masculinity under consideration in this paper, detachment from women.[4] Far from trying to operate independently of women, Pharaoh's success suddenly depends entirely upon whether these women will obey him. There are different ways of interpreting Pharaoh's decision to rely upon the midwives. Perhaps Pharaoh is offering a new vision of masculinity in which it is acceptable, perhaps even commendable, for men to depend upon and cooperate with women. But this option seems doubtful in light of the broader narrative bias that seeks to emasculate Pharaoh. Rather, his decision may be a subtle effort to emerge successfully in the realm of administrative wisdom by having others soil their hands with Israelite blood to thwart their burgeoning population while keeping his own hands clean. Simultaneously, Pharaoh's dependence upon women seems to underscore his failures as a man because he is so

---

4. I am indebted to the editor for an incisive comment that prompted this addition.

powerless that he must depend upon women. Thus, although Pharaoh breaks decorum on this point, it seems only to raise the issue of wisdom to set him up for further failure and emphasize his existing failures as a man. Indeed, in the other areas, persuasive speech and killing, where Pharaoh acts more appropriately, he fails. Whether the midwives are ethnically Hebrew or Egyptian is irrelevant here.[5] Either way, the narrator reports that the midwives 'did not do what the king *told* (דבר) them' (1.17). The use of דבר (word) for Pharaoh's communication with the midwives highlights his ineffectiveness as a persuasive leader. Pharaoh's words are not persuasive enough. Instead of being persuaded to kill, the midwives 'let the children live', which prevents Pharaoh from killing anyone (1.17). In Exod. 1.20, God rewards the midwives and the Israelites 'become more numerous (רבה) and were very mighty (עצם)'. The repetition of this phrase from what Pharaoh noticed in Exod. 1.9 recalls his original goal of wise dealing to curtail the population growth, which remains unachieved. Pharaoh's failures in masculinity are clearly growing.

In the final scene, Exod. 1.22–2.10, the evaluation of Pharaoh's ability to speak persuasively, kill, and be womanless continues. As with the preceding scenes, Pharaoh's speech establishes the parameters. After Pharaoh's previous failures confront him, he tries even harder to succeed in each area. The speaking increases from a simple 'telling' (אמר, 1.15) to a stern 'commanding' (צוה, 1.22). The audience widens from the midwives to '*all* his people' (כל־עמו, 1.22). By expanding the range of who is included in his command to kill beyond only the midwives to encompass *all* his people, Pharaoh seems to be attempting to circumvent the women he earlier depended on. In this sense, he is seeking to be free of women, who, from his perspective, plagued him earlier. Initially, even the scope of violence seems to increase from only the Hebrew sons to '*every* son born' (כל־הבן הילוד, 1.22). Pharaoh seems to mean every son born *to the Hebrews*, as the Samaritan Pentateuch and the LXX supply. But, if the MT is followed, then through this conspicuously omitted phrase, Pharaoh's fury emerges to reveal an even greater rage in the violence proposed. At the risk of redundancy, but for clarity in comparison: He commands (not simply speaks) all his people (not just the midwives) to kill every son born (not only Hebrews). He is trying to speak persuasively, be free of women, and kill. But his commands are disobeyed again, which shows that Pharaoh cannot persuade others with his words. And this time, the role of women increases in spite of his efforts to avoid relying on women. In the preceding scene, only the two midwives disobeyed. But in this scene, Moses' mother, sister, and Pharaoh's very own daughter collaborate to prevent him from accomplishing his goals. Even when Pharaoh tries to avoid relying upon women, he is still defeated by women working together. And

5. For a concise summary of the issue, see Childs 2004: 16.

although attention is focused on Moses, Pharaoh remains unable to kill. While Pharaoh tries harder to achieve success within certain assumptions about masculinity, he fails more than ever before.

In Exod. 1.8–2.10 assumptions about masculinity are a potent device in the narrator's arsenal for crafting the total defeat of Pharaoh. When Pharaoh later faces the onslaught of God, Moses, and the plagues, he does so as a thoroughly deconstructed and emasculated man. As the assumptions about masculinity are not challenged, but relied upon to deconstruct his power, they are subtly reinscribed until this point. But as the story continues a complex evaluation of these same assumptions also emerges.

Masculinity Reinscribed or Critiqued (Exodus 2.11–4.26)?

a. *Exodus 2.11-15a: Moses, Masculinity and Violence*
Physical violence abounds in Exod. 2.11-15a. It is a veritable lexicon of violent verbs. An Egyptian man 'strikes' (נכה) a Hebrew man (2.11). Moses 'strikes' (נכה) an Egyptian (2.12). Two Hebrew men are 'fighting' (נצה) together (2.13). Pharaoh seeks to 'slay' (הרג) Moses (2.15a). In the one verse where an act of violence is not committed or sought, violence is the topic of conversation. In Exod. 2.14, the Hebrew man confronted by Moses asks, 'Do you intend to *slay* (הרג) me as you *slew* (הרג) the Egyptian?' In each verse, an act of physical violence is committed, talked about, or sought.

While male violence abounds, Moses is the first character to rise unambiguously to the status of killer. Moses sees an Egyptian man 'striking' (נכה) a Hebrew man (2.11). But 'striking' does not always result in death because in laws dealing with 'striking', punishment depends upon whether the person lives or dies (e.g. Exod. 21.12-27). Clearly, the Egyptian violently strikes the Hebrew, but this does not necessarily cause the Hebrew's death. In response to seeing the striking, Moses looks to see if anyone is present (2.12). Seeing no one, Moses 'strikes' (נכה) the Egyptian (2.13). While the action is the same as the Egyptian's, two points suggest Moses is the first killer of the story. (1) Moses hides the body in the sand, which implies this was a mortal striking (2.13). Even if the striking did not bring immediate death, but perhaps incapacitation, burying the body in the sand ensures the Egyptian dies. Either way, Moses is a killer. (2) In Exod. 2.14, the Hebrew confronted by Moses asks, 'Do you intend to *slay* (הרג) me as you *slew* (הרג) the Egyptian?' Every occurrence of הרג (to slay) in the Hebrew Bible refers to a physical or metaphorical death.[6] That the confronted Hebrew uses הרג to refer to

---

6. הרג is used metaphorically to speak of death for humans in Job 5.2; Prov. 1.32; 7.26. הרג is used to refer to the death of plants struck with frost and hail in Ps. 78.47. For instances of הרג being used to refer to the actual or impending death of humans, see, for example, Gen. 4.18; 12.12; 20.4; 27.41; 34.25-26; 37.20; Exod. 13.15; Lev. 20.15-16.

Moses' action, reveals that the story circulating about Moses' action is that this is an instance of a striking that resulted in a death. With both points in mind, Moses is the first killer of the story. Pharaoh's unsuccessful attempt to 'slay' Moses invites a comparison between the two. In the arena of killing, Pharaoh remains a failure, but Moses emerges successful.

Initially it appears that killing is reinscribed as an ideal aspect of Moses' masculinity, but the text invites a careful evaluation. Olson argues that in the history of interpretation, Moses' killing of the Egyptian is generally viewed positively, but only by filling in certain gaps in the narrative and ignoring some details (2004: 138-41). For example, Moses' fear (Exod. 2.14) is one of the details Olson mentions that commentators often ignore (140). He incisively shows how the author of Hebrews simply contradicts this detail by instead claiming that Moses leaves 'without fear' (Heb. 11.27), which transforms Moses into an example of faith (140). As an example of a gap in the narrative that commentators fill in order to approve of Moses' action, Olson cites a midrashic tradition that is clearly not in the text, which claims Moses consulted with angels, who approved of his deed, before killing the Egyptian (140).[7] Instead of making these interpretive moves, Olson agrees with Brevard Childs in concluding that 'the narrative does not offer up a final verdict; instead it prompts the reader to ask difficult questions…' (146). This is prudent because it leaves indeterminate what is not clear, refuses to fill gaps, and accounts for important details often ignored. Yet, an explicit condemnation of Moses' action is unnecessary to prevent violence and killing from being reinscribed as an aspect of his masculinity because other textual details, such as Moses' fear and others explored below, can be seen as impeding these efforts.[8]

A portrayal of the cyclical nature of violence, which pushes Moses from the land, shows that violence is an unsustainable approach to conflict. An Egyptian 'strikes' a Hebrew and then Moses 'strikes' the Egyptian. One striking leads to another striking. The confronted Hebrew man supplies another word to clarify Moses' act: 'slaying'. As Moses 'slew' the Egyptian, Pharaoh then seeks to 'slay' Moses. One slaying leads to an attempted slaying. The story describes a believable situation in which people who commit acts of violence against others soon find themselves on the receiving end of that very

---

7. The tradition he cites is *Exod. R. 1.29*.

8. A collection of essays specifically addressing how the association of violence with masculinity can be resisted is especially insightful on how this can occur (Breines *et al.*: 2000). See especially Breines *et al.* (2000: 17), Najcevska (2000: 187) and Quisumbing (2000: 251) for additional specifics. A reoccurring theme is that showing the ineffectiveness of violence as a sustainable approach to conflict and presenting nonviolent alternatives can effectively resist the link between violence and masculinity. Similar features emerge in the story about Moses killing the Egyptian.

same action. The depiction of an escalating cycle of violence that pushes Moses from the land, allows readers to reconsider if violence is a sustainable response to conflict, and by extension, if killing should be a masculine ideal.

The preceding scenes show other ways of resisting oppression than violence. Olson suggests the primary purpose of Exod. 2.1-10 is to present an Egyptian, Pharaoh's daughter, acting righteously on behalf of a Hebrew, which 'prevents an easy painting of all Egyptians as evil' (2004: 144). While this is an important function of the preceding story, as with the earlier story of the midwives, it also shows oppression effectively resisted without the use of violence.[9] Lapsley highlights this contrast most incisively: 'The way the women's deliverance (completely nonviolent, effective resistance) and the incidents involving Moses (violent, ineffective resistance) are starkly juxtaposed suggests that a gendered critique of violence may be operative' (2005: 80). Clearly, these earlier scenes cannot offer a new vision of masculinity for Moses because it is women who opt for the nonviolent approach to conflict. But the narrative juxtaposition of the results of these two different approaches to conflict deconstructs the perceived importance and necessity of violence itself. Thus, while Moses remains a killer, the link between masculinity, including Moses' own masculinity, and violence is resisted because the narrative shows that this is an ineffective way of approaching conflict alongside examples of more effective ways of approaching conflict.

b. *Exodus 2.15b-21: Moses, Masculinity and Detachment from Women*
After fleeing Egypt, Moses settles in Midian near a well. Moses may be on foreign soil in a precarious setting, but this is familiar ground for audiences attuned to the conventions of betrothal scenes in the Hebrew Bible (e.g. Gen. 24.1-67; 29.1-20). Robert Alter points out a few elements to be expected: a future bridegroom in a foreign land, an appearance of a girl, someone drawing water, the girl rushing home, and then the betrothal (1981: 51-52). While these elements reoccur in similar scenes, divergences are artful ways of foreshadowing what is to come for the bride and bridegroom (47-62). Esther Fuchs explores the three instances of this type-scene in canonical order noting that a key difference is the 'gradual diminishment in the literary status of the bride and an increasing emphasis on the role of the groom' (1999: 46). She argues Exod. 2.15b-21, the shortest of the three, grants the least prominent role to women because of its brevity, which reflects the gradual phasing out of this type-scene before it disappears altogether in the Prophets (48-49). For Fuchs, the progressive disappearance of this type-scene serves a patriarchal ideology that upholds the unimportance of women in the lives of biblical leaders (49). If her argument is sustainable, then detachment from women is

---

9.   See also Lapsley (2005: 75-79) for additional details.

simply reinscribed as an ideal for some constructions of masculinity. But two divergences in this scene from the others suggest that the situation is not as clear as Fuchs argues.

A variation in Exod. 2.15b-21 from the other betrothal scenes is that the text reports the words of Reuel's daughters when they return from the well. It is customary for the woman to run and tell her family, but no other instance reveals her words. Rebekah 'runs and tells' all to her mother's household, but the content of her report is not given (Gen. 24.28). While Laban overhears her say, 'This he said to me', the actual content of her speech remains obscured (Gen. 24.30). Likewise, Rachel 'runs and tells' her father, but again the content of her report is absent (Gen. 29.12). Only Exod. 2.19 discloses the women's actual words: 'An Egyptian man delivered us from the hand of the shepherds and he also *certainly drew water* (דלה) for us and *watered* (שקה) the flock'. Where the other instances of this scene silence the women and prevent their voice from being heard, this scene gives the women full voice. And the scene does more than merely allowing audiences to hear their voices. In narratological terms, the scene allows the daughters to focalize their own experience at the well. Focalization, as a category of narratological analysis, refers to the idea that events are both seen and narrated from a particular perspective within texts (Bal 2009: 145-47). The focalization of this event through the eyes and voices of the daughters is clear because they diverge from the narrator's account of two textual events, both of which I only briefly note at this point, but comment on more extensively later. First, the narrator reports that Moses 'saves' (ישע) the daughters (2.17), but they say that he 'delivered' (נצל) them (2.19). Second, they also have a different version of who drew water at the well than what the narrator actually reports (2.16, 19). In both examples, the text allows the daughters to have a unique experience of the events and to audibly articulate that unique experience. Therefore, this scene not only allows readers to hear the women's voices, it also gives them a glimpse of a unique focalization of those events from the daughters' experience. While the scene is brief, the women are not mere peripheral figures, but play a significant part in it.

A second variation in this type-scene emerges when exploring the daughters' claim about who drew water at the well. In Exod. 2.16, the narrator reports that the daughters of Reuel, 'Came and *drew water* (דלה) and *filled* (מלא) the troughs *to water* (שקה) the flocks of their father'. Yet when they report back to their father, they tell him that Moses 'certainly drew water (דלה)' for them (2.19). They emphasize this point by the use of an infinitive absolute with a perfect verb. While the narrator states that Moses 'watered' (שקה) the flocks after saving them, the narrator does not report that Moses 'drew water' (דלה) for them as they stress to their father (2.17). In departing from the narrator's account, the daughters appear to be negotiating with their

father for a spouse, which is a significant deviation from the other occurrences of this type-scene. In Genesis 24, the unnamed male servant negotiates
with Rebekah's family to obtain Rebekah.[10] In Genesis 29, Jacob negotiates
with Laban for Rachel. In both scenes, men negotiate for women. But in
Exod. 2.15b-21, the roles are reversed. Women negotiate for the man, Moses.
Just as Moses saved the women, they save Moses by ensuring he will be
brought into their father's house.[11] Moses may remain a sojourner in a foreign land, but his situation is far less precarious now than at the opening of
this scene as a result of the daughters of Reuel. This motif of women saving
Moses, which emerges in the ways this type-scene diverges from the others,
foreshadows the role that Zipporah will have in saving Moses' life from an
attack by God (Exod. 4.24-26). It is also entirely consistent with what has
transpired previously in the text. Moses' mother, sister, and Pharaoh's daughter save Moses by working together and disobeying Pharaoh. Shiphrah and
Puah's decisive actions provide the foundation for this saving of Moses.[12]

These two variations reveal that the situation is more complicated than
Fuchs argues. The scene is laconic and the women fade when it closes, with
Zipporah's salvation of Moses being a notable exception. Still, the ways this
type-scene diverges from the others reveals that women have an important
role to play in saving Moses at critical junctures in his life. If Moses were
detached from women in the first four chapters of Exodus, he would be dead.
Thus, the text significantly challenges assumptions about masculinity that
would suggest detachment from women, in the sense of acting independently
of women or not relying upon women, is a masculine ideal for Moses. Indeed,
these chapters intimate the exact opposite. When Moses relies upon the
women in his life and is assisted by them, he lives. On the one occasion
Moses is not connected to women at this point in the text, he quickly becomes
embroiled in a cycle of violence that forces him to flee Egypt, narrowly escap-
ing alive. For Moses, the text portrays attachment to women far more positively than detachment from women.

Moses' rescuing of the daughters from the shepherds raises again the issue
of violence and masculinity. The narrator reports that Moses 'saved' (יֹשַׁע)

---

10. On the subtleties of this story, which are beyond the scope of this paper, see
Sternberg (1987: 143-52).

11. In a similar respect, Lapsley notes what she calls a 'pattern of reciprocal deliverances' (2005: 81). Her observation that this pattern involves baby Moses being saved by
women when they draw him from the river and Moses then saving women in this scene is
astute, but the pattern goes one step further than Lapsley notes (81-82). The pattern of
'reciprocal deliverances' comes full circle when these women, the daughters of Reuel,
save the adult Moses. Thus, while I am in full agreement with her observation, I suggest
that the pattern is continued one step farther than what she notes.

12. Again, for an account of these details, which are beyond the scope of this paper, see
Lapsley (2005: 72-79) and Frymer-Kensky (2002: 24-33).

them (2.17). Olson shows that although this verb is often used to describe 'savings' that use violence, this is not universal (2004: 143).[13] In exploring this argument, the daughters' experience of Moses' act is also important. They report that Moses 'delivered' (נצל) them (2.19). As with ישע (to save), נצל (to deliver) is often used in situations that use violence in delivering, but this is not always the case and it is even used specifically as deliverance from violence.[14] Thus, neither verb describing Moses' action requires violence. The emphasis of both is more on the end result of being saved or delivered than the method used to bring a person to that state. Indeed, there are almost deliberate moves made to obscure what Moses does to the shepherds. In Exod. 2.17, the narrator reports Moses saved 'them', a third person *feminine* plural suffix. The phrasing reveals what Moses does for the daughters and obscures what he does to the shepherds. Similarly in Exod. 2.19, the daughters report, 'He delivered *us*', again revealing what Moses does for the daughters, but not to the shepherds. As such, neither the narrator's description of Moses' action, nor the daughters' experience of it, offers any evidence on the manner in which Moses rescues the daughters. Is it possible that in obscuring the precise nature of Moses' action to the shepherds, the text prompts the audience to consider the possibility of resolving conflict without the explicit presence of violence? Moses' earlier efforts to address conflict were expressed in the unequivocally violent language of 'striking' (נכה) or 'slaying' (הרג) as interpreted by others who hear of Moses' action. But in this scene, conflict is addressed and these violent measures are not plainly evident. It is tempting to offer conjectures about how Moses 'saves' or 'rescues' the daughters, such as what Lapsley does when suggesting that Moses is 'progressively maturing, honing his mediating skills' (2005: 81). But the text's deliberate obscuring of the precise nature of Moses' action renders such tentative proposals as stable as their foundation. At the same time, by obscuring how Moses saves the daughters of Reuel, the text opens the possibility for imagining a masculinity, in which violence is not a prerequisite for conflict resolution as it was earlier.

c. *Exodus 3.1–4.17: Persuasive Speech and the Call of Moses*
Persuasive speech is a deceptively complicated theme in the call of Moses. From the beginning, God tries to persuade Moses to go to Egypt (Exod. 3.10). In the end, Moses goes. God is clearly a persuasive speaker. Moreover, as God's ability to sway Moses initiates the exodus from Egypt, the text portrays persuasive speech positively. But while this point is clear, associating God's persuasive speech with masculinity is more difficult. As previously discussed, other scholars argue that persuasive speech can be characteristic of

---

13. Important biblical examples that Olson cites include 2 Sam. 14.4-8; 22.3.
14. E.g. Gen. 32.12; 37.21-22; Josh. 2.13; 9.26; Jer. 22.3; Jon. 4.6.

both masculinity and femininity. For God's ability to speak persuasively to be a clear association of persuasive speech with masculinity, God needs to be imagined as a male in the text. While determining the textual portrayal of God's gender is a far more complex discussion than what is possible here, there is some evidence to problematize attributing God's ability to speak persuasively directly with masculinity.[15]

Moses also speaks persuasively, but what Moses attempts to persuade God of is not initially clear. The statement of Moses often relied upon to elucidate this ambiguity is exceedingly murky: 'Send through the hand of the one you will send' (שְׁלַח־נָא בְּיַד־תִּשְׁלָח, Exod. 4.13). Two possibilities exist: (1) Moses refuses to go and requests God send someone else, and (2) Moses acquiesces to God's call. Commentators often adopt the former and read Moses' prior statements as attempts to achieve this end (e.g. Childs 2004: 70-79). But even if this resolution of Moses' statement is plausible, it is similar to what Mieke Bal calls the 'retrospective fallacy' (1987: 108ff.). If Moses asks God to send someone else in Exod. 4.13, then it does not mean that his prior comments can be read from that perspective. While seemingly a minor point, it effects the evaluation of Moses as a persuasive speaker. If Moses has been trying to avoid going all along, then Moses is not a persuasive speaker. But if Moses never tries to evade his call, or only does so at the end, then Moses could be a

---

15. The focus of this paper is masculinity in Pharaoh and Moses. Thus, the factors that complicate efforts to gender God are formerly outside the scope of this paper. If God's behaviour fit well with other aspects that are indicative of masculinity under consideration in this paper (i.e. violence, detachment from women, persuasive speech), there could be an indirect way of gendering God's behaviour. But linking God's actions with these aspects of masculinity is difficult. Killing is not yet an issue in the story and is therefore not applicable here. Detachment from women is more complicated. Clearly, God chooses to rely upon Moses to liberate the people and Aaron is Moses' spokesperson, which suggests that God does not rely on women. Yet, in Exodus, the midwives are the first people that God depends on. Without the midwives, God would have no people to liberate. In this sense, God is dependent on the midwives. Moreover, God's liberation of the people from bondage by resisting the oppression of Pharaoh, finds its narrative prototype in the midwives' defiance of Pharaoh to intervene on behalf of targeted members of society (see also Lapsley 2005: 79). God can be seen as acting in a fashion similar to the midwives, so not entirely detached from women. Finally, both women (the midwives and Moses' sister) and men (Moses) engage in persuasive speech, so it is difficult to definitively link it with either masculinity or femininity. Thus, God's ability to speak persuasively does not necessarily make God masculine or male. God needs a sexed body to make this link clear. While God sees, hears, and appears in these chapters, the only body parts God has are a 'hand' and 'an outstretched arm', which can be euphemisms for male genitalia, but they do not have to be understood in this way. Thus, although it might initially seem that God is masculine in these chapters, there are significant impediments to adopting this position because of these textual details.

persuasive speaker. With this possibility open, it is evident that Moses moves God to adopt new aspects that were not part of the initial proposal made by God. Moses obtains a name for God (3.13-16), three signs to show the people (4.1-9), and Aaron as a spokesperson (4.10-17). Thus, Moses is a persuasive speaker because he moves God to adopt new elements that were not originally part of the proposal.

While Moses is a persuasive speaker, his claim that he is not 'a man of words' because of 'a heavy mouth and a heavy tongue' complicates the discussion of how this ability relates to his masculinity (Exod. 4.10). Leaving aside the irony of a persuasive speaker who avows ineptness with words, Moses' assertion is puzzling because the ability to persuade others with his words does not seem integral to his calling. When God sends Moses to Pharaoh to bring the people out of Egypt, God does not specify how to accomplish this task (3.10). Later, God makes it clear that although Moses will speak to Pharaoh, Moses' words will not persuade Pharaoh (3.18-19). Quite apart from Moses' words, it is God's outstretched hand and wonders that will persuade Pharaoh (3.20). In a similar respect, although Moses will speak to the elders of Israel (3.16), when Moses suggests that the people will not believe him, God provides signs, not words, to persuade them (4.1-9). In both instances, success for Moses occurs in spite of his inability to speak persuasively. Perhaps Moses makes his bewildering confession because he has noticed that if he fulfills the terms of God's calling, then he will not be a persuasive speaker, which would be an emasculating move in a setting where the ability is a sign of masculinity. Thus, Moses' statement seems to be an attempt to verify that persuasive speech will not be an intrinsic component of his calling and correspondingly that he will not unman himself if he does what God asks. Confirmation comes in two ways. First, Aaron becomes Moses' spokesperson (4.14-17). In this move, while persuasive speech may be more closely associated with Aaron's masculinity, it is disassociated from Moses' masculinity. Second, the place of Moses' words in relation to God's wonders is spelled out in Exod. 4.21-22. Moses will perform wonders as well as be an announcer and interpreter of God's actions against Pharaoh, but will not persuade Pharaoh with his own words. In the process, as gender is bound up in work, although Moses is a persuasive speaker, it does not seem to be an integral component to his masculinity.

d. *Exodus 4.24-26: Masculinity Revisited*
Exodus 4.24-26 is a perplexing scene. It describes God's sudden attempt to kill Moses and Zipporah's intervention that wards off God to save Moses. The scene is incredibly laconic, antecedents of pronouns are not entirely clear, and the portrayal of a murderous deity is surprising. While commentators bemoan the difficulties and obscurities of this text, they also do not

hesitate to suggest a few points.[16] In that spirit and in relation to the stated intentions of this essay, three are suggested here. (1) A woman saves a man. Without Zipporah's intervention, Moses would be dead. As alluded to earlier, her saving role, foreshadowed in the divergences of the betrothal scene, is enacted here.[17] If detachment from women is supposed to be a masculine ideal, this scene presents a significant challenge to that ideology. Without Zipporah's mediation, the text gives every impression that Moses would be dead. (2) A decisive action accomplishes as much or more than two chapters of persuasive speech. Zipporah simply takes action as opposed to engaging with God in a rhetorical debate. In so doing, she calls into question the necessity of persuasive speech in some situations by showing the effectiveness of a quick action to protect a targeted person. (3) Violence is not portrayed positively. The text says that God 'sought to kill him' (ויבקש המיתו, Exod. 4.24). Earlier Pharaoh 'sought to slay Moses' (ויבקש להרג, Exod. 2.15). Where God sought to 'kill' (מות), Pharaoh sought to 'slay' (הרג). While the verbs used are different, both Pharaoh and God 'seek' (בקש) the death of Moses. In 'seeking' the death of Moses, God and Pharaoh are cast in surprisingly similar terms. The depiction of God as acting aggressively towards Moses, just like Pharaoh, prevents God's action from being viewed entirely positively. The portrayal of violence in less than a positive light resists rescribing violence as a trait to be linked with the constructions of masculinity studied in this paper.

Conclusion

Exodus 1–4 offers a complex representation of certain traits associated with masculinity in the Hebrew Bible: (1) Violence, especially as expressed through killing, (2) Persuasive speech as part of dealing wisely, and (3) Detachment from women. In the characterization of Pharaoh, the narrator depicts Pharaoh trying to act in accordance with these assumptions, but consistently failing. The narrative effect of this portrayal is to emasculate Pharaoh and deconstruct his power. As no challenge is presented to these assumptions, they are initially reinscribed. But as the text focuses on Moses, a critical evaluation of the same assumptions was noted. Without explicitly condemning Moses for killing the Egyptian, the text invites a careful reconsideration of the merits of violence by depicting a realistic cycle of violence that pushes Moses out of the land alongside examples of effective nonviolent resistance. While Moses

---

16. Pardes has a particularly interesting analysis of this story (1992: 79-97). She suggests that this scene reflects an Israelite adaptation and repression of Egyptian myths about Isis and Osiris in an attempt to accommodate them to a patriarchal and monotheistic religion.

17. See also, Lapsley (2005: 84).

is a killer, the explosively rebounding effects of this action resist positively associating violence with his masculinity. Furthermore, the text problema-tizes any attempts to reinscribe detachment from women as a masculine ideal for Moses because the women in his life rescue him at important points of his life. And even though Moses is persuasive, it is difficult to definitively link this ability with his masculinity. The deconstruction of these assumptions about masculinity culminates in the scene where Zipporah, a woman, saves Moses from God's violent attack with a quick action, not an abundance of words. While the text relies upon assumptions about masculinity to decon-struct the power of Pharaoh, it also deconstructs the masculine values them-selves and subtly begins to construct a reconfigured, if not yet fully formed, gendered identity for Moses. In this emerging image of masculinity for Moses, violence is not necessarily a positive trait or a prerequisite for conflict resolution, both relying upon women and intervening on behalf of targeted others are traits to be valued, and persuasive speech is not clearly linked to masculinity.

Bibliography

Alter, Robert
    1981   *The Art of Biblical Narrative* (New York: Basic Books).
Bal, Mieke
    1987   *Lethal Love: Feminist Literary Readings of Biblical Love Stories* (Bloom-ington: Indiana University Press).
    2009   *Narratology: Introduction to the Theory of Narrative* (Toronto: University of Toronto Press, 3rd edn).
Bolger, Diane (ed.)
    2008   *Gender through Time in the Ancient Near East* (Lanham, MD: Altamira Press).
Breines, Ingeborg, Robert Connell, and Ingrid Eide (eds.)
    2000   *Male Roles, Masculinities and Violence: A Culture of Peace Perspective* (Paris: UNESCO).
Brenner, Athalya (ed.)
    1994   *A Feminist Companion to Exodus to Deuteronomy* (Sheffield: Sheffield Academic Press).
Childs, Brevard
    2004   *The Book of Exodus: A Critical Theological Commentary* (Louisville, KY: Westminster John Knox Press).
Clines, David J.A.,
    1995a   'David the Man: The Construction of Masculinity in the Hebrew Bible', in his *Interested Parties: The Ideology of Writers and Readers of the Hebrew Bible* (JSOTSup, 205; GCT, 1; Sheffield: Sheffield Academic Press): 212-43.
    1995b   'The Book of Psalms: Where Men are Men: On the Gendering of Hebrew Piety', online: http.//www.shef.ac.uk/bibs/DJACcurrres/PlayMan.html (accessed February 22, 2009).

1996   'Loin-girding and Other Male Activities in the Book of Job', online: http://
           www.shef.ac.uk/bibs/DJACcurrres/Loingirding.html (accessed February
           22, 2009).

1997   'Dancing and Shining at Sinai: Playing the Man in Exodus 32–34', in the
           present volume, and online: http://www.shef.ac.uk/bibs/DJACcurrres/
           Dancing.html (accessed February 22, 2009).

2002   'He-Prophets: Masculinity as a Problem for the Hebrew Prophets and their
           Interpreters', in Alastair G. Hunter and Philip R. Davies (eds.), *Sense and
           Sensitivity: Essays on Reading the Bible in Memory of Robert Carroll*
           (JSOTSup, 348; Sheffield: Sheffield Academic Press): 311-28.

Connell, R.W.
2005   *Masculinities* (Berkeley, California: University of California Press, 2nd
           edn).

Croucher, Karina
2008   'Ambiguous Genders? Alternative Interpretations: A Discussion of Case
           Studies from the Pre-Pottery Neolithic and Halaf Periods', in Diane Bolger
           (ed.), *Gender through Time in the Ancient Near East* (Lanham, MD:
           Altamira Press): 21-51.

Day, Linda
2006   'Wisdom and the Feminine in the Hebrew Bible', in Linda Day and
           Carolyn Pressler (eds.), *Engaging the Bible in a Gendered World: An
           Introduction to Feminist Biblical Interpretation in Honor of Katherine
           Doob Sakenfeld* (Louisville, KY: Westminster John Knox Press): 114-27.

Exum, Cheryl
1994a   'You Shall Let Every Daughter Live: A Study of Exodus 1.8–2.10', in
           Brenner 1994: 37-61.

1994b   'Second Thoughts about Secondary Characters', in Brenner 1994: 75-87.

Frevert, Ute
1998   'The Taming of the Noble Ruffian: Male Violence and Dueling in Early
           Modern and Modern Germany', in Pieter Spierenburg (ed.), *Men and
           Violence: Gender, Honor, and Rituals in Modern Europe and America*
           ([Columbus, OH]: Ohio State University Press): 37-63.

Frymer-Kensky, Tikva
2002   *Reading the Women of the Bible: A New Interpretation of their Stories*
           (New York: Random House).

Fuchs, Esther
1999   'Structure and Patriarchal Functions in the Biblical Betrothal Type-Scene:
           Some Preliminary Notes', in Alice Bach (ed.), *Women in the Hebrew
           Bible: A Reader* (New York: Routledge): 45-51.

Gesenius, H.W.F.
1910   *Gesenius' Hebrew Grammar* (ed. E. Kautzsch; revised and trans. A.E.
           Cowley; Oxford: Clarendon Press).

Goldingay, John
1995   'Hosea 1–3, Genesis 1–4, and Masculinist Interpretation', *HBT* 17: 37-44.

Hoffner, Harry A., Jr
1966   'Symbols for Masculinity and Femininity: Their Use in Ancient Near
           Eastern Sympathetic Magic Rituals', *JBL* 85: 326-34.

Lapsley, Jacqueline
    2005   *Whispering the Word: Hearing Women's Stories in the Old Testament*
            (Louisville, KY: Westminster John Knox Press).
Najcevska, Mirjana
    2000   'Education, Masculinity and Violence', in Ingeborg Breines *et al.* (eds.),
            Male Roles, Masculinities and Violence: A Culture of Peace Perspective
            (Paris: UNESCO): 181-87.
Olson, Dennis T.
    2004   'Violence for the Sake of Social Justice? Narrative, Ethics, and
            Indeterminacy in Moses' Slaying of the Egyptian (Exodus 2.11-15)', in
            Charles H. Cosgrove (ed.), *The Meanings We Choose: Hermeneutical
            Ethics, Indeterminacy, and the Conflict of Interpretations* (New York: T.
            & T. Clark International): 138-48.
    2006   'Untying the Knot? Masculinity, Violence, and the Creation–Fall Story of
            Genesis 2–4', in Linda Day and Carolyn Pressler (eds.), *Engaging the
            Bible in a Gendered World: An Introduction to Feminist Biblical Inter-
            pretation in Honor of Katherine Doob Sakenfeld* (Louisville, KY: West-
            minster John Knox Press): 73-86.
Pardes, Ilana
    1992   *Countertraditions in the Bible: A Feminist Approach* (Cambridge, MA:
            Harvard University Press).
Quisumbing, Lourdes R.
    2000   'Values Education toward a Culture of Peace', in Ingeborg Breines *et al.*
            (eds.), *Male Roles, Masculinities and Violence: A Culture of Peace Per-
            spective* (Paris: UNESCO): 249-55.
Spierenburg, Pieter
    1998a   'Knife Fighting and Popular Codes of Honor in Early Modern Amster-
            dam', in Pieter Spierenburg (ed.), *Men and Violence: Gender, Honor, and
            Rituals in Modern Europe and America* (Ohio: Ohio State University
            Press): 103-27.
    1998b   'Masculinity, Violence, and Honor: An Introduction', in Pieter Spierenburg
            (ed.), *Men and Violence: Gender, Honor, and Rituals in Modern Europe
            and America* ([Columbus, OH]: Ohio State University Press, 1998): 1-29.
Sternberg, Meir
    1987   *The Poetics of Biblical Narrative: Ideological Literature and the Drama of
            Reading* (Bloomington, IN: Indiana University Press).
Washington, Harold C.
    1997   'Violence and the Construction of Gender in the Hebrew Bible: A New
            Historicist Approach', *BibInt* 5: 324-63.
Weems, Renita J.
    1992   'The Hebrew Women Are Not like the Egyptian Women: The Ideology of
            Race, Gender, and Sexual Reproduction in Exodus 1', *Semeia* 59: 25-34.

DANCING AND SHINING AT SINAI: PLAYING THE MAN IN EXODUS 32–34[*]

David J.A. Clines

These days, I am teaching myself to say, every time I open a page of the Hebrew Bible, 'This is a male text'. And then, 'Where is its masculinity inscribed, where is it visible? How are the distinctives of masculinity expressed? What image of maleness, what profiles of masculinity, are embedded here? What message do the males inside this text receive about what it is to be a man? And what message do the males and females outside this text receive about how men should 'play the man'? This phrase[1] is the *mot juste*, I would suggest, for masculinity *is* a performance, a performance of a learned script. The Hebrew Bible, I am coming to understand, is written throughout in a language that is still imperfectly deciphered. It is written in *'ivrit* 'Hebrew'; we all know that. But who notices that it is also written in *gavrit* 'Masclish' (shall we say?), in the language of masculinity? *Gavrit* is of course not just a language with its own vocabulary (like כָּבוֹד 'honour' and בֹּשֶׁת 'shame', גָּדוֹל 'great' and גִּבּוֹר 'mighty one', הרג 'slay' and הֵמִית 'kill' and הִכָּה 'smite'), but a thought-world with its own ideals and standards and conventions. In this paper, I want to identify four distinctives of masculinity in Exodus 32–34: (1) The Warrior Male; (2) The Persuasive Male; (3) The Womanless Male; and (4) The Beautiful Male.

---

[*]   This paper was first read to the Biblical Law Section of the Society of Biblical Literature at its Annual Meeting, San Francisco, 22 November 1997.
   1.   The phrase comes from 2 Sam. 10.12, where Joab says to his brother Abishai when confronted by Syrians and Ammonites: 'Be of good courage, and let us play the man for our people, and for the cities of our God' (RSV). The phrase is perhaps most familiar to the English-speaking reader through the sentence of the Oxford martyr Hugh Latimer to his friend Nicholas Ridley at their execution, 'Play the man, Master Ridley; we shall this day light such a candle, by God's grace, in England, as (I trust) shall never be put out' (cited from *The Oxford Dictionary of Quotations* [1979: 310]). It is found also in *The Martyrdom of Polycarp*, 9, where Polycarp hears a voice from heaven: 'Be strong, Polycarp, and play the man' (in the translation of Lake 1925). In a modern setting, it is to be found in Ray Bradbury's novel *Fahrenheit 451* (1954: 36), with evident reference to the sentence of Hugh Latimer.

1. *The Warrior Male*

The fundamental characteristic of a man in Hebrew Bible literature, as I understand it, is that he should be a fighter, which means: capable of killing another man. And Moses is, at the most elemental level, such a man. The baby in the basket is in danger just because he is a male child, and the narrative of Exodus shows us how justified the pharaoh's fear of male children is: it only takes Moses two sentences to get from suckling at the breast to murdering an Egyptian (Exod. 2.9, 11).

Moses the lawgiver is not generally remembered as a killer. His youthful murder of an oppressive Egyptian is often waved away as a act of hotheadedness mingled with righteous indignation. In the commentators we can even observe, as Childs notes, 'a tacit approval of Moses' deed because of its passionate quality'.[2]

I do not need to linger over the many associations of Moses with death and killing, for it is a particular episode that is before us. What is special here is that it is not the enemies of Israel that are the objects of his violence, not Egyptians or Midianites, but members of the Israelite company itself.[3] Says Moses to the Levites:

> Buckle on your sword, each of you, and go up and down the camp from gate to gate, every man of you slaughtering brother, friend and neighbour (32.27 NJB).

If killing is the quintessential male characteristic in the Hebrew Bible, killing lots of other men in company with fellow killers has to be doubly so, and killing brothers, friends and neighbours is a triple masculinity. The narrative invokes the image of the 'troop', the collectivity of male warriors that moves in unison and overwhelms the fears and fatigue and conscience of the individual soldier.[4] Slaughtering brother, friend and neighbour is not a pretty picture, and all the worse because it is in the name of God. But it is the picture of masculinity this text presents us with, the image of the male that it inculcates into impressionable young Bible readers and confirms in more seasoned warriors who have long been gripped by the idea of killing, literally or metaphorically, brother, friend and neighbour for the sake of a cause. No

2. See Childs 1974: 42; he does mention a strain in the history of exegesis in which Moses' act was condemned (40-42).

3. There is an exegetical tradition that it was the 'mixed multitude' from Egypt rather than the Israelites themselves that were to blame for the making of the golden calf (so e.g. Saadia and Rashi; cf. Childs 1974: 576).

4. See for example the impressive descriptions of the 'troop as totality-machine' in Klaus Theweleit's *Male Fantasies*. II. *Male Bodies: Psychoanalysing the White Terror* (1989: 153-59); his analysis is that 'the surplus value produced by the troop is a code that consolidates other totality formations between men, such as the "nation"' (155).

one can be a disciple of Jesus, for example, without this very vision of masculinity: 'No one can be my disciple if he does not hate his father and mother and wife and children and brothers and sisters—and his own life!' (Lk. 14.26).

The narrative equally signifies the importance of a chain of command in military affairs and underscores that to be a soldier requires obedience: everyone carrying out this massacre is acting under orders. Moses makes it an issue of a specific divine prescription ('Thus says Yahweh', a phrase rare in the Pentateuch), and the Levites act 'according to the word of Moses', another uncommon locution (only in Exod. 8.13; Lev. 10.7). The common bloodguilt of the Levites bonds them, and sets them apart from the rest of the people.[5] 'Today', Moses said, 'you have consecrated yourselves (*mla yd*) to Yahweh, one at the cost of his son, another of his brother' (32.29 NJB). Some might think that the Levites were set apart or consecrated to Yahweh at some pacific ordination ceremony such as Numbers 8 represents, with washing and shaving and a change of clothes. Not according to Exodus 32, which portrays them as males, as warriors.

2. *The Persuasive Male*

When I was studying masculinity in the David story,[6] I came to realize that persuasive speech was in ancient Israel a typical mark of male behaviour. With great success, David, for example, persuades Saul that he is capable of withstanding Goliath (1 Sam. 17.34-36), explains to Saul why he did not kill him in the cave (1 Sam. 24.10-15), and even brings Saul to admit that he has done wrong (1 Sam. 26.21). These are effective examples of the power of words, not in any magical sense,[7] but as instruments of control. To be master of persuasion is to have another form of power, which is not an alternative to, and far less a denatured version of, physical strength, but part of the repertory of the powerful male.

Moses' masculine strength shows itself here in a speech of persuasion that has the effrontery to attempt to change the mind of *God*. Yahweh has announced that in revenge for the making of the molten calf he will annihilate the people and make Moses into a great nation (32.10). Moses displays his strength in a powerful speech (Exod. 32.11-13), and Yahweh 'repents' of the evil he had planned to do to his people (Exod. 32.14). Moses is not so

---

5. Whether the traditional violence of the patriarch Levi has anything to do with it (cf. Gen. 34.25; 49.5-7; Deut. 33.9) I do not know (cf. Hyatt 1971: 310).

6. 'David the Man: The Construction of Masculinity in the Hebrew Bible', in Clines 1995a: 212-43.

7. I am not claiming that, since I find convincing the analysis of Thiselton 1974: 282-99.

successful, it must be said, in his second speech to Yahweh (Exod. 32.31-32), though there is some confusion over whether this second speech was not altogether otiose: it seems that Yahweh, in repenting in v. 14 of the evil he planned against the Israelites, no longer needs to be called on to 'forgive' them, as Moses asks in v. 32.

Moses' third dialogue with Yahweh (Exod. 33.12-23) is also somewhat indistinct,[8] but it too represents an achievement for Moses' power. In this six-member dialogue, three speeches of Moses and three of Yahweh, it is Moses who makes the running and it is Moses who gets his way. It is an intercession in form, but it is also an act of power, for Moses wrests concession after concession from Yahweh. When he does not at first get his way, as when he is assured of Yahweh's mere 'presence' when what he wants to gain is knowledge of his 'ways' or purposes (Exod. 33.13),[9] he insists until Yahweh concedes, 'This very thing that you have spoken I will do' (Exod. 33.17)—a very submissive speech for a deity, is it not? Even when Moses demands to see Yahweh's 'glory'—a most outrageous desire,[10] which might be thought either to kill him or to make him divine—he is not entirely rebuffed; even if his request is not granted, it is not refused either. He may not see Yahweh's 'glory', but he sees his 'goodness' and hears his 'name'. This is how a 'real man' behaves, runs the text. He is so adept with the weapon of words that he can take on any opponent, even the deity, and win—or if not exactly win, then not be put to shame.

3. *The Womanless Male*

Male texts do not on principle exclude women, but it is characteristic of them nevertheless that women are invisible. In the male world, the presence of women can be assumed, but rarely needs to be signaled. Obviously, the two protagonists in this narrative, Moses and Aaron, are male, and so is the only other named person, Moses' attendant, the young man Joshua. Yahweh is male too, of course (as Moses would have seen only too well if he had glimpsed more than Yahweh's 'back parts'), and he remembers his dealings with the males of old, Abraham, Isaac and Israel/Jacob (Exod. 32.13; 33.1).

8. 'Perhaps the logical consistency of this dialogue should not be overworked', says Childs (1974: 594). But for an energetic attempt to establish its coherence, see Moberly 1983: 67-83.

9. I take a lead here from G. Henton Davies (1967: 241): 'Moses therefore implies that he is not satisfied with God's reply, and his own request still stands. In effect he says: "I know we have your Presence—even if it is outside the camp—but I want to know your ways—your purposes".'

10. Henton Davies denominates it 'The Daring of Moses' (1967: 242).

The (male) 'sons' of Levi, the ideological cleansers, are the other active players who catch our attention.

To be sure, the men of Israel have wives and daughters with gold earrings (Exod. 32.2), daughters who, they fear, will whore after foreign gods and make their brothers whore after them also (plainly, the males cannot go astray of their own accord, but only if they are seduced by women) (Exod. 34.16). Perhaps the women are there too in the scene by the golden calf, when the people 'sat down to eat and drink, and rose up to play' (Exod. 32.6)—if that שׁחק means what we suspect it does, as the Good News Bible (Today's English Version) puts it so delicately: 'The people sat down to a feast, which turned into an orgy of drinking and sex'.[11]

But on the whole, 'the people' (העם) in this narrative does not mean in Hebrew what it means for us. It is not the totality of the Israelites in the wilderness, but the males alone. We notice that it is the men who are focalized as the narrative opens: the 'people', that is, the *men*, saw that Moses was overdue in returning and urged Aaron to make gods for them. For Aaron responds to the 'people' by telling them to remove the earrings from their 'wives and sons and daughters' (Exod. 32.2). The 'people' can therefore only be the men. If we have a vision, when we read throughout this narrative of the 'people', of sisters and cousins and aunts converging upon Aaron to plead for a golden calf, of stiff-necked women as well as men (Exod. 32.9), of singing in soprano as well as baritone voices, of dancing as a mingling of the sexes, or of ground gold being forced down the throats of maidens and matrons and little old ladies—we have only to remember scenes of males-only education and entertainment and markets from Taliban-controlled Afghanistan to adjust our focus. This is a womanless world. (You can say that the presumptive women, through being invisible, at least escape the ideological slaughter: the sons of Levi mow down only brothers and companions and neighbours, men every one of them. The women escape with their lives, which they can then spend usefully bewailing their lost husbands and brothers and sons.)

Yahweh too has eyes only for males. Whether it is beast or human offspring, he claims the life of the first male to 'open the womb' (Exod. 34.19). If a female is the first offspring, Yahweh is not interested.[12] (I do not know if the first male, even if the second offspring, counts as 'firstborn'.) If you want to keep your firstborn son, and not let him go into service in Yahweh's house, like Samuel, you need to pay Yahweh for him. And even if your sons have been 'redeemed', they must show themselves to Yahweh three times a year in

---

11. But what if there were no women, and it were homosexual sex? That seems to be what the by-form *ṣḥq at* signifies in Gen. 21.9, where Ishmael is 'playing' with Isaac.

12. This must have been the case too in the slaying of the firstborn in Egypt (Exod. 12.12); though a gendered word is not used (I mean, בכור could in principle include females), we are meant to know that only males can be firstborn.

an all-male ceremony (Exod. 34.23).[13] In short, males are important in the eyes of God, females are not.

The manifestations are various, but the interpretation is one, as Joseph would say. What is worth remembering of the past is what men have done. What is therefore worthy of note in the present is what men are doing. This is authoritative, this is God's attitude. That is the message the text has for men and women alike.

4. *The Beautiful Male*

Beauty is a masculine ideal in the ancient world; the evidence is unassailable. But is it to be found in our chapters? There is an inkling of male beauty in the decoration of the men of Israel. Exod. 32.2 has Aaron inviting 'the people' (העם), who must be the men, to 'Take off the rings of gold which are in the ears of your wives, your sons, and your daughters' (RSV)—though saying nothing, as it happens, about gold rings that might be in their own ears. Exod. 32.3 has 'the people' taking off the gold rings from 'their' ears—which also is not entirely clear, since it might be from the ears of the wives, the sons and the daughters, or might be from their own ears. Exod. 32.24 is unequally unspecific, in that it has Aaron declaring that he asked 'anyone' with gold jewellery to strip it off. But I am assuming that it is purely accidental that the men of the people are not specifically said to be wearing gold earrings. For in Exod. 33.4-6, the 'people of Israel', the men, put off their ornaments in mourning. In Exod. 35.22 'both men and women' bring gold ornaments, brooches, earrings, signet rings and armlets, for the decoration of the taber-nacle. And it was both men and women who had 'borrowed' the jewellery from their Egyptian neighbours in the first place (Exod. 11.2). In any case, even if the men in our chapter are not specifically said to be wearing earrings, their 'sons' clearly are.

The point is that men are wearing jewellery, which means adornment, to enhance beauty. If you can't imagine being regarded as attractive, you don't decorate yourself. Dressing up means that you have a certain image of your-self as worth looking at. The men of ancient Israel evidently felt the same, and there was no conflict between the heroic male and the prettified male. In a world where there is, unlike our own, no important overlap in social role between men and women, there is no need for men to define themselves as masculine over against women, to follow what has been called the primary

---

13. The rule has appeared already in Exod. 23.17. Male commentators usually see nothing remarkable in this, nor even wonder *why* the males are appearing before Yahweh or what he might do to them when they do. I checked Henton Davies (1967), Hyatt (1971), Childs (1974), as well as Noth (1962) and Cole (1973).

rule for men of our own time: Don't be female.[14] There is therefore no inhibition on a man decorating his body.

Finally, a gendered reading of our text can perhaps offer an explanation for the famous crux in 34.30 about the shining of Moses' face. As a powerful male, who has had the supreme distinction of personal converse with God, Moses acquires astonishing beauty that not only dazzles his earthly conversation partners but perhaps also stirs in them unhealthy lusts. If the servant of Yahweh in Isaiah 53 had no beauty that males should desire (חמד) him, we may assume that if Moses has outstanding beauty of face he will be desired by other males.

The key term is the 'shining' of the face. It is an ordinary word for the shining of light, whether of the sun (e.g. 2 Kgs 3.22) or the moon (Isa. 60.19) or stars (Joel 2.10), a fire (e.g. Isa. 4.5) or a lamp (e.g. Job 29.3), or the wake left in the sea by Leviathan (Job 41.24 [38]). What can it mean when it is a 'face' that shines, or to be more precise, the 'skin of the face' (Exod. 34.29)? Either it must be that the skin is lit up from without, as when it is illuminated by a strong light, or that it seems lit up from within, as if the face itself is a light. The fact that Moses' face remains shining even when he is not gazing upon the light that is God's presence suggests that it is an internal light. Either way, the key question is, Does a shining face improve your appearance? If it does, we are in the realm of beauty.

An important text is Ps. 104.15: '…wine to gladden the human heart, oil to make the face shine, and bread to strengthen the human heart' (NRSV). This has to be oil as a cosmetic (note its use after the bath, Ruth 3.3; 2 Sam. 12.20),[15] and we have to assume that other people think you are more beautiful if your face is shining. If you are poor, oil is a food staple; if you can afford to splash it on your face you are well off. So a shining face is a sign of wealth, and we all know that in many cultures money is a powerful aphrodisiac.[16] An unoiled face, on the other hand, is a 'hard' face or a 'tough' (עַז) face, which is a sign of sadness or bad temper; if you are wise, you are happy, and your face shines and the natural 'hardness' of your face is transfigured, according to Eccl. 8.1: 'A man's wisdom makes his face shine, and the hardness (עז) of his countenance is changed' (RSV). A shining face is an attractive

---

14. J.A. Doyle calls this the 'negative touchstone' of men's role. Whatever women do is *ipso facto* what a real man must not do (1989), cited by Wood 1994: 77-81. Cf. Brittan 1989: 3: 'Masculinity…does not exist in isolation from femininity—it will always be an expression of the current image that men have of themselves in relation to women'.

15. J.C. Trever (1962: 592-93) notes the use of oil for 'anointing', but fails to say why people anointed themselves (and others). J.A. Balchin (1986: 585-86) does say that oil is a cosmetic ('In the desert regions of the East it kept the skin and scalp soft'—which is to say, I presume, not עז). The *ABD* has no entry under Oil or Anoint.

16. In an economy where oil is cheap and plentiful, it is not favoured as a cosmetic.

face, and to be as radiant as a bride is to be beautiful, especially if the light is coming from inside.[17] So too in Eccl. 13.25: 'The sign of a good heart is a radiant look'.[18]

When Yahweh's face shines, he blesses people, it is usually said, so that a shining face is said to be a sign of favour. That seems to be the implication of texts like:

> Restore us, O God; let thy face shine, that we may be saved! (Ps. 80.4, 8, 20 [3, 7, 19]).

> Let thy face shine on thy servant; save me in thy steadfast love! (Ps. 31.17 [16]).

> May God be gracious to us and bless us and make his face to shine upon us (Ps. 67.2 [1]).

But no one seems to ask what possible connection there can be between Yahweh's face shining and us being saved.[19] We are not to imagine, for example, a discharge of energy from the divine visage that drives a change of circumstances for the oppressed. It must be that a shining face on Yahweh is a sign of his happiness, that he is in a good and favourable mood, and so will prepared to help (similarly of humans in Prov. 15.13[20]). No one can expect a favour from a sour-faced god. But a happy face is a saving face.

Is a happy face an attractive face as well, a sign of beauty? I cannot say that I know a place where Yahweh is said to be beautiful, but he is very often glorious, which is perhaps not so very different (the Queen of England, according to the National Anthem, is 'victorious, happy and glorious'). And I suspect that the 'favour' (חן) of Yahweh (e.g. 1 Kgs 13.6; Ps. 90.17) has something to do with beauty also. Moses was a beautiful baby (Exod. 2.1); what wonder then that in the happy afterglow of intercourse with the divine he should wear a beautiful shining face.

These have been some notes for a gendered reading of the narrative of Exodus 32–34. I tried to keep out of my mind as I read the profiles of

17. Cf. Ogden 1987: 128: 'The wise person has a "glow" about him (*tå'îr pånåw*), a resource welling up from within'. I find Robert Gordis's explanation unconvincing, that what is in view here is *appearing* gracious in public, whatever one's true feelings (1968: 286); similarly Crenshaw 1987: 149.

18. Translation by Patrick W. Skehan 1987: 251.

19. R.N. Whybray is typical of most when he writes: '"Making the face shine"... denotes [God's] gracious approval... But here it probably has a somewhat different sense: the face is an index of the feelings; and a bright face is a sign of happiness or contentment' (Whybray 1989: 129).

20. Eccl. 7.13 expresses a deviant thought, that a sad face may accompany a cheerful heart.

masculinity I had drawn for other biblical texts,[21] and to let the contours of this narrative shape themselves in my mind. In the event, however, I found myself categorizing the evidence in much the same way as I had done in previous papers. It could be that I have let myself become locked into a grid of my own devising, or it could be that the image of masculinity in the biblical literature is really rather uniform.

I am very well aware that all these data need a lot more theorizing. I suppose that study of masculinity in the Bible is to some extent still in the stage that feminist biblical criticism was at in the 1960s and 70s, identifying and collecting the data, monitoring the language and the rhetoric of gendered discourse, and so on. The present volume will no doubt help to move the discussion of masculinity into a new phase.

Bibliography

Anon.
　　1979　　*The Oxford Dictionary of Quotations* (Oxford: Oxford University Press, 3rd edn).
Balchin, J.A.
　　1986　　'Oil', in *ISBE*, III: 585-86.
Bradbury, Ray
　　1954　　*Fahrenheit 451* (London: Ham–Davis).
Brittan, Arthur
　　1989　　*Masculinity and Power* (Oxford: Basil Blackwell).
Childs, Brevard S.
　　1974　　*Exodus: A Commentary* (London: SCM Press).
Clines, David J.A.
　　1995a　　'David the Man: The Construction of Masculinity in the Hebrew Bible', in his *Interested Parties: The Ideology of Writers and Readers of the Hebrew Bible* (JSOTSup, 205; Gender, Culture, Theory, 1; Sheffield: Sheffield Academic Press): 212-43.
　　1995b　　'The Book of Psalms, Where Men Are Men: On the Gender of Hebrew Piety' (presented at the Society of Biblical Literature Annual Meeting, Philadelphia, November, 1995), www.shef.ac.uk/bibs/DJACcurrres/GenderPiety.html.
　　1996　　'Loin-girding and Other Male Activities in the Book of Job' (presented at the Society of Biblical Literature International Meeting, Dublin, July, 1996), www.shef.ac.uk/bibs/DJACcurrres/Loingirding.html.
　　1998　　'"Ecce Vir", or, Gendering the Son of Man', in J. Cheryl Exum and Stephen D. Moore (eds.), *Biblical Studies/Cultural Studies: The Third Sheffield Colloquium* (JSOTSup, 266; Gender, Culture, Theory, 7; Sheffield: Sheffield Academic Press): 352-75.
　　2002　　'He-Prophets: Masculinity as a Problem for the Hebrew Prophets and their

---

21. In addition to the paper on David mentioned above (1995a), see also Clines 1995b, 1996, 1998, 2002, 2003, 2007.

Interpreters', in Alastair G. Hunter and Philip R. Davies (eds.), *Sense and Sensitivity: Essays on Reading the Bible in Memory of Robert Carroll* (JSOTSup, 348; Sheffield: Sheffield Academic Press): 311-28.

2003 'Paul, the Invisible Man', in Stephen D. Moore and Janice Capel Anderson (eds.), *New Testament Masculinities* (Semeia Studies, 45; Atlanta: Society of Biblical Literature): 157-68.

2007 'Being a Man in the Book of the Covenant', in J.G. McConville and Karl Möller (eds.), *Reading the Law: Studies in Honour of Gordon J. Wenham* (London: T. & T. Clark International): 3-9.

Cole, Alan
 1973 *Exodus: An Introduction and Commentary* (TOTC; London: Inter-Varsity Press)

Crenshaw, James L.
 1987 *Ecclesiastes: A Commentary* (OTL; Philadelphia: Westminster Press).

Davies, G. Henton
 1967 *Exodus: Introduction and Commentary* (Torch Bible Commentaries; London: SCM Press).

Doyle, J.A.
 1989 *The Male Experience* (Dubuque, IA: William C. Brown, 2nd edn).

Gordis, Robert
 1968 *Koheleth—The Man and his World: A Study of Ecclesiastes* (New York: Schocken Books).

Hyatt, J. Philip
 1971 *Exodus* (New Century Bible; London: Oliphants).

Lake, Kirsopp
 1925 *The Apostolic Fathers*, I (LCL, 24; Cambridge, MA: Harvard University Press).

Moberly, R.W.L.
 1983 *At the Mountain of God: Story and Theology in Exodus 32–34* (JSOTSup, 22; Sheffield: JSOT Press).

Noth, M.
 1962 *Exodus* (OTL; London: SCM Press).

Ogden, Graham
 1987 *Qoheleth* (Readings; Sheffield: JSOT Press).

Skehan, Patrick W.
 1987 *The Wisdom of Ben Sira* (AB, 39; New York: Doubleday).

Theweleit, Klaus
 1989 *Male Fantasies. II. Male Bodies: Psychoanalysing the White Terror* (Cambridge: Polity Press).

Thiselton, A.C.
 1974 'The Supposed Power of Words', *JTS* 25: 282-99.

Trever, J.C.
 1962 'Oil', in *IDB*, III: 592-93.

Whybray, R.N.
 1989 *Ecclesiastes* (New Century Bible; Grand Rapids: Eerdmans).

Wood, Julia T.
 1994 *Gendered Lives: Communication, Gender and Culture* (Belmont, CA: Wadsworth Publishing Company).

Masculinity and its Regimentation in Deuteronomy

Mark K. George

Deuteronomy is, among other things, a book of classifications and categorizations. Laws and legal systems are projects in classification and categorization. They declare certain actions, persons, times, places, and other things to be lawful or lawless, permitted or prohibited, establish the conditions under which something is permitted or prohibited, and make other such distinctions and divisions. Additionally, Deuteronomy asserts these laws and the classifications they establish are for all Israel, and that they come from no less of an authority than Moses, the man who spoke with Yhwh face to face, received these laws, and then instructed Israel in them (Deut. 4.5, 14; 6.1; 26.16; 34.10). This in and of itself is a classificatory distinction, comparing Israel over against all other peoples of the world, as Yhwh's treasured possession (Deut. 7.6-7; 10.15). In the making of such distinctions, Deuteronomy presents itself as unsurpassed; the text instructs Israel not to turn aside from it, to the right or to the left (Deut. 5.32; 28.14; so also the king, 17.20). Nothing is to be added to it (Deut. 4.2), and nothing need be; it is the last word.

Classification and categorization are social endeavors based on comparison and systems of organization. Comparison and organization are activities with which the book of Deuteronomy is greatly concerned, even obsessed. Laws, given their attempts to distinguish between certain behaviors, necessarily require comparison between two or more behaviors (or objects, ideas, actions, or other things). Furthermore, such comparisons require some system of organizing the behaviors or objects being compared, in order to distinguish between them, and such organization requires establishing criteria of evaluation. Evaluative criteria are not neutral or objective. Rather, they are a means of encoding social values, preferences, biases, conflicts, and other social factors into those organizational and ordering systems. Classificatory systems, in other words, encode social preferences into them, even if they profess to be the word of Yhwh.

Deuteronomy's classificatory project, along with its repeated proclamation that all its commandments and ordinances are to be carefully observed by

Israel, is an attempt to shape and control the lives of Israel.[1] It does this by asserting its own authority over Israel. Deuteronomy is, as Bernard M. Levinson argues, not simply *a* torah of Yhwh. Its claims are much bolder. Deuteronomy asserts it is *the* torah of Yhwh, or, more precisely, the *Torah* of Yhwh, provided by the deity for Israel's benefit.[2] By claiming it is the Torah of Yhwh, Deuteronomy asserts it is the definitive Torah, the unsurpassed religious authority for Israel. As such, it is socially normative for Israel's life, the answer and guide for Israel's self-understanding, its life in the land, its relationship to its deity, and its actions and behaviors.

By claiming the position of Torah for Israel, Deuteronomy claims the ability and right to regiment the lives of the people of Israel, to whom it refers as the assembly, קהל, who are the target of its commandments and ordinances. The verb 'regiment', according to the *OED*, means '[t]o bring or put (a group of things) into some definite order or system; to organize or systematize, esp. strictly or rigidly'; and '[t]o form (a group of people) into an organized group or body; to organize (a person or group), esp. according to a strict order or system; to cause to conform to such a system.'[3] Thus, Deuteronomy's attempt to regiment the assembly involves the implementation of a definite order (i.e., Torah), with the goal of causing the assembly to conform to that order. The social mechanisms it employs to bring about such order and conformity are the organization and classification of certain aspects of Israel's social life. This allows Deuteronomy to exert its authority in a comprehensive way. Deuteronomy determines where sacrifices are to be made: only at the place Yhwh chooses to place his name (Deut. 12.8-11). It determines time and the seasons of Israel's yearly life: three times each year—Passover, Weeks, and Booths—all the men of Israel are to present themselves 'before the LORD your God at the place that he will choose' (Deut. 16.16). Actions are regulated in town and open country (Deut. 22.23, 25). Whispered words encouraging the worship of a deity other than Yhwh are to be ignored and the whisperer must be put to death immediately and in public (Deut. 13.6-11 [MT 7-12]). Diet is to be closely monitored and controlled (Deut. 14.3-21). Warfare is to follow prescribed guidelines of behavior, both for Israelites and toward their enemies and land (Deut. 20). Along the way, Deuteronomy implicitly and explicitly compares actions, behaviors, conditions, and other aspects of social life against other possibilities, such as the worship practices

---

1. Israel is told 17 times to 'diligently observe' or 'observe diligently' (NRSV), שׁמר ועשׂה, the words of Deuteronomy: Deut. 4.6; 5.1; 6.3, 25; 7.11; 8.1; 11.22, 32; 12.1, 32 [MT 13.1]; 16.12; 19.9; 26.16; 28.58; 29.8; 31.12; 32.46.

2. Bernard M. Levinson, *Deuteronomy and the Hermeneutics of Legal Innovation* (New York and Oxford: Oxford University Press, 1997).

3. *OED Online*, s.v. 'regiment, *v.*', Dec. 2009, http://0-dictionary.oed.com.bianca. penlib.du.edu/cgi/entry/50201212, accessed 20 Feb. 2010.

of the peoples who are being given into Israel's hand (Deut. 12.2-4). These comparisons, and the preferences Deuteronomy expresses about those it commands Israel to do, are the means by which the regimentation of Israel's life is made clear. Do this. Do not do that. Understand time in this way. Eat this, but not that. As such, these comparisons present a definition of what it means to *be* Israel and a member of the assembly.

If comparison, whether implicit or explicit, is one way or social mechanism whereby Deuteronomy regiments Israel's life, the commandments and ordinances are another such mechanism. Each commandment or ordinance draws Israel's attention to itself merely by being identified and named. This makes them objects of social awareness ('So now, Israel, give heed to the statutes and ordinances that I am teaching you to observe…', Deut. 4.1), and once this happens, Deuteronomy repeatedly commands Israel to be vigilant about observing (שׁמר) and doing (עשׂה) them (e.g., Deut. 4.6; 5.1; 6.3; 7.11; 12.1; 28.1; 31.12).[4] Observing and doing take place at both the national, corporate level and at the individual level (the assembly), and involves both personal responsibility and responsibility for others. Each individual within Israel, as well as Israel as an assembly, is obligated to do what the commandments and ordinances require; they must observe them. Concurrently, each individual and the assembly of Israel is constrained to observe that others are observing and doing the commandments and ordinances. This is part of keeping and observing the Torah, and the constant, continuing observation becomes another means by which Israel's social life is regulated and regimented. Observation occurs in public and in private (e.g., Deut. 22.23-27), between the people and nation as a whole and its constitute parts (cf. Deut. 13.12-18 [MT 13-19]). By observing and doing what Deuteronomy commands, Israel and Israelites are regimented.

Discussion of classification and categorization in Deuteronomy, of how they depend on comparisons that in turn depend on social valuations and preferences, and how the classification of things is a means of regulation of social life, is important for understanding Deuteronomy's representations of Israelite masculinity. Articulated within the laws, commandments, and ordinances of this book is Deuteronomy's representation of Israelite men and, by extension, masculinity. Articulation of this cultural ideal is not especially hidden or obscured. Deuteronomy's attempts to categorize, classify, and thereby regulate Israel's social and religious identity and life is addressed to men, individually and collectively. Throughout the book, Moses' speeches are directed to an anonymous male audience by means of second masculine singular and second masculine plural verbal forms and object suffixes. As Moses recounts Israel's history from the exodus to its position on the east side of the

4. So also Miller 1990: 54.

Jordan (Deut. 1–4), reminds Israel of the commandments and ordinances it is to keep and observe (Deut. 4–26), emphasizes the covenant relationship into which it has entered with Yhwh (Deut. 27.1–31.29), and gives his final words to Israel (Deut. 29.30–33.29), he implicitly instructs Israelite men on what it means to *be* a man in Israel. Deuteronomy as Torah, in other words, includes instructions on what each and every male needs to know in order to be a man in Israel.

Deuteronomy's representation of what it means to be a man in Israel is perhaps best encapsulated in the concern with having a name in Israel. Ultimately, to be a man is Israel is to have a name in Israel and thus on the earth. It means to dwell in and on the land Yhwh promised that man's ancestors—Abraham, Isaac, and Jacob—to give to their descendents. As one of those descendents, each man in Israel is a recipient of the benefit of Yhwh's divine promise and promise-keeping, and therefore may live in and on that land. Yet in order to continue living on that land, he must observe and do the commandments and ordinances of Deuteronomy. Failure to do so results in Yhwh blotting out his name from under heaven (Deut. 29.20 [MT 29.19]). This curse is severe. Not only will his name cease to exist in Israel, both the assembly and the land, it will cease to exist 'under heaven', מתחת השמים, that is, from anywhere on the earth. Another classification and category appears here, that of heaven and earth, one that evokes Deuteronomy's cosmology. What is more, not having a name under heaven contrasts sharply (i.e., through comparison) with Deuteronomy's repeated references to that place where Yhwh will choose to place his name, a place implicitly on earth, since Israelite men may go there.[5] This comparison and contrast between the divine name and a man's name suggests that to have one's name blotted out from under heaven means, minimally, being blotted out from Yhwh's earthly presence. Learning and doing what Deuteronomy commands, in other words, is encouraged by a severe curse.

What, then, does Deuteronomy represent as the definition of a man in Israel? The answer to this question involves a number of elements, and a thorough analysis of Deuteronomy's representation of Israelite masculinity is beyond the scope of this essay. It is possible here to discuss a number of categories (i.e., my own classification system, reflecting my own preferences and biases) of what it means to be a man in Israel according to Deuteronomy. These include representations of a man's body; a man's place in society; how time is categorized; the spaces and places a man inhabits and passes through; and the relationship a man has with the deity, what in modern Western parlance is called 'religion'. This last category will inform much of what is

---

5. Most scholars assume this place to be Jerusalem and the Temple (cf. Tigay 1996: 120; Nelson 2002: 145-50, but other arguments as to the location of this place have been made (e.g., Monroe 2007: 318-41).

discussed in the other categories, in part because of Deuteronomy's self-representation as the Torah of Yhwh, and in part because the deity, who also has a name on the earth, provides another source of information on Deuteronomy's representation of being a man, or at least a male, in Israel.[6]

1. *The Male Body*

The Israelite male body is represented in a number of ways in Deuteronomy, even though an overall physical description of it, such as is found in the Song of Songs (e.g., Cant 5.10-16), is not one of them. Instead, the male body is represented in Deuteronomy by means of a series of intersecting elements, traits, practices, strictures, permissions, actions, and other social characteristics. The body emerges, in other words, not through the description of a dominant (ogling? panoptic?) gaze, but rather out of other discourses of characteristics which cross the body and thereby define it. Both within themselves, and in conjunction with others, these discourses of characteristics engage in comparison, categorization, and classification, with the result that standards or norms for the Israelite male body become clear. The Israelite male body, for example, is compared and contrasted to the bodies of Ammonites and Moabites (Deut. 23.3 [MT 4]), Hittites, Girgashites, Amorites, Canaanites, Perizzites, Hivites, and Jebusites (Deut. 7.1). When it comes to characterizing bodies by the socio-political characteristic of being a people, the Israelite male body is similar to these bodies in that is characterized in socio-political terms, but different because it most emphatically is an Israelite body. The corollary to this distinction is that the Israelite male body does not engage in the same behaviors or practices as those bodies. Israelite males are not to make covenants or intermarry with these people, turn away from Yhwh to follow their gods, or imitate their worship practices by building altars, pillars, sacred poles, or making idols (Deut. 7.2-6). On the contrary, Israelite men are to destroy both these people and their practices, and do so without mercy (Deut. 7.2). Moreover, these peoples are distinct from two other types of bodies, the resident alien (גר) and the foreigner (נכרי).[7]

There are many characteristics and discourses articulated in Deuteronomy that represent its ideal male body. There are five, however, I want to outline here. These five have particular attention given to them in Deuteronomy, and for that reason have been discussed and analyzed frequently by scholars,

---

6.   For the purposes of this essay, I assume and accept that the male pronouns and verbal forms used with respect to Yhwh in the text reflect a male representation for Yhwh, and that this representation is bound up with that of human men.

7.   Resident alien, גר: Deut. 1.16; 5.14; 14.29; 24.14; 29.11 [MT 10]; 31.12; the foreigner, נכרי: Deut. 14.21; 15.3; 17.15; 23.20 [MT 21]; 29.22 [MT 21].

although without much consideration of how they articulate a cultural understanding and standard of what it means to be a man in Israel.[8] These five are food, sex and sexual relations, war and conduct in battle, marriage and children, and having a name.

a. *Food*

The commandments about food are among the most debated in biblical scholarship. A number of theories have been put forth by scholars to explain why some foods are permitted Israelites while others are not.[9] That debate is not the concern here. Instead, how do the commandments and ordinances about allowed and prohibited foods function as representations of the Israelite male body? Several characteristics are evident.

To begin, Deuteronomy acknowledges that people must eat. Perhaps this is obvious, but the fact that Deuteronomy articulates commandments and ordinances about food indicates not only an acknowledgement of this need, but a concern to regulate and regiment it. What is more, this need is expressed especially for men, and, through the representation of their diet, then also for women, children, and others in the Israelite assembly (e.g., Deut. 14.26, 28-29; 16.11, 13-15; 24.19, 21; 26.12-13).

An Israelite male's diet is varied. Meat is allowed, whether from domestic animals (the herd or flock) or wild ones, as long as it conforms to certain guidelines (Deut. 14.3-8). So too are grains and wheat, olives and olive oil, milk and curds, strong drink and wine.[10] The good land into which Yhwh is bringing Israel is characterized by wheat and barley, vines and fig trees, pomegranates, olive trees, honey, and as a place where bread may be eaten without lack (Deut. 8.8-9). Certain types of seafood are permitted, as are certain insects and fowl (Deut. 14.9-21). It is notable that an Israelite male's diet is based on another classificatory system, that of space. The foods permitted him are those that draw upon the range of sub-spaces within the earthly zone: land (Deut. 14.3-8), water and sea (Deut. 14.9-10), and air (Deut. 14.11-20).

The fact that these dietary guidelines are included in Deuteronomy indicates that variety in a man's diet does not mean licentiousness, gluttony, or

8. Concern for how they function as a representation of Israelite masculinity, however, has not been the focus of these scholars' work.

9. The literature on this topic is vast and expanding. A few of the important works on the topic include Mary Douglas (1966), Howard Eilberg-Schwartz (1990), Jonathan Klawans (2000), Jacob Milgrom (1991), Saul M. Olyan (2000), although many more could be cited.

10. Cf. Deut. 7.13; 8.8; 11.14; 12.17; 14.23, 26; 16.9; 18.4; 23.25 [MT 26]; 28.51; 32.14; 33.28. It is worth noting here that the land itself is described as 'flowing with milk and honey' (NRSV; Deut. 6.3), in which case a prohibition on milk or honey would be quite ironic!

drunkenness are allowed. On the contrary, such behavior is explicitly condemned (Deut. 21.20). This suggests that an Israelite male eats with self-
control, both in terms of putting limits on what types of food he eats and
drinks, as well as how much he consumes.[11]

The ability to eat a variety of food comes with the expectation that Israelite men will work for that food, whether that involve planting and harvesting,
grinding and preparing, hunting and killing, raising and slaughtering, or
harvesting, crushing, and fermenting.[12] While they do this work, they must be
ever mindful that they once were slaves in Egypt, but now are delivered from
that slavery.[13] An Israelite male, then, not only works, but knows he once
worked as a slave to Pharaoh. This is why all Israelite men must work only
six days and observe the Sabbath on the seventh day and keep it holy, doing
no work on it (Deut. 5.12-15). The link between work and slavery is one
aspect of Deuteronomy's representation of Israelite masculinity. To be an
Israelite male is to be aware of that former status.

The work Israelite men do is presented as being something from which
they will benefit. By keeping the commandments and ordinances of the Torah
(Deuteronomy), they will receive the blessings of Yhwh in the form of
abundant food and wine (Deut. 8.10). Failure to keep those commandments
and ordinances will result in experiencing the curses of Yhwh, whereby their
work will be for naught: they will plant vineyards and tend their vines but not
enjoy their fruit, plant seed but gather little, see their oxen slaughtered before
their eyes, their donkeys stolen, and their sheep given to their enemies (Deut.
28.30-31, 33, 38-40, 42). Only when the Israelites enter the land Yhwh
promised their ancestors and kill all its inhabitants will they find 'a land with
fine, large cities that you did not build, houses filled with all sorts of goods
that you did not fill, hewn cisterns that you did not hew, vineyards and olive
groves that you did not plant' (Deut. 6.10-11). And what will they do when
they enter the land and find these things? Eat their fill, וְאָכַלְתָּ וְשָׂבָעְתָּ (Deut.
6.11). Israelite males are to work for their food, and then enjoy it.

b. *Sex and Sexual Relations*
Deuteronomy expects, as does much of the Old Testament, that an Israelite
male is married, something about which I will say more below. But sex and
sexual relations are not restricted to marriage for Israelite men. Several laws
prohibit a man having sex with a woman, be she married or promised in
marriage (Deut. 22.22-29), which means that Israelite men are having sex

---

11. Jeffrey Tigay comments, 'The Torah regards limitations on man's appetite as fundamental to a proper way of life', which he roots in the Eden and Flood stories (1996: 137).

12. Deut. 8.8-9; 11.14; 14.21-23; 20.6; 22.9-10; 23.24-25; 24.19-21.

13. Deut. 5.6, 14-15; 6.12, 21; 7.8; 8.14; 13.5 [MT 6], 10 [MT 11]; 15.15; 16.11; 24.18,
22.

with women, whether those women are single, virgin, or married. This being
said, it is only if the couple is found out (מצא 'caught' [NRSV], Deut. 22.22)
that the punishment is carried out, a situation which assumes there are couples
in Israel who are not caught. The risks of getting caught are higher in a town
than in a field (Deut. 22.23-27). These prohibitions assume that a man is looking to have sex, or at least to take advantage of a situation when it presents
itself (such as the presence of an engaged woman in the field, 22.25). An
Israelite male is a sexual being.

The sexual partners, willing or unwilling, in Deuteronomy's representation
of Israelite males, are varied. Married women, engaged women, and virgins
are not the only women with whom a man may have sex. Former wives (Deut.
24.1-4), father's wives (Deut. 22.30 [MT 23.1]), mother's-in-law (Deut. 27.23),
sisters (Deut. 27.22), virgin women who are not engaged (Deut. 22.28-29)—
all these women are potential sexual partners for Israelite men. So, too, are
temple prostitutes, whether female or male (Deut. 23.17-18).[14] Although no
Israelite woman or man is to play this role, according to Deuteronomy, that
does not mean an Israelite male may not have sex with a non-Israelite temple
prostitute.

Sex and sexual relations play an assumed role in warfare and military
campaigns. In this assumption, Deuteronomy is not terribly different from the
surrounding cultures and their definitions of what it means to be a male in
them. Deuteronomy explicitly states that all the men in an enemy town may
be killed if they refuse to surrender peacefully and become forced laborers
(Deut. 20.13). The women and children, as well as the livestock and everything else in the town, are deemed spoil to be plundered by Israelite males for
their enjoyment (Deut. 20.14). That rape (at least) is the fate assumed for
these women is suggested in the book of Judges by Sisera's mother, a
Canaanite from Hazor, as she gazes out her window, awaiting the return of
her son from war with Israel. As recounted in the Song of Deborah, Sisera's
mother waits and wonders why he is delayed, only to be reassured, by both
'her wisest ladies' and her own answer, 'Are they not finding and dividing
the spoil?—A girl or two for every man...' (Judg. 5.29-30). The Hebrew
phrase translated (politely) as 'A girl or two' is רַחַם רְחָמָתַיִם, which Koehler–
Baumgartner translates as, 'one or two laps, a euphemism for vaginas, meaning one or two women as spoils of war, bed-mates, in vulgar conversation of
soldiers.'[15] Women captured in war as spoil are available for the sexual use

---

14. There is scholarly debate about just what is being referred to in this verse, for both
the male and the female. For the female role, Tigay opts for 'prostitute' rather than 'cult
prostitute', the latter of which he argues is a modern term, and then concludes 'male
prostitute' may be the meaning for the male (Tigay 1996: 215-16). He provides a helpful,
brief summary of the issues. Cf. also Nelson 2002: 280-81.

15. Ludwig Koehler *et al.*, (2001), s.v. רְחָמָה, 2:1218.

and enjoyment of conquering soldiers, whether Israelite or Canaanite, as Sisera's mother so tellingly reveals.[16]

One other aspect of the male body that deserves mention here is the prohibition on a man wearing a woman's clothing, or vice versa (Deut. 22.5). This command is about as close as the text comes to taking up the issue of gender as such. The command may be an ancient equivalent to the modern phrase, 'the clothes make the man'. If so, then I assume the understanding here is that men wear a particular type of clothing, as do women. For a man to wear a woman's clothing confuses his identity as a man. Given Deuteronomy's concern, as the Torah of Yhwh, to establish permanent categories and classifications for Israel, such gender confusion cannot be allowed. Gender specific clothing becomes another social mechanism for regimenting Israel's life and behavior. Clothing signals a person's gender role in Israel, and Deuteronomy expects all Israelites to wear the clothing appropriate to their gender.

c. *War and Conduct in Battle*
In addition to being represented as a sexual being, an Israelite male is a fighter. War and warfare are presented as a reality in each Israelite male's life. Israelite males are expected to be warriors and fight the battles Yhwh tells them to fight, even if the theological explanation of such battles is that Yhwh fights for them (Deut. 3.22) to drive out the nations before them (e.g., Deut. 4.1; 6.10, 18, 23; 12.1). When they fight, Israelite men are to be ruthless, utterly destroying (החרם תחרים) the inhabitants of the land (Deut. 7.2). They are to be fearless when they go out to fight because they do not fight alone; Yhwh fights on their behalf against their enemies in order to give Israel victory (Deut. 20.1-4).

The expectation that an Israelite male goes to war is tempered by a humanitarian concern for other aspects of what it means to be a man in Israel. Exemptions from military service are made for those who have built a new house but not yet dedicated it (Deut. 20.5), for those who have planted vineyards but not yet enjoyed their fruit (Deut. 20.6), those engaged but not yet married (Deut. 20.7) and those newly married (Deut. 24.5). These exemptions represent important aspects of an Israelite male's life and identity as house builder, planter, and husband. Another humanitarian concern represented in the text is for those who are afraid. Israelite men are to have courage as they prepare for battle, but any who are afraid may return to their houses, lest they erode the courage of other men (Deut. 20.8).[17] And a humanitarian concern may motivate

16. An Israelite warrior may opt to marry one of these captured women, but she remains a woman taken as plunder.
17. Somewhat ironically, Deuteronomy repeatedly talks about fear. Fear of Yhwh is one kind of fear, and it has a positive valuation in the text; cf. Deut. 4.10; 5.29; 6.2, 13, 24;

the self-control Israelite men are to show in battle. When Israel goes to war, the army is to offer terms of peace when they draw up against a town to fight it (Deut. 20.11-12). So, too, are all the fruit trees of a besieged town to be spared the axe (Deut. 20.19-20).[18] In these ways, Deuteronomy presents a code of conduct for Israelite men in battle, one in which self-control on the part of the army is required.

Once battle begins, Deuteronomy represents Israelite men quite differently. If peace terms are refused by a town, then the men of that town are slaughtered once it is captured (Deut. 20.12-15). If, however, Israel fights one of the peoples of the land Yhwh is giving Israel, then no one is spared; every living thing that breathes—men, women, children, and animals—is killed (Deut. 20.16-18). No mercy is to be shown to those people (Deut. 7.2). Deuteronomy is adamant in this regard (cf. also Deut. 20.17), which may represent a certain textual anxiety on its part that Israelite males are prone to be merciful toward such people, even if the deity is not.

d. *Marriage and Children*

Throughout Deuteronomy, Israelite males are represented as married men with children. Marriage is the basic social situation in which Deuteronomy understands men to live. Men may have one or more wives, although Deuteronomy recognizes that multiple wives may cause social disruption and disharmony, since one wife may be favored over another, a situation with implications for their sons (Deut. 21.15-17).[19] Kings, however, are an exception to this situation. Deuteronomy warns a king against having many wives, 'or else his heart will turn away' from Yhwh (Deut. 17.17).

A man may find a wife from among the women captured from a defeated enemy, as long as he observes the regulations set forth in Deuteronomy: she is brought into his house, her head is shaved and nails are cut, she discards her captive's garments and mourns her father and mother a full month. Once this process is observed, the man may 'go in to her and be her husband' (Deut. 21.10-13).

8.6; 10.12, 20; 13.4 [MT 5]; 14.23; 17.19; 25.18; 28.58; 31.12-13. Fear also is something Israelites and others are understood to experience. In some instances, Israel is commanded not to fear; cf. 1.21, 29; 3.22; 31.6, 8. In these cases, Israelite males are represented as having fear, and are being encouraged. In others, the fear of Israel is placed on others by the deity; cf. Deut. 2.25; 11.25.

18. Self-interest also may motivate the prohibition on cutting down a town's fruit trees. Israel is told it will enter the land and receive, among other things, vineyards and olive groves it did not plant (Deut. 6.11). Sparing the fruit trees of towns Israel attacks may be a means of fulfilling this promise.

19. See the discussion about this situation in Nelson 2002: 260; Tigay 1996: 195-96.

Men are expected and encouraged to get married. The exemptions from military service for men who are engaged or newly married are exemplary in this regard. In such cases, they are excused from military service for one year, presumably in order to have a child with their new wives (Deut. 20.7, 24.5). At the same time, not all marriages are permissible. Men may not intermarry with any of the women from the peoples of the land Yhwh is giving Israel, 'for that would turn away your children from following me, to serve other gods' (Deut. 7.4).

Marriage, however, is represented as being a source of some anxiety for men. Wives are coveted by other men (Deut. 5.21). Other men try to have sex with a man's wife (Deut. 22.22). Engaged women also are objects of desire among some men, who try to have sex with them either in town or in the field (Deut. 22.23-27). The anxiety here is that the woman may *want* to have sex with another man. Such appears to be the assumption underlying the commandment of Deut. 22.23-24, in which both the man who sleeps with the engaged woman and the woman are stoned to death at the town's gate. She could have cried out for help, but did not, and thus she dies (cf. Deut. 22.25-27, where, if she has sex with a man in the open country, she does not die, presumably because she would not want to have sex with the man and would cry out). This anxiety about women who want to have sex may also be present in situations where men accuse their wives of not being virgins on their wedding nights (Deut. 22.13-21).

Children are the assumed purpose and result of marriage. This is suggested by the military exemptions a man may receive, and is made clear in the levirate laws of Deuteronomy 25. A married man who dies without leaving a male heir still has a chance of having a son to carry on his name. A brother is to marry the first man's wife and have sex with her so she might bear a son for the dead man and enable his name to continue in Israel (Deut. 25.5-6). Thus, men are supposed to have children. Children are a major responsibility for a man, especially sons. He is to teach his children (sons, בָּנִים) the Torah (Deut. 4.9-10; 6.2, 7, 20; 11.19), so they do not forsake Yhwh and serve other gods (Deut. 7.4). An Israelite male as father thus is represented in Deuteronomy as chief pedagogue for his children, responsible for instructing them in the Torah. This is so that they will do well in the land Yhwh is giving them, for they are the ones inheriting the land (Deut. 1.39; 4.40; 5.29; 6.2; 11.21; 12.28; 31.13; 32.46). As a father, therefore, Deuteronomy represents men as responsible for realizing the promise Yhwh made with their ancestors. In addition to teaching his children Torah, a man is explicitly required to observe the festival days of Weeks and Booths with them, both sons and daughters (Deut. 16.11, 14). This requirement suggests that a man's instruction of his children involves more than instruction in Torah, it also involves participation in the festivals and travel to that place where Yhwh chooses to place his name. A man is responsible for religious life, both religious instruction (Torah) and practice (festivals and rituals).

e. *Having a Name*

The concern Deuteronomy expresses for an Israelite male to have a son is so that each man might have a name in Israel. The purpose of the levirate laws is that a man's name 'not be blotted out of Israel' (Deut. 25.6). A son produced by a levirate marriage 'shall succeed to the name of the deceased brother', יקום על־שם אחיו המת, which indicates that having a name is one of the things Deuteronomy expects for Israelite males.

Deuteronomy is greatly concerned with names, especially the name of Yhwh. It is Yhwh's name that will dwell in a particular place of his choosing (e.g., Deut. 12.5, 11). It is by Yhwh's name that Israel is to swear (Deut. 6.13; 10.20) and in his name the Levites are to bless (Deut. 10.8; 21.5). It is at the place Yhwh chooses to place his name that Israelite males are to come three times each year for the festivals (Deut. 16.2, 11, 15). The name of Yhwh is not to be misused (Deut. 5.11). By comparison, the names of the gods of the nations Israel is about to dispossess are to be blotted out from their places (Deut. 12.3).

The concern Deuteronomy expresses for divine names, and the (dis-)respect and (ir-)reverence shown them, provides a way of representing to Israelite men the importance of creating, establishing, and maintaining a name in Israel.[20] For an Israelite male to have a respected name in Israel is to share something with Yhwh. It is a means of living in the land with honor and living beyond death itself. And Deuteronomy clearly represents this as an important part of what it means to be a man in Israel.

The levirate law is explicit about how an Israelite man accomplished having a name in Israel: children, or, more precisely, sons. The son born through a levirate marriage assumes his dead father's name (Deut. 25.6). By having descendents, a man has a name, one that is carried on after his death.[21] Beyond the levirate laws, however, the military and wartime exemptions for engaged or newly married men imply that they serve as a means for a man to create and establish his name in Israel, and to ensure its preservation after his death through children.

Creating and establishing a name for a man depends on having sons who can carry on that name after a man's death. It also depends on having honor

---

20. In addition to appearing three times each year at the place Yhwh chooses for his name, Israelite men are to bring their tithes to that place and eat those tithes there, an action I take as demonstrating respect for the deity and the deity's name, in addition to being a means of learning to fear Yhwh. Cf. Deut. 14.23-26; 26.1-15.

21. On this social practice, see Tigay 1996: 231-32, 482-83.

in the culture of ancient Israel, which many assume is a culture of honor–shame.[22] Children (i.e., sons) are to honor their father and mother (Deut. 5.16). Why? '[S]o that your (ms) days may be long and that it may go well with you in the land that Yhwh your God is giving you' (Deut. 5.16). A man must honor his dead brother. He must perform the duties of the levir when his brother dies and leaves no male heir, or else he and his sister-in-law must go to the elders at the gate. There she may accuse him of failing to do his duty for his dead brother, and if he continues to refuse to do it, she may pull off his sandal, spit in his face, and announce that he has failed in his duty. From that point on, his family will be known throughout Israel as that of the man whose sandal was pulled off (Deut. 25.7-10), a dishonor for him and his family. Other behaviors also grant or take away honor from a man, such as returning a poor man's garment to him at night if that garment has been taken as pledge for a loan. By doing so, the man who returns the cloak gains righteousness, צדקה, before Yhwh (Deut. 24.12-13). If a bride is accused by her new husband of not being a virgin, an issue of honor-shame is at stake. Her parents will display proof of her virginity to the elders of the gate, the husband will pay a fine to her parents, and he cannot divorce her (Deut. 22.13-19). The groom is dishonored, not the bride or her parents. On the other hand, if the parents cannot produce the proof, then the daughter is taken to the gate of her father's house and stoned to death for doing a disgraceful thing, נבלה, in Israel (Deut. 22.20-21). Both the bride and her parents are dishonored. An Israelite man must gain honor by his actions and the actions of his family, and by doing so, he establishes a name for himself in Israel.

If understanding the importance of what it means for an Israelite male to have a name on the earth is suggested by the importance Deuteronomy places on Yhwh's name, the converse also is true. An Israelite male needs to, indeed must, live on after his death by having his name carried on by his sons. If this is true for Israelite males, how much more so must this be true for Israel's deity, Yhwh? The deity, however, has no female deity partner, either wife, consort, or virgin, with whom he may procreate, at least according to Deuteronomy.[23] How does he perpetuate his name? Through his chosen people and their observance of his Torah. Should they fail to observe it, then Yhwh will blot out their names from upon the earth.[24]

Food, sex and sexual relations, war and conduct in battle, marriage and children, and having a name are represented in Deuteronomy as answers to what it means to be a man in Israel. These characteristics provide their own

22. See, for example, Clines 2007: 3-9, and bibliography therein.

23. Evidence such as the Kuntillet 'Ajrud inscriptions may suggest reality was otherwise, at least for some at certain periods of time, but this is not the case for Deuteronomy.

24. Of course, this raises the question of who will then perpetuate the 'name' of Yhwh, a question addressed by Joshua after Israel's initial defeat at Ai (Josh. 7.9).

ways of describing an Israelite man in terms of what he does, how he acts, and what it takes for him to conform to the commandments and ordinances articulated in Deuteronomy. These discourses intersect on his body, in the sense that they are things a man does with his body. By doing them and conforming to Deuteronomy's representation of an Israelite, a man becomes an Israelite male. Conversely, a man knows he is an Israelite because he conforms his actions to them. This is especially so since Deuteronomy claims for itself the status of Torah, the word of Yhwh, and therefore that it is the standard by which an Israelite male is measured.

2. *A Man's Place in Society*

It should be noted at the outset of this section that a male Israelite body is a social body because of the various social mechanisms and discourses that intersect and cross a man's body and thereby define it. Therefore, the section above, on the male body and its various aspects, must be presumed in discussing a man's place in Israelite society.

An Israelite male is, according to Deuteronomy, a brother/kinsman/neighbor/citizen (אח; e.g., Deut. 1.16, 28; 2.4; 10.9; 15.2; 17.20). He also can be a member of the assembly (קהל; Deut. 5.22; 9.10; 10.4; 18.16; 23.1-3, 8 [MT 2-4, 9]; 31.30). The idea of the assembly symbolizes the idea that each man stood before Yhwh at Mt. Horeb, where they heard the words of Yhwh (Deut. 4.10; cf. 5.22; 9.10; 10.4; 18.16; 29.10). They also are the ones who hear the words of the covenant that Yhwh made with Israel in the land of Moab, given in addition to those at Horeb (Deut. 29.1). Thus an Israelite male's place in the society of Israel is as a man who has heard and understood the words of Yhwh that comprise the covenant with Yhwh and agreed to that covenant (Deut. 5; 30.15-20; 31.9-13).

This being said, not every male qualifies as a member of the assembly. In one of the relatively few comments about a male body, any male with crushed testicles or whose penis is cut off is ineligible to be part of the assembly (Deut. 23.1 [MT 2]). Nor may those who are misbegotten (ממזר 'of an illicit union' [NRSV]) be part of the assembly, even to the tenth generation (Deut. 23.2 [MT 3]).[25] Similarly, no Ammonite or Moabite, to the tenth generation, may be a part of the assembly (Deut. 23.3-6 [MT 4-7]), although Edomites and Egyptians may, from the third generation onward (Deut. 23.7-8 [MT 8-9]).

Beyond these more formal aspects of what it means to be a member of the assembly, other factors are evident as well. A man can lose his place in the assembly, for a variety of reasons. If he seeks to persuade others in the

---

25. The meaning of the Hebrew term here is uncertain. See the discussion in Tigay 1996: 211.

assembly to serve gods other than Yhwh, he is killed (Deut. 13.6-12 [MT 7-13]), a punishment that, obviously, removes him from the assembly. So, too, if a man is a prophet and seeks to lead other men to worship other gods, he is to be removed from the midst of the other men (Deut. 13.1-5 [MT 2-6]).[26] Those who offer their sons or daughters to foreign gods not only threaten the continuation of their name in the land (because of the death of their children), but stand to lose their place in the assembly, because they are serving other gods (Deut. 12.31; 18.10). Complete loyalty (תמים) to Yhwh is demanded of all the men of the assembly (Deut. 18.13). Israelite men are represented as being keepers of their towns and neighbors, entrusted with the well-being of the community.

Deuteronomy sets forth certain behaviors of Israelite males as expected of them within society. Generosity with food and other types of material support for others in the community is one such expectation. They are to provide tithes of food for the Levite, resident aliens, widows, and orphans in their towns in order that their work might be blessed (Deut. 14.29). Similarly, they are to be generous toward those in need, giving liberally and lending enough to meet whatever need they find (Deut. 15.7-11). They shall serve as keepers of a sort with respect to their neighbors' livestock and other property, seeing to it that it is returned to the rightful owner (Deut. 22.1-4).

Men serve in various social roles within Israelite society. A social classification system distinguishes men from one another. When it became too burdensome for Moses to hear and settle all the disputes of the people himself, he created a regimented society, with leaders or commanders over thousands, hundreds, fifties, and tens, along with officials (שטרים) throughout the tribes (Deut. 1.9-15; cf. 16.18). He commanded judges to adjudicate fairly, without partiality (Deut. 1.16-17; cf. 16.19-20). Elders also are present in society, and it is to them that certain cases, such as that of the accused bride mentioned above, are brought. The Levites are their own class of individuals within Israel, with their own expectations for behavior as priests (e.g., Deut. 12.12; 14.27; 17.9; 18.1; 24.8; 31.25). Of course, serving in the army also is part of a man's expected service in and for Israel.

3. Time and Its Categorization

Time has a certain pattern and rhythm to it in Deuteronomy, because it, too, is a classificatory system. As such, it functions as a regimen for Israelite men. Three times each year, every male in Israel is to appear before Yhwh, in the place where he chooses to set his name: Passover, Weeks, and Booths (Deut.

---

26. Entire towns that served other gods were to be removed from the assembly by means of their utter destruction; Deut. 13.12-18 [MT 13-19].

16.16). Passover occurs in Abib and is to be observed for seven days, although men must be in this place only on the first day (Deut. 16.1-8). Seven weeks later, Weeks occurs, and again every male must journey to the place Yhwh chooses, along with his sons, daughters, male and female slaves, the Levites in his town, strangers, orphans, and widows (Deut. 16.9-12). During both Passover and Weeks, each Israelite male is to recall his experience of slavery in Egypt and Israel's escape at night (Deut. 16.1, 3, 6, 11). Booths also is observed for seven days (Deut. 16.13). These festivals create a regimen of time for Israelite males, marking the year for them as well as requiring their physical presence at a particular place at those times.

A similar regimentation of time is established by sacrifices from the flock, tithes, and the sabbatical year. Every year, the first born males of a man's flock and herd are to be consecrated to Yhwh and eaten at the place Yhwh will choose (Deut. 15.19-22). Every third year, the tithes males take of all the yield of the field is to be stored in their towns as provisions for Levites, orphans, widows, and resident aliens (Deut. 14.28-29; 26.12). Every seventh year debts are to be forgiven other Israelite males (Deut. 15.1-6). Likewise, Israelite slaves are to be released every seventh year (Deut. 15.12). Being a male in Israel is represented in Deuteronomy as ordering and conforming one's time in these ways.

4. *Space and Place*

Space also is classified and regimented for Israelite men. There is the land Yhwh is about to give them, which is the land Yhwh promised their ancestors (e.g., Deut. 1.8; 4.1; 12.1; 28.11). Within this land, Deuteronomy gives priority to the place where Yhwh will choose to set his name (e.g., Deut. 12.5, 11, 21; 14.23; 16.2). There are the three cities of refuge where (male) homicides may flee if they unintentionally kill someone (Deut. 19.1-13). A man's fields are another division of space in Israel, and each man is to observe and honor those divisions (Deut. 19.14). There are distinctions between different types of space in Israel: fields, vineyards, orchards, towns, and so on. At a larger scale, space is divided between heaven and earth.

It is important to note that all this space, with the exception of heaven, is presumed to be space a male can occupy and safely pass through. Such is not the case for women, or at least virgins. A woman raped by a man in a field (Deut. 22.25-27) is not condemned to death because the law assumes that there is no one around who can hear her cries for help. Implicitly, fields are dangerous spaces for women, but not for men. This may speak to the idea that a man's name can be blotted out from under heaven. The space under heaven—earth—is where a man's name is represented as being created and established. A man's name and the earth appear to be common elements in a particular cosmological category in Deuteronomy. Of course, this category also includes the presence of Yhwh's name, so it is not exclusive to men. But it does suggest why all the earth is male space, and therefore space within which males may move about (in contrast to women).

Houses represent yet another type of space in Deuteronomy. Houses can be spaces of slavery and bondage. Israel was delivered from Egypt, 'the house of slavery', by Yhwh (Deut. 5:6; 13:5). But they also are built by men (Deut. 20.5; 22.8; 28.30). Houses are where men are most intimately connected to family (Deut. 20.7; 21.12; 22.21; 24.1; 25.10), they are the spaces where the Torah of Yhwh is written on the doorposts (Deut. 6.9), and they are where executions of daughters who are found not to be virgins when they marry are carried out (Deut. 22.21). This indicates that, while a woman may be relatively safe within a man's house, outside it she faces increased danger.

5. *A Man's Relationship with the Deity*

Deuteronomy represents an Israelite male's relationship with the deity in several ways, and they shape the self-understanding of each man. Men in Israel are those who were slaves in Egypt and redeemed from that social position by Yhwh.[27] The actions of Yhwh towards Israel, and especially Israelite men, are accomplished with 'a mighty hand and an outstretched arm' (Deut. 4.34; 5.15; 7.19; 11.2; 26.8), language that is important for the suzerainty treaty form to which the book of Deuteronomy conforms. Yhwh's actions toward Israel are not due to anything it did or deserved. Rather, they are the actions taken by Yhwh for his own reasons. Israel is the smallest of the peoples of the earth, yet Yhwh chose them to be his people because of his love for Israel (Deut. 7.7; 10.14-15; 14.2). Because they were chosen by Yhwh, they are a people holy to him, that is, set apart by and for him (as compared with the other peoples of the world; Deut. 7.6; 14.2, 21; 26.19; 28.9).

The language of love in Deuteronomy represents something more, if not other, than an emotion on the part of the deity. Love is language used in the context of suzerainty treaties from the ancient Near East. As Moshe Weinfeld has demonstrated, the book of Deuteronomy conforms to the general shape of such treaties (Weinfeld 1972). These treaties establish a legal and political relationship between the dominant power (the suzerain) and the dominated power (the vassal). What this means for Deuteronomy's representation of masculinity in Israel is that Israelite males are the vassals of Yhwh. They once were slaves to Pharaoh in Egypt, but now they are slaves (servants) of Yhwh, and dwell in the land Yhwh promised to give their ancestors. The language of

---

27. Deut. 5.6, 15; 6.12, 21; 7.8; 8.14; 13.5 [MT 6], 10 [MT 11]; 15.15; 24.18.

covenant, which evokes the suzerainty treaty, is pervasive in Deuteronomy, and it becomes a means of continually reminding (male) readers and listeners that they heard the terms of the covenant, both at Horeb and in Moab, agreed to it, and now live under it (Deut. 5; 30.15-20; 31.9-13). Thus an Israelite man is a vassal of Yhwh, and to Yhwh he must remain loyal. It is why no Israelite male may turn to the right or the left from the Torah, it is a fundamental difference separating them from all other people (especially men), and it is why they cannot be bound to other people (wives), because they might lead them away from their relationship with Yhwh. As an earthly suzerain may demand loyalty from his vassal, so, too, may—and does—Yhwh demand loyalty from his vassal, Israel and Israelite men.

6. *Conclusion*

The representation of Israelite masculinity in the book of Deuteronomy emerges as a result of the book's concerns with categorization and classification. In order to know what Deuteronomy understands a man to be, one has to look at those other categories and classifications. By considering different ways in which the male body is classified (as something requiring food and sex, that engages in war, that marries and reproduces, and that has a name), and at society, time, space and place, and a man's relationship with Yhwh, Deuteronomy's representation of Israelite masculinity begins to emerge.

These things being said, there is much more work to be done on Deuteronomy's representations of masculinity and how it signifies what it means to be a man in Israel. The representation of an Israelite male discussed in this essay is the one Deuteronomy wants to present to Israel, that is, it is the dominant, hegemonic representation of the Torah. Yet other representations remain: the men who are afraid to go into battle (Deut. 20.8-9), those with certain physical disabilities or conditions (crushed testicles, penises that have been cut off, leprosy; Deut 23.1 [MT 2]; 24.7), being a glutton or drunkard (Deut 21.20), and the like. Categorization and classification involve comparison, and traces of those against whom Deuteronomy's idealized male is compared remain in Deuteronomy. They await further consideration, as do the categories I have used in this essay, which need to be expanded, challenged, and refined so that a clearer understanding of masculinity in this book is possible. Given Deuteronomy's claims for its own importance and status in Israel, as the Torah of Yhwh to which nothing is to be added or taken away (Deut. 4.2; 12.32), this material bears further investigation and analysis in Hebrew Bible masculinity studies. Also, given the continuing discussion and debate about a range of issues concerning the Deuteronomistic History, work remains to be done on the relationship of Deuteronomy's representation of masculinity to that of the other books in the Deuteronomistic History, if for no other reason than to determine whether those books add to, or take away from, Deuteronomy's representation of Israelite men.

Bibliography

Clines, David J.A.
    2007   'Being a Man in the Book of the Covenant', in J. Gordon McConville and Karl Möller (eds.), *Reading the Law: Studies in Honour of Gordon J. Wenham* (New York & London: T. & T. Clark): 3-9.
Douglas, Mary
    1966   *Purity and Danger: An Analysis of Concepts of Pollution and Taboo* (London: Routledge).
Eilberg-Schwartz, Howard
    1990   *The Savage in Judaism: An Anthropology of Israelite Religion and Ancient Judaism* (Bloomington, IN: Indiana University Press).
Klawans, Jonathan
    2000   *Impurity and Sin in Ancient Judaism* (Oxford and New York: Oxford University Press).
Koehler, Ludwig, Walter Baumgartner, and Johann Jakob Stamm (eds.)
    2001   *The Hebrew and Aramaic Lexicon of the Old Testament* (trans. M.E.J. Richardson; study edn, 2 vols; Leiden and Boston: Brill).
Levinson, Bernard M.
    1997   *Deuteronomy and the Hermeneutics of Legal Innovation* (New York and Oxford: Oxford University Press).
Monroe, Lauren A.S.
    2007   'Israelite, Moabite and Sabaean War-*herem* Traditions and the Forging of National Identity: Reconsidering the Sabaean Text RES 3945 in Light of Biblical and Moabite Evidence', *VT* 57: 318-41.
Milgrom, Jacob
    1991   *Leviticus 1–16: A New Translation with Introduction and Commentary* (AB, 3; New York: Doubleday).
Miller, Patrick D.
    1990   *Deuteronomy* (Interpretation; Louisville, KY: Westminster/John Knox Press).
Nelson, Richard D.
    2002   *Deuteronomy: A Commentary* (OTL; Louisville, KY: Westminster John Knox Press).
Olyan, Saul M.
    2000   *Rites and Rank: Hierarchy in Biblical Representations of Cult* (Princeton, NJ: Princeton University Press).
Tigay, Jeffrey H.
    1996   *Deuteronomy* (Jewish Publication Society Torah Commentary; Philadelphia: Jewish Publication Society).
Weinfeld, Moshe
    1972   *Deuteronomy and the Deuteronomic School* (Oxford: Clarendon Press).

VARIATIONS ON THE THEME OF MASCULINITY: JOSHUA'S GENDER IN/STABILITY IN THE CONQUEST NARRATIVE (JOSH. 1–12)[*]

Ovidiu Creangă

In contrast to a homogenous picture of masculinity sometimes assumed by feminist studies, mapping Joshua's masculinity in the Conquest Narrative (Josh. 1–12) is a challenge. This is partly so because of the changing features of Joshua's portrait at the level of literary sources (J, E, JE, D, P),[1] and partly because of the need to work selectively on the literary-diachronic level, where Joshua grows from a young minister of Moses (Exod. 33.11) to an arbiter of the covenant at Shechem near the end of his life (Josh. 24).[2] An aging Joshua provides opportunities to consider the expression of his masculinity at specific periods of his life. Finally, the position of prominence that Joshua enjoys in the Conquest Narrative is another hurdle. As well as falsely guiding us into thinking that the conquest is a one-man job, it also eclipses the development of other male characters. Eleazar, Phinehas, and even an aged Caleb still boasting about his warrior-skills (Josh. 14.11-12; 21; 22), suddenly appear as if from nowhere *after* the formal end of the conquest of the Land (Josh. 11.23).

The Conquest Narrative is an androcentric text.[3] In general, it tells the

---

* To my father Gheorghe, a man of few words, and to my good-old friend Nick: he knows why. A version of this paper was read at the SBL International Meeting in Rome (2009). I thank the audience for their comments, in particular Dr Nili Wazana for her comment regarding masculinity and the aging of Joshua.

1. With reference to past scholarship, Alexander Rofé (2006: 53-90) has recently examined a variety of portraits of Joshua according to the Deuteronomistic and Priestly sources of the Book of Joshua, listing no less than four distinct conceptions of Joshua that appear in the Conquest Narrative (autocratic-warrior, follower of Moses' commandments, fulfiller of the written Torah and the rabbi-like Joshua). Rofé also looked at pre-Deuteronomic sources, especially at the tradition about Joshua the seer endowed with magical powers (Rofé 2006: 83ff). As seer, Joshua stands in the tradition of other Pentateuchal practitioners of magic, like Moses and Aaron, and also Balaam (see Römer 2003: 12-22).

2. For the development of Joshua as a biblical character from the Pentateuchal narratives to the Book of Joshua, see Chirichigno 1987: 69-79.

3. I have showed elsewhere the androcentric nature of the Conquest Narrative in

story of one great man—Joshua, who conquers the Land of Promise with the help of his male god, Yhwh. It documents their words (monologues, speeches, commands) and actions. It depicts them as partners in wars, fighting side by side. It also uncovers the psychology of men in times of war, putting on display men's reactions (courage, fear) and solutions (resistance, trickery) to the threat of public humiliation and annihilation. Importantly, it profiles a variety of men: leaders and their followers, vocal and silent men, men heroic and fugitive, men saved (by a woman) and betrayed (by the same woman), winners and losers, compromisers and hard-liners who would rather die defending their ancestral lands than surrender.

In this study, I examine the representation of and resistance to Joshua's masculinity in two distinct traditions preserved respectively in the pre-Deuteronomistic (and pre-exilic) and Deuteronomistic (exilic/postexilic) strata of the Conquest Narrative (chaps. 1–12).[4] My aim is to examine how the masculinity of the autocratic warrior Joshua and the Mosaic Joshua exalts, allures, marginalizes and subordinates types of men and masculinities with whom he comes into contact, according to these two redactional layers.[5] Joshua's

relation to the absence of female celebratory singing to commemorate Israel's victories against its enemies (Creangă 2007: 106-23). This phenomenon is known throughout the Hebrew Bible (Exod. 15.1-18; Judg. 5; 1 Sam. 18.6-7) and indeed throughout the ancient Near East. The narrative's androcentrism is not immune to deconstruction. Rahab certainly challenges the pillars of male-centrality on the basis of access to the Torah of Moses and pre-conquest memories of Israel's victories and the recollection (by men) of those. However, her public speech and visibility (that is, her agency) are greatly reduced when the spies ask her not to divulge their intentions to anyone but remain indoors on the day of battle (Josh. 2.14-21). She withdraws from the narrative scene as soon as she joins the Israelite camp (Josh. 2; 6). See further, Creangă 2009a: 123-38.

4.   To carry out the task set out here I will follow the delineation of the literary strata proposed by Martin Noth in his *Überlieferungsgeschichtliche Studien* (2nd edn 1957; ET *The Deuteronomistic History* [2nd edn, 1991]), which is still generally followed many commentators (Gray 1967; Soggin 1972; Butler 1983; Nelson 1997; Creach 2003). There is ample disagreement among scholars about Noth's redactional choices or date of composition, and even ampler disagreements about the whole notion of the 'Deuteronomistic History' (DH). I wish not to engage this debate at this stage, primarily because my immediate concern here is Joshua's gender, not the redactional history of the Conquest Narrative. I will, however briefly, try to indicate when a different redactional view might alter Joshua's representation.

5.   It is not Joshua's leadership as such that is discriminatory, since I am not suggesting that the problem lies, at least not primarily, in having one supreme leader as opposed to shared leadership at the top. Rather, the discrimination lies in Joshua's *representation as a leader*. The phenomenon is comparable to the study of ancient Near Eastern portraiture. The standing sculpture of Gudea, ruler of Lagash, or the statue of King Assurnasirpal II of Assyria, for instance, portray idealistic images of men—strong, wise, imposing and

hegemony is tightly woven around specific models of gender behaviour and male sexual identity found throughout biblical and ancient Near Eastern literature, but, as I want to argue, these are destabilized by ambiguity and the absence of key masculine traits. Before proceeding, however, a word about the concept of masculinity underlying this investigation and its reverberation throughout Hebrew Bible masculinity studies is in order.

Men and Masculinities

In his influential book titled *Masculinities*, R.W. Connell (2005) disputes attempts to define masculinity in terms of an *essentialist* (a physical, psychological or behavioural feature around which masculinity revolves), *positivist* (a scientific indexing of facts that characterize men and women), *normative* (an ideal type of man that all men should strive to mimic) or, finally, a *semiotic* approach (an oppositional description of masculinity based on what is not-femininity) (68-71). None of these approaches, in Connell's opinion, captures the essential and dynamic feature of the masculine gender, namely the ordering of social practice in relation to bodily features (71-72). Connell's approach to masculinity is to be distinguished from other social constructionist approaches to gender precisely because of his stress on the physical, bodily dimension of maleness and the inherent possibilities and limitations of acting out that identity that the body causes (52-56). In giving the body an important role in the performing of gender, Connell is careful to distance himself from the notion that masculinity is biologically determined. For Connell, masculinity is a matter of positioning in a gender order, such as patriarchy for example, and of practices through which that social location is maintained and experienced bodily and culturally (71). Since one can position oneself, or is positioned by others, variously in any given gender order, Connell profiles four types of masculinity.

'Hegemonic masculinity' connotes the most dominant representation of what it means to be a man in a given gender order (77-78). What makes this type of masculinity hegemonic is a correspondence between cultural ideals and institutional power to enforce these ideals. Such an image of masculinity gives the appearance of permanence and naturalness, but it is vulnerable to change and fragile when its base is being eroded by new and competing ideas. At the opposite side of the male gender spectrum is a type of male identity that Connell calls 'subordinate masculinity' (78-79). It signifies the bottom of a gender hierarchy, the repository of whatever is repulsive and rejectable from the point of view of hegemonic masculinity. It is most clearly seen as

violent—made to overshadow and lessen the importance of features of the 'everyday man' (cf. Winter 1989; 2009).

the opposite of 'true masculinity', the most emasculated. The process of subordination of men at the hands of other men (or women) can involve cultural and social exclusion, legal and physical violence and economic discrimination, among other forms of abuse. Men in subordinated positions may resist their inferior status and strive to change it, but may not always succeed. In contrast to these two conflicting representations of masculinity is a third type of masculinity that Connell calls 'complicit masculinity'. Men who fit in this category are those who benefit from the domination of a particular type of masculinity and/or of men in general (79-80). This type of masculinity is to an extent parasitic, in the sense of harvesting the 'patriarchal dividend' without being the front-line trooper of patriarchy. Finally, 'marginalized masculinity' is a position that lacks the legitimation ('authorization' is Connell's term) that hegemonic masculinity claims, but it is loosely connected to it (80-81). This identity emerges from the interplay of gender and various other social structures, such as class, race, ethnicity or even health (disability).

Connell's typology of masculinity reveals tension and competition between various articulations of masculinity, not a universal model made a priori for all men to fit into. Hegemonic masculinity is embodied locally and changes across time and space. The pressures causing change in privileged and less privileged representations of masculinity have social, economic and cultural roots (see Segal 2006: 25-43; Cornwall and Lindisfarne 1994: 11-47).[6] The qualities selected to represent an ideal image of masculinity are arbitrarily chosen to maintain social and/or economic gains of those in power, as well as to reproduce key social and material institutions (e.g. kinship, military or state administrative structures) over which they rule.[7] Connell's observation that hegemonic masculinity discriminates not only between men *and* women, but also, and crucially, *between* different types of men has been echoed by feminist critics (Cornwall and Lindisfarne 1994: 11-47 [23-26]). Any idealized version of masculinity produces a contrast between men who display

---

6.   A relevant example here is Josephus's representation of Joshua (*Ant.* 5). Feldman (1989: 351-76) shows how Josephus departs from the biblical description of Joshua in significant ways. Unlike the biblical tradition, Josephus depicts Joshua as a state figure whose five key masculine traits are: wisdom, courage, temperance, justice and piety, all of which designed to 'improve' the image of the Jews before their Roman captors in the first century CE. As this example shows, historical circumstances determine what virtues are selected to idealize a man, not an a priori model.

7.   The successful application of Connell's theory has not gone without criticism. A number of important critiques brought against the concept of 'hegemonic masculinity' led Connell to respond with a critical review and reformulation of what the concept can and cannot do, and which areas need further development and which need to be abandoned. The best of these discussions is found in Connell and Messerschmidt 2005: 829-59.

such qualities, skills, attributes, etc, and those men who do not (see Hutchings 2008: 389-407, for a discussion of masculinity and war). While Connell describes many of the conscious strategies used to keep a representation of masculinity hegemonic, attention ought also to be paid to the less conscious mechanisms, what Jeff Hearn calls the 'taken-for-grantedness' of hegemony (2004: 59). Hegemonic masculinity remains normative only insofar as it is able to inculcate consent among large groups of men (and women), even as men who actually embody hegemonic masculinity are few, and co-opt, reduce or suppress their agency. Studying these processes of maintaining and/or resisting hegemony is of greater value than the categorization itself (though nowhere does Connell suggest that classifying types of male behaviour is a sufficient task in itself).

The above observations have reverberated throughout most of the biblical scholarship on masculinity. The tendency to outline and catalogue male traits as a way of getting at the essence of the 'biblical man' is particularly visible in the work of David J.A. Clines (1995; 1998; 2002; 2003; 2007). It has soon become apparent, not least to Clines himself, that there is a growing need to recognize the limitations of generalization that inevitably characterizes this portraiture of biblical men.[8] It is now especially clear that the social and sexual biases (elitist and heterosexual), the ideological foundations and asymmetry of Hebrew Bible's portraiture of men need to be exposed further, and in stronger terms, in order to uncover new possibilities of being a man. Indeed, the last decade has seen some remarkable advances in the area of queer-masculinity studies, due to works by Moore (1996; 2001), Boer (1999; 2001), Stone (2001a; 2005) and Jennings (2005), among others. But it is not an easy task: the Bible's gender (hetero)normativity carefully covers its back, as Polaski (2008: 435-51), to name one other scholar, finds in the Song of Songs' use of gender language and imagery.

Clines notes that violence, persuasive speech, beauty, maintaining male honour, and acting independent of women are the key markers of biblical men, and he illustrates this by looking at Moses, Aaron, David, the prophets, Job and his friends.[9] Even within this continuum of male attributes of select elite biblical figures, a certain inconsistency in representation can be observed. Traits are variously present in the depiction of biblical men. With the exception of a few remarkably beautiful men, like Adonijah (1 Kgs 1.6) or Absalom

---

8. Clines states: 'I am very well aware that all these data need a lot more theorizing', but he sees his job at that point, in the mid to late '90s when he sketched most of the studies that will appear later, as that of 'identifying and collecting data, monitoring the language and rhetoric of gender discourse…' (Clines in this volume).

9. For the last study on Job, see 'Loingirding and other Male Activities in the Book of Job', available online in pre-publication format at: http.//www.shef.ac.uk/bibs/DJACcurrres/Articles.html.

(2 Sam. 14.25), other men like Joseph (Gen. 39.6) or David (1 Sam.16.12) are only 'handsome' (תֹּאַר), 'beautiful' (יָפֶה) or 'good looking' (טוֹב רֹאִי), but most men's physical appearance, including that of Joshua's, is not noticed by the biblical writers.[10] Although violence seems to be an almost universal trait of Clines's men, it is not a defining attribute of all biblical men. Denis Olson (2006: 73-86) demonstrates that violence is not a definitive feature of the first men in the Creation and Fall narratives of Genesis, since Cain's killing of Abel is deconstructed by Cain's life as a fearful fugitive (Gen. 4.12-14). Persuasive speech, too, is a common trait among the men of the Bible, but it is not a universal male attribute (recall Moses' admission that he is not a man of words, Exod. 4.10). The realization that biblical men 'talk', and can even be good at it, will not surprise feminist scholars who have long showed that male logo-centrism is part and parcel of the reign of the phallus in the Bible (Brenner 1997: 31-51, 175-81). What needs further investigation—and this is just one area where feminist and masculinity scholars can join hands—are the ways in which a logo-centric phallus discriminates against those without a symbolic or biological phallus (emasculated men and women, respectively), as well as against those who wish to be recognized as fully-fledged men through practices and attributes outside the current hegemonic trend.[11] Not all adult males wish to, or will ever be, muscular, husbands, fathers, heterosexual, financially successful, and so on, but perhaps all aspire to be 'men' in their own way.

The remainder of this paper focuses on the portraiture of masculinity in the traditions of Joshua the warrior and the student of Moses' Law. I take these two portraits to represent hegemonic formulations of masculinity on which distinct notions of power and domination are modelled. I will pay attention to the negotiation of Joshua's hegemonic masculinity by Israelites and Canaanites coming under its spell.

Joshua's Hegemonic Masculinities (Joshua 1–12)

In the portraits of Joshua that I want to look at, as well as within the Conquest Narrative more generally, domination through sword and/or word is the main feature of masculinity. The form, intensity and scale of domination

---

10. The reasons for this may be because, as Macwilliam (2009) suggests, 'male beauty is uncomfortable for male writers and readers…because on the one hand it places the object of the male gaze in a female, passive position, and on the other it puts the male gazer under suspicion of illicit desire' (270-71).

11. For instance, the problems the presence of the phallus brings to the male priests are insightfully discussed by Rooke (2009) in relation to priestly breeches (19-37 [33]). For a critical assessment of biblical and (Western) cultural overemphasizing of the penis and its displacing onto other muscles of meaning, see Boer 2009: 35-44; Miller 1995: 1-26.

differ from the pre-Dtr to Dtr stratum, but it remains a point of definition in both.[12] It is important to note from the outset that <u>each of the portraits of Joshua is displaced at some point in the redaction of the Conquest Narrative, and hence loses its universal claim.</u> Still, I take the two portraits of Joshua as <u>examples of hegemonic masculinity</u> because of the high degree of control and power that Joshua, Yhwh's chosen leader, exerts over others. Each particular picture expresses an ideology that legitimizes people in positions like Joshua's to dominate other men (and women). <u>In what follows, I will also highlight which men are complicit in Joshua's hegemony, which men are marginalized by it, which men are subordinated to it, and how ultimately Joshua's hegemony is undermined by the very structure that sustains it.</u>

a. *Joshua the autocratic-warrior*

Although Joshua is nowhere in the pre-Dtr sources (or Dtr) explicitly called a 'warrior' (גבור) or a 'man of war' (איש המלחמה), his association with leading wars goes back a long way to a time before the conquest of the Land (Exod. 17.9-10). Even before the start of the conquest, he is remarked on for being courageous in war (Num. 14.6-9). Yhwh encourages Joshua to be fearless ('do not be afraid nor discouraged', אל־תערץ ואל־תחת, Josh. 8.1; 10.8), which in turn becomes his message to the troops in war (Josh. 10.25) (see Lohfink 1962: 32-44; Conrad 1985).[13] As a warrior-leader, he shows himself

---

12. L. Daniel Hawk (2009: 145-60) has recently shown that the Conquest Narrative concentrates on Israel's aggression against the kings of the Land, not against its inhabitants. With the exception of Jericho and Ai, no city is destroyed together with its inhabitants. As Lawson Stone (1991: 25-35) argued before Hawk, the Dtr redactors are showing an interest in making the conquest as ethical as possible to deal with the problem of genocide created by Deuteronomy's commandments of 'total destruction' against Canaanite population (Deut. 7.1-2; 20.16-18). One has to be conscious, however, that 'straightening things up', as it were, is done from Israel's point of view, not from the point of view of those who are defending their ancestral lands. Violence and the violent male leader carrying out the conquest are still left unchallenged, whether violence is done out of legal obligation (as in the case of the Gibeonites and the southern alliance defeated near Gibeon [Josh. 10]) or defensively (as in the case of the rebellious northern alliance crushed at Merom Waters [Josh. 11]). Ethically or not, Joshua is a violent man.

13. In the D layer, Moses and the people encourage Joshua with these words (Deut. 31.7, 23; Josh. 1.6, 7, 9, 18). It has been argued by Porter (1970: 102-32) that the use of the formula 'do not be afraid or discouraged' in Josh. 1.6-9 marks the transfer of office from Moses to Joshua in a dynastic succession. Porter's suggestion that the transfer of office depicts Moses and Joshua as royal figures found further support in Nelson's claim that Joshua is fashioned after King Josiah (1981: 531-40; also 1997: 21-22). Nelson's attempt to demonstrate that these similarities amount to a Josianic redaction of the Book of Joshua has been rightly criticized (cf. Eynikel 1996: 363). Nevertheless, the comparison of Josiah with Joshua proposed by Nelson led other scholars to read the Conquest Narrative against a Josianic context (for example, Rowlett 1996).

to be in charge of the entire people. His commands to them are short and firm, just as Yhwh's orders to him are brief and precise (Josh. 5.2-3). Joshua is obeyed down the entire chain of command (Josh. 2.1; 4.5-8, 17-18; also in 1.10-11, 16, 18 [D]), with one disastrous exception, Achan (7.1). In exchange for his devotion, Yhwh increases Joshua's fame (שֵׁמַע) throughout the Land (Josh. 3.7; 4.14; 6.27), so that Joshua is feared by all of his compatriots (4.14) and (some) enemies alike (2.11; 5.1; 10.3-4, 16). Joshua's relationship to Moses is unclear. There is no specific acknowledgement in the pre-D tradition of the Conquest Narrative that Joshua is Moses' personal aide. He is, however, known to be Moses' assistant (שָׁרֵת) in various sources outside the Conquest Narrative (Exod. 24.13 [E]; 33.11 [J]; Num. 11.28 [P]), and perhaps we can assume that such knowledge was implicitly supposed by the pre-Dtr collector/s at some point. We are hardly on better ground in respect to Joshua's succession to Moses. Most of the evidence linking Joshua to Moses exhibits strong Dtr language and could very well constitute later additions aimed at bringing the conquest and its hero into line with Deuteronomic theology (Josh. 2.9-11; 4.10, 12, 14; 8.30-35; 9.24; 11.12, 15, 20; 14.6-13). D is not alone responsible for portraying Joshua's succession in office after Moses; the P(riestly) source knows of this too (Num. 27.15-23), but, apparently, not J or E, or JE of the Book of Joshua.

This brief characterization of the autocratic warrior-leader makes no reference to Joshua's physiology because no mention of his anatomical features is made anywhere in the Conquest Narrative. With the exception of a few references to his old age in other literary strata (Josh. 13.1 [P]; 23.1-2 [D]), it is not revealed in this narrative whether Joshua was physically attractive, well-built, tall, or hairy—all traditional physical markers of masculinity. The absence of physical detail contrasts with the rabbinic tradition that attributes to Joshua both a gigantic stature and handsomeness, albeit lesser than that of Moses (*Sifre Num.* 146b, n. 11; *Yal. Deut.* 959).[14] However, the biblical writer's apparent lack of interest in Joshua's body does not mean that the body plays no role in the representation of his masculinity. The narrative deploys a metonymic use of Joshua's body members to express his masculinity. Joshua's 'mouth' and 'hand' are literarily connected with acts of transmission of instructions from Yhwh (Josh. 3.7-13; 4.15-17) and with Joshua's effort to memorialize Yhwh's great deeds at the Jordan River (Josh. 4.5-8, 20-24) (these organs will be instrumental in the commemoration of the Torah in D; cf. Josh. 1.12-15; 8.30-35). The same body-organs of Joshua (hand and mouth) are also associated with deadly acts of violence against the Land's inhabitants (Josh. 6.2; 8.1-2, 18, 26; 10.8, 12-13, 26; but also 5.13).

---

14. Cf. also Ginzberg 1994: 14; Hirsch and Pick 1901–1906: 281-84 (282).

What is more, if we take the references to Joshua's old age as belonging to later additions derived from other sources (Josh. 13.2 [P]; 23.1-2; Judg. 2.9 [D]), we are left with a portrait of Joshua in which he, apparently, never ages or dies. Joshua 24, which contains another note about Joshua's death (vv. 29-30), is a highly disputed text. Its origin has been tied to a subsequent D redaction.[15] If it is true that Joshua's death is not part of the early material, we are left with the image of a mythic hero whose beginnings and ending are, fittingly for a legendary figure, quite obscure. Joshua appears in this early source as an ever-potent military hero who assaults the Land and penetrates militarily its cities until the whole Land lies open before him (see Josh. 10.29-39; 11.10-14 in conjunction with 10.40-42; 11.16-20a).[16] He is, to put it rather bluntly, a 'conquest machine', lubricated by the divine assistance of his warrior god Yhwh before and during each battle (Josh. 10.8, 10-11).

The play on the sexual and sexist imageries of biblical wars (invasion as rape, battering as sexual intercourse) has been noted by others (Washington 1997: 324-63; Bergmann 2008: 129-42). I, too, have explored such undertones in the stories of Jericho, where the shutting (סגר) of Jericho, with none going in or out of the city, echoes the closing of a woman's womb (for example Hannah's, in 1 Sam.1.5-6); its penetration occurs in the end when the solders 'enter' her (cf. Josh. 24.11; see Creangă 2009a: 96).(The use of homosexual imagery to stigmatize a dispersing Amorite army before Joshua's troops ('harass them from the rear', as NJPS renders איביכם ונגבתהם in 10.19b), or to humiliate an army pursued from behind after turning its back to its pursuers (Josh. 7.4-5; 8.20),[17] constructs the heterosexual identity of the ideal leader Joshua. His (heterosexual) masculinity is measured by his capacity and skill to prevent his penetration, sexual as well as symbolical in war, and to keep the territories (and booty) taken. Men like Joshua penetrate militarily other men, or they are unmanned, but do they also penetrate sexually?

To complicate this picture, let us note that, while heterosexuality is attributed to Joshua by the language of war, Joshua's heterosexual identity is hard to establish. The silence surrounding Joshua's sexuality in the Book of Joshua

15. According to Römer (2007: 179-80), Joshua 24 is a collaborative work between D and P supporters who coalesced in the Persian period to promote the publication of the Hexateuch.

16. Noth sees Josh. 11.20b as Dtr addition (1991: 65), but see Creangă 2009b: 23-37 for a different view.

17. It is not uncommon for invasion or attack from behind to be depicted as an act of anal penetration: see Laukewish 1998: 212-20. Some rabbinic sages link the root זנב in Deut. 25.18 with the Hebrew word for 'tail' that was used in rabbinic Hebrew as a euphemism for 'penis'; Amalek's attack on Israel at Rephidim is read as a sodomizing of the Israelites, which of course attracted the severe injunction to 'blot out the name of Amalek from under heaven' (Deut. 25.19; Exod. 17.14). See further, Horowitz 2006: 111-12.

(or anywhere in the Hebrew Bible[18]) is truly astonishing. Did Joshua really not have a wife or a concubine prior to or during the conquest and settlement, and did he not father any children?[19] In biblical or other ancient Near Eastern traditions, fatherhood is not only a divine blessing, but a standard against which masculinity is measured (Hoffner 1966: 326-34).[20] Yet, this important marker of masculinity is seemingly denied Joshua. It is as if Joshua does not have a sexually active penis, or if he has one, it is carefully hidden. But why, and by whom? Coming to the aid of the biblical Joshua, the rabbinic sages erect his penis by marrying him to Rahab, with whom he enjoys both hus-bandry and fatherhood,[21] but it is noteworthy that such conjugal pursuits are absent from the biblical account. This observation becomes even more intriguing if we compare his case to that of other men in the Book of Joshua. Take the only other Israelite man mentioned by name (and genealogy) in the Conquest Narrative: Achan. His wife is not mentioned among his household belongings (though his sheep and oxen are!), but his children are (Josh. 7.24); Caleb's wife does not appear anywhere, but he has a daughter, Achsah, whom he marries to Othniel (Josh. 15.16-19); Eleazar's wife is not known, but his son, Phinehas, is a reputable leader (Josh. 22.13-32). Why, then, this impor-tant omission in the case of Joshua? How can it be that Joshua could have a hard military phallus, but not a procreative penis?

Hegemonic conceptions of masculinity in the Ancient Near East are not substantially different from dominant images of biblical masculinity. Military aggression, procreative sex, upholding of moral law/standards, defending the weak are common standards of elite masculinity (see the Semna Stela of the Middle-Kingdom Pharaoh Senwosret III). The absence of female companion/s and offspring from Joshua's life resembles to an extent the ancient Meso-potamian male-centred portraiture of war, according to which royal figures

---

18. Cf. also 1 Chron. 7.27, where Ephraim's genealogy stops at Nun and his son Joshua.

19. It is sometimes claimed that ביתי in Josh. 24.15 includes Joshua's wife and children in the same way Achan's deed affected his entire family (Woudstra 1981: 352 n. 6; Butler [1983: 274] speaks of Joshua's 'family' without explaining who the term includes). Other times it is thought to refer to the tribes of Joseph (Gray 1967: 196; Nelson 1997: 276), in which case no emphasis is put on women as part of Joshua's family. The latter view finds further affirmation in the Targum of Joshua, where the expression 'as for me and my house' is rendered 'I and the men of my house' (Harrington and Saldarini 1987: 55).

20. See, for instance, Ps. 78.51 (as captured in NIV). For a fuller discussion of the biblical and extra-biblical (ancient Near Eastern) traditions, with bibliography, see Sandra Jacobs (in this volume). Note in addition Herodotus's comment: 'After prowess in fighting, the chief proof of manliness [for Persians] is to be the father of a large family of boys' (*Hist.* 1.63.).

21. There is some debate about the identity of descendants resulting from Joshua's union with Rahab, but it is generally assumed to include mostly men (prophets and kings). See *Zeb.* 116; *Mek. Yitro; Rashi* to Josh. 2; *Yal. Josh. 9*. For further discussions, see Hirsch and Pick 1901–1906: 282-83; Ginzberg 1998: 5.

appear in public events unaccompanied by family members. Women and children, too, are regularly absent from reliefs, or are depicted as tribute or booty (as in the 'Black Obelisk' of Shalmaneser III from Nimrud). But sometimes members of the royal family *do* appear together on inscriptions (of the stela of Urnanshe, for example) (see Asher-Greve 1989: 175-95). It is admittedly hard to avoid thinking that the gaps in the portrait of the biblical Joshua are there to cast a shadow of doubt over the heterosexual identity of the military-autocratic figure of Joshua. If that were true, it would have some surprising implications for the very construction of heterosexuality and heteronormativity underlying much of the Hebrew Bible's notion of hegemonic masculinity.[22] We will return to this point with further questions in the next portrait of Joshua, but let us first look at those who normalize this exemplification of Joshua's dominant masculinities.

These men are, first, the שֹׁטְרִים, acting as a ring in the chain of command. They are Joshua's mouth for getting the people and the (Levitical) priests[23] ready to cross the Jordan River (Josh. 1.10; 3.2). Then, there are the spies, Joshua's eyes, as it were, sent out to gather intelligence (Josh. 2.1; 7.1). Also prominent are the קְצִינִם, army commanders, who share in Joshua's triumph over enemies by stepping upon the kings' necks (Josh. 10.24). Lastly, among the regular soldiers, אַנְשֵׁי הַמִּלְחָמָה (Josh. 5.4, 6; 6.3), and general armed forces, חָלוּץ (Josh. 6.7, 9, 13), is a unique contingent of Special Forces, the 'mighty warriors', גִּבּוֹרֵי הַחַיִל, always near Joshua in the thick of action at Ai and Gibeon (Josh. 8.3; 10.7).[24] These groups of men, united by war, advance the hegemony of the 'military hero' by themselves drawing their identity from performing tasks associated with the conquests. As far as one can tell, they freely consent to participate in the conquest and show no resistance to what they are doing or to Joshua, their superior. Their service is not without reward, since all stand to benefit materially (booty, land and women) from occupying Canaan. Their complicity is therefore a lucrative business.

b. *Joshua the student of Moses*
The undisputed Deuteronomistic additions to the received tradition are few but significant. Chapter 1 of the Book of Joshua adds new colours to Joshua's

---

22. This observation, of course, has implications for the imagining of divinity in whose image biblical masculinity, Joshua's in this case, is created. Cf. Schneider 2001: 201-27.

23. Joshua himself asks the priests (הכהנים) to pick up the Ark of the Covenant and move to the front of the people (Josh. 3.6, 8, 13, 14, 17), but this task is attributed to the Levitical priests (הכהנים הלוים) a few verses earlier (v. 3). On Mt Ebal, the Levitical priests are the custodians of the Ark (Josh. 8.33), so it is possible that Levitical priests are the target of Joshua's and his officers' commands.

24. These are praised elsewhere for their outstanding military skills. See 2 Sam. 23.20; 1 Chron. 12.9 [ET 8], 21.

portrait. The autocratic leader with whom Yhwh speaks directly in the received tradition is clearly introduced as Moses' assistant (שָׁרֵת), who is in a position of inferiority to Moses, the direct servant of Yhwh. He is charged with military duties (Josh. 1.3-5) and assured of divine assistance (vv. 5, 9), but success is made subject to his study of and obedience to the Book of the Law of Moses (vv. 7-8).[25] The fact that even Yhwh agrees to assist Joshua exclusively on the basis of his obedience to the Torah (Josh. 1.7-9; 11.23) is a notable deviation from the pre-D conception of divine assistance made available upon request (Josh. 10.12-14) or even unsolicited (Josh. 5.13-15; 6.2; 10.6-9; 11.6). While the Dtr has the people pledging to obey Joshua as they obeyed Moses (Josh. 1.16-17a), the offer becomes conditional on Yhwh being with Joshua as he was with Moses (v. 17b). The Dtr author ensures that Joshua's military and cultic achievements are seen as a direct fulfilment of Moses' instructions (Josh. 1.12-18; 4.12; 8.30-31, 33, 35; 11.12, 15, 20, 23) as well as a continuation of Moses' conquests in Transjordan (Josh. 12.1, 6-7), not as disconnected accomplishments of an autocratic warrior.

This student-like figure of Joshua is not first and foremost a warrior, but a spokesman of Moses. There is an overlap between the warrior and the spokesman Joshua, but there are also notable differences. Though both 'talk', the warrior Joshua commands whereas the spokesman Joshua seeks to convince. At critical junctures in the life of the nation, Joshua addresses the people in a way that exhibits his artfully constructed arguments. For example, before invading the western territories of Canaan, he seeks the support of the Transjordanian tribes. Mixing an appeal to male honour with a call to memory, he summons the Transjordanian tribes to remain true to the pledge once given to Moses (Josh. 1.13-15; cf. Num. 32.16-27). The speech inspires the Transjordanians, who respond overwhelmingly (Josh. 1.16-18) and cross the Jordan River for battle in large numbers (40,000, according to 4.13). During the conquest of southern Canaan, Joshua uses the opportunity of the public execution of five Amorite kings captured at Makkedah to convey, physically as well as verbally, the message of fearlessness and trust in the Divine Warrior fighting for Israel (Josh. 10.25, 42).

The wider use of memory as a rhetorical component of persuasion is a unique feature in male speeches in the D (and P) layer of the Book of Joshua, as elsewhere in the DH (Moses, Samuel, David). The recitation of the written Law, the recollection of specific instructions formerly given, the re-remembering of former things past and the care to memorialize the present are put to various rhetorical uses. They inspire and move the audience to desirable

---

25. This wears well with one rabbinic tradition in which the meeting with the angelic being near Jericho (Josh. 5.13-15) is prompted by Joshua's negligence of Torah study amid war preparations (cf. Ginzberg 1998: 7).

actions, but they also display ability on the part of the speaker. Not surprisingly, all the male leaders in the Book of Joshua make skilful use of the past as a rhetorical aid to secure something in the present. Caleb recalls the promise of inheritance he received from Moses in order to justify his request for inheritance on Mt Hebron (Josh. 14.6-12), Phinehas revisits the past sins and sinners who have brought trouble on Israel in order to prevent the Transjordanians from doing the same (Josh. 22.16-18, 20), while the spokesmen for the Transjordanian tribes justify their building project out of insecurity over the future memory of their contribution to the conquest (vv. 26-28). Persuasion is thus part of the repertory of the hegemonic male.[26] Their speeches are an instrument of control that they master just as well as their swords.[27]

We may be tempted to think that a man preoccupied with studying and teaching the Law is someone more inclined to words than swords. This may be true if we limit the notion of violence to the use of physical force against another party. Domination through words is just as powerful as domination through arms, especially when words are backed up by the speaker's capacity to exercise force. Giovanni Garbini argues that Joshua the 'pious rabbi who meditates on the law "day and night" (1.8)' is depicted not as 'a protagonist but as a subordinate' to Yhwh and to Moses (1988: 128-30). Implied in Garbini's view is the point that Joshua is less masculine because he moves exclusively on Yhwh's orders, and so is lacking David's independence, and takes Yhwh's word at face value, thus displaying the opposite of Gideon's retorts. But this is to fail to acknowledge Joshua's use of 'soft power', the inculcation of subordination through what Hearn calls 'peaceful domination' (2004: 65). The degree to which Joshua subjects all Israel to the Law and turns his constituents into accomplices of his own hegemony is nowhere more visible than during the ceremony on Mt Ebal (Josh. 8.34-35).[28] This

---

26. Persuading is not analogous with story-telling, though a story told well will persuade; yet there are features found in men's story-telling that apply to their persuasive speeches as well. It is commonly accepted that story telling is central to men's self-identity (cf. Coates 2002), but what is noteworthy is that men's stories (unlike women's stories) focus on male exploits and achievements. Stories told by men tend to promote camaraderie among men, not emotional intimacy. This feature is noticeable in Joshua's talks as well as in the talks of Caleb and Phinehas. Central to their speeches is the recounting of personal exploits or the exploits of others.

27. See Clines 1995: 219-21; and 'Dancing and Shining at Sinai: Playing the Man in Exodus 32–34' (section 2, 'The Persuasive Male', in this volume).

28. Other examples could be found. For example, Robert G. Boling (1983: 241-61) argued that the image of the skilful and peaceful negotiator Joshua who saves the Gibeonites from the hands of the angry Israelite mob (Josh. 9.22-26) originates from the Levitical families who have emigrated south in the wake of the Assyrian capture of northern Israel. These families, Boling claims, did not benefit from the privileges of the Zadokite priests

highly ritualized performance has at its centre an altar, the Law inscribed in stones, the Ark, the presence of all Israel and the voice of Joshua reading the Law out-loud. The atmosphere is one of sacrificial celebration aimed at restoring social cohesion after the extirpation of one family cell from Israel (v. 31; cf. 7.24-26). Unity is reconstituted through a hierarchical display of leadership, at the centre of which stands Yhwh represented by the Ark (8.33). The position of Joshua in relation to the Ark, the Levitical priests, and the people's elders, officers and judges is, curiously, unclear, though one can safely assume that he occupied a central position from where the Law was read (vv. 34-35). Violence is not an explicit feature of the ceremony, but it is tacitly encoded in the failure to occupy the right place in the symbolic hierarchy (Rowlett 1996: 157). There are also covenantal imprecations inscribed on stones and recited by Joshua (v. 33-34), not directed at any one particular individual or group, but reminding everyone, Israelite or non-Israelite, of Yhwh's violence against those who disobey the Law (Assmann 1992: 43-65). Without being coerced by physical force, people *en masse* consent to become 'subjects' of the Law in lieu of their being gathered before it and placing themselves under the authority of the one imparting such knowledge (Foucault 1980: 109-133).

The men keeping Joshua's company in this tableau and with whom leadership over Israel is shared are the people's elders (זִקְנֵי), officers/scribes (שֹׁטְרִים) and judges/governors (שֹׁפְטִים) (Josh. 8.33). We find them near Joshua in exactly this format during other public occasions (Josh. 23.2; 24.1), at which time Joshua's power of words is showcased. They are the primary recipients of his words, as well as those who are expected to pass them on after Joshua is gone (Judg. 2.27). Unlike earlier sources, the aging of Joshua's

and so they remained disillusioned with the monarchy and found the violence that characterized its kings repugnant. Being in favor of the old covenantal renewal movement, the only leader behind whom they could throw their support was a leader devoted to upholding the Law by peaceful means, a reconciliatory figure who resorted to dialogue rather than arms to secure peace with the Land's inhabitants. Regardless of what one thinks today of Boling's thesis about the Levitical origin of the DH, his study highlights Joshua's ambassadorial role in the pursuit of peaceful cohabitation. Indeed, some scholars attribute the absence of conquest reports in the highlands of Ephraim, Joshua's homeland, to his negotiating skills (Hamlin 1983: 104). As peace broker, Joshua implements his goals in a peaceful manner amid a dissatisfied mob bent on violence (vv. 18, 26) and the leaders' oath (vv. 21-22). This theme is reiterated in the voluminous commentary on Joshua by Boling and Wright (1982), at the end of which the authors conclude with these interesting words: 'To get a clear answer to the question "What sort of man was Joshua?" the persons to ask would be not the Dtr 1 or Dtr 2 but persons such as the family of Rahab, the residents of the Hivite towns of Gibeon, and the participants in the convocation at Shechem... With historical Joshua, we may be sure, persons came first and mattered most' (544).

body is carefully recognized in D.[29] Joshua has a finite life (Josh. 23.14a) and, depending on what we make of Joshua 24, he even dies after a long life (v. 29). The double note that Joshua was 'old and well advanced in years' (Josh. 23.1-2), which prefaces Joshua's farewell address (vv. 2-16), is significant in showing that knowledge-transfer has replaced other of his abilities (e.g., leading in war). In making speech a key feature of an elderly Joshua, the Dtr depicts Joshua as a wise aged man who still mobilizes the leaders' attention. They still respond to his call. To exercise such power is to be a 'true man' according to ancient standards of elders' masculinity (van Nortwick 2008: 122-23; also Berquist 1997: 47-68).[30]

One of the striking features in Dtr's representation of Joshua is, again, the absence of a female consort and/or offspring. As noticed above, Joshua is unaccompanied by a woman (or women) and without offspring in earlier sources, just as he is in this later source. Joshua's ability to deliver a good message and persuade people to keep the Law, not least those closest to him (Josh. 24.15), is the cornerstone of his masculinity in D, yet the question of 'the penis is difficult to leave alone...' (Miller 1995: 9). Joshua's penis ought to have been an important marker of his warrior or Mosaic (priestly) identity. After all, Moses, in whose image Joshua is fashioned, fathered children and had two wives (Exod. 4.20; 18. 2-4; Num. 12.1). Assuming the Dtr historian has broader knowledge of Moses and Joshua from 'Hexateuchal' sources, there are a few avenues that can be taken to get around the overlooked penis. One way is to see the transfer of Joshua's powers to elders after his death (Josh. 24.31; Judg. 2.7) as the ideal model of governance intended for Israel from the beginning, except that events leading to the prolonged wilderness sojourn (Num. 27.12-17) made it necessary for Moses to appoint a temporary successor (Joshua) to put Israel in possession of the Land (so Assis 2003: 25-42). According to this view, Joshua's political phallus would replace his biological penis—political descent over biological lineage, in other words. Another route is to deploy gender categories to configure the relationship between Joshua and Yhwh. Joshua's body, his mouth, is the receptor of

29. According to Josephus (*Ant.* 5.1.29), Joshua was 85 years old when he assumed command of the people at Shittim, an inference probably based on Caleb's age (Josh. 14.7-11). Joshua dies at the age of 110, according to the biblical tradition (Josh. 24.29).

30. Applying similar standards, P also depicts the old Joshua as manly. Joshua displays wisdom in the allocation of territories (Josh. 14.6-14; 18.1-10) and in resolving or easing internal disputes emerging from the allocation of land (17.3-4, 14-17). He blesses Caleb (14.13) and the Transjordanians (22.6-7), and encourages others to act without fear, even as he himself no longer takes part in the action (17.17; 18.2-3). The autocratic and bellicose Joshua of the pre-Dtr and Dtr sources vanishes behind the image of an aged man acting in concert with another elderly leader, Eleazar, and with the other tribal leaders to advance Israel's territorial interests in the Land in the company of another old man, Eleazar, and of other tribal leaders (14.1; 17.4; 21.1).

Yhwh's words transmitted through (an even more feminized) Moses (Josh. 1.8), in the same way a woman's body (vagina) is the recipient of the male sperm. The possession and transmission of the Torah is a masculine trait, especially in relation to other men who do not have the Torah or do not transmit it further, but its acquisition in relation to Yhwh evokes feminization (Jaffee 2004; Eilberg-Schwartz 1992: 17-46; Creangă 2009: 108-109). According to this view, the priestly teacher Joshua reproduces himself through his followers (remaining leaders, wider audiences of his speeches). They are his 'spiritual' seed, his (spiritualized) penis. Yet even for this rabbinic-like masculinity of Joshua, centred on the pursuit of the divine through Torah-study and teaching, the absence of biological descendants resulting from dis-ciplined sexual intercourse is still eye-catching (see Satlow 1996: 19-40). Finally, one might say that the biblical tradition sanctions Joshua because of homoerotic 'indiscretions' in which he is judged to have been implicated. To make this case, one would have to interpret Joshua's assistantship to Moses as consisting of both homosocial *and* homoerotic elements. The social bond-ing is clear: Moses takes Joshua with him for a long stay at Mt Horeb, the two spend regular time together in the Tent of Meeting and even fight together (Exod. 17.9; 24.13; 32.17; Num. 33.11). However, explicit evidence for homo-erotic acts between Moses and his younger servant Joshua, or between Joshua and Yhwh after Moses' death, are more difficult to find.

But let us linger here for a little longer. In *Jacob's Wound: Homoerotic Narrative in the Literature of the Hebrew Bible* (2005), Theodore W. Jennings, Jr, reveals the common practice of senior heroes and warriors using younger male companions, usually of lower status, to carry their arms ('arms-bearers') and provide various forms of assistance. Jennings claims that these men bonded homosocially and homosexually (3-12). Classical Greek antiquity, where the term pederasty defines an amorous relationship between adult males and younger, adolescent boys, provides ampler evidence of love between men, from the homoeroticism surrounding the warriors of the 'Sacred Band of Thebes' and the heroes Achilles and Patroclus in Homer's *Iliad*. Other examples can be found further away, in the earliest of Mesopotamian docu-mented close friendships, that between Gilgamesh and his younger friend Enkidu in the *Gilgamesh Epic* (for a discussion of these, see Halperin 1990: 75-87), but also, not mentioned by Jennings, the nocturnal affairs of Pharaoh Neferkare (Pepi II) with his general Sisene during the Sixth Dynasty (2460–2200 BCE) in the Old Kingdom. Using the joint homosocial and homoerotic bonding of the two male companions as an interpretative framework, Jennings turns, among other places, to the triangle of service and love between Saul, David and Jonathan, and to Yhwh's love towards his attractive-looking cho-sen leaders, Saul and David (1 Sam. 9.2-27; 10.14; 14.1; 16.21-22; 20.21). There is no denying that Jennings's homoerotic reading of the Saul–David saga contains some fanciful imagination,[31] of which my own attempt to tease out Joshua's absent phallus in homoerotic terms may be equally guilty. But let us, for the sake of this argument, pursue some comparisons. In each of these cases, the younger companion is loyal to his older, wiser or more powerful partner and survives him (Gilgamesh survives Enkidu, Achilles survives Patroclus, David survives Saul and Jonathan, and Joshua survives Moses). A vocabulary of intimate, close bondage and/or kinship relations is used to define and situate socially and emotionally the relationships in question: David is Saul's 'son' (1 Sam. 24.16), David 'loves' Jonathan (1 Sam. 20.17), Patroclus is Achilles' 'beloved companion' (*Iliad* 8.99), Enkidu is Gilgamesh's 'friend' (in the Akkadian version as well as in all Old Babylonian and Neo-Assyrian fragments), 'brother' (Tablet VII, line 20), but also 'servant' in one Sumerian version (Tablet XII, line 10).[32] Joshua remains Moses' 'assistant' throughout most of his life (Josh. 1.1; Deut. 1.38), receiving the higher title of Yhwh's 'servant' (עבד) only after his death (Josh. 24.29), but, as between Gilgamesh and Enkidu, the epithet 'servant' or 'assistant' can denote a loving relationship.

These similarities, in and by themselves, provide, at best, only conjectural evidence of love between Joshua and his master. Perhaps a stronger case can be made by turning to the meeting between Joshua and the Captain (שׂר) of Yhwh's hosts (Josh. 5.13-15).[33] The (nocturnal?) meeting of two men of an unequal standing in the vicinity of Jericho is narrated in a chapter already filled with images of adult naked penises (Israelites' circumcision at the hands of Joshua, 5.2-8) and piles of discharged foreskin (hence the name of the place, Gibeath Haaraloth, or 'hill of foreskins', 5.3). The gaze of Joshua's eyes is drawn, first, to the Captain ('he lifted up his eyes and saw, and behold, a man', וישׂא עיניו וירא והנה־אישׁ), then to the Captain's position ('standing in front of him', עמד לנגדו) and, finally, to his weapon/sword, which is 'drawn out in his hand' (וחרבו שלופה בידו). The expression 'he lifted up his eyes and looked, and behold' describes the meeting of David with the 'messenger' (מלאך) sent out to plague Israel, now approaching Jerusalem (1 Chron. 21.16), but it is also used to describe the moment Isaac sees Rebekah, a meeting also outdoors and in the evening (Gen. 24.63). Some (homo)erotic undertones, on account of this expression being used in romantic settings,

---

31. For a critical review, see Moore 2008: 478-83.

32. See Pritchard 1955: 72-97 and 1969: 67-71 for various renditions of the *Epic of Gilgamesh*.

33. The relationship of Josh. 5.13-15 to the Dtr redaction of the Conquest Narrative is difficult to define. The passage has been allocated to the J, JE, P (at least parts of it) and D source. Limitations of space prevent a survey of redactional history, but see for this Štrba 2008: 15-69. The view followed in this study is that the passage reflects an older tradition that Dtr received and reworked to inaugurate the conquest of the Land.

may be intended in Joshua's case, which cannot be said to apply to David's meeting with Yhwh's messenger in 1 Chronicles 21 (even less so in 2 Sam. 24.17). There the messenger is clearly an angelic creature, suspended between earth and heaven, and the mood between these men is one of deep anguish (David and the elders are dressed in sackcloth in 1 Chron. 21; detail is missing from 2 Sam. 24, but David's distress is retained in v. 14).

What is alluring about the Captain to make Joshua want to draw closer and find out who the stranger is? Is it the weapon adorning the image of the mysterious man, already 'drawn out' of its sheath? Swords, knives, arrows and spears are commonly recognized as phallic symbols expressing military power and sexual virility, so admittedly, when such objects appear in the hands of male heroes, the penis need not be exposed to convey sexual virility; one stands for both.[34] Attracted to the curious features of this phallic creature, Joshua approaches him inquisitively, asking about his identity (Josh. 5.13). Once identity is revealed, the answer causes Joshua to fall face down, not untypically (cf. David and the elders, 1 Chron. 21.16), exposing his back to the Captain (Josh. 5.14), but is that another hint of (homo)eroticism? In relation to the Captain, Joshua is feminized (submissive, not argumentative or wrestling; cf. Hess 1996: 125). The Captain's command that Joshua remove his footwear because 'the ground/place on which you stand is holy' (Josh. 5.15) denotes the sanctity of the place of meeting (between Gilgal and Jericho) or of the Land more generally, but could not the unsandaling of Joshua be read also as a form of 'uncovering the feet' known elsewhere to indicate sexual desire (Ruth 3.7-9)?

What this hypothetical reading uncovers is not actual sex occurring between Joshua and his Captain, but only homoerotic resonances surrounding their meeting near Jericho. It shows Joshua meeting in the heavenly Captain his conceptual pair (if not a soul-mate), a commander of armies defined by the sword in his hand but possessing no visible penis. The lack of narrative description of the area just beneath the loins of these two men is perhaps illustrative of homoerotic anxiety (or homophobia) that characterizes especially Priestly or Priestly-influenced redactors, but not only (see Eilberg-Schwartz 1994). Leaving Joshua single and childless in a culture predicated on heterosexual love and procreation, so destining him to genealogical oblivion but saving his memory by making him a reputable warrior hero, is no

---

34. Cf. Hoffner 1966: 337 ('In particular, those symbols which primarily referred to his military exploits often served to remind him of his sexual ability as well'). Joshua provides a classic example of the linkage between pointing military objects (swords, knives, spears) and the penis in the making of flint knives for circumcision (Josh. 5.2-3), with which Joshua apparently never departs as these are buried with him (Josh. 24.31, in the Septuagint text), but also a metaphoric linkage in the exposure of his 'javelin' (כִּידוֹן) as a symbol of Ai's penetration (Josh. 8.18-19, 26).

more than a unique representation of power (priestly/non-sexual over military/sexual, though this binary division is hardly applicable anywhere else since procreation is important in P). It can well be also a form of narrative castration for having been Moses' and the Captain's (so Yhwh's?) 'pal'.

Moving on, the types of masculinity discussed next are no less heroic or less stable than those studied above; they are pushed down the gender order encoded in the Conquest Narrative because they do not fit the model of domination exerted by Joshua.

Marginalized and Subordinated Masculinities in Joshua 1–12

More often than not, marginalized and subordinated men lack not heroism or good judgment, or other qualities woven into the tapestry of hegemonic masculinity, but power resulting from social, economic and political privileges. And for that reason, one way in which men in this position compensate for what is missing is through acts of cunning. In the Gibeonite story (Josh. 9) we have one particular example of marginalized men and masculinity working to establish their identity alongside Joshua's. In choosing trickery to deal with Joshua's threat, the Gibeonites (Josh. 9) are likened to Rahab (and to other biblical men and women), who also lacks other means to save herself from destruction. The Gibeonites devise a trick (Josh. 9.3-5), Rahab takes advantage of Joshua's spies in a moment of vulnerability (Josh. 2.2-7). Writing about the trickster Jacob, Susan Haddox (11 in this volume) correctly notes that 'While intelligence and persuasiveness is associated with masculinity in the biblical texts, the cunning of the trickster is a different matter... Thus when Jacob is portrayed as a trickster, it points out his position of subordination' (Chapter 1 in this volume). I prefer to speak of the Gibeonites in terms of 'marginalization' rather than 'subordination' for reasons of terminology, since above I defined 'subordination' as that which is wholly rejectable from the hegemonic point of view; by comparison, marginalized men are within the hegemonic framework, but outside its privileges. The Gibeonites appear willing to settle for a low position when asking to reside among the Israelites ('we are your servants, make a covenant with us', 9.11). The jobs to which they are assigned are clearly feminizing them. Drawing water and splitting wood are things associated with women and the lowly,[35] but that seems acceptable in their eyes as long as their lives are spared. The pretext for taking this humble position is a desire to worship Yhwh of whose name/fame they have heard (9.9-10). Of course, when the truth about their

---

35. The feminization of the Gibeonites becomes further evident in the curse that appoints the Gibeonites to tasks usually performed by women. In the biblical world, women were the drawers of water (cf. Gen. 24.11) and extra-biblical sources show wood-cutting to be a job done by women. See, for a fuller treatment, Gordon 2003: 163-90.

identity comes out (9.16-17), it is fear for their lives that drives them to the negotiating table, not faith in the Israelite god (9.24-25).

It is noteworthy that the Gibeonite negotiators speak on behalf of their 'elders' (זקנים), who thus surrender their power to Joshua (9.11, 25). The elders' decision to submit rather than oppose Joshua shows some reasonable thinking and even a degree of heroism, especially as they consider their plan against the fate of Jericho and Ai (9.3). The Gibeonites' display of courage and determination to succeed (in staying alive) illustrates the fluidity of praiseworthy traits across the divide of hegemonic and marginalized masculinities.

However, like the other accomplices in Joshua's hegemony (army personnel, scribes, elders, judges, heads of tribes, *et al.*), the Gibeonite leaders too extend its normativity by becoming its subjects, even without standing to benefit from it materially or socially. Life alone is a worthy price, but it is going to be a humble life. The covenant made with the Israelite leaders in the name of Yhwh grants the Gibeonites the status of 'insiders', except that the Gibeonites are going to be a different kind of members. The inequalities resulting from this transaction are seldom given the right attention by those who study the construction of identity in Joshua 1–12 (for example, Mitchell 1993; Rowlett 1996; Hawk 2000a). At the heart of the Gibeonite story may rest the question of what to do with 'good' foreigners and what consequences follow from letting them 'in' (Hawk 1997; 2000b). Nevertheless, the message of the story is clear: *if* you (Hivite or other non-Israelite) do get in, all you can hope for is a place of servitude with very limited access to power, if any. Socially, economically and politically the Gibeonites remain marginal members of Israel for a long time, becoming exceptionally vulnerable under King Saul (2 Sam. 21.1-3). Their status may be comparable to that of the 'stranger who walks in your midst' (הגר ההלך בקרבם), to put it generously, which is a position comparable to that of women and children (8.33, 35). It clearly is not that of a native Israelite male. What this example shows, then, is their emasculation as a result of submitting to Joshua's hegemony which, though not exactly good news, provides them with a shelter against the anger of the mob (9.26). The Gibeonites shows no resistance to Joshua (only to other inhabitants of the Land), but use their agency effectively to devise a way in.

The kings of the Land, furthermore, represent that which Joshua/Yhwh rejects. What constitutes their 'deviance' from the point of view of masculinity represented by Joshua is the display of fear (Josh. 5.1) and, when enough courage is mobilized to put up a fight, loss in the contest of war (Josh. 8.29; 10.16-27, 30, 33, 37, 39, 40, 42; 11.1-12). In the case of the Canaanite kings who actually confront Joshua we see an element of unsuccessful resistance and failed agency. The kings show the capacity to organize themselves in large coalitions (Josh. 10.1-5; 11.1-5), which is an expression of their masculinity that resembles Joshua's. The call and mobilization for war shows they have the nerve to prevent Joshua's advancement into the southern and northern areas of Canaan. It also displays strategic thinking on the part of the head-king, in uniting otherwise fragmented city-states. From their point of view, surrender without a fight is unacceptable and life in servitude a disgrace not worth living with (a thinking unlike that of the Gibeonites). These are qualities and strategies that Joshua himself displays. The crushing of their opposition by Joshua, however, is due to direct divine intervention (Josh. 10.10-11) and shortcomings in their military strategy.[36] In the end, the kings are unable to protect their bodies and their people, which is tantamount to being emasculated. Their failure illustrates the subordination of this type of men (some fearful, some courageous, but all unsuccessful in stopping Joshua) and of this type of body (penetrated by sword [Josh. 10.26], hanged and buried unceremoniously [Josh. 8.29; 10.27]) to the type of man and masculinity that rules successfully over others and maintains bodily integrity. Unlike the Gibeonites' agency manifested in their crafted response to Israel's approach, the kings called up by Adoni-zedek of Jerusalem and Jabin of Hazor simply follow that which is proposed to them. Having submitted their agency to Adoni-zedek or Jabin, they resist Joshua without avail. One final example: Achan's choice to retain and hide the forbidden items from Jericho may be seen as an assertion of his agency (acting independently from and contrary to other Israelites) and resistance to Joshua's orders (Josh. 7.20-21; cf. 6.18), but it gets him and his family killed (7.25-26). And the reason for that is his failure to note—a warning intended for the text's audience as well—that submission to Yhwh and Joshua is intrinsic to the legitimate notion of masculinity. Achan, like the kings called up for battle, shows a type of resistance and agency deemed illegitimate in the eyes of Yhwh.

These examples illustrate the inability of subordinated masculinity to gain in standing before the dominant type of masculinity as a result of active resistance; but they also expose hegemony's limited success to inculcate consent among and co-opt the agency of all groups of men, raising questions about other vulnerable points existing within and outside itself. The struggle Joshua voices at the end of the Book, and one about which he is uncertain, is whether Israel will keep t/his hegemony hegemonic (Josh. 23.6-16; 24.19-20).

Conclusion

The configurations of male gender uncovered in this study illustrate the re/construction of normative masculinity from the warrior Joshua in the pre-exilic literary stratum to the Mosaic figure in the exilic/postexilic layer.

---

36. For a study of these, see Malamat 1975: 35-55.

While the hegemonic base of Joshua's normative masculinity is changing and even vulnerable to erosion, as in the case of Joshua's heterosexual identity, in each instantiation a dynamic of co-option/refutation/discrimination against alternative versions of masculinity and men occurs. The fashioning of Joshua's body in each portrait (warrior, student of the Law) is a projection of, and for, the social body and the body politic of Israel in each of these historical periods (pre-exilic and exilic/postexilic). The changing emphasis of Joshua's power from military to religious is aimed at subjecting a new readership/audience to its grip. The absence of Joshua's penis in both portraits has wide implications for the flow and distribution of that power, of course. Single and childless, Joshua eschews the conventional heteronormativity of (most) biblical men, and so he fits only in part under other hegemonies (Priestly, especially). Whether his sexual state (infertile? undesiring of women? or both?) causes the neglect of his penis, or whether the absence of female consort/s and offspring is a sanction against his indiscreet use of the penis, the sex is lost, and with it, it seems, the heterosexual Joshua. And that, undoubtedly, is a subject of further investigation.

Bibliography

Asher-Greve, Julia M.
   1989   'Observations on the Historical Relevance of Visual Imagery in Meso-
            potamia', in Albert de Pury (ed.), *Histoire et conscience historique dans
            les civilisations du Proche-Orient ancien* (CCEPOA, 5; Leuven: Peeters):
            175-95.
Assis, Elie
   2003   'Divine versus Human Leadership: An Examination of Joshua's Succes-
            sion', in M. Poorthuis and J. Schwarz (eds.), *Saints and Role Models in
            Judaism and Christianity* (Leiden: Brill): 25-42.
Assmann, Jan
   1992   'Inscriptional Violence and the Art of Cursing: A Study of Performative
            Writing', *SLR* 9/1: 43-56.
Bergmann, Claudia D.
   2008   'We have seen the enemy, and he is only a "she": The Portrayal of Warriors
            as Women', in Kelle and Ames 2008: 129-42.
Berquist, Jon L.
   1997   'The Biblical Age: Images of Aging and the Elderly', in William J. Carl, Jr
            (ed.), *Graying Gracefully: Preaching to Older Adults* (Louisville, KY:
            Westminster John Knox Press): 47-68.
Boer, Roland
   1999   *Knockin' on Heaven's Door: The Bible and Popular Culture* (Biblical
            Limits; London: Routledge).
   2001   'Yahweh as Top: A Lost Targum', in Stone 2001: 75-105.
   2009   'Skin Gods: Circumcising the Built Male Body', *JMMS* 1/1: 35-44.

Boling, Robert G.
1983   'Levitical History and the Role of Joshua', in Carol L. Meyers and M.
        O'Connor (eds.), *The Word of the Lord Shall Go Forth: Essays in Honour
        of David Noel Freedman in Celebration of his Sixtieth Birthday* (Winona
        Lake, IN: Eisenbrauns, 1983): 241-61.
Boling, Robert G., and G. Ernest Wright
1982   *Joshua: A New Translation with Notes and Commentary* (AB, 6; Garden
        City, NY: Doubleday).
Brenner, Athalya
1997   *The Intercourse of Knowledge: On Gendering Desire and 'Sexuality' in
        the Hebrew Bible* (Leiden: Brill).
Butler, Trent C.
1983   *Joshua* (WBC; Waco, TX: Word Books, 1983).
Chirichigno, G.C.
1987   'The Use of the Epithet in the Characterization of Joshua', *TJ* 8/1 (Spring):
        69-79.
Clines, David J.A.
1995   'David the Man: The Construction of Masculinity in the Hebrew Bible', in
        his *Interested Parties: The Ideology of Writers and Readers of the Hebrew
        Bible* (JSOTSup, 205; GCT, 1; Sheffield: Sheffield Academic Press, 1995):
        212-41.
1998   '"Ecce Vir", or, Gendering the Son of Man', in J. Cheryl Exum and
        Stephen D. Moore (eds.), *Biblical Studies/Cultural Studies: The Third
        Sheffield Colloquium* (JSOTSup, 266; GCT, 7; Sheffield: Sheffield Aca-
        demic Press): 352-75.
2002   'He-Prophets: Masculinity as a Problem for the Hebrew Prophets and their
        Interpreters', in Alastair G. Hunter and Philip R. Davies (eds.), *Sense and
        Sensitivity: Essays on Reading the Bible in Memory of Robert Carroll*
        (JSOTSup, 348; Sheffield: Sheffield Academic Press): 311-28.
2003   'Paul, the Invisible Man', in Stephen D. Moore and Janice Capel Anderson
        (eds.), *New Testament Masculinities* (SBLSS, 45; Atlanta: Society of Bib-
        lical Literature): 181-92.
2007   'Being a Man in the Book of the Covenant', in J.G. McConville and Karl
        Möller (eds.), *Reading the Law: Studies in Honour of Gordon J. Wenham*
        (London: T. & T. Clark International): 3-9.
n.d.   'Loingirding and Other Male Activities in the Book of Job', unpublished
        paper available online: http.//www.shef.ac.uk/bibs/DJACcurrres/Articles.
        html.
Coates, Jennifer
2002   *Men Talk: Stories in the Making of Masculinities* (Oxford: Blackwell).
Connell, R.W.
1995   *Masculinities: Knowledge, Power and Social Change* (Berkeley, LA: Uni-
        versity of California Press).
Connell, R.W., and James W. Messerschmidt
2005   'Hegemonic Masculinity: Rethinking the Concept', *Gender and Society*
        19/6: 829-59.
Conrad, Edgar W.
1985   *Fear Not Warrior: A Study of 'al tîra' Pericopes in the Hebrew Scriptures*
        (Chico, CA: Scholars Press).

Cornwall, Andrea, and Nancy Lindisfarne
  1994   'Dislocating Masculinity: Gender, Power and Anthropology', in A. Cornwall and N. Lindisfarne (eds.), *Dislocating Masculinity: Comparative Ethnographies* (London and New York: Routledge): 11-47.
Creangă, Ovidiu
  2007   'The Silenced Songs of Victory: Gender, Power and Memory in the Conquest Narrative of Joshua (Josh. 1–12)', in Deborah W. Rooke (ed.), *A Question of Sex? Gender and Difference in the Hebrew Bible and Beyond* (HBMS, 14; Sheffield: Sheffield Phoenix Press): 106-23.
  2009a   *The Conquest of Memory: Israel's Identity and the Commemoration of the Past in Joshua's Conquest Narrative (chs. 1–12)* (PhD dissertation, King's College, London.
  2009b   'Symmetric and Asymmetric in the Summaries of Joshua's Military Campaigns in the Land: A Short Note on Joshua 11.16-23', in C. Constantineanu and M. V. Măcelaru (eds.), *Bible, Culture, Society: Postgraduate Explorations* (Osijek: Evanđeoski Teološki Fakultet): 23-37.
Eilberg-Schwartz, Howard
  1992   'The Problem of the Body for the People of the Book', in Howard Eilberg-Schwartz (ed.), *People of the Body: Jews and Judaism from an Embodied Perspective* (Albany: State University of New York Press): 17-46.
  1994   *God's Phallus: And Other Problems for Men and Monotheism* (Boston: Beacon Press).
Eynikel, Erik
  1996   *The Reform of King Josiah and the Composition of the Deuteronomistic History* (Leiden: Brill).
Feldman, Louis H.
  1989   'Josephus's Portrait of Joshua', *HTR* 82: 351-76.
Foucault, Michel
  1980   'Truth and Order', in C. Gordon (ed.), *Power/Knowledge: Selected Interviews and Other Writings, 1972–1977* (New York: Pantheon Books): 109-33.
Garbini, Giovanni
  1988   *History and Ideology in Ancient Israel* (trans. John Bowden; London: SCM Press).
Ginzberg, Louis
  1998 [1913] *The Legends of the Jews* (4 vols; Baltimore and London: Johns Hopkins University Press).
Gordon, Robert
  2003   'Gibeonite Ruse and Israelite Curse in Joshua 9', in Ernest W. Nicholson and Robert B. Salters (eds.), *Covenant and Context* (Oxford: Oxford University Press): 163-90.
Hamlin, E. John
  1983   *Joshua: Inheriting the Land* (ITC; Grand Rapids, MI: Eerdmans).
Harrington, Daniel J., and Anthony J. Saldarini (eds.)
  1987   *Targum Jonathan of the Former Prophets. Introduction, Translation and Notes* (Edinburgh: T. & T. Clark).
Hawk, L. Daniel
  2009   'Conquest Reconfigured: Recasting Warfare in the Redaction of Joshua', in Kelley and Ames 2008: 145-60.

2000a   *Joshua* (Berit Olam: Studies in Hebrew Narrative and Poetry; Collegeville, MN: Liturgical Press).

2000b   'Fixing Boundaries: The Construction of Identity in Joshua', *ATJ* 32: 1-12.

1997   'The Problem with Pagans', in Timothy K. Beal and David M. Gunn (eds.), *Reading Bibles, Writing Bodies: Identity and the Book* (London and New York: Routledge): 153-63.

Hearn, Jeff

2004   'From Hegemonic Masculinity to the Hegemony of Men', *FT* 5/1: 49-72.

Hess, Richard S.

1996   *Joshua: An Introduction and Commentary* (TOTC; Downers Grove, IL: Intervarsity Press).

Hirsch, Emil G., and Bernard Pick,

1901–1906 'Joshua', in *JEnc* 7: 281-84.

Hoffner, Harry

1966   'Symbols of Masculinity and Femininity: Their Use in Ancient Near Eastern Sympathetic Magic Rituals', *JBL* 85: 326-34.

Horowitz, Elliot

2006   *Reckless Rites: Purim and the Legacy of Jewish Violence* (Princeton and Oxford: Princeton University Press).

Hutchings, Kimberley

2008   'Making Sense of Masculinity and War', *Men and Masculinities* 10: 389-407.

Jaffee, Martin S.

2001   *Torah in the Mouth* (Oxford: Oxford University Press).

Jennings, Theodore W., Jr

2005   *Jacob's Wound: Homoerotic Narrative in the Literature of the Hebrew Bible* (New York: Continuum).

Kelle, Brad E., and Frank R. Ames (eds.)

2008   *Writing and Reading War: Rhetoric, Gender, and Ethics in Biblical and Modern Contexts* (SBLSympS, 42; Atlanta: Society of Biblical Literature).

Laukewish, Vincent A.

1998   'Assault from Behind: Sodomy, Foreign Invasion and Masculine Identity in the Roman d'Eneas', in Sylvia Tomasch and Sealy Gilles (eds.), *Text and Territory: Geographical Imagination in the European Middle Ages* (Philadelphia: University of Pennsylvania Press): 212-20.

Lohfink, Norbert

1962   'Die deuteronomistische Darstellung des Übergangs der Führung Israels von Moses auf Josua', *Scholastik* 37: 32-44.

Macwilliam, Stuart

2009   'Ideologies of Male Beauty and the Hebrew Bible', *BibInt* 17: 265-87.

Malamat, Abraham

1975   'Israelite Conduct of War in the Conquest of Canaan according to the Biblical Tradition', in Frank Moore Cross (ed.), *Symposia Celebrating the Seventy-Fifth Anniversary of the Founding of the American Schools of Oriental Research (1900–1975)* (Cambridge, MA: American Schools of Oriental Research): 1.35-55.

Miller, Toby

1995   'A Short History of the Penis', *Social Text* 43 (Autumn): 1-26.

Mitchell, Gordon
    1993   *Together in the Land: A Reading of the Book of Joshua* (JSOTSup, 134; Sheffield: JSOT Press).

Moore, Stephen D.
    1996   *God's Gym: Divine Male Bodies of the Bible* (New York and London: Routledge).
    2001   *God's Beauty Parlor: And Other Queer Spaces in and around the Bible* (Contraversions: Jews and Other Differences Series; Stanford, CA: Stanford University Press).
    2008   'Review of Jacob's Wound: Homoerotic Narrative in the Literature of Ancient Israel', *JHS* 17: 478-83.

Nelson, Richard D.
    1997   *Joshua: A Commentary* (OTL; Louisville, KY: Westminster John Knox Press).

Nissinen, Martti
    1998   *Homoeroticism in the Biblical World* (trans. Kirsi Stjerna; Minneapolis: Augsburg Fortress Press).

Noth, Martin
    1991   *The Deuteronomistic History* (2nd edn; Sheffield: JSOT Press).

Olson, Dennis T.
    2006   'Untying the Knot? Masculinity, Violence, and the Creation–Fall Story of Genesis 2–4', in Linda Day and Carolyn Pressler (eds.), *Engaging the Bible in a Gendered World: An Introduction to Feminist Biblical Interpretation in Honor of Katherine Doob Sakenfeld* (Louisville, KY: Westminster John Knox Press): 73-86.

Polaski, Don
    2008   'Where Men are Men and Women are Women? The Songs of Songs and Gender', *RevExp* 105: 435-51.

Porter, J. Roy
    1970   'The Succession of Joshua', in John I. Durham and J. Roy Porter (eds.), *Proclamation and Presence: Old Testament Essays in Honour of Gwynne Henton Davies* (London: SCM Press): 102-32.

Pritchard, James B. (ed.)
    1955   *Ancient Near Eastern Texts Relating to the Old Testament* (2nd edn; Princeton, NJ: Princeton University Press).
    1969   *The Ancient Near East. Supplementary Texts and Pictures Relating to the Old Testament* (Princeton, NJ: Princeton University Press).

Rofé, Alexander
    2006   'Giosuè figlio di Nun nella storia della tradizione biblica', *RSB* 18: 53-90.

Römer, Thomas C.
    2003   'Competing Magicians in Exodus 7–9: Interpreting Magic in the Priestly Theology', in Todd Klutz (ed.), *Magic in the Biblical World: From the Rod of Aaron to the Ring of Solomon* (JSNTSup, 245; London: T. & T. Clark International): 12-22.
    2007   *The So-Called Deuteronomistic History: A Sociological, Historical and Literary Introduction* (London: T. & T. Clark).

Rooke, Deborah W.
    2009   'Breeches of the Covenant: Gender, Garments and the Priesthood', in

Deborah W. Rooke (ed.), *Embroidered Garments: Priests and Gender in Biblical Israel* (HBM, 25; KCLSBG, 2; Sheffield: Sheffield Phoenix Press, 2009): 19-37.

Rowlett, Lori L.
1996   *Joshua and the Rhetoric of Violence: A New Historicist Analysis* (JSOTSup, 226; Sheffield: Sheffield Academic Press).

Satlow, Michael L.
1996   '"Try To Be a Man": The Rabbinic Construction of Masculinity', *HTR* 89: 19-40.

Schneider, Laurel C.
2001   'Yahwist Desires: Imagining Divinity Queerly', in Ken Stone (ed.), *Queer Commentary and the Hebrew Bible* (JSOTSup, 334; Sheffield: Sheffield Academic Press): 201-27.

Segal, Edwin S.
2006   'Variations in Masculinity from a Cross-Cultural Perspective', *AGR* 10: 25-43.

Stone, Ken (ed.)
2001   *Queer Commentary and the Hebrew Bible* (Sheffield: Sheffield Academic Press).
2001a   'Queer Commentary and Biblical Interpretation', in Stone 2001: 11-34.
2005   *Practising Safer Texts: Food, Sex, and Bible in Queer Perspective* (London and New York: T. & T. Clark).

Stone, Lawson G.
1991   'Ethical and Apologetic Tendencies in the Redaction of the Book of Joshua', *CBQ* 53: 25-35.

Štrba, Bjažej
2008   *Take off your Sandals from your Feet! An Exegetical Study of Josh 5,13-15* (ÖBS, 32; Frankfurt: Peter Lang).

Van Nortwick, Thomas
2008   *Imagining Men: Ideals of Masculinity in Ancient Greek Culture* (Westport, CT: Praeger).

Washington, Harold C.
1997   'Violence and the Construction of Gender in the Hebrew Bible', *BibInt* 5: 324-63.

Winter, Irene J.
1989   'The Body of the Able Ruler: Toward an Understanding of the Statues of Gudea', in H. Behrens *et al.* (eds.), *Dumu-E₂-Dub-ba-a: Studies in Honor of Åke J. Sjöberg* (Philadelphia: Occasional Publications of the Samuel Noah Kramer Fund, 11 / The University Museum): 573-83.
2009   'What/When Is a Portrait? Royal Images of the Ancient Near East', *PAPS* 153: 254-70.

'AND HIS SKIN RETURNED LIKE A SKIN OF A LITTLE BOY': MASCULINITY, DISABILITY AND THE HEALING OF NAAMAN

Cheryl Strimple and Ovidiu Creangă

2 Kings 5 recounts the story of Naaman, the Aramean general, who, upon the advice of a captured Israelite servant girl, travels to Samaria in order to cure his 'leprosy'.[1] The narrative is typically read as a story about Naaman's conversion and, thus, God's universality, Naaman being characterized as an arrogant foreigner who is transformed into a gracious convert.[2] Naaman, however, embodies a complex representation of disability and masculinity within the struggle for power among male characters in the narrative. The union of physical ability and masculinity is not as straightforward as one might expect it to be, and the story's contrasts, transformations and antitheses epitomize the complicated nature of this relationship. Naaman's story uses 'disability'[3] to manipulate male identity in order to present and reinforce a version of normative Israelite masculinity fully in keeping with Deuteronomistic ideology.

Disability is integral to the artistry and ideological weight of the story. Naaman's disability not only moves forward the plot of the story, but also serves as a narrative hinge upon which his miraculous conversion turns. In 2 Kings 5, male bodies become the textual site of contestation for male power and religious identity. Naaman's healing and conversion solve the 'problem' of his disability and normalize his identity as one who serves and worships Yhwh. For Gehazi and the king of Aram, however, disability tempers their status and power in the story.

---

1.   The term 'leprosy' is used in quotations marks to emphasize the socially constructed nature of a highly stigmatized discourse that this term represents as a translation of צרעת. Although quotation marks will not be used around each occurrence of the term 'leprosy', or even around more general terms like 'illness' and 'disease', the unmarked terms are considered to indicate this social-cultural construction throughout this essay (cf. Pilch 2007: 135-40 (137), and 2008: 635-37).

2.   See: Nelson 1987: 176; Long 1991: 69; Wiseman 1993: 207; Provan 1995: 191; Fretheim 1999: 153.

3.   Like the term 'leprosy', we place 'disability' in quotation marks at the beginning of this essay to denote the social construction of 'able-bodied' as a norm or unmarked term and 'disabled' as the marked term that stigmatizes variations in mental and physical variations in human embodiment.

Lennard J. Davis argues that the construction of 'normalcy' creates the 'problem' of disability. He explains, 'the "problem" is not the person with disabilities; the problem is the way that normalcy is constructed to create the "problem" of the disabled person' (Davis 2006: 3). Davis traces the development of the concept of a 'norm' from its late entry into the English language in 1840 through its incorporation and presentation of mental and physical 'ideals' as the standard to which all bodies and intellects should conform. Early statisticians who also held eugenicist values contributed to this ideal of the human body that grouped 'disabilities' among undesirable traits in people, like criminality and poverty (6-9). Foucault (1973) proposes the concept of the 'medical gaze' to describe not only the meticulous processes by which illness is mapped out – defined, measured, named, classified, anatomized – but also the circumstances in which disease is constructed as something different from, but part of, a healthy physical condition. Davis's and Foucault's explication of the (precarious) emergence of the 'normal' or 'healthy' allows us to consider how normative identity is constructed and presented in biblical texts and, specifically, what health-norms are implicit in the ideological trend/s of a particular text. What might the theological and historical goals of the Deuteronomistic History (DH hereafter) communicate about expectations of Israelite masculinity? How does disability impact this expectation? This study will employ a narrative-critical approach to 2 Kings 5 in order to show that the language used in this story draws implicit connections with Deuteronomy and the DH to establish a hierarchy of male power in line with its religious and political goals.

Masculinity and 2 Kings 5

Masculinity, like disability, is a contested concept, and studies in masculinity emphasize the socially constructed, culturally determined nature of masculinity—or more aptly, masculinities—within a given society. Throughout the three waves of Masculinity Studies, an increasing awareness emerged concerning the groups of people that challenge a singular concept of masculinity (Edwards 2006: 2-3). During the first wave in the 1970s, the sex role paradigm argued for the social construction of masculinity through socialization that taught and reinforced sex roles that were considered limiting or even harmful to men. In the 1980s, oppressed masculinities involving race, class, and sexuality critiqued the assumed white, middle class, Western representation of masculinity underpinning the first wave. A third wave, informed by post-structuralism, emphasizes the historical and contemporary representations of masculinity in terms of 'normativity, performativity, and sexuality' (Edwards 2006: 3). Notably absent, however, in most Masculinity Studies books is a treatment of disability and masculinity. While studies in masculinity may include disability within the list of attributes that add complexity to concepts of masculinity (Edwards 2006: 140; Whitehead 2002: 88, 189-90), few engage disability and masculinity in an in-depth or detailed way.[4] In one of the few studies on biblical masculinity and disability, Hentrich points out that the disability question tends in the first instance to overshadow traditional gender categories, so that a person with a disability is often seen as a disabled person before being seen as a man or a woman (2007: 73). That may be true, yet even in Hentrich's study, which aims to correct this shortsightedness, more reflection is needed on how disabled men in the Bible perform masculinity, that is to say, how they negotiate between or contest established norms of masculinity.[5] When the topic of disability arises in masculinity studies, it does so in relation to agency and experiences and perceptions of the physical male body (Connell 2005: 54-55; 2006: 58), omitting the intersection of cognitive disability and masculinity (but see Olyan 2008).

The concept of hegemonic masculinity casts the discussion in largely heterosexual, dualistic terms, in which social relations of power are woven into a model of masculinity based on intellectual (intelligent, persuasive) and physical abilities (muscular, healthy, attractive) that are exalted up to the point that they become an ideal which only a very small number of men can truly attain (Carrigan *et al.*, 1985: 592; Cornell 2005: 54-55). This does not mean, however, that disabled men are automatically and necessarily cast outside hegemony or positioned at its opposite side, alongside women, children, effeminate and homosexual men. That may appear to be the case at times, depending on the nature and severity of one's disability, but various positions within the hegemonic schema can be occupied by the (heterosexual) disabled, for example a position of complicity where hegemonic standards are reinforced and benefited from, or a position of marginalization from where some advantages over others may still be harvested.[6]

The retention of real power by disabled men becomes more evident when we note that disabled men are characterized by some of the same traits as able men. A growing body of literature examining the representation of masculinity in the Hebrew Bible emphasizes the link between masculinity and

4.   Many books in the category of Masculinity Studies include only minor comments on masculinity and disability, often no more than a couple of pages (Brod 1994; Whitehead 2002; Beynon 2002; Connell 2005; 2006).

5.   Helpful examples include the study by Gerschick and Miller (1995: 183-204) on how men who are disabled from birth or have become disabled as a result of accident or illness respond to hegemonic masculine ideals, and also the study by Shakespeare (1999: 53-64) on sexuality and disabled masculinity.

6.   For a discussion of hegemony and its structure, see Connell 2005: 77-81. For a critical application of Connell's typology to the Conquest Narrative (Josh. 1–12), see Creangă (in this volume).

violence, persuasion, beauty and independence from women (Clines 1995; Washington 1997; 1998; Haddox 2006; but see Olson 2006). Naaman is described as a 'mighty warrior' (2 Kgs 5.1), just as is David (1 Sam. 16.18). His disability did not prevent him from achieving high military status (צבא שׂר), even though his military exploits remain implied. David is 'intelligent in speech' (1 Sam. 16.18) and uses this attribute as an element of control (Clines 1995: 219-20), yet Naaman is not far behind. He is articulate in his complaint against Elisha (2 Kgs 5.11), movingly persuasive when he embraces Israelite monotheism (2 Kgs 5.15, 17), trusting of the servant (Gehazi) of his beneficiary, restrained in the use of unnecessary violence (not using Elisha's slight as a pretense for war). He listens to the advice of women (and servants) who play a small but integral role in the story, but he acts alone. David is a 'beautiful man' (אישׁ תאר, 1 Sam. 16.18). Naaman's skin becomes after healing 'like the skin of a little boy' (2 Kgs 5.14), suggesting an idealized contrast to the previous appearance of his skin and, perhaps, beauty (cf. Olyan 2008: 16). The single adjective מצרע—a highly stigmatized skin condition to an Israelite—undoubtedly operates as a negative counterpart to his otherwise positive characterization and functions to lessen his overtly positive masculinity, but this should not detract from the common features a disabled Naaman shares with other hegemonic men of the Bible.

2 Kings 5 avoids an overtly gendered discourse that contrasts the masculine and feminine in order to critique male power. Instead it achieves that through disability. Although 2 Kings 5 subtly feminizes Naaman, in that warrior language describes both Naaman and his wife (2 Kgs 5.1, 3) and diminutive language is used of the Israelite servant girl and Naaman once he is cured, it is the *removal of his disability* that effects his emasculation, as he appears before other men with the skin of a 'little boy' (2 Kgs 5.3, 14). Thus, the story uses Naaman's disability and its removal to impose a hierarchy of legitimate male power—a hierarchy supported in part by the purity standards in Leviticus and reinforced within Dtr's worldview that values the able-bodied, Israelite adult male obedient to Yhwh as fashioned by the Deuteronomic law. The positioning of Naaman within that hierarchy can be traced by following his journey to and from Elisha (and Yhwh). As we will see in more detail below, 2 Kings 5 deploys a variety of interlocking strategies to establish a hierarchy of male power in the story and to position Naaman as an ideal example for other Israelite men. These strategies include: (a) the use of disability as a narrative device that can be imposed or removed to denote male status, (b) Deuteronomistic resonances that reinforce a normative Israelite male identity, and (c) the structuring language of loyalty that establishes Yhwh and then Elisha as the most powerful characters in the narrative.

Naaman's Disability in Priestly and Deuteronomistic Worldviews

Priestly and Deuteronomic texts share similarities in their portrayal of disability, both assuming that 'everything about the body can be categorized in religiously relevant terms' and 'both locate disability primarily in the individual body' (Raphael 2008: 29). The skin, that thin layer separating the inside of our bodies from the outside world, functions in Leviticus (for example, Lev. 13.1-46) as an 'ideal boundary' in the sense that only 'a certain kind of surface represents holiness' (Raphael 2008: 37). The priestly categories of pure and holy represent merely two aspects of the 'Normal' (Raphael 2008: 39), with the help of which the 'abnormal' is imagined, described and dis/placed away from the former (Num. 5.1-5; 12.14-15; 2 Chron. 26.21). In the same way, according to Raphael (2008.48), Deuteronomy constructs as Normal the idea of belonging to Yhwh's covenant community, where health and ability become not only signs of acceptance but also rewards for loyalty to Yhwh (Deut. 7.15; 24.8; disloyalty brings about physical and mental illness, cf. Deut. 28.21-22, 27-28). In both Leviticus and Deuteronomy, then, the impure and unholy, the 'abnormal', despite being placed outside the Norm/al, remains part of it in so far as it allows demarcation to take place.

2 Kings 5 echoes some of these ideas. The story holds Naaman to Israelite purity standards and priestly conceptions of the Normal as represented in Leviticus and, moreover, casts Naaman's skin condition as an individual disability in need of eradication prior to his standing before Elisha and Yhwh. That Naaman has צרעת immediately frames this story within terms of Israelite cultic purity; he is not 'cured', אסף, but becomes 'clean', טהר (2 Kgs 5.14). The צרעת on Naaman's skin is not something to be washed away in the Abana or Pharpar rivers but laundered in the Jordan River so that he can be ritually clean. Naaman, as his question in v. 12 reveals, understands his healing in terms of washing/bathing, רחץ, but the text frames his healing in terms of cleanliness. Before he can in effect become part of the covenant community, perhaps understood here as coming face to face with Elisha, Naaman's skin must emulate this ideal boundary. Naaman's return journey from the Jordan River to Elisha's house is suggestive of the language of joining the covenant community, where the new member 'comes' or 'enters' (בוא) (Josh. 9.8, 9) and 'stands before' (עמד לפני, but sometimes נצב לפני, Deut. 4.11; 29.10), or in a place from where a proclamation is expected (Deut. 27.12, 13), and confesses 'I know that ... God...' (Deut. 4.39; Josh. 2.9). Thus, although Naaman is an accomplished man in many ways, he begins the story at a disadvantage. His marginal social status according to Israelite standards of purity places his masculinity in question from the beginning. Once this marginal status marker is removed and his skin becomes healthy, the story is keen to bring this now even more powerful masculinity under check through a

language of loyalty to Yhwh that places him not only within the covenant community but also as a servant who stands before Elisha and Yhwh. Olyan rightly suspects that biblical authors use disability or other tropes of 'weakness and ineffectuality' to further the plot of a story and highlight a favorite theme, typically that of Yhwh's agency and power (Olyan 2008: 9). In this way, Naaman's skin condition is co-opted by the Dtr author/s and made to drive the plot of Naaman's story towards his miraculous healing and conversion, but concomitantly also towards a legitimate notion of masculinity.

Deuteronomistic Resonances Reinforcing Normative Israelite Masculinity

Since Martin Noth's Deuteronomistic History hypothesis,[7] scholars have conceptualized the provenance of the Elijah–Elisha cycle as an existing compilation forming a post-Deuteronomistic addition.[8] Although the Elisha cycle contains Deuteronomistic formulas[9] and shows considerable Deuteronomistic reworking in the placement of the three victories over Aram[10] and the retelling of Jehu's revolt (Miller 1966: 447-50), the Naaman story stands as part of the Elisha cycle (2 Kgs 4.1–8.6 and 13.14-21) and is thus considered unrelated to the DH. Yet, certain language within the Naaman story resonates with

7. Martin Noth identified a 'Deuteronomistic' author (Dtr) within Joshua–Kings on the basis of language use and perspective in line with Deuteronomic Law (DL), a theological interpretation of Israel's history, and the use of rhetorical speeches like those in Deuteronomy (Noth 1981: 4-5). This author, according to Noth, incorporated existing traditional sources and linked them together by way of 'connecting narrative' (Noth 1981: 10). Noth considered Dtr's theological themes implicit: most importantly that the Israelite people had a special relationship with Yhwh that obligated them to uphold DL. For Noth, worship as prescribed by DL provided the core of Dtr's historical account, but Dtr was not so much interested in outlining correct forms of worship as identifying illicit ones and, thus, Israelite apostasy (Noth 1981: 92). Noth calls the 'real theme' of the DH the 'the conduct and fate of the people once they had settled in Palestine' and characterizes Yhwh as a God who 'acted at the beginning of Israelite history and... repeatedly intervened to help' (Noth 1981: 91-93). Therefore, according to Noth, the end of Israel as a nation, which Deuteronomy forewarned, was final and decisive with no hope for a future, a restored monarchy or even a nation (Noth 1981: 93).

8. Noth considered the Elijah–Elisha cycle traditional material reproduced though divided by Dtr. According to Noth, the Elijah–Elisha cycle consisted of 'originally independent episodes and a short series of anecdotes, welded together into a more or less unified continuous narrative before Dtr.'s time. Dtr. incorporated it into his history, splitting it up into parts' (Noth 1981: 68, also 71). Otto and others view it as post-Deuteronomistic additions. See Otto 2003: 497 n. 33.

9. 2 Kgs 1.18 and 2 Kgs 3.1-3.

10. McKenzie attributes this reworking to the Prophetic Historian. See McKenzie, 'Prophetic History', 216.

themes in Deuteronomy and by extension reinforces the theological world-view of Dtr. This language serves as a kind of signpost of how to read the story to an audience already familiar with Deuteronomy. As Philip Satter-thwaite explains in his approach to 2 Kings 2–8:

> The artless and disjointed surface appearance of some biblical narratives con-ceals implicit connections between events which readers are expected to note and make sense of. As they do so, they uncover a wealth of significance and pointed evaluation. This narrative strategy may be summed up in the phrase 'implicit commentary': explicit interpretative and evaluative comments are regularly withheld, the narrator instead suggesting interpretations and evalu-ations by implicit analogies and contrasts (1998: 6-7).

In the same way, 2 Kings 5 provides an implicit commentary that resonates with and reinforces Deuteronomistic cultic, as well as normative masculine, ideals. This is not to argue that 2 Kings 5 is a Deuteronomistic compilation but rather to suggest that a story without explicit Deuteronomistic editing and additions can nonetheless support Deuteronomistic ideology through analo-gous language.

Moshe Weinfeld identifies nine theological themes in Deuteronomy that provide the context of Deuteronomistic vocabulary.[11] Of these, four inform the Naaman story: the struggle against idolatry, centralization of the cult, monotheism, and observance of the law out of loyalty to the covenant. Lan-guage within the Naaman story resonates with Deuteronomistic vocabulary and ideas and situates this story within a Deuteronomic frame that implicitly supports the aims of the DH. This language includes references to *other gods*, אלהים אחרים (2 Kgs 5.17), *bowing down*, שחה (2 Kgs 5.18), and *clinging*, דבק (2 Kgs 5.27).

---

11. These nine themes are the struggle against idolatry; the centralization of the cult; exodus, covenant, and election; the monotheistic creed; observance of the law and loyalty to the covenant; inheritance of the land; retribution and material motivation; fulfillment of prophecy; and the election of the Davidic dynasty (Weinfeld 1972: 1). Weinfeld argues that 'what makes a phrase deuteronomic is not its mere occurrence in Deuteronomy, but its meaning within the framework of deuteronomic theology' and that much of the terminology that is Deuteronomic is not new but reflects the specific context of Dtr (Wein-feld 1972: 1-2). For example, the expression 'other gods', אלהים אחרים, occurs in Deu-teronomy but is not necessarily Deuteronomistic, according to Weinfeld, in that it is 'part and parcel of the common Hebrew vocabulary' (Weinfeld 1972: 2). However, if Weinfeld identifies the struggle against idolatry as a central theme of Deuteronomy, then the phrase 'other gods' for an Israelite audience would have associative meaning and provide an implicit commentary in line with this theme in the DH. This resonance, in fact, holds together the separate traditions included within the DH. These same resonances allow for the implicit nature of Deuteronomistic themes with which, according to Noth, the audience would already be familiar (Noth 1981: 89).

The language of bowing down to other gods points to the theme of the struggle against idolatry (Weinfeld 1972: 321).[12] Deuteronomy 8.19 warns, 'If you do forget the LORD your God and follow other gods to serve and bow down to them, I solemnly warn you today that you shall surely perish'. Likewise, Joshua's Deuteronomistic speech reminds his hearers that 'If you transgress the covenant of the LORD your God, which he enjoined on you, and go and serve other gods and bow down to them, then the anger of the LORD will be kindled against you, and you shall perish quickly from the good land that he has given to you' (Josh. 23.16). 'Servant' and 'bowing down' language come together in Naaman's speech in a positive reformulation of Dtr's discourse against apostasy: 'For this thing, may the LORD forgive *your servant*: when my lord goes into the house of Rimmon *to bow down* there and he leans on my arm and *I bow down* [in] the house of Rimmon, *when bowing down* in the house of Rimmon, may the LORD forgive *your servant* this thing' (2 Kgs 5.18). Bowing down figures prominently in Naaman's request for forgiveness of future, unintended sin, in that the verb חחש appears three times in this single verse.

Deuteronomistic language that relates to observance of the law and loyalty to the covenant is expressed by the phrase 'to cleave to Yhwh', דבק ביהוה (Weinfeld 1972: 333).[13] Deuteronomy identifies Yhwh as the one to whom the Israelites should cling. In Deuteronomy, the language of clinging also relates to illness and disease as divine punishment.[14] In the DH, the language of clinging appears in the criticism of Solomon as one who clung to his foreign wives (1 Kgs 11.2) (Campbell 1994: 58). This same language, however, also occurs in the Elisha cycle within another Deuteronomistic addition:

12. This language occurs in Deut. 8.19; 11.16; 29.26 and in the DH (Josh. 23.16; Judg. 2.19; 1 Kgs 9.6; 16.31).

13. The idea of clinging to Yahweh occurs in Deut. 4.4; 10.20; 11.22; 13.4; and 30.20, and this same language is used by Dtr in Josh. 23.8 (cf. also 22.5); and 2 Kgs 18.6.

14. Deuteronomy promises protection to Israelites from the 'diseases of Egypt': 'The LORD will turn away from you every illness; all the dread diseases of Egypt that you experienced, he will not inflict on you, but he will lay them on all who hate you' (Deut. 7.15). Later in Deuteronomy, Yhwh warns that pestilence will cling to the Israelites if they disobey the covenant (Deut. 28.21) and that Yhwh will cause the 'diseases of Egypt' to cling to the Israelites (Deut. 28.60). In the same way, Naaman's leprosy clings to Gehazi. When Elisha asks Gehazi, 'Is this a time to take silver and to take clothing and olive trees and vineyards and flocks and cattle and servants and female slaves?' (2 Kgs 5.26), Gehazi had only taken the first two of the eight items, but for this Elisha proclaims, 'Naaman's leprosy will cling to you and your descendants forever' (2 Kgs 5.27). By taking these things, Gehazi has disobeyed the covenant and Elisha, acting as Yhwh's representative, punishes him in accordance with the warnings in Deuteronomy 28.

2 Kgs 3.3 describes Jehoshaphat as clinging to the sin of Jeroboam: worshipping other gods. 'Clinging' language thus implies that if an Israelite male does not cling to Yhwh, then illness or disease will cling to male bodies. The language of clinging brings together the construction of disability and Israelite religiosity in 2 Kings 5; Israelites who cling to Yhwh avoid stigmatizing and marginalizing illnesses. Likewise, in the case of Gehazi, those who cling to sin are subject to clinging diseases.

The resonances of the language of serving other gods, bowing down and clinging in the Naaman story are not neutral in respect to the construction of masculinity but seek to normalize male behavior and male bodies. Deuteronomistic masculinity involves adherence to the positively valued behaviors to which Deuteronomistic themes point (see George in this volume). Through his confession, Naaman embodies ideal Israelite male behavior in that he proclaims Yhwh as the one, true God and vows to serve only Yhwh. Elisha, too, exhibits unwavering devotion to Yhwh when he refuses to take gifts from Naaman (Gehazi's actions are discussed below). Once Naaman's leprosy has been cured, he is now fit to worship Yhwh and works to secure what he thinks he will need to do so. Although Naaman does not seem on the face of things to understand Israelite worship when he asks for the two mule-loads of earth, he perhaps understands better than anyone what worship of Yhwh requires. In line with Deuteronomic and Deuteronomistic thinking, correct worship of Yhwh takes place in a central location. For him the ground (אדמה) provides a palpable connection with the Land where Yhwh dwells. This soil is a site of memory and devotion, a place of worship that facilitates Naaman's participation in the centralized cult. It is clearly not an alternative to the altar in Jerusalem, but only a mere extension of the Land that enables Naaman to connect with Yhwh. His unusual participation in the cult, in turn, elevates his sense of masculinity, not in the sense of becoming the normative model of masculinity, but in being placed immediately under it (represented by Elisha) and disrupting Gehazi's former standing within that male order.

Hegemonic Masculinity and the Language of Loyalty in 2 Kings 5

Attention to the use of 'servant' and 'standing before' language in 2 Kings 5 further reveals the structure of male power and hegemony, as it distinguishes between Israelite and non-Israelite and between adult males and young men. The narrative consistently uses two different terms for 'servant' throughout the story, עבד and נער. The use of servant language resonates with Deuteronomy's language about 'serving other gods' and brings Naaman from his lofty social position in Aram to the status of a servant and worshipper of Yhwh. The narrative uses 'young woman' and 'young man' language of Israelite servants and reserves the typical Hebrew word for servant, עבד, for non-Israelites in the story.[15] The Israelite servant girl is a 'little girl', נערה קטנה (2 Kgs 5.2) and Gehazi is Elisha's 'young man', נער (2 Kgs 5.20). The use of נער renders the narrator's description of Naaman's skin as that of a little boy, נער קטן, all the more astonishing for it aligns Naaman with Israelites: the Israelite servant girl, Gehazi, and the unnamed servants sent by Gehazi. The king of Aram calls Naaman 'my servant', עבדי (2 Kgs 5.6), but Naaman refers to himself only as 'your servant', עבדך, in relation to Elisha after his healing and conversion (2 Kgs 5.17-18). <u>Thus, the narrator uses 'young man' language and 'servant' language to signal Naaman's inclusion but also his place within the hegemonic hierarchy.</u> Elisha is no one's servant, or better, no man's servant, for he is איש־האלהים, 'the man of God' (v. 8; cf. also for this title 2 Kgs 4.16, 22, 25, 40), but immediately after him is the self-proclaimed 'servant' Naaman, then the 'young man' Gehazi.

The preposition 'before', לפני, provides another structuring motif for the entire story, furthering the theme of loyalty with which the story is concerned. In the first three verses, לפני establishes hierarchical social and political relationships. The syntactic structure of the first verse begins with Naaman's name followed by an appositional phrase and two parallel phrases introduced by היה: 'And Naaman, the commander of the army of the king of Aram, was a great man *before* his lord and his face was lifted because by him the LORD gave deliverance to Aram; and the man was a mighty warrior—leprous' (2 Kgs 5.1, emphasis added). In this single verse, the reader learns a great deal about Naaman's identity and allegiance: he is the commander of the Aramean army, an important man in the eyes of his king, a mighty warrior who also had leprosy.[16] He is not only a non-Israelite but also belongs to the ethnic group that holds increasing political dominance over Israel and serves as the means by which Yhwh will punish them (1 Kgs 19.15-18). In the second verse, the Arameans go out in bands and return with a little Israelite girl, נערה קטנה, who is *before* Naaman's wife. It is the little Israelite captive who articulates the Deuteronomistic vision of hegemonic male power in the story when she says to her mistress, 'O, that my lord [was] *before* the prophet in Samaria! Then, he would cure him of his leprosy [literally: gather him from his leprosy]' (2 Kgs 5.3, emphasis added). The words of the little Israelite girl

15. The only deviation from this use appears in Gehazi's answer to Elijah's question in 2 Kgs 5.25; however, Gehazi's reference to himself as an עבד supports the division of power demarcated in the story by the terms עבד and נער. When he refers to himself as an עבד, he is claiming the same social power and status as Naaman.

16. Naaman's leprosy is attached to the end of the first verse as a single adjective, but translations emphasize his disability by treating this single word as a disjunctive phrase. Some examples include, NRSV: 'The man, though a mighty warrior, suffered from leprosy'. RSV: 'He was a mighty man of valor, but he was a leper'. KJV: 'He was also a mighty man in valor, but he was a leper'. NKJV: 'He was also a mighty man of valor but a leper'. NJB: 'But the man suffered from a virulent skin-disease'.

foreshadow the plot and intent of the story. When the story begins, Naaman is *before* his lord, the king of Aram; the little Israelite girl is *before* the wife of Naaman; and she states her desire that Naaman be '*before* the prophet in Samaria' (2 Kgs 5.3). When the story approaches its climax, Naaman stands before Elisha.

The verb 'to stand', עמד, used with לפני, further structures the narrative according to loyalty and male power. When Naaman travels to Samaria, the king of Israel perceives his request as a pretense for war. Elisha reassures him by asking the king to send Naaman to him so that he might know that there is a prophet in Israel. Naaman stands at the entrance to Elisha's house, but Elisha sends only a messenger to tell him to bathe in the Jordan seven times and be clean. Naaman responds, 'I thought that for me, he would surely come out and stand (עמד) and call on the name of Yhwh his God and wave his hand over the spot and cure the leprosy!' (2 Kgs 5.11). As a powerful man, Naaman expected Elisha to stand before him, but Elisha asserts his male power in the story by failing to appear. Once Naaman accedes to Elisha's superior power by following his instructions, his leprosy is healed and his skin 'returned to him like the skin of a little boy and he was clean' (2 Kgs 5.14). Naaman then returns to Elisha and 'stands before him' (2 Kgs 5.15). Now that Naaman, the great man, has become like a little boy and cleansed of his leprosy, he meets Elisha in person. When Naaman tries to give Elisha gifts, however, Elisha refuses, swearing an oath by Yhwh's name 'whom *I stand before*' (2 Kgs 5.16). Elisha refuses Naaman's gifts along with the recognition of Naaman's equal or, perhaps, higher social status. In fact, the opposite occurs. Naaman presses Elisha to take gifts from him because he wants something from Elisha: 'If not, please let be given to *your servant* two mule-loads of earth because *your servant* will not again offer burnt offerings or sacrifice to other gods except to Yhwh' (2 Kgs 5.17). Elisha refuses to be indebted to Naaman. Instead, the giving and accepting of gifts along with Naaman's healing places Naaman in Elisha's debt and situates Elisha in a more powerful position than Naaman.

Conversely, the use of לפני and עמד in relation to Gehazi exposes his attempt to acquire power by illegitimate means. In contrast to Elisha's refusal to be beholden to Naaman, Gehazi swears an oath by Yhwh's name to run after and take something from Naaman. He enlists his own young men as servants to accompany him, placing himself on a par with Elisha. Once Naaman gives gifts to the two young men, they carry them *before* Gehazi (2 Kgs 5.23). Upon returning, Gehazi, like Elisha, *sends* the young men away. When Gehazi appears before Elisha, he literally 'stands to' his lord, אל־אדניו ויעמד (v. 25).[17] This is the only time when עמד is used with the preposition אל in

---

17. This oppositional stance is well documented in the literature. See Cohn 2000: 41.

the story, signaling Gehazi's attempt to meet Elisha as an equal who stands next to, not before, him. Prior to Gehazi's deception of Naaman, he and Naaman shared the same social position in the story; however, Elisha's punishment relegates Gehazi to a status below the now clean and more faithful Naaman. Elisha's question to Gehazi judges his actions in light of Deuteronomistic themes. The first part of Elisha's question, 'Is this a time to take silver and to take garments?' (2 Kgs 5.26), refers to the actual items Gehazi takes in the story. However, Elisha continues, 'And olive trees and orchards, and flocks and cattle, male and female slaves?', resonating with the language in 2 Same. 8.14-17, where Samuel warns that a king

> will take the best of your fields and vineyards and *olive orchards* and give them to his courtiers. He will take one-tenth of your grain and of your vineyards and give it to his officers and his courtiers. He will take your *male and female slaves*, and the best of your *cattle* and donkeys, and put them to his work. He will take one-tenth of your *flocks*, and you shall be his slaves [emphasis added].

In Elisha's compact use of these three pairs, he evokes one strand of Deuteronomistic thinking about the monarchy that views it negatively. Gehazi's crime is not one of simple greed contrasted to the now gracious Naaman. His crime consists of the crime of kings who appropriate goods from the people, become wealthy and worship other gods. For this reason, Elisha speaks the performative words, 'The leprosy of Naaman will *cling*, דבק, to you and your descendants forever' (2 Kgs 5.27). The language of clinging punctuates the seriousness of Gehazi's crime. Gehazi clings not to Yhwh but to the ways of wealthy kings. That is why Elisha intends to punish him so severely. Gehazi, like Israel's disobedient kings, exemplifies what an Israelite man ought not to be. The insider who becomes an outsider serves as the shocking antithesis to Naaman, the foreigner who stands out as an ideal Israelite. The idealization of Naaman against Gehazi continues in v. 18 where, unlike the unrepentant Gehazi, Naaman asks forgiveness for future sins against Yhwh that he might inadvertently commit: 'This thing may LORD forgive: when my lord goes into the House of Rimmon to bow down there and he leans on my arm and I bow down in the House of Rimmon, when I bow down in the House of Rimmon, may the LORD forgive your servant this thing' (2 Kgs 5.18). Naaman's speech is all the more remarkable for its depiction of the king of Aram. After Naaman's healing and conversion, the once gracious, competent king is now enfeebled. The verb 'to lean', שׁען, can denote actual leaning on someone or something or it can be used to describe the one on whom the king depends.[18]

However, it is not linked to the socio-political structuring function in contrast to the use of לפני in the story.

18. Samson asks to lean on the pillars of the house in Judg. 16.26. The young man

The story disables the king of Aram by portraying him as one who requires Naaman's help in order to bow down before his god. Now that Naaman's disability has been neutralized, and his position within Israelite male hierarchy established, the narrative disables the one greater and more unfaithful to Yhwh than him: the king of Aram. Disability language, then, comes in the end to characterize the two male characters in the story not loyal to Yhwh, Gehazi and the king of Aram, and signals their low place within the male hierarchy.

Elisha's severe punishment of Gehazi, one of the least powerful men in the story, and healing and elevation of the foreigner Naaman provides a window into the internal strategies of hegemonic masculinity. There we see resistance criticized and complicity rewarded. Though Elisha couches his condemnation of Gehazi in Deuteronomistic terms, one cannot but wonder if Gehazi's attempt to challenge Elisha's power motivates Elisha's punishment. This undercurrent that sees Israelite men emasculated to provide a telling contrast with non-Israelites runs through other texts. In the Book of Joshua, for example, Achan epitomizes the loss of masculinity, unable in the end to protect himself, his children and his property due to pollution from חרם (Josh. 7), whereas other former inhabitants of Canaan survive the conquest and dwell in the Land (Josh. 9). Gehazi and Achan complicate Deuteronomy's link between masculinity, ethnicity and membership in the covenant community, exposing its vulnerable loopholes. Both Gehazi and Achan are able-bodied males, both are Israelites, both are submissive and obedient up to a point, but both are greedy and are punished for it. The first (Gehazi) is struck with a disabling skin-disease, the second (Achan) with death. The first will live in shame and disgrace, the second with disrepute in the collective memory created by the DH (Josh. 22.20).

Instead of Conclusion: Disability, Narrative Prosthesis and Material Metaphor

David Mitchell and Sharon Snyder identify what they call 'the shared characteristics in the literary representation of disability', namely the tendency of most cultures to consider disability as a 'problem in need of a solution'. The representation of disability in literature, also true for Naaman's story, tends to function in two primary ways: as a 'stock feature of characterization', but even more importantly, as an 'opportunistic metaphorical device' (Mitchell and Snyder 2006: 205). They call this use 'narrative prosthesis', because disability serves as the means by which a character is distinguished from the

reports that he saw Saul 'leaning' on his spear in 2 Sam. 1.6, 2 Kgs 7.2 and 7.17 describe a captain 'on whose hand the king leaned' in the sense of the one upon whom the king depends or the second in command.

norm and at the same time performs a metaphorical function by drawing a connection to a more abstract concept and saying something about it (2006: 205). Mitchell and Snyder name this process the 'materiality of metaphor' where an abstract concept like illness or disability is represented as a cognitive or physical variation from a culturally determined norm (2006: 205). Narrative in this sense depends upon disability, like a strange feature that stimulates one to reflect upon oneself, and disability in turn contributes to the artistry and richness of the story.

Disability as a narrative prosthetic has many uses and operates on many levels. In this study, it was used as part of the normalizing discourse that values a certain notion of masculinity. Even if an anomaly according to Israelite purity standards, Naaman's leprosy is the narrative prosthetic that gives the author a reason to tell the story, but one that also must be removed in order to give purchase to the abstract conceptualization of legitimate Israelite masculinity. Naaman's leprosy as a narrative prosthesis functions almost as a material object that is gathered and later applied to Gehazi; it is not simply leprosy that clings to Gehazi but *Naaman's* leprosy. Gehazi's leprosy, therefore, exposes his disloyalty towards Yhwh and Elisha on the surface of his skin. It functions as the material metaphor that signifies the cost of resistance to hegemony and hegemonic males. The portrait of normative Israelite male identity conveyed by this story of healing and illness is one in keeping with the Deuteronomistic themes of obedience to the law, worship of Yhwh alone, and the rejection of apostasy. Naaman is the Deuteronomistic man *par excellence*, articulating and upholding key Deuteronomistic themes: knowledge that Yhwh is the only god (2 Kgs 5.15), worship of Yhwh alone (2 Kgs 5.17) and disavowal of other gods (2 Kgs 5.18). Since only a few Israelite men could be prophets like Elisha, this post-conversion depiction of Naaman guides the male audience to identify with and emulate him, and place itself under the authority of Yhwh and of his chosen prophets.

Bibliography

Avalos, Hector
    1995   *Illness and Health Care in the Ancient Near East: The Role of the Temple in Greece, Mesopotamia, and Israel* (HSM; Atlanta: Scholars Press).
Avalos, Hector, Sarah J. Melcher and Jeremy Schipper (eds.)
    2007   *This Abled Body: Rethinking Disabilities in Biblical Studies* (SemeiaSt; Atlanta: Society of Biblical Literature).
Campbell, Antony F.
    1994   'Martin Noth and the Deuteronomistic History', in Steven L. McKenzie and M. Patrick Graham (eds.), *History of Israel's Traditions* (Sheffield: Sheffield Academic Press): 31-62.
Carrigan, T., R.W. Connell and J. Lee
    1985   'Toward a New Sociology of Masculinity', *TheorSoc* 14: 551-604.

Clines, David J.A.
      1995   'David the Man: The Construction of Masculinity in the Hebrew Bible', in
                his *Interested Parties: The Ideology of Writers and Readers in the Hebrew
                Bible* (JSOTSup, 205; GCT, 1; Sheffield: Sheffield Academic Press): 212-
                43.
Cohn, Robert L.
      2000   *2 Kings* (Berit Olam; Collegeville, MN: Liturgical Press).
Connell, R.W.
      2005   *Masculinities* (2nd edn; Berkeley: University of California Press).
      2006   *The Men and the Boys* (Berkeley: University of California Press).
Cross, Frank M.
      1973   *Canaanite Myth and Hebrew Epic: Essays in the History of the Religion of
                Israel* (Cambridge, MA: Harvard University Press).
Davies, D.
      1977   'Interpretation of Sacrifice in Leviticus', *ZAW* 89: 387-39.
Davis, Lennard J.
      2006   'Constructing Normalcy: The Bell Curve, the Novel, and the Invention of
                the Disabled Body in the Nineteenth Century', in Lennard J. Davis (ed.),
                The Disability Studies Reader (New York: Routledge): 3-16.
      2006   *The Disability Studies Reader* (New York: Routledge).
Edwards, Tim
      2006   *Cultures of Masculinity* (New York: Routledge).
Foucault, Michel
      1973   *The Birth of the Clinic: An Archeology of Medical Perception* (London:
                Tavistock Publications)
Fretheim, Terence E.
      1999   *First and Second Kings* (Westminster Bible Companion; Louisville: West-
                minster John Knox Press).
Fritz, Volkmar
      2003   *1 and 2 Kings: A Continental Commentary* (CC; Minneapolis: Fortress
                Press).
Gerschick, Thomas J., and Adam S. Miller
      1995   'Coming to Terms: Masculinity and Physical Disability', in Donald F.
                Sabo and David F. Gordon (eds.), *Men's Health and Illness: Gender,
                Power and the Body* (Research on Men and Masculinities Series, 8; Thou-
                sand Oaks, CA: Sage Publications): 183-204.
Gray, John
      1970   *I and II Kings: A Commentary* (OTL; London: SCM Press, 2nd edn).
→ Hentrich, Thomas
      2007   'Masculinity and Disability in the Hebrew Bible', in Hector Avalos *et al.*
                (eds.), *This Abled Body: Rethinking Disabilities in Biblical Studies*
                (SemeiaSt; Atlanta: Society of Biblical Literature): 73-87.
Long, Burke O.
      1991   *2 Kings* (FOTL, 10; Grand Rapids, MI: Eerdmans).
McKenzie, Steven L.
      1985   'The Prophetic History and the Redaction of Kings', *HAR* 9: 203-20.
Melcher, Sarah J.
      1998   'Visualizing the Perfect Cult: The Priestly Rationale for Exclusion', in

Nancy L. Eiesland and Don E. Saliers (eds.), *Human Disability and the Service of God* (Nashville, TN: Abingdon Press): 55-71.

Miller, J. Maxwell
1966   'The Elisha Cycle and the Accounts of the Omride Wars', *JBL* 85: 441-54.

Mitchell, David, and Sharon Snyder
2006   'Narrative Prosthesis and the Materiality of Metaphor', in Lennard J. Davis (ed.), *The Disability Studies Reader* (New York: Routledge): 205-16.

Nelson, Richard D.
1987   *First and Second Kings* (IBCTP; Atlanta: John Knox Press).

Noth, Martin
1981   *The Deuteronomistic History* (Sheffield: JSOT Press).

Olson, Dennis T.
2006   'Untying the Knot?: Masculinity, Violence, and the Creation–Fall Story of Genesis 2–4', in Linda Day and Carolyn Pressler (eds.), *Engaging the Bible in a Gendered World: An Introduction to Feminist Biblical Interpretation in Honor of Katharine Doob Sakenfeld* (Louisville, KY: Westminster John Knox Press): 73-86.

Olyan, Saul M.
2008   *Disability in the Hebrew Bible: Interpreting Mental and Physical Differences* (New York: Cambridge University Press).

Otto, Susanne
2003   'The Composition of the Elijah–Elisha Stories and the Deuteronomistic History', *JSOT* 27: 487-508.

Pilch, John J.
2007   'Disease', in *NIBD*, 2: 135-40.
2008   'Leprosy', in *NIDB*, 3: 635-37.

Provan, Iain W.
1995   *1 and 2 Kings* (New International Biblical Commentary / Old Testament Series; Peabody, MA: Hendrickson Publishers).

Raphael, Rebecca
2008   *Biblical Corpora: Representations of Disability in Hebrew Biblical Literature* (London and New York: T. & T. Clark International).

Satterthwaite, Philip E.
1998   'The Elisha Narratives and the Coherence of 2 Kings 2–8', *TynB* 49: 1-28.

Shakespeare, Tom
1999   'Sexual Politics of Disabled Masculinity', *Sexuality and Disability* 17: 53-64.

Weinfeld, Moshe
1972   *Deuteronomy and the Deuteronomic School* (Oxford: Clarendon Press).

Whitehead, Stephen M.
2002   *Men and Masculinities* (Cambridge: Polity Press).

Wilkinson, John
1978   'Leprosy and Leviticus: A Problem of Semantics and Translation', *SJT* 31: 153-66.

Wiseman, D.J.
1993   *1 and 2 Kings: An Introduction and Commentary* (Leicester: Inter-Varsity Press).

Wright, David P.
    1987   *The Disposal of Impurity: Elimination Rites in the Bible and in Hittite and Mesopotamian Literature* (Atlanta: Scholars Press).
Zucconi, Laura M.
    2008   'Aramean Skin Care: A New Perspective on Naaman's Leprosy', in Shawna Dolanskya (ed.), *Sacred History, Sacred Literature: Essays on Ancient Israel, the Bible, and Religion in Honor of R.E. Friedman on his Sixtieth Birthday* (Winona Lake, IN: Eisenbrauns): 169-78.

'I AM NOT AFRAID OF ANYBODY, I AM THE RULER OF THIS LAND': JOB AS MAN IN CHARGE IN THE *TESTAMENT OF JOB*

Maria Haralambakis

At first glance it may seem that the *Testament of Job*, with the scholarly attention it has attracted during the last two decades in relation to the women who feature in it, is an unlikely composition to feature in a volume on masculinity. However, this essay will argue that, although women are present in the *Testament of Job*, they occupy subordinate roles and that it is Job who remains at the centre of attention throughout this patriarchal story. The protagonist is portrayed as a man in charge; he has control over his own life and over that of others. He fulfils different masculine roles, such as a father and husband, a wealthy king, a wrestler in combat and a benefactor of the poor. Job in the *Testament of Job* confirms the expectation of masculinity as 'a man's capacity to exercise power and control' (Kaufman 1994: 142).

This portrayal of Job as a patriarch can be contrasted with the presentation of Job as a pawn of God and Satan in the Book of Job. A detailed comparison of these two compositions about Job is beyond the scope of this essay, but it is noteworthy that the difference between them often forms the point of departure in studies about the women in the *Testament of Job*. Van der Horst, for example, first mentions that 'women definitely do not play a prominent role' in the biblical book of Job. He subsequently contrasts this with the situation in the *Testament of Job*: 'no fewer than 107 out of 388 verses in *Testament of Job* deal with women, i.e., almost thirty times as much space as in the biblical book' (van der Horst 1989: 94-95). Van der Horst's essay is the first of a significant number of studies about the *Testament of Job* which focus on the topic of 'women'. This pseudepigraphon lends itself to this concern, like several other compositions which remained 'outside the canon',[1]

---

1. One might see a connection between the role of women and the fact that these works literally remained on the margin, outside the established canon. Schüssler Fiorenza states in the introduction to the volume *Searching the Scriptures*: 'this commentary seeks to transgress canonical boundaries in order both to undo the exclusionary kyriarchal tendencies of the ruling canon and to renew the debate on the limits, functions and extent of the canon... Revitalizing this debate is necessary because the historical silencing and

because of the presence of women in it. The most prominent questions addressed in studies on women in the *Testament of Job* are whether or not the portrayal of women (Job's wife[2] and female servant) in chaps. 1–45 is different from that in chaps. 46–53 (Job's daughters), and if so, whether or not the first is negative and the second positive.[3] Scholars who take the daughters of Job to be an example of a positive portrayal of women tend to look from the text to the historical context and ask the question whether the *Testament of Job* is related to a community where the role of women was more elevated than in society as a whole (see for example Chesnutt 1991). The issues of gender inequality and power structures remain largely unaddressed in these studies. That these issues are at the centre of the study of masculinity (as well as of gender studies in general) becomes clear for example in this explanation: 'gender is not simply a system of classification, by which biological males and biological females are sorted, separated, and socialized into equivalent sex roles. Gender also expresses the universal inequality between women and men. When we speak about gender we also speak about hierarchy, power, and inequality, not simply difference' (Kimmel 2004: 1).[4]

In the studies on 'women' in the *Testament of Job* it is generally not pointed out that all these women remain dependent on the male protagonist of the narrative. That this is the case can be highlighted here by briefly summarizing Job's dealings with women in the *Testament of Job*. Job suppresses the sense of initiative in his female servant (chaps. 6–7). When she decides to give the beggar not the burnt loaf of bread that Job told her to give him, but her own good loaf, Job chastises her. She is made to believe that she is a

textual marginalization of women are the by-products of the so-called patristic kyriarchal selection and exclusionary canonization process' (Schüssler Fiorenza 1994: 5).

2.   Who receives the name Sitidos in the Greek manuscripts (although the name is mentioned only once, in 25.1, the introduction to a lament about her), but remains nameless in the Slavonic witnesses (in the Coptic 25.1 has not been preserved (see Schenke 2009: 84 for the Coptic text). The servant is unnamed, she is only referred to by her occupation as door maid.

3.   Van der Horst recognizes two contrasting images of women, leading to 'discrepancy and tension' in the Testament between the negative portrayal of Sitidos and the door maid and the positive view on Job's daughters (van der Horst 1989: 116). Chesnutt does not regard the portrayal of Job's servant and wife as purely negative, but he still perceives the role of the daughters in chaps. 46–53 as 'radically different'. His view is that the *Testament of Job* 'as it now stands offers an exceptionally positive portrayal of women' (Chesnutt 1991: 124-25). Susan Garret strongly disagrees with both these views and suggests instead that 'a fundamentally negative view of females as preoccupied with that which is earthly and corruptible underlies the document from beginning to end' (Garret 1993: 57).

4.   This is not to say that masculinity can be understood as exclusively being about power, a statement emphasized for example by Seidler 2006.

disobedient servant. She also appears as somewhat naïve and imperceptive, because unlike Job, she does not realize that this beggar is Satan in disguise. After Job has been forced out of the city and sits in sickness and poverty on a dung heap, Job's wife suffers for her husband and works as a servant and later beggar to bring him his bread (chaps. 21–25). She lives for him, not for herself.[5] This is made clear especially by her anticipation of her own freedom as she advises Job to 'say some word to (against) the Lord and die. Then I too shall again be free from weariness arising from (my) labours for your body' (25.1). In the last section of the *Testament of Job*, Job remains at the centre of attention as his brother describes the last days of Job's life, including his death and funeral. In the funeral scene the other characters surround Job's body, just as throughout the part of the story told by Job (chaps. 1–45) they surrounded Job on his death bed, listening to his farewell address. Even though the main topic of chaps. 46–50 concerns the inheritance of the daughters, it hardly justifies the view that in chaps. 46–52 'Job's three daughters are the centre of attention... Job is practically forgotten' (Nicholls 1982: 110-11). The daughters are portrayed as dependent on their father. It is Job who decides whether they receive an inheritance or not. The power is in his hands, not in theirs. It is true that they take the initiative to protest against receiving none of Job's worldly possessions. Unlike in the case of the servant, their initiative is not punished but rewarded, as Job listens to their complaint and engages in a dialogue with them. But in this dialogue it is clear that Job is in charge. His first response indicates that he has anticipated his daughters' protests: 'I have already selected for you in inheritance better than that of your brothers' (46.3).[6] Next he instructs one of his daughters to go and get the boxes which contain their inheritance. The dialogue soon turns to a monologue of Job addressing his daughters (chap. 47). It is only during the short descriptions of each daughter girding herself[7] and receiving changed hearts

---

5. Which is similar to the portrayal of this woman in the Book of Job, as noticed by Klein: 'woman's desire is not directed towards herself, but is focussed on the male's needs...woman is expected to deny herself and concentrate totally on her husband' (Klein 1995: 194).

6. Unlike mentioned otherwise, the citations from the *Testament of Job* are from the edition of Kraft *et.al.* 1974, and the verse numbers follow the edition by Brock (the numbers of which Kraft mentions in parenthesis), which is also used in most other translations.

7. In the Book of Job the girding of the loins is presented as a masculine activity, part of God's challenge to Job (Job 38.3, 40.7; see also Clines, 'Loingirding'). In the *Testament of Job* this challenge is not part of the very short appearance of God (42.1-6). When Job reminds his daughters of the value of these chords, he tells them how God gave him these chords, which healed his body from the worms and diseases (*T. Job* 47.3-10). He tells them how God told him to 'arise, gird your loins like a man' (47.5). Subsequently Job distributes these chords as an inheritance to his daughters tells them to 'rise, gird them around you before I die in order that you may be able to see those who are coming for my

and singing angelic songs that the focus is on these women. Even here the women are not in charge and their story is not told by them, but (as becomes clear in chap. 51) by their uncle, who witnesses this scene. Whether the daughters' inheritance of Job's spiritual insight, while the sons walk off with all his worldly possessions, constitutes a positive portrayal of women or not remains a debatable issue.[8]

It has to be concluded that the *Testament of Job* 'does not offer a visionary precedent to feminism' (Garret 1993: 70).[9] Although it features female as well as male characters, it does not challenge power structures and inequality between men and women but simply reproduces them. The male characters are the ones who are presented in positions of power, especially the protagonist himself. That the topic of 'women in the *Testament of Job*' has attracted so much scholarly attention proves one of the key issues in the study of masculinity. Women are immediately visible as women (as 'other'), but men remain invisible as men, because they are perceived as the norm, as the general human being. This is exactly what scholars working in the area of masculinity studies aim to expose (see for example Edley and Wetherell 1995: 2-3, Collinson and Hearn 2001, Whitehead 2001, and Kimmel 2004: 5-8). The invisibility of men as men relates to the power they have: 'Not talking of men is a major and structured way of not beginning to talk of and question men's power in relation to women, children, young people, and indeed other men, or perhaps more precisely men's relations within power' (Collinson and Hearn 1994: 97).

The remainder of this essay will examine the way Job is portrayed as a patriarchal 'man' in the *Testament of Job*. He is not a generic human being, but a member of the male sex and masculine gender.[10] While recognizing the importance of paying attention to the ancient society that may have produced this literature and the notions of gender therein, my concern here is exclusively with the *Testament of Job* as a literary production. This essay is envisioned not as an historical critical study, but as an exercise in reading the *Testament of Job* as a story about a 'man' through the lens of constructs of

departure' (47.12). The girding is thus literal, with cords which become instruments of healing and of spiritual insight.

8.   To my knowledge there is only one study that focuses explicitly on the issue of the daughters' inheritance. Peter Machinist argues that the presentation of heavenly chords as an inheritance to the daughters is the solution of the author of the *Testament of Job* to reconcile the information given in the biblical book of Job (the daughters receive an inheritance) with the 'dominant Biblical rule for male inheritance' of the father's worldly possessions (Machinist 1997: 76).

9.   Céline Mangan concludes the same about the Targum of Job; see Mangan 1996: 110.

10.   For the significance of the distinction between the biological (sex) and the social (gender) see for example Coltrane 1994: 45.

masculinity informed by recent research in the area of gender studies.[11] This reading will focus especially on the crucial issue of power expressed through the image of Job as a 'man in charge'. As Tolson makes clear: 'the "promise to power" is at the centre of a network of conventional masculine characteristics: authority, self-assertion, competitiveness, aggression, physical strength' (1977: 8). These characteristics can all be recognized in the portrayal of Job within the different roles he embodies. He occupies positions of authority as father, king, and one of the wealthiest men around. He is self confident, capable of aggression and shows physical (and mental) strength, especially as he competes with other males in what can be described as two conflict stories. The first of these conflicts is between Job and Satan (chaps. 17–27), the second between Job and three fellow kings who come to visit him (28.1–44.1).

Job embodies the roles of father, husband, athlete for God, king and benefactor (mostly) at the same time. There is considerable overlap between these roles. Nevertheless going through them one by one provides an opportunity to highlight the different components of the way in which Job is portrayed as a man in charge.

Job as Father

The first role in which the reader encounters Job is that of father. The *Testament of Job* starts with an introductory statement by an anonymous external narrator[12] which makes clear that the last day of Job's life is the starting point of the narrative. Job is presented as ill and about to die as he calls his children to stand around him so that he can settle his affairs. The reader (or hearer in the case of oral communication) thus imagines an elderly father in a bed of some kind, presumably located in a room in a house. After the introduction by the anonymous narrator, who mentions how Job calls his children, the first words of the protagonist are 'gather round my children, gather around me' (1.4). Much emphasis has thus been placed on the calling of Job's children to stand around him. With this action Job places himself literally at the centre of attention. He also proves himself as man in charge from the beginning of the story as he calls his children, expecting them to obey. That they did so seems to be taken for granted, apparently it is not even necessary to mention that the children dropped whatever they were doing to respond to their father's request (or command). Although they are present as listeners throughout the story

11. By making this perspective explicit, it is hoped that the charge of anachronism (attributed to scholarship on the role of women in the *Testament of Job* by Kugler and Rohrbaugh 2004: 45) can be avoided.

12. 'External narrator' is more precise equivalent to the traditional term 'third-person narrator'. A speaker who utters text is grammatically always a first person, not a third person. See Bal 1997: 22.

that Job tells, neither they nor Job's first set of ten children play a large part in the events.[13] Not much emphasis is placed on Job's relationship with his children. The children listen to their father, but scarce mention is made of the father listening to his children. The only exception to this has already been mentioned, namely Job listening to his daughters' protest (chap. 46). They speak (a little) and act in the last section of the narrative. Although the daughters seem to take some initiative, they are mainly responding to the plans their father has for them as inheritors of his spiritual insight. Whether this is what they themselves want, or whether they would rather share in the material inheritance of their brothers remains an unasked question. As in 'the traditional family' the father has 'a right to be obeyed…but was 'not expected to relate closely to their children' (Seidler 2006: 94).

Job's (second set of) children thus function mainly as part of the setting in which Job narrates his life-story, as receptors of this story and instructions (which seem to be addressed more to his sons than to his daughters, chap. 45). The portrayal of Job as father is important for the nature of the literary work as a farewell address embedded into a story about the end of the hero's life. The children are present as listeners and receivers (of an inheritance), but it is the father who decides what he tells them and what he gives to whom. Job's role as father is thus one area of life in which he is firmly in charge.

Job as Husband

Although the presence of children is thus important for the setting of the story, their mother receives sparse attention. She does not feature as a character in the story. She is not described, she does not act or speak. Job merely mentions her in his opening speech to his children: 'and your mother is Dinah, from whom I begot you; for my former wife died with ten other children in a bitter death' (1.6).[14] She is thus mentioned only as mother of the children.

The 'former wife' features as a character in the story Job tells, but not until chap. 21. She does not play a role in his account of his quest for the true god, nor in the description of his wealth and lifestyle before Satan's attack, nor in his mourning about his children and his expulsion from the city. Presumably his wife was there during these (good and bad) times, but in Job's retelling of these events on his death bed there is apparently no need for him to elaborate on her presence. It is his story, and apparently his role as husband is not a priority to him.

The wife finally appears as part of Job's description of his suffering, as he

---

13. To keep the length of this essay under control no attention will be given at this point to Job's first set of ten children, who 'perished by a bitter death.'

14. For an explanation of the merging of two traditions regarding Job's wife in the *Testament of Job*, see Legaspi 2008.

sits outside of the city on a dung heap. In chap. 21 she does not tell her own story; Job describes her fate as part of his reflection on his losses. Having lost all his wealth, his children, the loyalty of his subjects and his throne in the city, on top of all of this, he also sees his 'humbled wife' working as a servant to earn him bread. But after his brief shocked outburst he again takes up his 'cool pose' (21.4).[15] He is thus in charge of his own emotions, in the face of extraordinary suffering. How she feels is apparently not important enough to be mentioned, although she is allowed to express her emotions in chap. 24. Here she also tells Job about her encounter with the bread seller (which Job has already mentioned in the previous chapter) and she speaks the famous words which constitute her only speech in the biblical Book of Job. She is presented as an object of pity, an unfortunate woman (queen turned beggar). For Job it seems her disgrace is part of Satan's attack on him. One of the ways in which Satan gets at Job is via his wife. After Job has defeated Satan (chap. 27), his wife is not mentioned again until chap. 39, after Job and his three fellow kings have been engaged in their intellectual conflict (competition). Job the narrator mentions how she comes 'in tattered garments, fleeing from her servitude' (39.1).[16] She dramatically throws herself at the kings' feet, to request that they dig up the bones of her children, so that they can be given a decent burial. In the Coptic version she expresses her desire even more: she wants to have a final look at the bones of her children, she wants to bury them, and she wants to understand their death (Schenke 2009: 148-49).

This is not a 'story about Job's wife' as an 'excursus'.[17] Her request and the kings' willingness to comply is an integral part of the conflict between Job and his colleagues. Job demonstrates, at the expense of his wife's desires, that his spiritual insight is superior to the earthly concerns of the other characters in the story.[18] He is the man in charge. He forbids the kings' soldiers to dig

15. 'And after these things I resumed my rational "composure"'. In the Slavonic tradition it is not Job's stoic coolness that is being invoked, but his faith in God: 'Then I placed all on the compassion of God.' The term 'cool pose' is in (post)modern masculinity studies used to refer specifically to the experiences of black men, subject to disadvantages due to racism: 'cool pose is an attempt to carve out an alternative path to achieve the goals of dominant masculinity' (Majors 2001: 211). As such it does not have much to do with Job in the *Testament of Job*, other than that Job on his dung heap in worms has also become a social outcast in a disadvantaged position. I use it here merely as a better sounding synonym of 'rational composure'.

16. In the Slavonic version the garments are not mentioned.

17. Contra Schaller, who identifies both chaps. 21–26 and 38–39 as such. He calls the first story 'Fürsorge und Verzweiflung der Frau Hiobs' and the second 'Das Ende der Frau Hiobs' (Schaller 1979: 304). I argue instead that the story of the wife is an integral part of the conflict stories between Job and Satan, and between Job and his fellow kings.

18. This has been recognized as an important theme of the *Testament of Job*, for example by Collins (1974).

for the bones. Instead he shows his wife and the kings that the children are in heaven. Job is right, the kings are wrong. The wife seems to forget her own wish, to ensure the children's burial, and instead draws comfort from the sight of her children happy in heaven. She dies peacefully and is mourned by the cattle and by the people of the city (not by her husband).

The death of Sitidos is the last mention made of a wife. The second wife, Dinah, is not present (at least not mentioned as being present) at Job's death and funeral. It can thus be concluded that Job's role as husband is not a very prominent one. He is an independent man, not in need of women.[19] They are largely effaced from his story, in spite of the presence of his first wife in his stories of male competition and conflict.

Job as an Athlete/Wrestler (for God)

The roles of husband and father are of comparatively nominal significance for the events of the story. The roles that are more important for determining the narrative are that of athlete, of king and of benefactor. These are the roles that relate to Job's work and vocation and that present him as a hero and in competition with other males. Brittan states in the opening line of his Chapter on 'Masculinity as Competitiveness': 'perhaps the most popular image of masculinity in everyday consciousness is that of man the hero, the hunter, the competitor, the conqueror' (Brittan 1989: 77). Competition between men in the *Testament of Job* is most visible in Job's conflicts first with Satan and later with his fellow kings. These conflicts relate to Job's role as an athlete (or wrestler) for God. This role is probably the most dominant one, with the greatest significance for the story Job tells.

It begins with what can be called Job's quest for the true God. As Job starts to retell his story to his children, he first explains to them that he used to be called Jobab. He lived near an idol and saw people making offerings to it (in the Greek version). In the Slavonic tradition he himself used to participate in the worship of this idol. Job next describes how he questions the nature of this idol and wonders if this is the 'God who made heaven and earth and the sea and all that is in it' (2.4).[20] In the Slavonic version he subsequently utters a short prayer: 'take care (of me) Lord, let me know'.[21] This prayer is answered in chap. 3, as Job narrates how he heard a voice while he was sleeping. It is the following dialogue between Job and an angel that determines the plot of the story.

19. Clines in his work on the David story identified 'the womanless male' as an aspect of masculinity in the Hebrew Bible (Clines 1995a: 225-27).
20. The last item differs in various manuscripts; one Slavonic manuscript does not have 'that is in it', Greek has 'and us ourselves'.
21. In the Greek text he wonders 'how then shall I know?'

Job is in charge in his quest for the true god. He first expresses his desire to know the creator god. Then, when the angel explains to him that the one served in the temple 'is not God, but this is the power of the Devil who deceives human nature' (3.7), Job responds with a request for permission to destroy this temple. He himself takes the initiative for this destructive violent action. It is not required of him, but apparently he feels the need to demonstrate his gratitude to the one 'who came for the salvation of my soul' (3.5). This episode shows that Job is in charge of his own life and that of others. He only needs to ask permission from God, fellow humans do not have anything to say over him. He exclaims in the Greek version: 'who is there to stop me, since I rule this region' (3.7). The rendering in the Slavonic places more emphasis on Job as a fearless hero: 'I am not afraid at all, I am the ruler of (this) land.' Job is thus a true masculine hero: in charge, fearless, not shunning violence where necessary and working for 'the greater good'. That his family may suffer in the process is apparently less relevant. The angel warns him that if he goes ahead and destroys the temple, Satan 'will angrily rise against you for battle…he will inflict many misfortunes on you and he will take away all your possessions; he will carry off your children (or: servants)' (4.4). The angel explains that Job will be 'like an athlete, who spars and endures labours and wins the crown' (4.10-11). In this same speech the angel promises Job rewards if he perseveres: honour ('I shall make your name renowned in all generations until the end of time') and wealth ('I shall restore you again to your possessions and you will receive double').

What can be understood as religious zeal thus plays in important role in the *Testament of Job* as a motivation for Job's actions. His firm belief is demonstrated in his persevering in his suffering (inflicted on him by Satan as part of their combat) and in the convictions he expresses in his verbal conflict with his friends. In the battle between Job and Satan a contrast can be observed between Job's fair play and Satan's foul play. Satan uses disguises and approaches Job obliquely, first via his female servant (chaps. 6–7) and subsequently via his wife (chaps. 23–26). In what turns out to be their final confrontation, Job bravely challenges Satan: 'Come up front! Stop hiding yourself! Does the lion show his strength in a case? Does a fledgling take flight while in a basket? Come out and fight!' (27. 1, translation of Spittler 1983: 551). Job's skill as being clever with words is demonstrated by his use of rhetorical questions. He also shows himself to be heroic, not afraid of a fight. In their only face to face confrontation Job wins, Satan admits defeat and departs ashamed. Job overcomes Satan with his perseverance, his 'standing firm in battle', 'toughness' and 'patience' (see Haas 1989[22]).

---

22. Haas recognizes these three distinct concepts in what is usually translated with perseverance; each concept relate to a different (but synonymous) Greek verb used in specific passages of the *Testament of Job*. In the light of the current study it is worth mentioning

Both Job and Satan commit acts of aggression[23]: Job as he destroys Satan's temple and Satan as he destroys Job's possessions and kills his children. Nevertheless they do not take on each other in a physical fight, although metaphorical reference to wrestling is made (especially by Satan in chap. 27). The competition between Job and the other males is mainly mental and spiritual, but the language used (especially in the conflict with Satan) is reminiscent of physical fighting.

In the conflict between Job and his fellow kings there is less reminiscence of physical combat. Instead it seems to be about the power of words, about rhetorical skills. Job proves himself as a persuasive speaker, as being good with words.[24] As Clines observes, 'to be master of persuasion is to have another form of power, which is not an alternative to, and far less a denatured version of, physical strength, but part of the repertory of the powerful male' (Clines 1995a: 220).

Job is thus presented as a strong man with the power to overcome Satan and the soundness of mind and rhetorical skills to silence his fellow kings, in spite of him being in a disadvantaged situation, sitting on a dung heap, apparently in humiliation.

Job as King

As in the Book of Job, in the *Testament of Job* the protagonist is a wealthy man.[25] In the Book of Job of the Hebrew Bible the exact occupation of the

that each of these terms is active. The first two (standing firm in battle and toughness) relate to different types of fighting, and patience in Job's case 'is no passive resignation, but implies a waiting intently for God's saving intervention founded on one's hope in God' (Haas 1989: 128). Job's perseverance, although a different word, is similar to the notion of self-control which is part of a common expression of masculinity in the Second Temple Period, see for example Moore and Anderson 1998: 249-73.

23. Aggression, violence and competition are prominent themes in the study of men and masculinities. For a few examples see Morgan 1994, Kimmel 2004: 264-87, and Seidler 2006: 49-61.

24. In contemporary (Western) societies being good with words is sometimes seen as a feminine trait; it is believed that girls are quicker to develop verbal skills than boys. However in modern studies on gender/masculinity it has been discovered that the evidence of this apparent gender difference is minimal; see for example Edley and Wetherell 1995: 22 and Kimmel 2004: 35.

25. About the Book of Job as 'a rich man's story—not only a story *about* a rich man but also *by* a rich man' see Clines 1995b: 125-28. Some of his arguments seem to be less applicable to the *Testament of Job*, for example the portrayal of Job as a poor man on a dung heap seems more realistic, at least he does not have servants and it is mentioned that he has to reside on a dung heap outside of the city, dependent on his wife to bring him bread. Death of starvation is mentioned as a realistic possibility (in the dialogue between Job's wife and Satan disguised as bread seller in 23.8 and 24.9).

hero is not mentioned. The Greek Book of Job (Septuagint) makes Job and his visitors kings. The significance of the royal status of its protagonist for the story of the *Testament of Job* can be debated. Seidel emphasizes its importance as he states that due to this portrayal of Job as a king everything in the *Testament of Job* has to be understood in a royal framework (Seidel 1992: 227). This statement can be disputed on the grounds of lack of prominence given to the status of Job as king within the narrative. For example, it is not mentioned in the setting of the scene by the anonymous narrator or by Job in chap. 1. Job first mentions it in the dialogue with the angel in 3.7 to affirm his power as he suggests to destroy Satan's temple. Nobody will stop him, and he is not afraid, because he is the king of this region. However, in his lengthy description of his wealth and lifestyle before Satan's attack, Job does not mention his role as king, nor is it mentioned at the end of the narrative. In chap. 44 Job narrates how he, after his restoration, resumed his good deeds. From this it seems that his role as benefactor of the poor is more significant than his role as king. The royal status of the protagonist does not play a role in the division of the inheritance to the children, nor in the funeral scene.

It seems that Job's role as king becomes significant mainly in competition with other kings. In chap. 17 Satan disguises himself as a king, 'a rival power capable of claiming rulership of the area' (according to Kirkegaard 2004: 9). By pretending to be the king of the Persians he manages to undermine Job's authority and deceive his subjects. He convinces them to turn against their king Job even to the point of looting his palace (chap. 18). In this example the role of king relates to power and rivalry.

In the story of the visit of the other kings, Job's role as king features especially at the beginning of this section. Here his royal status seems to relate especially to the issue of identity. The visiting kings take their time in their effort to find and identify Job. That to them his royal status is part of Job's identity is noticeable in their questions as they search for him. They first ask the citizens for 'Job who rules over all of Egypt' (28.8) and later approach Job with the question 'are you Job, our fellow-king?' (29.3b; 31.5). They refuse to recognize Job (30.3, 31.1). When they finally believe that this poor man is indeed Job, Eliphaz laments his fate. This song contrasts the former glorious throne with the present situation. As Job remembered in chap. 28, the other kings used to admit that he was more wealthy and noble than them (this passage seems to reveal some rivalry between the kings). Chapters 29–32, with all the repetition it contains, emphasizes the shock that the fellow kings seem to experience. There is a sharp contrast between the past, where Job outshone the other kings, and the present, where the other kings come to visit with their whole entourage (soldiers, doctors etc) and Job sits in sores on a dung heap, abandoned by his people.

However, in Job's response to Eliphaz's lament it turns out that he does not recognize himself as being inferior to them. He commands them to be silent, so he can tell them about his throne. Subsequently he proudly declares that his throne is in heaven and that it is eternal (chap. 33). In his claim to possess an eternal kingdom, he thus affirms his royal status and proclaims his kingdom superior to theirs. That this is not the sort of reaction the other kings seem to expect from their former colleague, is evident from Eliphaz's angry outburst in chap. 34.

The competitive element between the kings shows that Job's role as king is closely related to his role as athlete for God. As mentioned before, in the conflict with his friends Job asserts his superiority through clever rhetorical skills. An example can be provided from the dialogue between Baldad and Job that follows the verbal aggression of Eliphaz. Baldad's aim is to try to establish whether 'Job's heart is in a stable condition' (36.2). They discuss this for a while, including the question of on whom Job places his hope.[26] Job's keeps drawing attention to the heavenly realms, and outsmarts Baldad with a question about the functions of the human body which he cannot answer (chap. 38). In his encounter with his fellow kings Job asserts himself by demonstrating abundant self-confidence and resistance to their questions and intimidations.

It can thus be observed that in his role as king Job is in charge. Although Satan succeeds in deceiving his citizens and forcing Job from his throne, his victory is only temporary. Job knows that the (temporary) loss of his throne and everything associated with it is part of his test. Job's fellow kings still respect him, based on his former grandeur as a king who used to outshine them. To their initial fury he still claims to be superior to them, as he maintains the conviction that his throne is in heaven and that his kingdom is forever. The presentation of Job as king is a clear manifestation of his position of authority. It reinforces the image of a man in charge (already, but not only) by virtue of his position.

Job as Benefactor of the Poor

The portrayal of Job as a philanthropist may have been (at least partially) responsible for the success of the *Testament of Job* later in its history of reception and for the perception of Job as a saint.[27] It is in his role as a

---

26. In the *Testament of Job*, more than in the Book of Job, the men listen to each other and answer each other's questions. On the absence of this basic pattern of communication in the canonical text see Bechtel 1995: 236.

27. Job in the *Testament of Job* has been described as like a saint, for example by Glatzer (1966: 197), Collins (1974: 37) and Nicholls, who recognizes in the portrayal the protagonist a 'progress from puzzled inquirer to mystic saint' (1982: 108). Kohler already mentioned that Job, like Abraham, 'became the type of a saint, the very model of a grant

benefactor that Job is presented as an example worthy to be followed. However, most 'ordinary readers' would not have the means to distribute as much to the poor as Job did: Job's generosity is directly related to his riches. The role of benefactor is thus related to that of wealthy king and to his position of authority. A prominent theme in the story is the way in which he uses this authority and wealth for the benefit of the less fortunate.

After Job has told his children about his encounter with the angel, his destruction of Satan's temple, and Satan's visit to his house he mentions that Satan asked the Lord for permission to take Job's possessions. Before Job narrates how Satan attacked him, he elaborates on his extensive wealth and exemplary lifestyle. In chaps. 9–15 the image is presented of a wealthy man managing his estates. He has in abundance and he gives in abundance. He is again presented as being at the centre of the action. From his house (or palace; no description of the place has been offered) 3000 camels go to distribute 'good things' to the poor ('the helpless, the unfortunate and the widows' (9.5)) and oxen go to plough in the fields of whoever needs their service (10.5). To his house people come to meet Job and to receive help. Job sits at his door and allows anybody to come and 'take as much as they need' (9.7). He also enables others to set up charitable services (chap. 11).

Although caring for the needy may be seen as a feminine role, the acts of a benefactor do not necessarily affect the image of Job as a man in charge. As king he has enough wealth to distribute to the poor and the fact that he does that makes him all the more respectable. His charity thus affirms his power. In addition to this it can be observed that what Job does as a benefactor is not the same kind of 'caring' commonly associated with femininity. He does not seem to be involved with the more mundane tasks; mention is made of servants who must have done most of the work. King Job instead sits at the door managing the whole enterprise. It is also mentioned that he played music for the widows after they were fed, and they would sing to 'glorify the lord' (14.2-3). He also uses his music to calm down murmuring servants (14.4-5). Job plays a sixed stringed instrument (*kitharas*) which he apparently uses to accompany the singing of psalms. Clines observes that in the David story 'the playing of stringed instruments...seems to have been largely a male activity' (Clines 1995a: 227-28). Although in the *Testament of Job* not only men play a stringed instrument (in chap. 52 Job presents this same musical instrument to his daughter Hemera),[28] here in chap. 14 the musicality

philanthropist' (Kohler 1897: 270). On the reception of the *Testament of Job* as a composition similar to a Saint's Life in Byzantine Christian contexts, see Haralambakis 2009.

28. It may be possible to perceive Hemera's playing of a stringed instrument (as a spiritual activity; part of the daughters' welcoming of the otherworldly beings that came to collect Job's soul) as part of the argument that the daughters, with their changed hearts, have become like males (as argued for example by Garret).

of Job can be perceived as a masculine trait, as an aspect of Job being in charge. He has the power to influence the lives of others through charitable giving as well as through music. He thus 'cares for' the poor from a position of power and authority, as a man in charge.

It is only when Job has that he can give. As in the Book of Job, the first thing that Satan takes from him is his wealth. Job is then no longer able to be the benefactor of the poor, having become one of them himself (chaps. 16–43). That the role of benefactor of the poor is important to him is evident from the statement at the end of Job's story. After God has spoken to him, the three kings have been restored and Elious has been condemned, the whole company returns to the city. The only aspect of his 'new life' that is mentioned is that Job resumed his good works for the poor (44.2).

Conclusion

It can thus be concluded that Job is portrayed throughout the *Testament of Job* as a patriarch, a 'man in charge'. His masculinity is expressed in different roles, and there is diversity in his experiences as a man, but what is constant is his capacity to control, resist and endure. He does occasionally show emotions, especially as he mourns the death of his children and the humiliation of his wife. But this does not undermine the portrayal of the protagonist of this narrative as a man in charge. Even when he is forced out of his city and from his throne and resides on a dung heap in sores and worms he has lost much of his wealth and status, he is still in charge.

At first sight it may appear that the image of a man in charge as a powerful king, a father leading his family and a wealthy philanthropist must be in tension with—what seems to be—the defeated, humiliated man on the dung heap outside of the city. How can this poor man in stench and worms be in charge of anything? It seems that Job's suffering at the hands of Satan, his loss of his status and wealth must have resulted in a crisis similar to 'the experience of unemployment, when a man's whole existence is thrown into crisis' (Tolson 1977: 55). To some extent Job's 'existence is thrown into crisis'. This is evident especially from the slow narration of events in chaps. 18–20. Job expresses his emotions as he compares his suffering to a 'woman paralyzed in her loins by the magnitude of birth pangs' (18.4-5). He admits to being 'deeply disturbed' by the news of the death of his children (19.2). But, after these brief emotional outbursts, he puts himself together and 'resumed his rational composure'. It is in this resumed rational state that he remains steadfast in battle with Satan, and proves to his fellow kings that he has 'his wits about him'.

The dung heap does not represent a loss of his masculinity; it rather resembles an arena in which he wins his victories. He has lost his wealth, his loyal citizens and the power that came with his throne, but seated on a dung heap he is still in charge. He still exercises power over his wife, who lives to meet his needs. He still has enough self confidence to beat Satan and to exhibit superiority in the competition with his fellow kings. He knows what he is worth and stands firm under (physical and verbal) pressure. After his trial he receives his reward for persevering in battle: the doubling of his former possessions. At end of his life he receives the honour that was promised to him before he took on the combat with Satan, 'a name renowned in all generations forever' (53.7). Whereas Job's wealth is lost and regained, his masculinity is maintained throughout the story. This masculinity is dominating and controlling: it silences the stories of the 'secondary characters' in the *Testament of Job*, particularly of the women, children and servants. Reading this ancient story through the lens of issues raised in masculinity studies reveals a patriarchal figure at the heart of the *Testament of Job*.

Bibliography

Bal, Mieke
    1997   *Narratology: Introduction to the Theory of Narrative* (2nd edn; Toronto: University of Toronto Press).
Barrett, Frank J., and Stephen M. Whitehead (eds.)
    2001   *The Masculinities Reader* (Cambridge: Polity Press).
Bechtel, Lyn M.
    1995   'A Feminist Approach to the Book of Job', in Brenner (1995): 222-51.
Brenner, Athalya (ed.)
    1995   *A Feminist Companion to Wisdom Literature* (Sheffield: Sheffield Academic Press).
Brittan, Arthur
    1989   *Masculinity and Power* (Oxford: Basil Blackwell).
Brock, Sebastian (ed.)
    1967   *Testamentum Iobi* (Pseudepigrapha Veteris Testamenti graeca, 2; Leiden: Brill).
Brod, Harry, and Kaufman, Michael (eds.)
    1994   *Theorizing Masculinities* (Thousand Oaks, CA: Sage Publications).
Chesnutt, Randall D.
    1991   'Revelatory Experiences Attributed to Biblical Women in Early Jewish Literature', in Amy-Jill Levine (ed.), '*Women like This': New Perspectives on Women in the Greco-Roman World* (Atlanta: Scholars Press): 107-25.
Clines, David J.A.
    n.d.   'Loingirding and Other Male Activities in the Book of Job'. Unpublished paper available online at: http.//www.shef.ac.uk/bibs/DJACcurrres/ PublicationsHome.html.
    1995   *Interested Parties: The Ideology of Writers and Readers of the Hebrew Bible* (JSOTSup, 205; GCT, 1; Sheffield: Academic Press)
    1995a   'David the Man: The Construction of Masculinity in the Hebrew Bible', in Clines (1995): 212-43.

1995b   'Why Is There a Book of Job, and What Does It Do to You If You Read It?', in Clines (1995): 122-44.

Collins, John J.
1974   'Structure and Meaning in the Testament of Job', in George MacRae (ed.), *Society of Biblical Literature: 1974 Seminar Papers* (Cambridge, MA: Society of Biblical Literature): 35-52.

Collinson, David L., and Jeff Hearn
1994   'Theorizing Unities and Differences between Men and between Masculinities', in Brod and Kaufman (1994): 97-118.
2001   'Naming Men as Men: Implications for Work, Organization and Management', in Barrett and Whitehead (2001): 144-69.

Coltrane, Scott
1994   'Theorizing Masculinities in Contemporary Social Science', in Brod and Kaufman (1994): 39-60.

Edley, Nigel, and Margaret Wetherell
1995   *Men in Perspective: Practice, Power and Identity* (London: Prentice Hall/ Harvester Wheatsheaf).

Garret, Susan R.
1993   'The "Weaker Sex" in the Testament of Job', *JBL* 112: 55-70.

Glatzer, Nahum N.
1966   'The Book of Job and its Interpreters', in Alexander Altmann (ed.), *Biblical Motifs: Origins and Transformations* (Cambridge, MA: Harvard University Press): 197-220.

Haas, Cees
1989   'Job's Perseverance in the Testament of Job', in Knibb and van der Horst (1989): 117-54.

Haralambakis, Maria
2009   'The Testament of Job: From Testament to Vita', in Eugenia Russell (ed.), *Spirituality in Late Byzantium: Essays Presenting New Research by International Scholars* (Newcastle: Cambridge Scholars Publishing): 55-96.

Horst, Pieter van der
1989   'Images of Women in the Testament of Job,' in Knibb and van der Horst (1989): 93-116.

Kaufman, Michael
1994   'Men, Feminism and Men's Contradictory Experiences of Power', in Brod and Kaufman (1994): 142-63.

Kimmel, Michael S.
2004   *The Gendered Society* (2nd edn; Oxford: Oxford University Press).

Kirkegaard, Bradford A.
2004   'Satan in the Testament of Job: A Literary Analysis', in Craig A. Evans (ed.), *Of Scribes and Sages: Early Jewish Interpretation and Transmission of Scripture. II. Later Versions and Traditions* (Library of Second Temple Studies, 51; London/New York: T. & T. Clark): 4-19.

Klein, Lillian R.
1995   'Job and the Womb: Text about Men, Subtext about Women', in Brenner (1995): 186-200.

Knibb, Michael, and Pieter W. van der Horst (eds.)
1989   *Studies on the Testament of Job* (SNTSMS, 66; Cambridge: Cambridge University Press).

Kohler, Kaufmann
    1897   'The Testament of Job, an Essene Midrash on the Book of Job', in George
           Alexander Kohut (ed.), *Semitic Studies in Memory of Rev. Dr Alexander*
           Kohut (Berlin: Calvary): 264-338.

Kraft, Robert A. *et al.* (eds.)
    1974   *The Testament of Job according to the SV Text* (Missoula, MT: Scholars
           Press).

Kugler, Robert A., and Rohrbaugh Richard L.
    2004   'On Women and Honor in the Testament of Job', *JSP* 14: 43-62.

Legaspi, Michael C.
    2008   'Job's Wives in the Testament of Job: A Note on the Synthesis of Two
           Traditions', *JBL* 127: 71-79.

Machinist, Peter
    1997   'Job's Daughters and their Inheritance in the Testament of Job and its
           Biblical Congeners', in William G. Dever and J. Edward Wright (eds.),
           The Echoes of Many Texts: Reflections on Jewish and Christian Traditions.
           Essays in Honor of Lou H. Silberman (Atlanta: Scholars Press): 67-80.

Majors, Richard
    2001   'Cool Pose: Black Masculinity and Sports', in Barrett and Whitehead
           (2001): 209-17.

Mangan, Céline
    1996   'The Attitude to Women in the Prologue of Targum Job', in Kevin J. Cath-
           cart and Michael Maher (eds.), *Targumic and Cognate Studies: Essays in*
           Honour of Martin McNamara (JSOTSup, 230; Sheffield: Sheffield Aca-
           demic Press): 100-10.

Moore, Stephen D., and Janice C. Anderson
    1998   'Taking It like A Man: Masculinity in 4 Maccabees', *JBS* 117: 249-73.

Morgan, David H. J.
    1994   'Theatre of War: Combat, the Military, and Masculinities', in Brod and
           Kaufman (1994): 165-82.

Nicholls, Peter H.
    1982   *The Structure and Purpose of the Testament of Job* (PhD dissertation,
           Hebrew University, Jerusalem).

Poliva, Jiři
    1891   'Apokrifna priča o Jovu', *Starine* 24: 135-54.

Schaller, Berndt
    1979   *Das Testament Hiobs* (JSHRZ, 3; Gütersloh: Gerd Mohn).

Schenke, Gesa
    2009   *Der koptische Kölner Papyruskodex 3221, Teil I: Das Testament des Iob*
           (PC, 33; Paderborn: Ferdinand Schöningh).

Schüssler, Elisabeth Fiorenza
    1994   'Introduction: Transgressing Canonical Boundaries,' in Elisabeth S. Fio-
           renza (ed.), *Searching the Scriptures. II. A Feminist Commentary* (London:
           SCM Press): 1-16.

Seidel, Hans
    1992   'Hiob, der Patron der Musiker', in Jutta Hausmann and Hans-Jürgen Zobel
           (eds.), *Alttestamentlicher Glaube und biblische Theologie. Festschrift für*
           Horst Dietrich Preuss zum 65. Geburtstag (Stuttgart: Kohlhammer): 225-
           32.

Seidler, Victor J.
    2006   *Transforming Masculinities: Men, Cultures, Bodies, Power, Sex and Love* (London: Routledge).
Spittler, Russell P.
    1983   'The Testament of Job', in James H. Charlesworth (ed.), *The Old Testament Pseudepigrapha* (New York: Doubleday): 1.829-68.
Tolson, Andrew
    1977   *The Limits of Masculinity* (London: Tavistock Publications).
Whitehead, Stephen M.
    2001   'Man: The Invisible Gendered Subject?', in Barrett and Whitehead (2001): 351-68.

Part III

Lo(o)sing It in Sex and Tears

DIVINE VIRILITY IN PRIESTLY REPRESENTATION: ITS MEMORY AND CONSUMMATION IN RABBINIC MIDRASH

Sandra Jacobs

This paper explores the representation of male sexuality in the Priestly depiction of the covenant of the rainbow and examines its relationship to the requirement of circumcision.[1] Carole Fontaine's observation, that 'all representation is *purposive*; it is not an accident when the human body is sculpted, drawn, carved, painted, decorated or indicated by iconic symbols (like stick figures or glyphs)' (2008: 35), is relevant also to the construction of the biblical imagery. The view advanced here is, first, that the Priestly representation of masculinity is based largely upon perceptions of fertility and virility, and that this representation characterizes the subsequent rabbinic gendering of memory. Secondly, for the later midrashic sages ideal masculinity is defined quite differently: not by its potential for prolific fertility or sexual virility, but rather by virtue of its being the chosen object of divine desire, realized in only the form of the circumcised male.

1. *The Figurative Representation of the Bow in the Clouds*

The concrete image of the rainbow as a קשת בענן, 'a bow in the clouds', describing the self-perpetuating sign that appears after the flood,[2] does not, of course, preclude its figurative representation. As such, the bow and arrow provided a readily communicative analogy for the process of seminal emission, as attested on a widespread basis in Egyptian, Babylonian, Hittite and Ugaritic texts, as Harry Hoffner (1966: 337) explains: 'Masculinity of the ancient was determined by two criteria: his prowess in battle and his ability

---

1. Diana Lipton kindly pointed out the significance of the symbolism of the rainbow in a series of personal communications on 20 and 21 March 2007. I wish to also thank Adrian Curtis and Bernard Jackson at the University of Manchester, who initially reviewed this material during the first year of my doctoral research. I would also like to thank Shani Berrin-Tzoref, Ovidiu Creangă, Shula Medalie and Nick Wyatt for additional feedback.
2. Gen. 9.13: 'I have set my bow in the clouds and it shall serve as a sign of the Covenant between me and the earth'.

to sire children. Because these two aspects were frequently associated with each other in the mind of the early Near Easterner, the symbols which represented his masculinity to himself and his society often possessed a double reference. In particular, those symbols which primarily referred to his military exploits often served to remind him of his sexual ability as well'.[3]

The earliest use of the figurative representation of the bow is attested in the Sumerian potency incantations, designed to induce virility, as witnessed in the *SÀ.ZI.GA. Ancient Mesopotamian Potency Incantations*: 'May the [qu]iver not become e[mpt]y! May the bow not become slack! Let the batt[le of] my love making be waged! Let us lie down by night!' (Biggs 1967: 37),[4] where the spell was recited by women to increase the desire and virility of the relevant male.[5] This image was not evoked exclusively as a metaphorical or literary abstraction. Rather, the accompanying ritual, on occasions, provided clear instructions also for making a bow, which together with an arrow, was then to be placed at the head of the participating man and woman (Biggs 2003: 73-74).

This symbolism was also inherent in the ideological framework of royal descent at Ugarit 'with its enormous emphasis on the procreation of a son, the filial duties incumbent on a son, the prestige of a divinely-constructed bow with its indulgence in hunting and falconry',[6] additionally informs Anat's insatiable desire to secure Aqhat's bow.[7] This bow, constructed by the divine agent Kothar-wa-Hasis, was given to Aqhat with the following blessing: 'You must surely bless him Bull El my father, you must surely give blessing to him, O Creator of creatures, so that he may beget a son in his house, a scion in the midst of his palace';[8] a request that clarifies not only the perceived effects of the bow as a mechanism for guaranteeing fertility and progeny, but also the more desirable means of royal succession, legitimised only in the birth of a son. Possibly the Ugaritic symbolism reflects also the divine prerogatives that Inanna obtained from Enki in Mesopotamian mythic tradition. As Gwendolyn Leick explains, these include 'the standard, the quiver, the wielding of the penis, the kissing of the penis, (and) the art of

---

3. See also Biggs (1967: 37-38). As was also the case (for example) in Ps. 127.3-5a: 'Sons are the provision of the Lord; the fruit of the womb, his reward. Like arrows in the hands of a warrior are sons born to a man in his youth. Happy is the man who fills his quiver with them'.

4. Ritual Nr. 18, lines 3-5.

5. Further examples are provided in Biggs 2003: 72.

6. Wyatt 2005: 473. For comparative use of this motif in Ugaritic literary texts such as the tale of Aqhat and in Baal/Anat mythological traditions, see Hoffner 1966: 327-30.

7. In the Story of Aqhat KTU 1.17-1.19. See also Hillers 1937: 71-80.

8. Wyatt 1998: 254, KTU 1.17, lines I.23-25.

prostitution', where the 'standard' and 'quiver' were the obvious metaphors for penis and vagina (1994: 151).[9]

It is the awareness of this symbolism that foregrounds the figurative representation of the bow, as understood in Gen. 9.8-17 and Gen. 49.22,[10] for example,[11] and provides the additional basis for post-biblical conceptions of male reproductive potency and sexuality.[12] This stated, the accompanying arrow representing the seminal emission was, nonetheless, absent in account of the covenant of the rainbow in Gen. 9.8-17. Its effect in conveying the potency of the divine seminal emission could still, however, be represented by the promise never to destroy all living creatures by a flood in Gen. 9.15:

I will remember My covenant between me and you	וזכרתי את־בריתי אשר ביני וביניכם
and every living creature among all flesh, so that the waters shall never again become a flood	ובין כל־נפש חיה בכל־בשר ולא־יהיה עוד המים למבול
to destroy all flesh.[13]	לשחת כל־בשר

9. Similarly Ben Sira (26.10-12) confirms recognition of these metaphors in second Temple Jewish tradition, as follows: 'Keep strict watch over a headstrong daughter, or else, when she finds liberty, she will make use of it. Be on guard against her impudent eye and do not be surprised if she sins against you. As a thirsty traveler opens his mouth and drinks from any water near him, so she will sit in front of every tent peg and open her quiver to the arrow'.

10. 'Joseph is a wild ass, a wild ass by a spring; wild colts on a hillside. Archers bitterly assailed him, they shot at him and harried him (ותשב באיתן קשתו) yet his bow stayed taut'. For my discussion of the reception of this tradition in 4Q 254 (4Q CommGen C) Fragment 7, see Jacobs forthcoming).

11. This symbolism is also be identified in prophetic traditions, as in Ezek. 1.26-28, where vision of the divine form is recalled: 'From what appeared his loins up, I saw a gleam, as of amber—what looked like fire encased in a frame; and from what appeared his loins down I saw what looked like fire. There was radiance all about him, like the appearance of the bow (כמראה הקשת) which shines in the cloud on a day of rain, such was the appearance of the surrounding radiance'. See also 'The Song of the Bow' in 2 Same. 1.17-27. Diana Lipton further considers that this symbolism is evident in the context of seed, offspring and disrupted dynasties in Hos. 1.6 and also Isa. 49.1-2.

12. As in also Talmudic tradition: והאמר שמואל: כל שכבת זרע שאינו יורה כחץ אינו מזרעת, 'Samuel said: "A spermatic emission that does not shoot forth like an arrow cannot germinate"' (TB *Hagigah* 15a). Further in TB *Sotah* 36b, where Rabbi Yochanan (commenting on Joseph's bow in Gen. 49.24) states in the name of R. Meir 'his bow (i.e. penis) subsided', while the TJ (*Horayot* 2, 46d), prefers the view of Rabbi Shmuel, who states: 'his bow stretched forth and retracted'. Tradition cited with comment by Shalom Paul (2002: 494).

13. See also Jub. 6.15: 'He set his bow in the cloud for a sign of the eternal covenant that there should not again be a flood on the earth to destroy it all the days of the earth'.

The account that Ishmael, Abraham's first-born and first-circumcised son, 'grew up and became a bowman',[14] is also relevant. No other male in biblical tradition is characterized as an archer in this specific way,[15] which rather suggests that the fulfilment of God's blessing to 'make him fertile and exceedingly numerous',[16] was again, represented by the image of the bow that guaranteed reproductive continuity to all mankind in the Noachic covenant. Given also the patriarchal nature of the bible text, are we then to understand that the promise made to Noah and to 'all flesh that is on earth',[17] indicate that only all male flesh was addressed? And is this confirmed by the concomitant Priestly requirement of circumcision, identified as בריתי בבשרכם, ' my covenant in your flesh', in Gen. 17.13?

2. ברית בבשרכם *'The flesh of your foreskin' and its Relationship to Fertility*

The Priestly requirement of circumcision, as part of a divinely bestowed covenant, appears to have little (if any) connection with the sign of the rainbow, in either its literal or figurative representation. Indeed David Bernat (2009), in his recent monograph, *Sign of the Covenant: Circumcision in Priestly Tradition*, provides a discussion subtitled 'Circumcision Has No Fertility Implications' (50-52), where he asserts: 'The fact that circumcision is performed on the penis does enable the Priestly author to perpetuate a patriarchal ethos. Beyond this, circumcision in P has nothing to do with the penis and its function' (50). This is, strictly speaking, correct only if one detaches the Priestly requirement of circumcision in Gen. 17.9-14[18] from the broader context of the patriarchal blessings, where fertility was certainly a highly significant concern.[19] One would also have to ignore the obvious

14. Gen. 21.20b: ויגדל וישב במדבר ויהי רבה קשת.

15. See אבן-שושן 2000: 1057.

16. Gen. 17.20: 'As for Ishmael, I have heeded you. I hereby bless him and make him exceedingly numerous. He shall be the father of twelve chieftains and I will make of him a great nation.'

17. Gen. 9.16-17: 'When the bow is in the clouds, I will see it and remember the everlasting covenant between God and all living creatures, all flesh that is on earth, so that the waters shall never become a flood to destroy the earth'. 'That', God said to Noah, 'shall be the sign of the covenant that I have established between me and all flesh that is on earth'.

18. Where Gen. 17.9-11 states: 'God said to Abraham, "As for you, you and your offspring to come throughout the ages shall keep my covenant. Such shall be the covenant between me and you and your offspring to follow which you shall keep: every male among you shall be circumcised. You shall circumcise the flesh of your foreskin and than shall be the sign of the covenant between me and you"'.

19. As (for example) in Gen. 13.16: 'I will make your offspring as the dust of the earth,

150   *Men and Masculinity in the Hebrew Bible and Beyond*

connections between Genesis 15 and 17, since 'the 'covenant in the flesh' has much in common with the 'covenant between the pieces' of chap. 15, presupposing it and supplementing it in various ways' (Sarna 1989: 123). This limitation raises a further dilemma: what would be the point in specifying 'an everlasting covenant',[20] if issues of succession and heredity were of no importance? Given also the preceding discussion of the sign of the rainbow, is it acceptable to unequivocally reject all symbolic interpretations of circumcision and the allusions to fertility therein?

The relationship between circumcision and fertility is first indicated in Gen. 17.2, where God states: 'I will establish my covenant between me and you and make you exceedingly numerous'.[21] The emphasis of the subsequent promises to Abram is nothing if not redolent of fertility: 'I will make you exceedingly fertile and make nations of you; and kings shall come forth from you' (Gen. 17.6). Secondly, circumcision is inferred from its virtual cause-and-effect relationship, presented in the Priestly narrative. In Gen. 17.9-14, its specification by God to Abraham is followed immediately by the promise of a son to his otherwise barren wife,[22] who we are told is aged 90 (Gen. 17.18). Thirdly, the promise of the covenant of circumcision is addressed 'to you and your offspring to come', on six separate occasions in Gen. 17.1-21.[23] As such, the ideal conception of masculinity, according to the formulation of these promises, is its ability to reproduce prolifically.

The association between circumcision and fertility in Priestly tradition is, however, fully recognized in contemporary scholarship,[24] and as Harvey

so that if one can count the dust of the earth, then your offspring too can be counted', and in Gen. 15.2, where the concern is articulated by Abram: 'O Lord what can you give me seeing that I shall die childless?' See further Gen. 15.4-5, 18; 16.9.

20. לאחזת עולם in Gen. 17.7.

21. The basis of this promise is explained by Westermann (1985: 259-60) as follows: 'Israel's existence in the exile takes its stand on the succession of generations; Israel continues to live in its families after the political collapse, from parents to children and to their children. Were no more children to be born, Israel would be cut off. This new situation gives a further nuance to the old promise: it now means not primarily that many derive from one, but that the generations continue into the future'.

22. 'I will bless her; indeed, I will give you a son by her. I will bless her so that she shall give rise to nations: rulers of peoples shall issue from her' (Gen. 17.16).

23. As Nahum Sarna (1989: 124) has noted: '"To you and your offspring to come": This expression occurs six times in this chapter (vv. 7[2], 8, 9, 10, 20) and appears also in 35.12 and 48.4 in connection with the covenantal promises. It too is legal terminology, as shown by the Aramaic legal papyri from the Jewish military colony at Elephantine (Aswan), Egypt (6th–5th centuries BCE). The inclusion of the phrase in the documents relating to the devolution of property upon the death of the owner assured that the real estate automatically passed on from generation to generation without restriction'.

24. This includes Claus Westermann (1985: 265), Victor Hamilton (1990: 470), Robert Hall (1992: 1026) and Lawrence Hoffman (1996: 38-39). See also Michael Fox's account

Goldberg concludes, 'Fruitfulness, the overall text seeks to teach us, ultimately is in the hands of God' (1996: 25). Maybe also, as Lawrence Hoffman suggests, 'perhaps the strongest part of the argument linking circumcision to fertility is the Bible's application to circumcision terminology to horticulture' (1996: 39).[25] Nor is it unreasonable to infer that the prohibitions against wasteful (non-productive) seminal emission (שכבת־זרע)[26] were also relevant precisely because fertility was crucial to the Priestly perception of masculinity.[27]

Not unreasonably, therefore, Howard Eilberg-Schwartz develops this association further, when he argues that 'the removal of the foreskin symbolically readies the organ for reproduction' (1990: 148), since the cut evokes infant male circumcision as akin to the pruning of the immature fruit trees to encourage prolific growth.[28] This symbolism is not unique to biblical literature, but is evident also in Ugaritic tradition. In KTU 1.23 El's prolific sexual activity was preceded by the necessary symbolic cut: 'the vine pruners prune him, the vine binders bind him, they cause his shoots to fall like a vine'.[29] Nicolas Wyatt explains: 'it still allows puns and double-entendres between the staff the god holds at this point and both the staff he later throws away, perhaps at the arrow he shoots at the bird and certainly his own "staff", that is, his penis. Uncircumcised he is unfertile. What is about to be pruned is an infertile plant, transparently a metaphor for his penis' (1992: 426).[30] Eilberg-Schwartz further suggests that the role of the Nazirites, described as 'untrimmed vines',[31]

---

of 'one etiological aspect of P.'s reinterpretation of the progeny promise' (1974: 591) and 'Be Fruitful and Without Blemish' (Glick 2005: 17-20).

25. See also Bernat's discussion (2009: 91-95) of this motif in 'Leviticus 19: Foreskinned Fruit Trees'.

26. Lev. 15.15, 18; 18.20; 20.15.

27. This also runs counter to Bernat's (2009: 51) evaluation: 'It is well-established that circumcision has fertility connotations in many cultures. Moreover, even if there is no available data to suggest it, circumcision may have been a fertility ritual in ancient Canaan or Israel. However, it has definitively no such significance in the Priestly literature'.

28. These are designated as 'uncircumcised' in Lev. 19.23, where the prohibition of not eating the produce of an immature fruit tree appears: 'When you enter the land and plant any tree for food, וערלתם ערלתו את־פריו you shall regard its fruit as forbidden', where the verb ערל 'to count as foreskin, i.e. as uncircumcised' (BDB 2000: 790) is rendered as 'forbidden'.

29. Wyatt 1990: 48, where the vine is denoted by the expression 'the blood of trees', indicating the juice of the grape in Ugaritic tradition.

30. In this tradition the 'hand' is the lexeme used to denote the penis. See also Delcor 1967: 230-40, and Robert Allan's interpretation (1995: 20-23) of *qz* in KTU 1.24, a hymn designated 'The Wedding of Nikkal-and-Ib', for corroboration of Wyatt's interpretation (1992: 426).

31. Lev. 25.5: 'you shall not reap the after growth of your harvest, ואת־ענבי נזירך לא תבצר, or gather the grapes of your untrimmed vines', and in 25.11 where the

provides 'an incontrovertible instance where the priests recognize an analogy between not cutting part of the human body (i.e. the hair) and not pruning grape vines' (1990: 151). This motif of pruning to encourage vigorous growth is frequently articulated in midrashic tradition, as here in *Tanhuma-Yelammedenu*:

> *I will establish my covenant between me and thee:* He was not aware of which part of his body was to be circumcised and so the Holy One Blessed Be He indicated the place of circumcision when he said: *And I will make thee exceedingly fruitful.* That is to say at the place through which *you increase and multiply* you are to be circumcised. However Bar Kappara was of the opinion that Abraham decided upon the place of circumcision by analogy. He said to himself: "Which part of the tree is subject to the law of עורלה [*Orlah*]?[32] It is that part of the tree which produces fruit, and so I must be circumcised from which I will produce my fruit.[33]

Certainly for the rabbinic sages who generated these traditions, circumcision was clearly perceived as a symbolic mechanism for enhancing fertility in concrete, physical terms, in the same way that a young vine is pruned to increase its yield. Bernat adds (2009: 50): "Eilberg-Schwartz, with his claim that circumcision was a fertility rite (1990: 141-148), completely misapprehends the character of the Priestly literature". Yet Bernat ignores both the corroborations in Lev. 19.23 and 25.5 (not to mention all the relevant midrashic traditions) that Eilberg-Schwartz has provided to substantiate his case. His critique (Bernat 2009: 51) of Eilberg-Schwartz continues as follows:

> He fails to recognize, however, that circumcision in P. is all but devoid of such symbols or ritualization. He further buttresses his thesis with a 'measure for measure' scenario, based upon the fully valid idea that the *karet* penalty may carry the sense of extirpation of one's offspring. Eilberg-Schwartz reasons that, since an uncircumcised Israelite will incur the *karet* punishment and be rendered infertile, the opposite, increased fertility, must attach to those who do comply with the circumcision commandment. Implicit in the logic of his argument is the invalid assumption that circumcision is the only precept whose abrogation brings *karet* upon the violator.

prohibition for harvesting נזריה, untrimmed vines, in the jubilee year appears. See also Isa. 5.6; Judg. 9.13; Joel 1.12; 2.22; Ezek. 15.2, 6.

32. עורלה is the Mishnaic tractate dealing with the prohibition of pruning young fruit trees.

33. Here the Midrash *Tan·uma-Yelammedenu* has amplified the tradition in בראשית רבה where R. Huna in the name of Bar Qappara states: 'Just as in the case of a tree, when the word עורלה "foreskin" is used it refers to the place which produces fruit, so too here "foreskin" with reference to man speaks of a place which produces fruit'. See also *Pirke de Rabbi Eliezer* on Lev. 19.23.

However this interpretation of the *karet* penalty and its relationship to circumcision is not unique to Howard Eilberg-Schwartz. For example, Nahum Sarna (1989: 126) also states: 'Certainly, the general idea that one who deliberately excludes himself from the religious community cannot be a beneficiary of the covenantal blessings and thereby dooms himself and his line to extinction'.[34] Nor has Eilberg-Schwartz, on any occasion, claimed that circumcision was 'the only precept whose abrogation brings *karet* upon the violator' (Bernat 2009: 51). That no further discussion of crimes that qualify for *karet* was provided by Eilberg-Schwartz may be because this is clarified elsewhere.[35] Moreover, even if this alleged omission had been provided, it would still not diminish the elementary logic in both Priestly and prophetic traditions that 'uncircumcised hearts, ears and lips are organs that cannot do what God intended them to do'. By extension, the removal of a man's foreskin symbolically enables the penis to more effectively discharge its divinely allotted task. That task, as suggested by the content of the covenant, is to impregnate women and produce offspring (Eilberg-Schwartz 1990: 149).[36] This view accords fully with Talmudic convention, as evident also in this forthcoming discussion of the gendering of memory (see below).

Accordingly, there is no reason to concur that Eilberg-Schwartz has misapprehended the significance of circumcision in Priestly tradition. Nor should any comparative analysis of midrashic materials be dismissed entirely because 'circumcision in P is all but devoid of such symbols or ritualization' (Bernat 2009: 51). Rather, as Lawrence Hoffman (1996: 38) has argued, 'meanings can be public without being official, and an additional, though unofficial, meaning was related to fertility'.[37] It is more constructive, therefore, to consider how, exactly, the 'official' Priestly designation of the penis was indicated, particularly in Gen. 17.10b-11:

Every male among you shall be circumcised.   המול לכם כל־זכר
You shall circumcise the flesh of your foreskin[38]   ונמלתם את בשר ערלתבם

---

34. See also Ilona Rashkow (1993: 92) for similar observations.

35. Admittedly Wold's comprehensive analysis (1997: 1-45) of the penalty of כרת (*karet*) was published only after Eilberg-Schwartz (1990). See also Horbury 1985: 14-38, and Olyan 2003: 34-51.

36. The significance of this task is summarized by Charlotte Fonrobert (2000: 116) as follows: 'Judaism, as framed by the rabbis of the Talmudic period based on biblical culture, is in a very fundamental sense a civic religious culture. That is to say, the rabbis and almost any other Jewish cultural formation post-dating them understand it to be a divinely ordained mandate for humanity to settle the world and cultivate it as it is humanly known. One of the most significant aspects of this mandate, if not the most important one, is reproduction. Thus the rabbis of the talmudic period (the second through seventh century CE) consider the first divine commandment "to be fruitful and multiply" (Gen. 1.28)'.

37. In his discussion, 'Bible and Birth: Some Priestly Public Meanings' (1996: 27-48).

38. Where ערל means 'uncircumcised' as indicated by וערל זכר in Gen. 17.14. Although

and that shall be the sign of the covenant   והיה לאות ברית
between me and you.   ביני וביניכם

Here the euphemism בשר, meaning 'flesh', denotes the penis,[39] as is attested also in Lev. 15.2: 'When any man has a discharge from his member, he is unclean',[40] where מבשרו is literally 'from his flesh'.[41] It is in this context that the recollection of the promise of the rainbow, to כל־בשר אשר על־הארץ, 'all flesh that is on earth' (Gen. 9.16) becomes, almost unnoticeably בריתי בבשרכם, 'my covenant in your flesh'. On this basis, moreover, Nahum Sarna describes circumcision as a 'Covenant in the Flesh' (1989: 122), and similarly Tikva Frymer-Kensky, 'The Ancestor Covenant: The Covenant of the Flesh' (2006: 143-44).

The use of this Priestly euphemism recalls also Sumerian convention, as (for example) in the Inanna/Dumuzi lyric traditions where, as Jarrold Cooper (1989: 88) observes, 'the unabashed sexuality of these texts notwithstanding, sexual intercourse is hardly ever mentioned by name, nor is the male organ, and even when the latter is referred to metaphorically, the reference is often ambiguous'.[42] Rabbinic sources also attest the use of בשר to denote 'bodily intimacy, and the touching of skin during sexual intercourse',[43] explicit in the Talmud: 'Rav Yosef cited a Tannaitic tradition: "Flesh": This means the intimacy of the flesh, namely that he should not behave with her in the manner of the Persians, who have intercourse while dressed'.[44] One cannot dismiss this use of בשר 'flesh' in P, let alone the relationship between circumcision and fertility, irrespective of the figurative interpretation of the rainbow that abounds by its association. As Ilona Rashkow (2000: 75) concludes: 'Characterizing biblical/ancient Israel as a phallocentric society is by no means an empty generalization. The Hebrew Bible posits the human penis as the explicit, emblematic and exclusive symbol of religious identity and membership of the

---

בשר ערלתכם is literally 'his uncircumcised flesh' or 'his uncircumcised penis', modern translations provide 'the flesh of his foreskin' (NJPS, NRSV and The Oxford Study Bible [1992 Revised Edition]).

39. Alternative biblical designations of the male reproductive organs include יד, 'hand', רגל, 'foot' and עקב, 'heel'. See also 'genitalia' in Pope 1992: 720-23.

40. איש איש כי יהיה זב מבשרו זובו טמא הוא.

41. The use of בשר as penis is explicit in Gen. 17.11, 14, 23-25; Exod. 28.42; Ezek. 16.26. Ezek. 23.19-20 also states: 'But she whored still more, remembering how in her youth she had played the whore in the land of Egypt; she lusted for concubinage with them whose members (בשר־חמורים) were like those of asses and whose organs were like those of stallions'. For further discussion of this euphemism, see Bratsiotis 1975: 319; Milgrom 2000: 1534; Glick 2006: 26-27.

42. Similarly also in Akkadian love lyrics (see Groneberg 2003: 69).

43. See discussion in Boyarin 2004: 43.

44. TB *Ketubot* 48a, as also indicated in the tradition cited by Ezra Melamed: מלמד 1968: 138 (בשר [תוס׳ מקואות פ״ו ה״ה] המהרהר בלילה ועמד ומצא בשרו חם טמא).

communal order. Thus, the penis symbolizes the special link between the society's God and the (male) members of the community. It serves as a physical reminder both of inclusion *in* the community and *from* it'; or as Eric Kline Silverman prefers: 'Circumcision and the covenant in Genesis 17 are the true "erection" of patriarchy' (2003: 45).

So what else was conveyed by this representation of the rainbow, as a manifestation of divine virility? And what of its effects upon בריתי בבשרכם 'my covenant in the flesh' with its explicit promise of fertility?

3. כל־זכר *and the Gendering of Memory*

So far I have argued that in the Priestly depictions of the rainbow and circumcision, masculinity is conveyed primarily by its ability to procreate successfully. As such, the Noachic 'covenant to all flesh',[45] represented by the figurative image of the bow and בריתי בבשרכם ברית עולם, 'my covenant in your flesh as an everlasting pact' with Abraham, clearly evoked the deity's inherent masculinity and sexual potency, specifically to the ancient reader (or listener) familiar with Mesopotamian, Ugaritic and Hittite symbolic convention.

Yet this is not all. When God announces: 'I have set my bow in the clouds and it shall serve as a sign of the covenant between me and the earth' (Gen. 9.13), what is further represented is the image of the divine phallus and its procreative powers. As part of this *'ôt*-etiology schema',[46] the rainbow, in representing the divine phallus, stimulates human memory not only of God's reproductive powers, but also of his divine beneficence that assures male sexuality and fecundity. The significance of this Priestly conception of memory is very much as Victor Hamilton (1990: 470) clarifies: 'God will see the circumcised penis of the Israelite before and during sexual congress, and will then "remember" his promise to Abraham and make them very fertile'. This explains, furthermore, why the prescription was not addressed to כל איש, 'every man', which might otherwise indicate the generic 'every person',[47] but rather only to כל־זכר 'every male' in Gen. 17.13-14:

Thus shall my covenant be marked in your flesh	והיתה בריתי בבשרכם
as an everlasting pact	לברית עולם
and if any male who is uncircumcised	וערל זכר
fails to circumcise the flesh of his foreskin,	אשר לא־ימול את־בשר ערלתו
that person shall be cut off from his kin;	נכרתה הנפש ההוא מעמיה
he has broken my covenant.	את־בריתי הפר

---

45. Evoked in Gen. 9.15-17.
46. This is defined in Fox 1974: 570-74.
47. Where איש is preferred in the Holiness Code, as in Lev. 15.2-16.

The use of כל־זכר also recalls the divine promise to remember the Covenant of the Rainbow, וזכרתי את־בריתי ('I will remember my covenant', Gen. 9.15) and לזכר ברית עולם ('remember the everlasting covenant', Gen. 9.16). Did, therefore, the sign of circumcision then represent the final Priestly refinement in a series of ever more specific rituals that symbolize God's physical restraint in that he will 'no longer cut off all flesh on earth',[48] once his bow is visible to all humanity? Is God not asking Abram to perform circumcision on himself to represent his own promised restraint against further human destruction? Or is the purpose of this rite as Tikva Frymer-Kensky (2006: 14) suggests: 'it demystifies the phallus, for the circumcised penis looks like the erect phallus in miniature'? Although each of these questions may each be answered in the affirmative (nor are they mutually exclusive), what is apparent is that God does not necessarily remember כל־נפש חיה בכל בשר, 'every living creature', in the aftermath of the flood, but only every male member, as the address to כל־זכר, 'every male', confirms.

Accordingly, in matters of procreation 'circumcision is not a *recognition* of male descent and dominance but an *assertion*, a re-(production) of this domination',[49] where such an assertion was vital because, as Eilberg-Schwartz explains (1990: 163), 'paternal identity is never as obvious as maternal'. Clearly the use of the verb זכר in the Priestly *'ôt*-etiology schema and its designation of all that is 'male' is no incidental play on words,[50] if we agree with Brevard Childs's observation (1968: 68) that 'the *zikkāron* stimulates God's memory and his acts of memory are synonymous with his acts of intervention. The *zikkāron* also stimulates Israel's memory, which produces participation in the sacred order.'[51] These memories allow for both the figurative representation of the bow in the clouds, and the euphemism of בשר, 'flesh', to filter from within biblical tradition,[52] almost undetected, into the continuum of subsequent rabbinic tradition, where masculinity remains still inextricably related to fertility, but becomes also the authoritative vehicle (and voice) for collective Jewish memory.

48. Gen. 9.11: 'I will maintain my covenant with you; never shall all flesh be cut off by the waters of a flood', where ולא־יכרת כל־בשר עוד occurs.

49. Anidjar 1997: 371. Anidjar's own italics.

50. זכר *zᵉkar* / זכור *zᵉkhûr* 'male' is cognate with the Akkadian *zikaru(m)*, where *zikru* / *zikkaru* means 'male' and 'virile' (cf. Black, George and Postgate 2000: 447). This use is witnessed in Ezek. 16:17b: ותעשי־לך צלמי זכר ותזני־בם, 'and you made yourself phallic images and fornicated with them'.

51. The separate root זכר (*zᵉkar*) 'to remember' is differentiated in vocalization in Akkadian as *zakᵃru(m)*. See Black, George and Postgate 2000: 443, and also Eisling 1990–1992: 77-79.

52. As in Ps. 78.38-39: 'He being merciful, forgave iniquity and would not destroy. He restrained his wrath, time and time again and did not give vent to his fury, for he remembered that they were but flesh (ויזכר כי־בשר המה), a passing breath that does not return'.

The most striking example of this symbolism is in the *Zohar*, where, as Elliot Wolfson (1998: 226) explains, 'an intrinsic link is forged between the phallus, memory and history: The circumcised phallus, which bears the mark of the divine covenant in the flesh, is the locus of collective memory that renders history meaningful'.[53] As is additionally characteristic of rabbinic tradition, 'both the language and gesture are geared to spur, not so much a leap in memory as the fusion of past and present. Memory here is no longer recollection, which still preserves a sense of distance, but reactualization' (Yerushalmi 1982: 44). Such 'reactualizations' are evident also in contemporary Jewish liturgical tradition, where the blessing on seeing a rainbow states 'Blessed are You, Lord our God, King of the Universe, who remembers the covenant, is faithful to the covenant, and fulfils his word',[54] recalling the divine promise not to destroy 'all flesh on earth'.

Yet as Yosef Haim Yerushalmi (1982: 5) adds, 'memory is always problematic, usually deceptive, sometimes treacherous'. Equally unavoidably, 'memory is, by its nature, selective, and the demand that Israel remember is no exception' (Yerushalmi 1982: 10). Such selectivity is manifest in the Hebrew language, which provides a classic example (if not, the classic example) of what Lawrence Hoffman (2001: 61) defines as 'the genderization of language'. Here 'the Hebrew words for male and female are iconic, as we see from *nekevah* ("feminine"), which is the passive participle of *nakev* = "to pierce, to split"'.[55] So too, a man (*zakhar*) is one whose sexual organ points: so that *zekher le* is construed by the Rabbis as pointing to something (Hoffman 2001: 61). Eilberg-Schwartz (1994: 172) adds: 'In Arabic, one of Hebrew's cognate languages, the word for male also means "male organ" and "call upon in worship"'. The priestly symbol of the covenant ties together these themes, for only a male's body can bear the symbol of the covenant. To put it another way, in the priestly community, remembering the covenant requires having the appropriate member'.

Moreover, the designation נקבה, 'female', accurately depicts the penetration of a woman's vagina during intercourse and is indicative of how her physical sexuality was conceived in rabbinic thought: as purely a passive

53. Similarly he notes: 'The covenant, biblically, is called a "sign" for it functions as that which reminds one of the relationship between God and Israel. Memory is thus linked fundamentally to the masculine because the site of the covenantal incision is the phallus. The more specific link between memory and the membrum virile is a bedrock of kabbalistic speculation. The correlation between *zakhar* and *zakhor*, first expressed in *Sefer ha-Bahir*, is developed and applied to various exegetical contexts by the author of the *Zohar*' (1998: 224).

54. From 'Blessings on Various Occasions', in *The Authorized Daily Prayer Book of the United Hebrew Congregations of The Commonwealth: Fourth Edition* (Hebrew 2006: 782 [ET 2006: 783]).

55. See further Clements 1990–1992: 84-85, and אבן-שושן 2000: 779.

receptor. This is apparent in the Talmudic discussion of martyrdom, where the requirement of a Jew to give up his life, rather than to transgress biblical law, is recommended in three separate cases: enforced idolatry, murder, or illicit sexual relations.[56] As the sages observed, this posed an inevitable dilemma for Esther, and they therefore ask:

But did not Esther transgress publicly?[57]	והא אסתר פרהסיא הואי
Abaye answered: Esther was merely natural soil.	אמר אביי אסתר קרקע עולם היתה
Raba said, "[Since] this was just for their pleasure it is different".[58]	רבא אמר הנאת עצמן שנאי

As Michael Satlow (1995: 326) explains, 'the rhetoric of apologetics, used to exculpate biblical characters who appear to have violated rabbinic sexual restrictions, is used only in the discussions on incest and sex between Jews and Gentiles'.[59] More relevant to our discussion, however, is the footnote in the Soncino edition of the Talmud, which clarifies that קרקע עולם היתה indicates '[she was] merely natural soil'. Esther is no more than that 'which is tilled, i.e. she was only the passive object of his embraces'. This recalls also the teaching of R. Samuel b. Onia that was credited to Rav: 'A woman is a shapeless lump, and can make a covenant only with him who makes her into a vessel',[60] i.e., it is only by means of a sexual relationship with a man that a woman achieves any useful purpose. And this is exclusively as a receptacle for the conception of children. As Ilona Rashkow concludes over the rabbinic tradition, 'woman is the soil in which male seed is planted'.[61]

It is in the light of such perceptions that the significance of the covenant of circumcision to כל-זכר, 'all males', and its homonymous relationship to memory recurs. Circumcision is, therefore, the single rite that stimulates, if not guarantees, divine memory and with it human fertility, precisely as was conveyed by the Priestly sign of the rainbow.

---

56. BT *Sanhedrin* 73a-74b.

57. In her marriage to Ahasuerus which would inevitably entail sexual intercourse with a non-Jew, rather than by suggesting that she committed an act of sexual indecency or impropriety in public.

58. BT *Sanhedrin* 74b. The argument here is that since Ahasuerus made Esther transgress to satisfy his personal desire (as Esther 2.17) rather than because he wished to disgrace or violate her religious tradition, it was therefore acceptable to save her own life, by acquiescing to his sexual demands.

59. See also Cynthia Baker's (2005: 133) comments.

60. TB *Sanhedrin* 22b: אשה גולם היא ואינה כורתת ברית אלא למי שעשאה כלי

61. Rashkow 1993: 92 (= 2000: 76). Rashkow adds (1993: 92 = 2000: 77): 'Of course, this idea of conception is not unique to the Hebrew Bible. Aeschylus expresses the Greek view: "The mother is no parent of that which is called her child, but only the nurse of the new-planted seed that grows. The parent is he who mounts".'

4. *Male Sexual Desire: The Danger and Potential of Vision*

In rabbinic tradition male sexual desire, in and of itself, is not considered to be inherently negative or evil, but rather a necessary prerequisite for the existence of humanity; it is understood also as a natural force created by God in his design of the universe. Its destructive capacity is apparent only when it is activated without restraint and thereby results in sin, as Charlotte Fonrobert explains: 'Since sexual desire has to remain a part of the fabric of human life to preserve the continuity of life, its transgressive potential has to remain part of the package deal' (2000: 117).[62]

The 'transgressive potential' of what appears to be no more than the sight of male exposure, evoked immediately after the flood (Gen. 9.18-27),[63] where 'Ham, the father of Canaan, saw his father's nakedness' (Gen. 9.22). Here the views of Rav and Shmuel (TB *Sanhedrin* 70a), that the crime was either castration, or anal intercourse, prefigure a number of more recent interpretations.[64] Eilberg-Schwartz also observes that 'in a culture in which masculinity is defined by procreation, by the fathering of children, the son's erotic gaze should not be directed at his father. Thus gazing and desiring are linked' (1995a: 147).[65] This is the understanding, also, of the sages in TB *Nedarim* 20a:

Rebbi Aha from [the school of] Rebbi Josiah said:	רבי אחא ברבי ישיאה אומר
He who gazes at a woman	כל הצופה בנשים
will eventually come to sin	סופו בא לידי עבירה
and he who looks even at a woman's heel	וכל המסתכל בעקבה של אשה
will beget degenerate children.	הויין לו בנים שאינן מחוגנים
R. Joseph said: Even one's own wife when she is *niddah*.[66]	אמר רב יוסף ובאשתו נדה

62. Where transgressions include adultery, incest and sexual intercourse with a menstruant, for example.

63. This immediately follows the promise of the rainbow in Gen. 9.8-17.

64. See Jacob Milgrom's discussion of the incest laws in Lev. 18 (Milgrom 2000: 1534-39), where two options are considered: First, Ham's homosexual crime with his father and, secondly, that of incest with his mother: 'A liaison with mother is tantamount to having sex with one's father—a taboo so deeply embedded in the Israelite (and universal) psyche that it requires no legislation'. Here Milgrom prefers to conclude that 'Genesis 9.22a really intends to say that Ham committed incest with his mother (*'erwat 'ābîw = 'erwat 'immô*) and that Canaan was a product of this incest' (2000: 1537).

65. See also Rachel Biale's discussion (1992: 40-59).

66. *Niddah* is the rabbinic term for the period of female menstrual bleeding, which renders a woman impure also for a further seven days after her final show of blood. The halakhic implications of this tradition are evident also in TB *Berakhot* 24a, where the sight of even a minimal section of a woman's body or uncovered hair is prohibited to any man who is about to recite the Shema.

Yet it is not 'the son's erotic gaze', but rather any vision of the divine image that is inherently dangerous (if not fatal) in biblical memory, as not only the Priestly sources indicate. In Exod. 20.21 God informs Moses: 'Go down, warn the people not to gaze, lest many of them perish' and explicitly states further: 'You cannot see my face, for man may not see me and live' (Exod. 32.20).[67] Fuhs additionally confirms that 'seeing the king' or 'seeing the face of the king', is a formula used when requesting an audience at a royal court, where 'never is a meeting with the king devoid of danger'.[68] Proprietary sensitivity also dictates that if the sign of the rainbow does indeed represent God's phallic reproductive powers, then no sustained gaze at this nakedness can be permitted. It is in this light that the Talmudic prohibition to look or gaze upon a rainbow is thus witnessed in TB *Hagigah* 16a,[69] and is codified in Jewish law, in the שולחן ערוך where הרואה הקשת, 'the one who sees a rainbow',[70] must recite the appropriate blessing but is forbidden to gaze excessively at it.[71]

This figurative representation of the rainbow and the perception of divine sexuality is particularly developed in mediaeval kabbalah.[72] In this interpretative realm 'scripture is less the intersection of the divine with human

67. Compare also: 'let not [the Kohathites] go inside and witness the dismantling of the sanctuary, lest they die', in Num. 4.20, and Judg. 13.21b-22: 'Manoah then realized that it had been an angel of the Lord. And Manoah said to his wife, "We shall surely die, for we have seen a divine being".' See also Elliot Wolfson's analysis (1994: 45-46) of the tradition in *Pirke de Rabbi Eliezer* (32:72b) and the parallels in Targum Pseudo-Jonathon on Gen. 27.1, which explain that Isaac's blindness in his old age was on account of his seeing the divine presence when he was bound upon the altar, about to be sacrificed.

68. Examples provided include: 1 Kgs 18.1-2, 15; cf. 1 Sam. 25.23; 2 Sam. 24.20; 2 Kgs 11.14 = 2 Chron. 23.13; Jer. 32.4; 34.3, in Fuhs 1990–1992: 224. See also the chapter on 'The Averted Gaze', where a discussion of 'God's Sightings' is provided by Eilberg-Schwartz 1994: 60-73.

69. See also TJ *Megillah 1.12.72b.*

70. הרואה הקשת אסור להסתכל בו ביותר *Orach Hayyim* א רכט. In contemporary Chabad (Lubavitch) tradition, the reluctance to teach this blessing to the uninitiated is commonly explained as preferring to avoid recollection of a time when the earth warranted destruction.

71. The status of the שולחן ערוך as the normative halakhic code of Jewish law cannot be underestimated, as Passamaneck (1996: 343) explains in his description of R. Joseph Karo, its author: 'As a legal authority, he was known throughout the Jewish world. His *Bet Yosef*, which he began in Adrianopole, was completed in 1542 in Safed; and from that monumental work came the seed of the *Shulcan Arukh* which Karo produced in his later years. He lived and worked among the mystics of Safed and his reputation as a respondent and as an authority in all areas of Jewish Law is undimmed after more than 400 years.'

72. 'Kabbalah represents a radical departure from any previously known version of Judaism, especially in the realm of theology. While kabbalists remain loyal followers of normative Jewish praxis, as defined by *halakha,* the theological meaning system that undergirded their Judaism was entirely reconstructed' (Green 2006: 215).

history, than the revelation of human history as divine life' (Fishbane 1989: 99). It is in this framework also that 'beholding the face of the *Shekhinah*,[73] in the Zohar, becomes an actual embrace or penetration of the mystic into the divine feminine' (Wolfson 1995: 30), so that the act of gazing becomes synonymous with the act of divine intercourse. Although the symbolism, of 'beholding the face of the *Shekhinah*', like representation of the rainbow, is avoided in mainstream rabbinic tradition, the Ramak,[74] in his clarification of the Divine attribute of the יסוד, conveys this figurative understanding of the rainbow as follows:

Since *yesod* also corresponds to 'the Covenant of the Rainbow'	שהיסוד היא אות ברית הקשת
which is the bow that is arched above	והקשת אינה דרוכה למעלה
only to shoot arrows at the attribute of *malchut*,[75]	אלא לשלח חצים למדת המלכות
the target of arrows.	שהיא מטרה לחץ
This refers to the guarding of the seminal drop	שומרת טפה
which shoots from him like an arrow	היורה כחץ
'to produce branches and bear fruit' (Ezek. 17.8).	*לעשות ענף ולשאת פרי* [יחזקאל יז·ח]
And as a 'bow' in the higher world is never drawn	וכשם שמעולם לא ידרוף הקשת העליון
except when aimed at the aforementioned target	אלא לנוכח המטרה
accordingly a man should not draw his bow	כף האדם לא ידרוף הקשת
—that is, cause himself to have an erection	ולא יקשה עצמו בדומצד
unless it is drawn towards its proper target—	אלא לנוכח המטרה הראויה
his wife, when she is in a state of purity,	שהיא אשתו בטהרה
at the time of union.[76]	שהיו עת הזווגות

Elliot Wolfson (1995: 30) further clarifies the symbolism conveyed by בריתי בבשרכם 'my covenant in the flesh', in kabbalistic tradition as follows: 'Circumcision is not simply an incision of the male sex organ; it is an inscription, a notation, a marking. This marking, in turn, is the semiological seal, as it were, that represents the divine imprint on the human body. The physical opening therefore, is the seal that, in its symbolic valence, corresponds to the opening of God'. This association recalls also the interpretation of Daniel Boyarin (1992b: 492-500), who suggests that Abraham's circumcision is realized as the essential 'peeling away' of skin that enables him to receive his

---

73. This is the rabbinic term for the indwelling of the divine presence, which in kabbalistic tradition is personified as God's bride.

74. This is the acronym for Rabbi Moshe Cordovero (1522–1570); kabbalistic scholar and student of R. Joseph Karo and R. Shlomo haLevy Alkabetz.

75. מלכות (or 'kingdom') is the realm over which the divine king rules, and is also another name for the tenth *sefira* (which is also designated as the *shekhina*).

76. The Hebrew text as reprinted in Cordovero 1993: 122.

vision of God.[77] Inevitably, according to Boyarin, 'the physical act of *circumcision in the flesh*, which prepares the male Jew for sexual intercourse, is also that which prepares him for divine intercourse' (1992b: 493).

Such climactic moments are described also in the midrashim on שיר השירים (Song of Songs) where 'to be sure the lover was a divine lover but the beloveds were actual human beings and the moment of erotic communion was mystical and visionary' (Boyarin 1992b: 498). What is also remarkable is that 'circumcision is understood by the midrash as feminizing the male, making him open to receive the divine speech and the vision of God' (1992b: 495).[78] If in the primaeval histories the sign of the rainbow evoked the divine phallus and the sign of circumcision 'represented the divine imprint on the human body' (Wolfson 1995: 30), the rabbinic response is not unpredictable:

> When the Rabbis read the Song of Songs, they do not translate its 'carnal' meaning into one or more 'spiritual' senses; rather they establish a concrete, historical moment in which to contextualize it. It is a love song, a love dialogue to be more specific, that was actually (or fictionally, according to some views) uttered by a lover and a beloved at a moment of great intimacy, at an actual historical moment of erotic communion, when God allowed himself to be seen by Israel, either at the Crossing of the Red Sea or at Mount Sinai (Boyarin 1992b: 498).

It is in this context that the legacy of the Song of Songs, not merely as intimate love poetry, but as overt 'egalitarian erotic',[79] merited canonization, as Rabbi Akiva emphasized: '*Shir haShirim* is the Holy of Holies'.[80] Is it that for man, who is specifically created in the image of God,[81] the most natural, symbolic representation must then the feminization of his beloved, Israel? Moreover if, indeed, the sign of circumcision 'represented the divine imprint on the human body', as argued by Eliot Wolfson (1995: 30), the circumcised penis would then be opened (or pierced), symbolically enabling the male Israelite to become the chosen recipient of divine penetration.[82] This is the

---

77. Boyarin (1992b: 492-500) bases his use of this metaphor upon Job 19.26: 'This after my skin will have been peeled off, but from my flesh I will see God'.

78. See also Rashkow 1993: 93-95, and Eilberg-Schwartz 1995: 166-80.

79. As particularly advocated by Burres and Moore 2004: 51.

80 שיר השירים קדש קדשים in M. *Yadayim* 3.5, where Rabbi Akiva's protest against any possible question of the scroll's canonical status is stated as follows: 'No man in Israel ever disputed that the Song of Songs does not render the hands unclean, for the entire universe is not worth the day on which the Song of Songs was given to Israel: for all the writings are holy, but the Song of Songs is the Holy of Holies'. See further Biale (1992: 31-32, 59) and Fonrobert (2000: 120-21).

81. As Gen. 1.27; 2 Cor. 4.4; Heb. 1.3.

82. In contrast to its representation in both the Midrash *Tan·uma-Yelammedenu* and בראשית רבה, where the circumcised penis enabled the male, rather, to become prolifically fertile.

very means by which the circumcised male achieves the most perfect expression of דבקות (literally 'cleaving') or closeness to God available, as is fully appreciated in kabbalistic tradition.

This use of this symbolism also provides a convenient solution to counteract the potential tension: Does the maleness of God and his control of human fertility undermine Israelite masculinity?[83] This may be, as Howard Eilberg-Schwartz (1994: 142) suggests, because 'on the one hand, it establishes male authority. On the other, it threatened to make human masculinity redundant'.[84] In the midrashic imagination, however, these fears are never articulated. It is only human femininity that becomes redundant,[85] reconfigured only as the necessary physical form through which ultimate perfection of the circumcised male can be achieved. The benefit of this symbolism counteracts, further, the inevitable danger of homoerotic gazing, also never explicitly admitted in rabbinic discourse.

5. *Conclusion*

The divine promise never to destroy 'all flesh that is on earth' (Gen. 9.16-17) represented in the sign of the rainbow, together with the purposive designation of circumcision as 'my covenant in the flesh', indicate that circumcision represented not only the physical ratification of the covenanted promises bestowed upon Abraham, but recalled the image of the divine bow and its reproductive potency, that would assure the fertility of the circumcised Israelite male. Furthermore, the deliberate address to 'every male' (Gen. 17.13) and its interchangeable use of the homonym זכר 'to remember') is highly effective in subsequent rabbinic discourse, because while it does automatically exclude, or prohibit, female memory, it ensures that the subsequent and most valued recollections remain only those that are inherently male.[86] The most striking development of this interpretation is found in the writings of

83. To what extent is this fear presupposed by the prohibition of portraying the divine image is discussed in Eilberg-Schwartz 1995a: 137-48 ('God's Body: The Divine Cover Up').

84. See also 1994: 15-29 ('The Divine Phallus and the Dilemmas of Masculinity').

85. Since only male circumcision is required in biblical law, and, as Elliot Wolfson (1995: 30) clarifies: 'Given the normative halakhic sexual mores, it follows that only one who is circumcised can have such a visionary experience. Circumcision is thus an act of opening that not only ushers the circumcised into the covenantal community of God, but places the individual into an immediate—visual—relationship to the divine'.

86. Its definitive success is achieved (at least until 1918, when Sarah Schneirer pioneered education for Jewish women) further, by virtue of the fact that rabbinic tradition is normatively recalled and transmitted only by men. Its impact is reflected additionally in the exclusion of women from classical, Talmudic learning, if not also, in the prohibition of women holding public positions of office in contemporary Orthodox Judaism.

the medieval kabbalistic masters, and crystallizes in the conception of the *Zohar*, where 'the circumcised phallus, which bears the mark of the divine covenant in the flesh, is the locus of collective memory that renders history meaningful' (Wolfson 1998: 226). In the midrashic imagination these representations also generated the desire to 'feminize' the male, thereby 'making him open to receive the divine speech and the vision of God', as Daniel Boyarin (1992b: 495) has argued. As such, the symbolism of the cut of circumcision further enabled the reconfiguration of only the male Israelite, as the chosen recipient of divine penetration.

The origins of this hermeneutic emerged initially, I suggest, in the late Tannaitic and early Amoraic period, where the rabbinic sages—having faced the loss of the Second Temple and the failure of both the Hasmonaean and Herodian dynasties, and also having experienced the reality of direct Roman rule in Judaea—reconfigured their ultimate, ideal, representation of masculinity to include singularly more than the benefits of fertility and sexual virility, idealized in Priestly tradition. This was a particularly bold response, since it is during the Hellenistic period, c. 133 BCE, that epispasm was first recorded among Jews.[87] It is also particularly relevant that only during the Graeco-Roman period was circumcision used to identify a member of the Jewish people: 'circumcision is likewise singled out in Hellenistic Jewish, pagan and Christian literature as the premier mark of the Jew, and specifically of the convert to Judaism' (Fredriksen 1991: 536).[88]

The midrashic symbolism may also have been generated in response to the teachings of Paul, specifically in his abrogation of circumcision for early Christians. It is in this light that the Priestly representation of male sexuality, based so heavily on qualities of fertility and virility, became less relevant to the early rabbinic sages. Their reconfiguration of masculinity ensured that male perfection would rather be defined as being the chosen object of divine desire, realized exclusively in the form of the circumcised male. For the medieval kabbalists, male (human) sexuality is further idealized through the act of 'feminization', where the figurative opening of the circumcised 'flesh' of the Jew qualifies him exclusively, as the worthy recipient of divine penetration. In response to the teachings of the early Christian gospels and in the wake of the subsequent persecutions advanced by the Church, the logic of this hermeneutic is, maybe, inevitable. And it is in this historical context that only the circumcised Jewish male becomes the ideal human partner for the

---

87. This was a surgical procedure designed to disguise the circumcised penis, which would otherwise be noticeable in Roman bath-houses and gymnasia. See 1 Macc. 1.11-15; 1 Cor. 7.18; and Tosefta, *Shabbat* 15.9. See, for more, Hall 1988: 71-86 and 1992b: 52-57.

88. As evident in Tacitus (*Hist.* 5.2), Petronius (*Satyricon* 102.14) and Suetonius (*Dom.* 12.2), as translated in Rabello 1995: 178-81.

symbolic consummation of God's love. And it is in reaction to these historical realities that the circumcised Jewish male is transformed from the Priestly
ideal into nothing less that the chosen human partner for the symbolic consummation of divine love.

Bibliography

Allan, R.
    1999   'Now That Summer's Gone: Understanding QZ in KTU 1.24', *SELVOA*
        16: 19-25.
Anidjar, G.
    1997   'On the (Under) Cutting Edge: Does Jewish Memory Need Sharpening?',
        in Jonathan Boyarin and Daniel Boyarin (eds.), *Jews and Other Dif-*
        ferences: The New Jewish Cultural Studies (Minneapolis and London:
        University of Minnesota Press): 360-96.
Baker, C.
    2005   'When Jews Were Women', *HR* 45: 114-34.
Bernat, D.
    2009   *Sign of the Covenant: Circumcision in the Priestly Tradition* (Ancient
        Israel and its Literature Series, 3; Atlanta: Society of Biblical Literature).
Biale, D.
    1992   *Eros and the Jews: From Biblical Israel to Contemporary America* (New
        York: Basic Books).
Biggs, R.D.
    1967   *SÀ.ZI.GA. Ancient Mesopotamian Potency Incantations* (Locust Valley,
        NY: J.J. Augustin).
    2002   'The Babylonian Sexual Potency Texts', in S. Parpola and R.M. Whiting
        (eds.), *Sex and Gender in the Ancient Near East: Proceedings of the 47th*
        Rencontre assyriologique internationale, Helsinki, July 2-6, 2001, Part I
        (Helsinki: The Neo-Assyrian Text Corpus Project): 71-79.
Black, J., A. George and N. Postgate
    2000   *A Concise Dictionary of Akkadian: Second Correct Printing* (Wiesbaden:
        Harrassowitz).
Blenkinsopp, J.
    1992   *The Pentateuch: An Introduction to the First Five Books of the Bible*
        (London: SCM Press).
Boyarin, D.
    1998   'What Does a Jew Want? The Political Meaning of the Phallus', in Chris-
        topher Lane (ed.), *The Psychoanalysis of Race* (New York: Columbia
        University Press): 211-40.
    1992a   'Behold Israel according to the Flesh: On Anthropology and Sexuality in
        Late Antique Judaism', *YJC* 5/2: 27-57.
    1992b   '"This We Know To Be the Carnal Israel": Circumcision and the Erotic
        Life of God and Israel', *CI* 18: 474-505.
Bratsiotis, N.S.
    1977–1999 'בשׂר: bāśār', in *TDOT*, 2:317-22.

Burrus, V., and S.D. Moore
2004   'Unsafe Sex: Feminism, Pornography and the Song of Songs', *BibInt* 11: 24-51.
Childs, B.S.
1962   *Memory and Tradition in Israel* (London: SCM Press).
Clements, R.E.
1990–1992   'זכר zākar; זכור zᵉkhûr; (נקבה nᵉqēbhāh)', in *TDOT*, 4:82-87.
Cooper, J.S.
1989   'Enki's Member: Eros and Irrigation in Sumerian Literature', in H. Behrens, D.M. Loding and M.T. Roth (eds.), *DUMU-E2-DUB-BA-A: Studies in Honor of Åke W. Sjöberg* (Philadelphia: University Museum): 87-89.
Cordovero, M.
1993   תומר דבורה *The Palm Tree of Devorah* (trans. M. Miller; Southfield, MI: Targum Press).
Delcor, M.
1967   'The Special Meaning of the Word יד in Biblical Hebrew', *JSS* 12: 230-44.
Dressler, H.
1975   'Is The Bow of Aqhat a Symbol of Virility?', *UF* 7: 217-20.
Eilberg-Schwartz, H.
1990   *The Savage in Judaism: Anthropology of Israelite Religion and Ancient Judaism* (Bloomington and Indianapolis: Indiana University Press).
1992   'The Problem of the Body for the People of the Book', in H. Eilberg-Schwartz (ed.), *People of the Body: Jews and Judaism from an Embodied Perspective* (New York: State University of New York Press): 17-47.
1994   *God's Phallus and Other Problems for Men and Monotheism* (Boston: Beacon Press).
1995a   'God's Body: The Divine Cover Up', in J.M. Law (ed.), *Religious Reflections on the Human Body* (Bloomington and Indianapolis: Indiana University Press): 137-48.
1995b   'The Nakedness of a Woman's Voice, the Pleasure in a Man's Mouth: An Oral History of Ancient Judaism', in H. Eilberg-Schwartz and W. Doniger (eds.), *Off with her Head: The Denial of Women's Identity in Myth, Religion and Culture* (Berkeley: University of California Press): 165-84.
Eisling, H.
1990–1992   'זכר zākar; זכר zēkher; זכרון zikkārôn;' אזכרה azkārāh', in *TDOT*, 4:64-82.
Elman, Y.
2007   '"He in his cloak and she in her cloak": Conflicting Images of Sexuality in Sassanian Mesopotamia', in R. Ulmer (ed.), *Discussing Cultural Influences: Text, Context and Non-Text in Rabbinic Judaism* (Lanham, MD: University Press of America): 129-63.
Shoshan-Even, A.
2000   קונקורדנציה חדשה לתורה נביאים וכתובים (Jerusalem: Kiryat Sefer).
Fishbane, M.
1998   *The Exegetical Imagination: On Jewish Thought and Theology* (Cambridge, MA, and London: Harvard University Press).
Fonrobert, C.E.
2000   'Taming the Powers of Desire: Love and Sex in Jewish Culture', in

J. Runzo and N.M. Martin (eds.), *Love, Sex and Gender in the World Religions* (Oxford: Oneworld): 113-27.

Fontaine, C.
2008   *With Eyes of Flesh: The Bible, Gender and Human Rights* (Sheffield: Sheffield Phoenix Press).

Fox, M.V.
1974   'The Sign of the Covenant: Circumcision in the Light of the Priestly *'Ôt* Etiologies', *RB* 81: 567-96.

Fredriksen, P.
1991   'The Circumcision of Gentiles and Apocalyptic Hope: Another Look at Galatians 1 and 2', *JTS* 42: 532-64.

Frymer-Kensky, T.
2006   'Covenant: A Jewish Biblical Perspective', in Tikva Frymer-Kensky (ed.), *Studies in Biblical and Feminist Criticism* (Philadelphia: Jewish Publication Society): 133-57.

Fuhs, H.F.
1990–1992 'ראה rā'â', in *TDOT*, 13:208-42.

Glick, L.B.
2005   *Marked in your Flesh: Circumcision from Ancient Judea to Modern America* (Oxford and New York: Oxford University Press).
2006   'The Life of Flesh is in the Blood', in G.C. Denniston *et al.* (eds.), *Bodily Integrity and the Politics of Circumcision: Culture, Controversy and Change* (New York: Springer Science and Business): 17-36.

Goldberg, H.E.
1996   'Cambridge in the Land of Canaan: Descent, Alliance, Circumcision and Instruction in the Bible', *JANES* 24: 8-34.

Green, A.
2006   'Intradivine Romance: The Song of Songs in the Zohar', in P.S. Hawkins and L. Cushing Stahlberg (eds.), *Scrolls of Love: Ruth and the Song of Songs* (New York: Fordham University Press): 215-27.

Groneberg, B.
2003   'Searching for Akkadian Lyrics: From Old Babylonian to the "Liederkatalog" KAR 158', *JCS* 55: 55-74.

Hall, R.G.
1988   'Epispasm and the Dating of Ancient Jewish Writings', *JSP* 2: 71-86.
1992a   'Circumcision', in *ABD*, 1:1025-1031.
1992b   'Epispasm: Circumcision in Reverse', *BibRev* (August): 52-57.

Hamilton, V.
1990   *The Book of Genesis: Chapters 1–17* (Grand Rapids, MI: Eerdmans).

Hillers, D.
1973   'The Bow of Aqhat: The Meaning of a Mythological Theme', in H.A. Hoffner (ed.), *Orient and Occident: Essays Presented to Cyrus Gordon on the Occasion of his Sixty-Fifth Birthday* (Kevelaer: Butzon & Bercker, and Neukirchen–Vluyn: Neukirchener Verlag): 71-80.

Hoffman, L.
1993   'How Ritual Means: Ritual Circumcision in Rabbinic Culture and Today', *StudLit* 23: 78-97.

1996   *Covenant of Blood: Circumcision and Gender in Rabbinic Judaism* (Chicago: University of Chicago Press).

2001   'Does God Remember? A Liturgical Theology of Memory', in M. Signer (ed.), *Memory in Jewish and Christian Traditions* (Notre Dame: University of Notre Dame Press): 40-72.

Hoffner, H.
1966   'Symbols of Masculinity and Femininity: Their Use in Ancient Near Eastern Sympathetic Magic Rituals', *JBL* 85: 326-34.

Horbury, W.
1985   'Extirpation and Excommunication', *VT* 25: 13-38.

Jacobs, S.
forthcoming 'Disqualifying Signs: The Sign of the Rainbow and the Covenant of Circumcision at Qumran', in A. Lange, E. Tov and M. Weigold (eds.), *The Dead Sea Scrolls in Context: Integrating the Dead Sea Scrolls in the Study of Ancient Texts, Languages and Cultures* (VTSup; Leiden: Brill).

Keuls, E.
1985   *The Reign of the Phallus: Sexual Politics in Ancient Athens* (Berkeley, CA: University of California Press).

Kline Silverman, E.
2003   'The Cut of Wholeness: Psychoanalytic Interpretations of Biblical Circumcision', in E. Wyner Mark (ed.), *The Covenant of Circumcision: New Perspectives on an Ancient Jewish Rite* (Hanover and London: Brandeis University Press): 43-57.

Kogan, L., and A. Militarev
2002   'Akkadian Terms for Genitalia: New Etymologies, New Textual Interpretations', in S. Parpola and R. M. Whiting (eds.), *Sex and Gender in the Ancient Near East: Proceedings of the 47th Rencontre assyriologique internationale, Helsinki, July 2-6, 2001, Part I* (Helsinki: The Neo-Assyrian Text Corpus Project): 311-21.

Kronholm, T., and H.J. Fabry
1990–1992 'קשת qešet', in *TDOT*, 13:201-208.

Leick, G.
1994   *Sex and Eroticism in Mesopotamian Literature* (London and New York: Routledge).

Margalit, B.
2007   'On Canaanite Fertility and Debauchery', in W.G.E. Watson (ed.), *'He unfurrowed his brow and laughed': Essays in Honour of Nicolas Wyatt* (Münster: Ugarit-Verlag): 177-92.

Melamed, Z.E.
1968   ספר זכרון לבנימין דה־פריס 'לישנא מעליה וכינויי סופרים בספרות התלמוד' (Jerusalem: Tel Aviv Research Authority): 119-48.

Milgrom, J.
2004   *Leviticus: A Book of Ritual and Ethics* (Minneapolis: Fortress Press).

Olyan, Saul M.
2003   '"We are utterly cut off": Some Possible Nuances For נגזרו לנו in Ezekiel 37:11', *CBQ* 65: 43-51.

Passamaneck, S.M.
1996   'Towards Sunrise in the East 1300–1565', in N.S. Hecht, B.S. Jackson,

S.M. Passamaneck, D. Piatelli and A.M. Rabello (eds.), *An Introduction to the History and Sources of Jewish Law* (Oxford: Oxford University Press): 323-57.

Paul, S.M.

1997   'A Lover's Garden of Verse: Literal and Metaphorical Imagery in Ancient Near Eastern Love Poetry', in M. Cogan, B.L. Eichler and J.H. Tigay (eds.), *Tehillah le-Moshe: Biblical and Judaic Studies in Honor of Moshe Greenberg* (Winona Lake, IN: Eisenbrauns): 99-110.

2002   'The Shared Legacy of Sexual Metaphors and Euphemisms in Meso-potamian and Biblical Literature', in S. Parpola and R.M. Whiting (eds.), *Sex and Gender in the Ancient Near East: Proceedings of the 47th Rencontre assyriologique internationale, Helsinki, July 2-6, 2001, Part II* (Helsinki: The Neo-Assyrian Text Corpus Project): 489-99.

2007   'An Akkadian-Rabbinic Sexual Euphemism', in D. Golinkin *et al.* (eds.), *Torah Lishma: Essays in Jewish Studies in Honor of Professor Shamma Friedman* (Jerusalem and Ramat Gan: Schechter Institute of Jewish Studies, The Jewish Theological Seminary of America and Bar Ilan University Press): xi-xiii.

Pinker, A.

2009   'On the Meaning of šgl', *JSIJ* 8: 1-16.

Pope, M.

1992   'Euphemism and Dysphemism in the Bible', in *ABD*, 1:720-25.

Rabello, A.M.

1995   'The Ban on Circumcision as a Cause of Bar Kokhba's Rebellion', *ILR* 29: 176-214.

Rad, G. von

1972   *Genesis: A Commentary* (London: SCM Press).

Raskow, I.N.

1993   *The Phallacy of Genesis: A Feminist Psychoanalytic Approach* (Louis-ville, KY: Westminster John Knox Press).

2000   *Taboo or Not Taboo: Sexuality and the Family in the Hebrew Bible* (Min-neapolis: Fortress Press).

Sarna, N.M.

1989   *Genesis: בראשית The Traditional Hebrew Text with the New JPS Transla-tion and Commentary* (Philadelphia: Jewish Publication Society).

Satlow, M.L.

1994   'They Abused Him like a Woman: Homo-Eroticism, Gender Blurring and the Rabbis in Late Antiquity', *JHistSex* 5: 1-25.

1995   *Tasting the Dish: Rabbinic Rhetorics of Sexuality* (Brown Judaic Studies Series, 303; Atlanta: Scholars Press).

1997   'Jewish Constructions of Nakedness in Late Antiquity', *JBL* 116: 429-24.

2001   *Jewish Marriage in Antiquity* (Princeton and Oxford: Princeton University Press).

Schwartz, S.

2008   'Memory in Josephus and the Culture of the Jews in the First Century', in W.O. McCready and A. Reinhartz (eds.), *Common Judaism: Explorations in Second Temple Judaism* (Minneapolis: Fortress Press): 185-94.

Veenhof, K.R.
 1995   'Seeing the Face of God: The Use of Akkadian Parallels', *Akkadica* 95: 33-37.
Veenker, R.A.
 2001   'Forbidden Fruit: Ancient Near Eastern Sexual Metaphors', *HUCA* 70–71: 57-73.
Westermann, C.
 1994   *Genesis 1–11: A Continental Commentary* (trans. J.J. Scullion; Minneapolis: Fortress Press).
Wold, B.G.
 2007   'Memory in the Dead Sea Scrolls: Exodus, Creation and Cosmos', in Stephan C. Barton, Loren T. Stuckenbruck (eds.), *Memory in the Bible and Antiquity: The Fifth Durham–Tübingen Research Symposium, Durham, September 2004* (Tübingen and Atlanta: Society of Biblical Literature): 47–74.
Wold, D.J.
 1997   'The "Kareth" Penalty in P: Rationale and Cases', in P.J. Achtemeier (ed.), *Society of Biblical Literature Seminar Papers*, I (Missoula, MT: Scholars Press): 1-45.
Wolfson, E.R.
 1994   *Through a Speculum That Shines: Vision and Imagination in Medieval Jewish Mysticism* (Princeton, NJ: Princeton University Press).
 1995   'Circumcision, Vision of God and Textual Interpretation: From Midrashic Trope to Mystical Symbol', in E.R. Wolfson (ed.), *Circle in the Square: Studies in the Use of Gender in Kabbalistic Symbolism* (New York: State University of New York Press): 28-48.
 1998   'Re/Membering the Covenant: Memory, Forgetfulness and the Construction of Identity in the Zohar', in E. Carlebach, J.M. Efrom and D.N. Meyers (eds.), *Jewish History and Jewish Memory: Essays in Honor of Yosef Haim Yerushalmi* (Hanover and London: Brandeis University Press): 214-46.
Wyatt, N.
 1992   'The Pruning of the Vine in KTU 1.23', *UF* 24: 425-27.
 1994   'The Meaning of El Roi and the Mythological Dimension of Genesis 16', *SJOT* 8: 141-51.
 1998   *Religious Texts from Ugarit: The Words of Ilimilku and his Colleagues* (Sheffield: Sheffield Academic Press).
 1999   'The Story of Aqhat', in W.G.E. Watson and N. Wyatt (eds.), *Handbook of Ugaritic Studies* (Leiden: Brill): 234-59.
 2009   'Circumcision and Circumstance: Male Genital Mutilation in Ancient Israel and Ugarit', *JSOT* 33: 405-31.
Wyschogrod, M.
 1983   *The Body of Faith: Judaism as Corporal Election* (Minneapolis: Winston Press).
Yerushalmi, Y.H.
 1982   *Zakhor: Jewish History and Jewish Memory* (Seattle and London: University of Washington Press).

SAMSON: MASCULINITY LOST (AND REGAINED?)*

Ela Lazarewicz-Wyrzykowska

The Samson narrative (Judg. 13–16) is rich in motifs of sexuality and gender. These motifs have been taken up in a number of studies, including the influential essays by Mieke Bal (1987) and Cheryl Exum (1993). While Exum uncovered the androcentric (1993: 89), indeed, sexist agenda of this text, Bal identified in Samson 'a prototype…of a typical category of man that emerges at a specific moment in the history of our culture', whose central feature is sexual insecurity (1987: 63).

Bal's and Exum's readings are focused primarily on female characters in this narrative, their portrayal and role in the plot, and Samson's relationships with them. In this essay I build upon these scholars' observations, but my goal is to revisit the issue of Samson's masculinity. It is important to emphasize that masculinity is something different from 'maleness' (that is, being of the male sex), and it is not the sum total of all physical, psychological or behavioural features of a given man, or of men in general. Rather, it is a cultural construct. In other words, it is a complex of values, behaviours and other features, including physical ones, culturally recognized as masculine, that is, ascribed to men and regarded as appropriate for them.[1] Accordingly, in this reading I do not analyse all aspects of Samson's behaviour, but indicate the ways in which his masculinity corresponds with a certain model of

*   I want to thank Ovidiu Creangă for the thought-stimulating and very enjoyable conversations, which led to the initial version of this essay being written and presented at the SBL International Meeting in Rome, 4 July, 2009. Moreover, I am extremely grateful to him for his patience and help when I grappled with preparing its final version. I thank also Diana Lipton, Daniel Davies, George Wilkes, Will Kynes and Tul'si Bhambry, who at different stages of my work on this essay provided me with helpful and inspiring comments.
1.   This is, of course, a simplified definition. The debate regarding the nature of masculinity, its relation to femininity, the importance of the sexed body in defining both categories of 'masculinity' and 'femininity', and many other related issues, has accumulated a substantial body of literature. Representative samples of voices in this debate can be found, e.g., in Berger, Wallis and Watson (1995) and Adams and Savran (2002). Anderson, Moore and Kim (2004) provide a comprehensive annotated bibliography of relevant works up to 2004.

masculinity, tightly connected with a particular understanding of male honour, and discuss how it is used in the narrative's ideology.[2]

Masculinity and Honour

The anthropological understanding of the concept of honour is comprised of 'an individual's sense of self-worth' (the 'sentiment of honour'), and one's reputation and status in the group (Stewart 2001: 6904; Pitt-Rivers 1968: 503). Studies conducted in the region of the Mediterranean and the Middle East demonstrated that the notion of honour, and the corresponding notion of shame, are highly gender-specific. At early stages of research, honour was identified exclusively with men, while women were thought to be mostly in the domain of shame: while men actively defend their own and their group's honour, women are to guard their own chastity, the loss of which brings shame upon them and the men under whose protection they remained (for example, Peristiany 1966b; Bourdieu 1966: 221-28; Abou-Zeid 1966). Even though some aspects of these findings were later modified, the strong link between masculine honour and a 'competitive notion of masculine sexuality' (Stone 1996: 42) in Mediterranean and Middle Eastern societies has rarely been questioned.[3]

In studies describing small rural communities of these regions, the parameters of masculine honour often include 'physical force and courage' (Blok 1984: 59), the former frequently identified with sexual potency, testified by the ability to sire many, preferably male, children (Blok 1984: 57-59; Gilmore 1987b: 10; Gilmore 1987c: 96-97). Such a notion of honour belongs to the key components of masculinity. For example, in Andalusian communities,

---

2. The hero's relationship with his parents, as well as Judges' theology reflected in his prayers and in his status as a nazirite, are of limited relevance to this reading. The story's 'preface' in Judges 13, with its emphasis on the 'birth of a hero' story (Niditch 2001: 185), is only briefly considered towards the end of this essay.

3. Studies of communities with a strong division between female and male groups have shown that also within female groups criteria of honour were used, albeit different from those used within male groups (Wikan 1984). At the same time, it has been argued that in some studies of masculine honour the sexual aspects have been overemphasized, at the expense of values such as hospitality, honesty and cooperation (Herzfeld 1987; Gilmore 1987c; Stone 1996: 43). It was also observed that only a few of the studies on Mediterranean and Middle Eastern societies have in their vocabularies words directly corresponding to the understanding of honour suggested by the anthropologists (Stewart 2001: 6906). Still, the complex of values and behaviours coherent with the postulated notion of masculine honour was consistently noted throughout those regions and, as Gilmore (1987b; 1987c: 101-102) demonstrated, it was the sexual component of honour that recurred in most of the studied communities (see also Stone 1996: 43).

the word *hombría*, 'manliness', was used to designate the ideal of an honourable man, while male genitals (*cojones*) were invoked to affirm the status of a honourable male (Pitt-Rivers 1966: 45; but compare Gilmore 1987c: 97). The link between honour and masculinity is evidenced also in the fact that men who are dishonoured, either through an erotic defeat, or 'an equivalent social submission' (Gilmore 1987b: 11) can be considered as 'lacking in manliness'. This can be understood as being 'castrated, tame' (Blok 1984: 57-58; Pitt-Rivers 1966: 45), or as 'sexual reversal', 'feminization' (Gilmore 1987b: 11). A dishonoured male 'in a sense…surrenders his own masculine identity and *becomes* woman who is victimized and penetrated… So male dishonour implies more than loss of social prestige; it also implies loss of male social identity, of masculinity' (Gilmore 1987b: 11; see also Brandes 1987: 122).

Masculine honour, like masculinity itself (Gilmore 1987b: 9-10), has to be constantly maintained, defended and protected: 'the individual is constantly forced to prove and assert himself' (Peristiany 1966b: 11). It can be impugned in the case of any kind of defeat, in a fight, or even in a game (Gilmore 1987b: 11), or by infringement of a man's property rights: 'when the chastity of a woman is violated, when living-stock or crops have been stolen, when part of the harvest is damaged' (Blok 1984: 58). In serious offences, the only way to reassert one's honour, and masculinity, is through violence against the offender. For example, 'the deceived husband cannot, without having rehabilitated himself through violence, easily show up in the public domains dominated by competitive men' (Blok 1984: 57). Furthermore, groups tend to possess a sense of 'collective honor, in which the individual members participate' (Pitt-Rivers 1968: 506). When the honour of an individual from one group is challenged by a member or members of a different social group, he does not represent just himself anymore, but becomes 'his group's protagonist' (Peristiany 1966b: 11; Bourdieu 1966: 201).

The usefulness of these notions of honour and shame for approaching the Hebrew Bible has already been noted by a number of scholars, including for example Ken Stone and David J.A. Clines. Stone (1996) discusses the notions of honour and shame among other anthropological categories, such as structures of prestige and 'traffic in women', and fruitfully employs them in the reading of a number of texts from Deuteronomistic History. Combining anthropological insights with a narratological method of analysis, Stone ably demonstrates how in the narratives that include references to sexual activity (Judg. 19; 2 Sam. 3.6-11; 2 Sam. 11–12; 2 Sam. 13; 2 Sam. 16.20-23), or that have been perceived as relating to sex in the history of interpretation (1 Kgs 2), sexual activity functions as an instrument of competition for status and power between the male characters. Clines, in turn, employs the notion of honour in his study of prophetic texts (2002). It is included among the parameters of masculinity, alongside other features such as the messenger function, strength, violence, holiness, negative attitude towards women and the role of standard-bearing. Clines uncovers the ways in which the masculinity of the authors of prophetic books is reflected in their work, in order to demonstrate how problematic such a gender bias is when new, more inclusive, ways of interpreting the Bible are concerned (see also his unpublished essays on Job and Psalms, available online).

It is, of course, important to recognize that, just as some social phenomena lend themselves better to analysis from this perspective, so too some biblical texts can be more fruitfully read using the notion of masculinity outlined above. The Samson narrative is one such text. Not only did Samson's strength and exploits make him an epitome of virility, but also the motif of 'status and power games' in male society is consistently present throughout the story (Niditch 1990: 620-21).

Masculinity Challenged

Male competition takes centre stage in the story of Samson's marriage to a Philistine woman from Timnah (Judg. 14.1-18). The hero sees a woman in Timnah and announces to his parents his intention to marry her (vv. 1-2). The parents protest (v. 3), but finally marriage is settled and Samson throws a wedding feast (v. 10). The people of Timnah bring to the feast thirty *mere 'im*: male guests, wedding 'companions' (v. 11).[4] Samson puts to them a riddle connected with a wager (vv. 12-14): if the men solve the riddle before the end of the feast, he will give them thirty linen garments and thirty changes of clothes, but if they fail to provide the answer, they will have to give him the same amount of items of clothing.

Bal (1987: 43) argues that in myths and fairy tales riddles are connected with sexual maturity: 'whoever knows the answer knows the mystery of woman and sexuality'. Samson's riddle, revolving around sexual symbols discussed by Crenshaw (1974: 490; 1978: 115) and Camp and Fontaine (1990: 141-42), can also be seen as his symbolic assertion that his, the groom's, sexual knowledge surpasses that of his thirty male wedding companions (Bal 1987: 45; 1988: 139). The riddle is a challenge to their masculinity.

There would be nothing unexpected about the groom being celebrated as the most masculine man at the wedding party. It is, after all, in the community's best interest to celebrate the groom's virility, since reproduction leads to the perpetuation of the community. Thus, we would expect the wedding companions to readily accept their role as the background against which the

---

4.   All biblical quotations, unless indicated otherwise, are from NRSV. On the custom of appointing the groom's 'companions', see van Selms 1950: 71

groom can shine. However, as it is underscored in the later exchange between Samson and the bride (v. 16b), the wedding guests represent *her* (and not *his*) people (Bal 1987: 42): 'You have asked a riddle of *my* people, but you have not explained it to me'. With his riddle Samson challenged not only 'other males', but 'males from the "other" group', for whom Samson's masculinity is a potential threat.

Even in situations of exogamous marriages challenges of this kind can be benign (Bourdieu 1966: 203; Niditch 2008a: 157), but in this case, instead of accepting their failure to solve the riddle (Niditch 2008a: 157), the men threaten the bride into extracting the answer from Samson (v. 15).[5] She finds out the answer and explains it to them (v. 17). The riddle was based on Samson's encounter with the lion in the vineyard (vv. 5-9), his private experience (Bal 1988: 135-42), not known to anybody else. Consequently, when the men finally provide the answer to Samson, he realizes that his bride had disclosed it to them. Thus, his honour is not only challenged by the sheer fact that his riddle was solved (he lost the bet), but also, and more importantly, it is offended by the bride's betrayal (compare Bourdieu 1966: 216-21). As Samson puts it, they 'ploughed with his heifer' (v. 18b). The sexual overtones of this phrase are easily detectable, and attested also in other biblical and Mesopotamian sources (Crenshaw 1974: 493-94). A heifer is an immature cow, a virgin: '[t]hat heifer was Samson's property, a right that has been violated by the men' (Bal 1987: 43).

Samson responds with violence. In order to 'avenge himself' (Bal 1987: 44-45), he kills thirty other Philistines, takes their garments as spoils and uses them to pay the wager debt (14.19a). Then, full of anger, Samson returns to his father's house (v. 19b). After some time he comes back to visit the bride (15.1), bringing with him a 'peace offering' (Niditch 2001: 186). However, he finds out that his bride was given to his best man (v. 2a), one of the wedding companions (van Selms 1950: 71-74), and thus one of those who benefited from the wager. Samson is offered, as a replacement, her younger and more beautiful sister, but declines (v. 2b). Instead, he sets the Philistines' crops, vineyards, and olive groves on fire (vv. 4-5). It could be argued that he acted out of frustrated sexual desire (Exum 1993: 78). His marriage was

---

5.   The text poses some chronological difficulties. Both in the Masoretic text and in LXX the men cannot find the answer for three days (v. 14). According to the Masoretic text, they approached the bride on the seventh day (v. 15), while LXX has fourth day. Verse 17 poses additional problems. It states that the bride tried to find out the answer for the whole seven days of the feast. As one may expect, there is a tendency to explain this discrepancy with the bride's curiosity: even before she was approached by her angry compatriots, she wanted to find out the answer for herself (thus for example Ryan 2007: 108). However, the exact chronology of these events is not relevant to this reading. For a discussion see Moore 1908: 335-36; Soggin 1981: 241-42

never consummated: the consummation of marriage took place only after the wedding feast (van Selms 1950: 71) and the Philistines offer the answer to the riddle on the seventh day of the festivities, just before 'the sun had set' (v. 18), or, as the text it is often emended, 'before he went into the chamber' (Moore 1908: 337; Exum 1993: 71). His later 'visit', at the time of harvest, traditionally connoted as a time of fertility (Niditch 2001: 186), has an obviously sexual intent. In Judg. 15.1 he explicitly declares 'I will go in to my wife (אבאה אל־אשתי) in the chamber'. As Exum (1993: 70) notes, the verb בוא is here used to indicate sexual intercourse. But, as we know, her father would not let him go in.

Even more importantly, whether or not in v. 18 'ploughing' meant 'taking advantage of the wife's weakness rather than actual sexual intimacy' (Crenshaw 1974: 494), when Samson finds out that his bride was already given to his best man, the figurative saying ironically takes on an explicitly sexual meaning. And, since 'the one who has the woman has the status' (Niditch 1990: 621), this is a further blow to Samson's honour: he is now being cuckolded by one of the men who had beaten him at the challenge he himself set. Accepting the offer of the younger sister would symbolize Samson's acceptance of his weakened position; it would bring closure to the cycle of challenges, but on conditions non-favourable to him. Instead, Samson attempts to strengthen his position. The destruction of the Philistines' property, the crops, is a response to the offence to Samson's honour constituted by the violation of his property, the bride.

He perceives such a response as thoroughly justified (15.3),[6] but the violence spirals out: the Philistines come and burn Samson's bride and her father (v. 6). The same pattern is present in the well-known chilling story of the Levite and his concubine in Judg. 19, where the men of Gibeah attack the man by way of his woman, and thus 'convey the message [to him] that their power will prevail over his' (Stone 1996: 82). Here, the Philistines clearly understand that Samson still perceives the bride as his property. Killing *her*, they avenge their loss of their crops and show disrespect to *him*, and thus pose a further offence to his honour. Samson responds by confronting the Philistines. He 'strikes them down...with a great slaughter' (v. 8), in what he describes as a vengeance (the root נקם, v. 7).

The exchange of acts of violence continues in Judg. 15.9-17. The Philistines make a raid on Lehi to seek their vengeance ('to bind up Samson, to do

---

6. NRSV translates the word רע in Samson's declaration in 15.3 as 'mischief', but the rendition 'harm' (as in Gen. 26.29) seems more appropriate. It is possible that in v. 3 there is a play on words מרעהו/מרעך (his/your companion, 14.20; 15.2), רעה לו (his best man, 14.20) and רע (harm).

to him as he did to us', v. 10), and the threatened men of Judah agree to deliver Samson to them. He frees himself from the bonds and kills another thousand Philistines (v. 15). One more display of Samson's virile energy follows in 16.1-3: after a sexual encounter with a prostitute in Gaza (the verb בוא again), he pulls up the city gates and carries them all the way to the hills of Hebron (16.3), while the Philistines lie in wait. Bal (1987: 49) comments on Samson's departing from the prostitute's house at midnight that 'he had to break off prematurely', but I follow the majority of commentators in interpreting this adventure as yet another example of his extraordinary masculine energy. In Exum's paraphrase: 'In the middle of a night of sexual activity, his vigor apparently undiminished, he struts off, carrying the Gaza gates on his shoulders, right under the Philistine's noses' (Exum 1993: 79). The act of carrying the gates away from the Philistines, to a place within Israel's sphere, symbolizes the 'removal of power and status' of the Philistines (Niditch 2008a: 168). Samson's position is strengthened and his masculinity is reasserted. But then, of course, he falls in love with Delilah (v. 4).

Masculinity Lost

Delilah, commissioned by the lords of the Philistines, extracts from Samson the secret of his strength. The way in which Delilah obtains this knowledge, and the literary structure of this section of the narrative have attracted attention of commentators. Particularly noteworthy are Bal's subtle analysis (1987: 49-58) and Lori Rowlett's suggestion that the interaction between Samson and Delilah resembles a 'classic S/M bondage game' (Rowlett 2001: 110). For the purposes of this reading it is sufficient to point out that in his confession Samson draws the link between his strength, his hair, and his nazirite status: 'A razor has never come upon my head, for I have been a nazirite to God from my mother's womb. If my head were shaved, then my strength would leave me; I would become weak, and be like anyone else' (v. 17). In the whole narrative the motif of Samson's naziriteship is mentioned only twice: in the annunciation story (chap. 13) and in his confession to Delilah. As I argue elsewhere (Lazarewicz-Wyrzykowska 2009: 128-30), the nazirite status could have been imposed on Samson in the process of the text's edition, through the association with his long hair. This can be seen as the editor's attempt to employ Samson's exploits in the service of the book's ideology. I return to this issue towards the end of this essay.

Having found out the truth about the source of Samson's strength, Delilah 'lets him fall asleep' (NRSV), or rather, 'brings him to sleep' (Sasson 1988: 334), 'on her lap' (עַל־בִּרְכֶּיהָ) or, as the Greek text has it, 'between her knees' (16.19). Most commentators, scholars and artists alike, have recognized the sexual setting of the scene, and identified Samson's sleep with post-coital lethargy,[7] while some point out the uses of the expression עַל־בִּרְכֶּיהָ in Gen. 30.3 and 2 Kgs 4.20 to highlight other possible nuances.[8] In any case, Samson's hair is then shaved (v. 19) by Delilah herself (Sasson 1998). The result of the shaving is the (seemingly permanent) loss of Samson's extraordinary physical strength. In folkloristic tales hair is frequently indicated as the seat of powers of a superhumanly strong hero (Niditch 1990: 612-13; 2008; Mobley 1997).[9] This motif operates in connection with the symbolic association of hair with masculine vitality and power, and in particular with sexual potency (Bal 1987: 54-55; Niditch 1990: 616-17; Exum 1993: 77). The probable sexual setting of the scene, the symbolism of hair, and the far-reaching results of the shaving have led a number of scholars to describe the shaving of Samson's hair, 'the symbol of his particular manliness' (Niditch 2001: 187), as symbolic castration.[10] Most importantly for this reading, Niditch describes the shearing of his hair as 'a sexual stripping and subjugation' and 'symbolic castration or womanization', symbolizing his 'defeated status' (1990: 617).

In the narrative, Samson's status as a defeated, unmanned, warrior is symbolized by several other 'womanizing' images (Niditch 1990: 617).[11] The weakened Samson is seized by the Philistines, who gouge out his eyes, bind him with bronze shackles and send him to prison, where he grinds at a mill

---

7.   The sexual setting of this scene is clear in Rubens's interpretation of Samson's sleep in his painting *Samson and Delilah* (1609–1610) showing the hero naked and asleep on his lover's lap. The post-coital nature of his slumber is suggested also by Delilah's naked breasts and disordered clothing.

8.   Bal (1987: 58-63) sees the whole scene as Samson's symbolic re-birth. Sasson (1988: 334) points out that עַל־בִּרְכֶּיהָ is where the Shunemite woman placed her sick child (2 Kgs 4.20). According to him, there are no sexual overtones in the discussed passage.

9.   Mobley (1997: 223-24; 2006: 22-25) observes that Samson's habit of wearing his hair in seven locks can be seen as an Israelite version of the six locks worn by the Mesopotamian *lakhmu*, 'hairy one'.

10.   Bal (1987: 59) comments that 'by cutting off his locks, the temporary weakness of the penis is made permanent.' In her psychoanalytical interpretation, she sees Samson's symbolic castration as part of his regression to infancy on Delilah's lap, and the reversal of the birth trauma (Bal 1987: 58-63). Exum argues that Samson's symbolic emasculation sends a message to the Israelite male: a man, who surrenders himself to a woman, puts himself in grave danger of emasculation and loss of potency. At a more general level, the story testifies to 'the male fear of losing the penis to the woman' (Exum 1993: 83).

11.   Niditch (2008a: 169-70) identifies Samson's 'feminization' with this exposure to the realm of culture. Thus, according to her, the process commences already with the series of Delilah's questions and the hero's 'false revelations'. With each attempt to bind, or overpower him, he moves closer to culture (from gut cords, through ropes, to weaving of his hair) and the process is completed with the shaving of his hair with the razor, a 'manmade tool'.

(v. 21). Grinding was the work done usually, though not exclusively (more on this below), by women (Crenshaw 1974: 501; Niditch 1990: 617; 2001: 188; Exum 1993: 84). It has long been noted that, consistently with the masculinist character of the rhetoric of war shared by the Hebrew Bible and other ancient Near Eastern literatures (Washington 1997), ancient Near Eastern prisoners of war were often subjected to this form of punishment. Its purpose was not only to exploit, but also to humiliate them, by putting them in a female role (van der Toorn 1986; Exum 1993: 84). Van der Toorn (1986: 249) asks us rhetorically: 'Could a warrior be more ridiculed than by making him do the work traditionally assigned to slaves and women?' As we shall see, he could.

It has been noted that 'grinding' (טחן) is in the Hebrew Bible used as a sexual *double entendre* (Niditch 2001: 188; 2008a: 171; Exum 1993: 79). The most explicit example is Job 31.10: 'If my heart has been enticed by a woman, and I have lain in wait at my neighbour's door; then let my wife grind for another; and let other men kneel over her' (compare Isa. 47.2-3). In Judg. 16.21 Samson is put in the position Job assigns to his wife (Niditch 1990: 617). The sexual innuendo of the verb takes his 'womanization' one step further: in doing the woman's work, he is not only 'like a woman', but like a *sexually subdued* woman (Niditch 1990: 617). Even more concrete language of sexual violence is introduced already in the question that Delilah asks Samson: 'How could you be bound, so that one could subdue you?' (16.6). She repeats the Philistines' question from the previous verse (v. 5); effectively, then, it is a question that the Philistines ask of Samson. As Exum (1993: 79) notes, the verb ענה, translated here as 'subdue', is elsewhere[12] used of raping a woman. Here, the identification of Samson with a sexually subdued woman is even more direct, not mediated by the double meaning of grinding.[13]

In the light of the above, it is important to point out that the verb צחק used to describe what Samson does before the Philistines gathered in the temple of Dagon in Judg. 16.25 (ויצחק לפניהם) also has sexual overtones (Exum 1993: 80; Niditch 1997: 617; 2001: 188; 2008a: 167, 171).[14] The reader is never informed what exactly it was that Samson did to 'entertain' (שחק) the

---

12. Gen. 34.2; Deut. 21.14; 22.24, 29; 2 Sam. 13.12, 14, 22, 32; Ezek. 22.10-11; Lam. 5.11.

13. Exum (1993: 79, 84) includes in the repertoire of vocabulary serving Samson's symbolic emasculation also the application of the verb 'entice' (פתה) to Samson as its object in 16.5.

14. It is used in Gen. 26.8-9 to describe what Isaac did to or with Rebekah that disclosed to Abimelech the truth about the nature of their relationship. Compare also Michal's jealousy when David 'makes sport' with dancing maidens before the ark in 2 Sam. 6.5, 21-22; 1 Chronicles 15.29 (see Niditch 1990: 617), and Gen. 39.14, 17 (see Lipton 2008).

Philistines. However, it is illuminating to recall here as intertext the already invoked story about the Levite and his concubine, with its motif of a threat of homosexual rape. In Judges 19 the men of Gibeah express desire to have intercourse with the Levite (v. 22). Ken Stone has shown in his insightful analysis that what is at stake in this story is not (homo)sexual desire, but a challenge to the Levite's masculinity and honour: in the Hebrew Bible 'the male who allows himself to be (or is unable to prevent himself from being) *acted upon* sexually shows himself to be the object of another man; he therefore becomes "feminized"' (Stone 1996: 76). It is, then, possible that behind the text's ambiguity there is a suggestion of yet another stage of Samson's emasculation: that he is not only defeated and humiliated, but also sexually subdued like a woman, through actual intercourse, or at least through forcible exposure of genitalia. Without pressing further this point, the boundaries between homosexual rape and more general 'homosocial' conflict are indeed fluid (Stone 1996: 84).[15] Thus, in the narrative Samson symbolically becomes a woman (Exum 1993: 83-84).

But there is a possibility that his blinding by the Philistines hints at an additional aspect of his emasculation.[16] I suggest that the gouging out of Samson's eyes should be considered in the context of his work at a mill: grinding was done not only by woman, but also by slaves and fettered animals (Crenshaw 1974: 501; Niditch 1990: 617; 2001: 188; Exum 1993: 84). And it is important to keep in mind that one of the oldest cattle-keeping techniques was castration, achieved by removal of the animal's testicles (Taylor 2000: 52-56; 166-68). Some of the males in cattle herds, designated to serve as fettered animals, were castrated to make them less aggressive and more easily manageable, and in order to control breading (Taylor 2000: 55, 166-68). Castrating cattle later gave rise to the practice of castrating slaves, especially those captured at war. They were thus prevented from continuing

15. As is well known, forcing male prisoners to perform simulated or actual homosexual activities continues to belong to the most widespread ways of their mistreating (be it the captured terror suspects, or fellow college students in the famous Stanford Prison Experiment). The latest well-documented graphic examples of torturing (male) prisoners in Abu Gharib, by forcing them to sexual activities are analysed by one of the leading American social psychologists Philip Zimbardo from the perspective of the results of the Stanford Prison Experiment (SPE). In the experiment, conducted by Zimbardo and his research team in 1970, volunteers recruited from among male college students were divided into two groups, 'guards' and 'prisoners', and located in conditions mimicking actual American prison. The experiment, originally planned for two weeks, had to be interrupted after seven days, due to the escalating aggression and violence of the 'guards' towards the 'prisoners'. The experiment is described in detail in Zimbardo 2007: 23-258. About the sexual harassment during the SPE, see for example 171-72.

16. Exum (1993: 79, 83) includes Samson's blinding in his symbolic emasculation, but does not discuss it further.

their lineage, and from burdening the society of their masters with the costs of bringing up their not-yet-productive offspring. Moreover, they were unable to enter the kinship networks, either within the slave group, or in the society of their masters. Condemned in this way to permanent alienation from the culture of their masters ('defamilied, depersonalized, desexed, decivilized', Taylor 2000: 172), they nevertheless retained their life and usefulness to the new masters by contributing to production (Taylor 2000: 171).[17]

In the Hebrew Bible body parts such as a hand (Isa. 57.8), a thigh (Gen. 24.2-3) or feet (Isa. 7.20; Ruth 3.4, 7) are used as euphemisms for male genitals (Englert 1974). It is possible that in the discussed text the gouged-out eyes, a double, symmetric, round organ, on some level of meaning serve as euphemism for the removed testicles.[18] Following this association would introduce a somatic aspect to Samson's hitherto symbolic emasculation (being defeated, subdued, humiliated). Such a connotation is strengthened by his being sent away to do the work of gelded animals and slaves.[19]

Masculinity Regained

In the narrative as a whole Samson's masculinity is undermined in spheres that are narrowing down: from the symbolic weakening of his position through beating him in the challenge set by himself, through the attack on his property, to his actual physical subduing, mutilation of his body and subjecting him to humiliating activities. The super-manly warrior is 'womanized' (possibly to the point of sexual abuse) and symbolically, if not physically, castrated. How does Samson's death alter the situation?

Renate Jost (1999) argues that the 'vengeance' (נקם) Samson invokes in his prayer (Judg. 16.28) should be understood in a legal context, as the

17. Gary Taylor (2000: 56-57) insists that with some exceptions, such as mutilating enemies at war, as well as punishment for treason, and medical surgeries, castration consisted primarily of removal of testicles, resulting in the victim's inability to procreate, but preserving his life. According to him, Freud's 'phallocentric' theory of the castration complex could have taken place only as a result of many significant changes in numerous fields of culture (Taylor 2000: 49-62, 65-66, 109).

18. Numerous literary examples of blinding, including of course the famous case of Oedipus, have been interpreted by Freud as a metaphor for castration (1955: 231; 1968: 190; 1971a: 162; 1971b: 130). Freud's insistence on castration as the removal of the penis, rather than testicles, is not completely consistent with his interpretation of blinding. Nevertheless, the latter supports the present argument. For a critique of Freud's perception of castration, see Taylor 2000. See also footnote 17.

19. This is not to argue that Samson's blinding should be definitely and unequivocally interpreted as an euphemism for his physical castration. For example, on the level of the narration, his blindness is invoked in Judg. 16.26, where he is unable to navigate his way around the temple unassisted.

restitution of his violated rights (similarly Exum 1981: 42). God answers the hero's prayer by restoring his superhuman strength and thus enabling him to kill his enemies (16.28-30). Of course, as well as the Philistines, Samson kills himself. Clearly, it is not the hero's life that is the most important value at stake, but the 'recovery of Samson's lost honor' (Crenshaw 1974: 501-502), and it is the latter that elicits God's intervention.

According to one of the rules of honour, connected with social pressure, '[t]he person who fails to take revenge ceases to exist for other people' (Bourdieu 1966: 211-12). Samson ceases to exist physically, but having rehabilitated himself in the eyes of his male society, he is posthumously accepted as part of it. There is 'a declaration of admiration for Samson's final deed (v. 30)' (Niditch 2001: 188), and his brothers and his family (lit., the whole house of his father, כל־בית אביהו) come to collect his body, and bury him in his father's tomb (v. 31).[20] The emphasis on the information that Samson killed more Philistines at his death than he did during his life (16.30) is not incidental: in order to rehabilitate himself from the enormous dishonour he suffered, he had to surpass his enemies in violence.

Thus, the Samson story concludes with a paradoxical happy end. First his hair starts to grow back, then God restores his physical strength, and finally the vengeance itself symbolically restores his honour and masculinity. He loses his life in the process, but ultimately he is vindicated.

Masculinity Manipulated

The spiral of violence connected with the honour/dishonour dynamic, which eventually led Samson to killing a record number of Philistines, started with his sexual interest in the woman from Timnah. His parents are far from happy when he announces his plan to marry her, but the narrator informs us: 'she was from Yhwh' (מיהוה היא, 14.4; my translation). This passage suggests that God may have been controlling everything that happened, including the final scene of Samson's suicidal vengeance (Exum 1993: 89; similarly Crenshaw 1978: 135). Indeed, the prologue with the annunciation scene gives us an image of Samson being conceived and dedicated for the particular

---

20. Exum (1993: 85) interprets the story's conclusion from a psychoanalytical perspective. Throughout the story female 'otherness' is amplified by being cast in terms of 'foreignness'. The story's overall message is that sexual women are dangerous and are not to be trusted, but controlled (Exum 1993: 83, 89-90). Samson's symbolic reincorporation into the male Israelite society is conditioned by his symbolic destruction of the female other, with whom he has been temporarily identified. His own death testifies to the insolubility of the problem of the female other in the framework of patriarchal binary thought. The other, to whom Samson is irresistibly drawn, is necessary for defining self, but is also threatening to the self's identity. Compare Bal 1987: 62-63.

purpose of fighting with the Philistines (Judg. 13.5). Samson's parents do not realize that his personal life is also subordinate to this purpose. Verse 14 leaves it open to question whether or not Samson himself is aware of this. However, elsewhere it is made clear that he is driven by sexual attraction (14.3; Bal 1987: 42; Exum 1987: 70), love (16.4), and, as I have demonstrated above, he is also motivated by the desire to defend his honour. It is only from the narrator's perspective that all of this turns out to serve 'a larger divine purpose' (Niditch 2008a: 155). Samson can be seen as an unaware executor of the divine plan, or, to put it more strongly, a victim of divine manipulation.[21]

If we look at the notion of God in this narrative as the projection of the author's/editor's ideological agenda (Rowlett 2001: 112-15), it becomes evident that Samson's actions in defence of his honour are here employed in the framework of the ideology of war. Not only do they defend the collective honour, but they also serve the purpose of killing large numbers of national enemies. Thus, the man's private vendetta, affirmed as the fulfilment of a prophecy and indirect working of God, becomes in this text the vehicle for achieving a public aim. Paraphrasing Exum (1993: 83), the text's message to an Israelite man is not only 'Do not trust women!', but also, 'It is all right to be violent and kill in defence of your masculine honour. And when you do that, you might actually be fulfilling God's plan'.

Yet, even though Samson's violence is sanctioned in the text in a variety of ways,[22] the narrative is not free from ambivalence towards him. Firstly, the aftermath of the displays of his rage is not always immediately beneficial to his own group, as is evidenced by the Philistine raid on Lehi (Niditch 2001: 186).[23] Samson's withdrawal to the cave (Judg. 15.8) and his binding by the Judahites signal the problematic status of the warrior, on the fringes of society.[24] Indeed, his final words 'Let me die with the Philistines' (Judg.

---

21. Samson's prayer in Judg. 15.18 ('You have granted this great victory by the hand of your servant') does not prove his conscious participation in the divine plan. He simply acknowledges his deity's role in this victory, but this does not mean he perceives the whole situation a 'pretext to act against the Philistines' (14.4) orchestrated by the deity.

22. One of those ways has just been discussed. The remaining ones include his nazirite dedication and the identification of his warrior's rage with the spirit of God rushing upon him (Judg. 14.6, 19; 15.14), or stirring him (13.25), and of course by his being one of the judges of Israel (15.20, 16.31).

23. Boling (1975: 238), explains that the inhabitants of Judaea are here regarded 'as constituent members of the Israel whom it was God's intention...to rescue from the Philistines'.

24. Samson's liminal status has been noted by Exum (1993: 77), who accentuates his being caught up between Israel and the Philistines. Niditch (2008b: 66-67) and Mobeley (1997, 2006) discuss Samson's liminality it in terms of opposition between culture and nature.

16.30) can be seen to convey the awareness that while the warrior's reintegration into civilian life can be problematic (Mobley 1997: 219, see also Creangă 2009: 99-102), the return of the *wounded* warrior might be not possible at all. He is acceptable only as a dead hero.

Also the fact that Samson dies childless, or at least the text is silent about any offspring he might have produced (Crenshaw 1974: 498), testifies to the narrative's ambivalence towards the character. It is surprising that the procreative abilities of a super-manly hero like Samson should not be emphasized, since the parameters of masculinity in the ancient Near Eastern paradigm included not only a man's military prowess, but also his ability to produce offspring (Hoffner 1966). Taylor's observation that one of the functions of castration was its being 'a legal or pseudo-legal punishment (usually for violation of local sexual customs)' (2000: title page, see also p. 165) can shed some light on this issue. By depriving the victims of the ability to procreate, castration served the purpose of 'ensuring that the future belongs to someone else'. Although Samson's sleeping with the enemy is, as I have just discussed, employed positively in the text's ideology, his childlessness can perhaps be seen as a symbolic punishment inflicted on him by the biblical authors for engaging in prohibited relationships with foreign women. The message is that those in whose eyes the Philistine women are 'right' (14.3b) eventually have their eyes taken out (16.21). Vindicated Samson may be, but the future of Israel belongs to those who do not take wives from the uncircumcised Philistines (14.3a).

Conclusion

In this essay I applied an anthropological understanding of masculine honour to engage with the model of masculinity represented by Samson. The sense of insecurity inherent in such a notion of honour is evidenced by the fact that the character's masculinity is constantly endangered: it is first challenged and temporarily reasserted, then lost, and finally regained, but at the cost of his life. This approach allowed me to demonstrate how such a model of masculinity, focused on violent defence of honour, is in the narrative depicted as a means to fulfil God's plan for Israel, and thus is employed in the book's ideology of war. Finally, I indicated the narrative's ambivalence towards Samson, connected with its attitude to his liaisons with foreign women and his status as a (wounded) warrior.

A close reading of the Samson story focused on his masculinity does not, of course, answer all the questions posed by the text. However, I hope to have demonstrated that such a reading allows us to understand better the logic of the character's behaviour, and to discover the connection between the model of masculinity he represents, and the ideology of war in which he is involved. On a different level, using the lens of masculinity reveals Samson's gender instability, which is connected in particular with his status as a warrior. This instability undermines the popular perception of biblical masculinity as a uniform, secure and stable feature of biblical men.

Bibliography

Abou-Zeid, Ahmed
    1966   'Honour and Shame among the Bedouins of Egypt', in Peristiany (1966a): 243-59.
Adams, Rachel, and David Savran (eds.)
    2002   *The Masculinity Studies Reader* (Oxford: Blackwell).
Anderson, Janice C., Stephen D. Moore and Seong Hee Kim
    2004   'Masculinity Studies: A Classified Bibliography', in Stephen D. Moore and Janice C. Anderson (eds.), *New Testament Masculinities* (SemeiaSt, 45; Leiden: Brill): 23-42.
Bal, Mieke
    1987   *Lethal Love: Feminist Literary Readings of Biblical Love Stories* (ISBL; Bloomington, IN: Indiana University Press).
    1988   *Death and Dissymmetry: The Politics of Coherence in the Book of Judges* (CSHJ; Chicago: University of Chicago Press).
Berger, Maurice, Brian Wallis and Simon Watson (eds.)
    1995   *Constructing Masculinity* (London: Routledge).
Blok, Anton
    1984   'Rams and Billy-Goates: A Key to Mediterranean Code Honor', in E. Wolf (ed.), *Religion, Power and Protest in Local Communities: The Northern Shore of the Mediterranean* (New York: Mouton): 51-70.
Boling, Robert G.
    1975   *Judges: Introduction, Translation, and Commentary* (AB; Garden City, NY: Doubleday).
Bourdieu, Pierre
    1966   'The Sentiment of Honour in Kabyle Society', in Peristiany 1966a: 191-241.
Brandes, Stanley
    1987   'Reflections on Honor and Shame in the Mediterranean', in Gilmore 1987a: 121-34.
Camp, Claudia V., and C.R. Fontaine
    1990   'The Words of the Wise and their Riddles' in Susan Niditch (ed.), *Text and Tradition: The Hebrew Bible and Folklore* (Semeia Studies 20; Atlanta: Scholars Press): 127-51.
Clines, David J.A.
    2002   'He-Prophets: Masculinity as a Problem for the Hebrew Prophets and their Interpreters', in A.G. Hunter and P.R. Davies (eds.), *Sense and Sensitivity: Essays on Reading the Bible in Memory of Robert Carroll* (JSOTSS, 348; London: Sheffield Academic Press): 311-28.
    n.d.   'Loingirding and Other Male Activities in the Book of Job', cited 30 October 2009. Online:

http.//www.shef.ac.uk/bibs/DJACcurres/Articles/Loingirding.html.

n.d.   'The Book of Psalms, Where Men Are Men: On the Gender of Hebrew Piety', cited 30 October 2009. Online: http.//www.shef.ac.uk/bibs/ DJACcurres/Articles/GenderPiety.html.

Creangă, Ovidiu
2009   *The Conquest of Memory: Israel's Identity and the Commemoration of the Past in the Conquest Narrative of Joshua (1–12)* (PhD dissertation, King's College, London).

Crenshaw, James L.
1974   'The Samson Saga: Filial Devotion or Erotic Attachment?', *ZAW* 86: 470-504.
1979   *Samson: A Secret Betrayed, a Vow Ignored* (London: SPCK).

Englert, Donald M.C.
1974   'Bowdlerizing the Old Testament', in Howard N. Bream, Ralph D. Heim and Carey A. Moore (eds.), *A Light unto my Path: Old Testament Studies in Honor of Jacob M. Myers* (Philadelphia: Temple University Press): 141-44.

Exum, Cheryl J.
1981   'Aspects of Symmetry and Balance in the Samson Saga', *JSOT* 6: 3-29.
1983   'The Theological Dimension of the Samson Saga', *VT* 33: 30-45.
1993   *Fragmented Women: Feminist (Sub)Versions of Biblical Narratives* (JSOTSup, 163; Sheffield: JSOT Press).

Freud, Sigmund
The Standard Edition of the Complete Psychological Works of Sigmund Freud (trans. J. Strachey, in collaboration with A. Freud, assisted by A. Strachey and A. Tyson; London: The Hogarth Press and the Institute of Psycho-Analysis).
1955   'The Uncanny', in S. Freud, *An Infantile Neurosis and Other Works (1917–1919)* 17: 217-56.
1968   'An Outline of Psychoanalysis', in S. Freud, *Moses and Monotheism, An Outline of Psycho-Analysis and Other Works (1937–1939)* 23: 139-208.
1971a   'The Economic Problem of Masochism', in S. Freud, *The Ego and the Id and Other Works (1923–1925)* 19: 155-72.
1971b   'Totem and Taboo', in S. Freud, *'Totem and Taboo', and Other Works (1913–1914)* 13: 1-162.

Gilmore, David D. (ed.)
1987a   *Honor and Shame and the Unity of the Mediterranean* (Washington, DC: American Anthropological Association).
1987b   'Introduction', in Gilmore 1987a: 2-21.
1987c   'Honor, Honesty, Shame: Male Status in Contemporary Andalusia', in Gilmore 1987a: 90-103.

Hoffner, Harry A.
1966   'Symbols for Masculinity and Femininity: Their Use in Ancient Near Eastern Sympathetic Magic Rituals', *JBL* 85: 326-34.

Lazarewicz-Wyrzykowska, Elzbieta
2009   *Aesthetic Form and the Book of Amos: The Application of a Bakhtinian Category to a Biblical Text* (PhD dissertation, University of Manchester).

Lipton, Diana
2008   'Longing in Egypt: A Solution for Male Infertility in the Joseph Story

(Genesis 39)', Cambridge: CRASSH Seminar, 27 October.

Mobley, Gregory
    1997   'The Wild Man in the Bible and the Ancient Near East', *JBL* 116: 217-33.
    2006   *Samson and the Liminal Hero in the Ancient Near East* (LHB/OTS; New York: T. & T. Clark).

Moore, George F.
    1908   *A Critical and Exegetical Commentary on Judges* (ICC; Edinburgh: T. & T. Clark).

Niditch, Susan
    2001   'Judges', in John Barton and J. Muddiman (eds.), *The Oxford Bible Commentary* (Oxford: Oxford University Press): 176-91.
    1990   'Samson as Culture Hero, Trickster, and Bandit: The Empowerment of the Weak', *CBQ* 52: 608-24.
    2008a   *Judges: A Commentary* (OTL; Louisville, KY: Westminster John Knox Press).
    2008b   *'My Brother Esau is a Hairy Man': Hair and Identity in Ancient Israel* (Oxford: Oxford University Press).

Peristiany, J.G. (ed.)
    1966a   *Honour and Shame: The Values of Mediterranean Society* (London: Weidenfeld & Nicolson).
    1966b   'Introduction', in Peristiany 1966a: 9-18.

Pitt-Rivers, Julian
    1966   'Honour and Social Status', in Peristiany 1966a: 19-77.
    1968   'Honor', in *IESS* 6 (New York: Macmillan): 503-11.

Rowlett, Lori
    2001   'Violent Femmes and S/M: Queering Samson and Delilah', in Ken Stone (ed.), *Queer Commentary and the Hebrew Bible* (JSOTSup, 334; Sheffield: Sheffield Academic Press): 106-15.

Ryan, Roger J.
    2007   *Judges* (Readings: A New Biblical Commentary; Sheffield: Sheffield Phoenix Press).

Sasson, Jack M.
    1988   'Who Cut Samson's Hair? (and Other Trifling Issues Raised by Judges 16)', *Prooftexts* 8: 333-39.

Selms, A. van
    1950   'The Best Man and Bride—From Sumer to St. John With a New Interpretation of Judges, Chapters 14 and 15', *JNES* 9: 65-75.

Soggin, J. Alberto
    1987   *Judges: A Commentary* (2nd edn; OTL; London: SCM Press).

Stewart, C.
    2001   'Honor and Shame', in *IESBS* 9: 6904-6907.

Stone, Ken
    1996   *Sex, Honor, and Power in the Deuteronomistic History* (JSOTSup, 234; Sheffield: Sheffield Academic Press).

Taylor, Gary
    2000   *Castration: An Abbreviated History of Western Manhood* (New York: Routledge).

Toorn, K. van der
   1986   'Judges xvi 21 in the Light of the Akkadian Sources', *VT* 36: 248-53.
Washington, Harold C.
   1997   'Violence and the Construction of Gender in the Hebrew Bible: A New Historicist Approach', *BibInt* 5: 324-63.
Wikan, Unni
   1984   'Shame and Honour: A Contestable Pair', *Man* 19: 635-52.
Zimbardo, Philip
   2007   *The Lucifer Effect: How Good People Turn Evil* (London: Rider).

JEREMIAH, MASCULINITY AND HIS PORTRAYAL AS THE 'LAMENTING PROPHET'

C.J. Patrick Davis

For many with any sort of cursory biblical knowledge, the picture conjured of the prophet Jeremiah is one of deep remorse and anguish: of a man whose message fell on deaf ears and who was last seen quietly grieving the destruction of his beloved Jerusalem. For me, it was always Rembrandt van Rijn's unforgettable 'Jeremiah', in which the aged prophet sits in dejection and helpless resignation while his city burns in the background. A typical, religious response to the painting may be one written by Dr Alex Tang of the Johor Specialist Hospital at the Monash University School of Medicine in Malaysia. In his blog subtitled 'My Adventures with Christian Spirituality, Spiritual Formation and Transformation', he recounts his reaction to seeing Rembrandt's masterpiece in Amsterdam's Rijksmuseum:

> As I gaze on Jeremiah's face and hands, I felt the pain and disappointment of a man who served God but met with much opposition and ridicule. No one listened to him. Everyone did what seemed right in their own eyes. Jeremiah had talked and scolded and cajoled but it all fell on deaf ears. And because of this, he had to watch as his beloved country was sacked, Jerusalem burnt and the temple destroyed. He had failed as a prophet of the Lord to convince his people. Though the fault was not his, the guilt must have weighted heavily on his mind. The guilt and the pain of a prophet as revealed in this painting.[1]

This psychological connection between Jeremiah's lamenting activity and his own internal struggles is an interesting one, especially in light of some of the recent scholarship conducted in the topic of gender in the Hebrew Bible, and masculinity in particular. These are demonstrated most saliently in recent studies by David J.A. Clines (1995a; 1995b; 2002), Athalya Brenner, Fokkelien van Dijk-Hemmes (Brenner and van Dijk-Hemmes 1996; Brenner 1997), and Susan E. Haddox (2006). What these studies overwhelmingly show is—among a variety of other features—the aggressive and violent characteristics of masculinity in the ancient Near Eastern world that would appear in total contradistinction to Rembrandt's much more passive vision of Jeremiah.

---

1. Cf. also the critical assessment in Budick 1988.

Thus, the question presents itself: how is it that Jeremiah was perceived as the 'Lamenting Prophet' amid such a fiercely virile social climate as in ancient Israel? And how was this feature developed through—or rather in spite of— the engendered language in the book of Jeremiah?[2] These questions will form the substance of this paper, which will consist of three separate components. First, I shall explore briefly the characteristics and emergence of Jeremiah as the 'Lamenting Prophet' in Second Temple Judaism. It is in the Second Temple Jewish literature that images and perceptions of the lamenting Jeremiah appear to have taken shape, and this will help to provide some diachronic orientation to this study. Second, I shall study more closely the concept of ritual mourning in the Book of Jeremiah with relation to the composition's particularly aggressive language. Third, I shall consider the presentation of women in the Book of Jeremiah in contrast with the common ideals of ancient Near Eastern masculinity, and how this relates to the above motifs of lament in Jeremiah and elsewhere in Second Temple Jewish literature. In the final section of this paper, I shall offer some thoughts on the connection between Jeremiah and his reputation for lament; how these are largely informed by the feminized language of the Book of Lamentations, and how they are incompatible with the portrayal of prophet's masculinity in the Book of Jeremiah.

1. *Jeremiah the 'Lamenting Prophet'*

Already in the period prior to canonization, it is clear that Jeremiah was known for composing and/or singing laments. The prologue to LXX Lamentations reads: 'And so it was after Israel was taken into captivity, and Jerusalem was laid waste; Jeremiah sat weeping, and he performed this dirge over Jerusalem'. The passage reflects a tradition that dates to at least the early third century BCE, despite the notion that the ascription of Lamentations to Jeremiah is generally regarded as false (Kraus 1960: 13-15; Hillers 1972: xix-xxiii; Holladay 1989: 84). Jeremiah appears to have never composed any recorded laments, as none exists in any part of the book of Jeremiah;[3] nevertheless, his reputation for having done so formed the basis for attributing the Lamentations directly to him. Further justification for this accreditation may

---

2.   The question is anticipated by R.E.O. White, who complains that Jeremiah is 'scandalously…best known as "the weeping prophet". His very name is grossly distorted and misused as a derogatory epithet for complaining weakness, pessimism, and self pity: a "jeremiad"' (White 1992: 1).

3.   Some have—rightly or wrongly—identified a series of 'confessions' in Jeremiah 11–20 as 'laments', for example, Jer. 11.18–12.6; 15.10-21; 17.14-18; 18.18-23; 20.7-18; cf. Holm-Nielsen (1960): 310, 356. For an inventory of the .prominent poetic metaphors' in this section, cf. Moore (2007): 236-46. However, it should be noted that the designation of this material according to a single genre is far from certain.

be in the literary dependence of Lamentations 2 on portions of the book of Jeremiah (Driver 1956: 462; Löhr 1894). In particular, Lam. 2.8-9 preserves an expansion of Jer. 14.2, and Lam. 2.11 may be a variation of Jer. 8.21, 23. Lam. 2.14 is an indictment of false prophets that reads suspiciously like Jeremiah's own description of the prophets from Samaria in Jer. 23.13 who are similarly called 'unsatisfying' (פלהת; cf. חזו לך שוא ותפל, Lam. 2.14).[4] Even though the book of Lamentations was probably compiled from a variety of different dirges, their connection to the prophet Jeremiah became palpable enough to have included the whole composition as part of the corpus of Jeremianic literature in the much later LXX codices. This is not only observed in the superscription of the book, but was confirmed in the Syriac title for the book as the 'Lamentations of the Prophet Jeremiah' (*'wlyth d 'rmya nby*). The Aramaic translation for Lamentations has shortened the superscription but likewise attributed the text to Jeremiah, who is called 'prophet and high priest' (*Tg. Ket.* Lam. 1.1).

The tradition of Jeremiah's authorship of Lamentations was later demonstrated in its placement in LXX immediately following the Book of Jeremiah and Baruch, thus cementing Jeremiah's reputation as the 'Lamenting Prophet'. It was also attested in *b. B.Bat.* 15a, where it states that 'Jeremiah wrote the book which bears his name, the Book of Kings, and Lamentations'. The tradition was perpetuated in the Targumim, where not only Jeremiah's authorship is presumed, but in addition, he is noted for his involvement in ritual laments. In *Tg. Ket.* Lam. 1.18, the text reads as follows: 'The Lord is righteous, for I have transgressed against his Word. Hear now all peoples the lament which Jeremiah pronounced over Josiah' (Alexander 2008: 123). Tracing the origin for Jeremiah's specific reputation for lament is complicated. However, it appears to be fixed at the earliest stage in the early Persian period, and with the notion that Jeremiah conducted a lament (or laments) for Josiah. 2 Chron. 35.25 reads: 'Jeremiah also uttered a lament for Josiah (ויקונן ירמיהו על יאשיהו), and all the singing men and singing women have spoken of Josiah in their laments to this day. They made these a custom in Israel; they are recorded in the Laments (והנם כתובים על-הקינות)'.[5] The reason for the introduction of a tradition such as this was probably part of a broader programme of Temple reform and royal propaganda.[6]

4. Cf. also Jer. 2.8b, however, in this passage an alternative lexeme יעל is used to describe the prophets who 'went after things of no profit'.

5. Cf. Hillers 1972: xx-xxi.

6. Cf. Knoppers, who suggests that in the strong emphasis placed on the liturgical elements of the Temple cult—to which the tradition of Jeremiah's lament belongs—Chronicles is probably not inventing new traditions for music as part of Temple worship, but is rather reinforcing an element of the cult which has been predominantly ignored in the Pentateuch and Dtr.: '[Chr.'s] work provides an impeccable precedent for a certain

In Ben Sira 49.7 (c. 180 BCE) Jeremiah is lauded for his perseverance in the face of persecution, and this passage also contains an implicit allusion to his reputation for lament.[7] The second stich of 49.6 reads: 'They set fire to the chosen city of the sanctuary, and made desolate its streets'.[8] This is a mild echo of Lam. 1.4: 'the ways of Zion mourn; no one is coming to the festivals, all her gates have been desolated'.[9] Ben Sira appears most interested in the veracity of Jeremiah's prophecies, but also seems to have embraced the notion that the contents of the first dirge in Lamentations at least were prophetically uttered by Jeremiah.

More recently, Jeremiah's reputation for lament has been observed in a previously unknown text from Qumran, in which the prophet's exploits in the land of Egypt from Jeremiah 43–44 [LXX Jeremiah 50–51] and his long-distance relations with the Babylonian exiles are prominently featured. Six copies of the *Apocryphon of Jeremiah* C (4Q385a, 4Q387, 4Q387a, 4Q388a, 4Q389, 4Q390) have been identified, and the text generally has been described as a 'Jewish historical apocalypse' having been dated to the early- to mid-second century BCE (Dimant 2001: 99-100, 115-16). One of the largest fragments from the *Apocryphon* manuscripts preserves an exchange between the prophet Jeremiah and the Egyptian Jewish community in Tahpanes:

1. in Tahpanhes w[hich is in the land of Egypt ...]
2. And they said to him, 'Inquire [on our behalf of G]od[... But]
3. Jeremi[ah did not listen] to them, not inquiring of Go[d] for them, [nor lifting up]
4. a song of rejoicing and a prayer. Jeremiah lamented [... laments]
5. [ov]er Jerusalem. *vacat*
   (4Q385a 18 ii. 1-5)[10]

The pericope is based on Jer. 42.1-6 [LXX Jer. 49.1-6], but the phrase of interest occurs in line four where Jeremiah is pictured 'lamenting' over Jeru-salem (ויהי ירמיה מקנן). Lutz Doering has commented regarding this fragment

---

kind of worship at the Jerusalem Temple. The central role given to the Levitical singers during the reign of David justifies an integral liturgical role for their descendants in the author's own time' (Knoppers 2003: 621). Cf. also Klein 2006: 44-46.

7.   However, Ben Sira would most likely not have the same elevated view as Chr. of the liturgical priests. Gabriele Boccaccini has called him an "enthusiastic supporter" of the officiating, Zadokite priesthood (Boccaccini 2008: 29-34).

8.   Patrick W. Skehan and Alexander A. Di Lella suggest that the citation of this passage implicates Jeremiah as a member of the royal court, perhaps because of the kings and their failure to listen to divine instruction in v. 4 (Skehan and Di Lella 1987: 499-500).

9.   Cf. a similar allusion in 4Q179 1.i.10-11: הוֹי כל ארמונותיה שממו [ ] ובאי מועד [אין בם בם כל ערי]; it is mentioned by Christian Wolff, but without any reference to Ben Sira 49.6 (Wolff 1976: 5-6).

10.   Translation by Martin G. Abegg (Wise, Abegg and Cook 2005: 446).

that it represents perhaps the earliest explicit 'literary proof' for Jeremiah's lament over the city and the ruins of the Temple (Doering 2003: 64). What is particularly intriguing is that—as in 2 Chron. 35.25—the verb used to indicate Jeremiah's activity is the polel participle קין, which is most commonly used in instances of ritual mourning (Moberly 1997: 867).[11] What the pericope in the *Apocryphon* represents is not only a tradition of Jeremiah's lament for Jerusalem that dates to at least the early second century BCE, but also the early establishment of Jeremiah in the performance of lament in what is possibly a liturgical setting. While Jeremiah refuses to 'inquire' after God (דרוש),[12] neither offering any 'songs of rejoicing' (רנה; or 'piercing cries') nor any 'prayers' (ותפלה),[13] he responds to the people's request in the ritual performance of a dirge.

Scholars have attempted to trace Jeremiah's reputation for lament back to the Book of Jeremiah, and have arrived at a variety of solutions.[14] Nevertheless, these remain implicit deductions, and the long-standing tradition is still one that is as mysterious as it is taken for granted. It prompts the question: to what extent was Jeremiah actually the 'Lamenting Prophet', and how does he acquire this reputation? For the present study, the query needs to include how closely his reputation for lamenting is in keeping with Jeremiah's own masculinity. After all—particularly of the modern Western world—

---

11. Doering notes that the periphrastic construction with היה + the participle stresses the duration of Jeremiah's action of lament, perhaps in contrast to his refusal to perform intercession on behalf of the Egyptian Jewish residents in ll. 3-4 (Doering 2003: 64).

12. On the cultically oriented uses and functions of שדר in the Hebrew Bible see Denninger 1997: 996-97.

13. The appearance of רנה and תפלה together in the Hebrew Bible is found in 1 Kgs 8.28 (2 Chron. 6.19), as part of King Solomon's dedication address of the first Temple. Solomon entreats Yhwh that he might 'attend to your servant's prayer and his supplication...heeding the piercing cry and the prayer (אל הרנה ואל התפלה) that your servant utters (מתפלל) before you this day'. Also twice, in Jer. 7.16 and 11.14, Jeremiah is instructed by God to 'offer up' on behalf of the people 'neither piercing cries nor prayers' (ואל-תשׂא בעדם רנה ותפלה) because of their participation in the cult of the Queen of Heaven (Jer. 7.18), and then because of their acts of covenant breach (11.1-13). In Ps.17.1; 61.2; 88.3 the terms appear together as part of petitions before Yhwh, that he 'listen' (שׁמעה, Ps. 61.2), 'give ear' (האזינה, Ps. 17.1; הטה-אזנך, Ps. 88.3) and 'attend' (הקשׁיבה, Ps. 17.1; 61.2) to the Psalmist's entreaties. 4QApocrJer C represents the only instance in which these terms are accompanied by the petitionary use of שדר and the ritual performance of lament מקונן.

14. For example, Sara Japhet has noted that the tradition of Jeremiah's mourning for Josiah may be traced to his prophecy concerning Jehoahaz in Jer. 22.10 (Japhet 1993: 1043). In a more popular commentary, John M. Bracke has suggested connections between Jeremiah's 'reported' weeping and mourning for the immanent destruction of Jerusalem in such texts as Jer. 7.29 and 8.22–9.1 and his traditional association with Lamentations (Bracke 2000: 182).

'lament' is hardly an aspiring characteristic for those of us who are male. As one of my colleagues commented to me in jest, should one 'set the masculine character of Jeremiah in the context of his feminine side? *Wasn't he crying all of the time?*'[15] Was Jeremiah indeed 'crying all the time'?[16] If so, how did this impact his perceived masculinity? If not, how and why did later interpreters create this feature of Jeremiah's portrait?

2. *Mourning and Anguish in the Book of Jeremiah*

R.W.L. Moberly in his entry 'Lament' in *NIDOTTE* has drawn a distinction between two concepts of lament in the Hebrew Bible.

> On the one hand there is the usage of the specific term for lament, expressed in Heb. by the nom. קינה and the derived vb. קונן, which invariably in the Old Testament is related to contexts of death and disaster and accompanied by a range of various terms for grief and mourning... On the other hand, there is the phenomenon that has been labeled "lament" by modern scholars, that is, a certain type of prayer, always addressed to God and looking at least in part to the future. This is prominent in the Psalter and also present elsewhere in the Old Testament, especially Isaiah, Jeremiah, and Habakkuk (Moberly 1997: 866-67).[17]

It is this second presumed genre that has prompted some to label a series of 'confessions' in the Book of Jeremiah specifically as 'laments'.[18] On the confessions themselves, Moberly says that they reflect the prevailing image of a prophet whose ministry was characterized by little more than suffering, mockery and public abuse, and that his own personal ignobility was paradigmatic for the entire nation of Judah and its own preponderance of their unfortunate state in occupation and exile (Moberly 1997: 878). While these

---

15. Personal communication with Dorothy M. Peters, 28 July 2009.

16. For the purposes of this study I shall restrict my investigation only to those instances dealing with ritual lament, as this is from where the Second Temple Jewish perception of the 'Lamenting Prophet' appears to emanate. It should be noted that while there are numerous Hebrew Bible depictions of men weeping, particularly in 2 Samuel (e.g. David for Saul and Jonathan in 2 Sam. 1.17-27; Paltiel for Michal in 2 Sam. 3.15-16; David and the people for Abner in 2 Sam. 3.32-34; David for Absalom in 2 Sam. 18.33) this does not ever appear to be the sort of activity in which the prophet Jeremiah in the Book of Jeremiah is engaged. Jeremiah is never portrayed in the scriptural text in the activity of בכה like David in 1 Sam. 20.41; 2 Sam. 15.30; 18.33, nor does he perform קין (cf. 2 Sam.1.17). In the one instance where קין appears in Jer. 9.16, it is important to note that the dirge performance is handled by a professional class of lamenting women (see below).

17. Cf. also Saul Olyan, who distinguishes between ritual and 'petitionary' mourning (Olyan 2004: 62-64).

18. Cf. e.g. Jer. 11.18–12.6; 15.10-21; 17.14-18; 18.18-23; 20.7-18, and n. 7 above. For a detailed discussion of these texts as a unit, cf. McConville 1993: Chapter 3.

emotive sorts of prophetic outbursts and expressions of personal anguish are far more prevalent in the book of Jeremiah, there are some instances in the text featuring the first, liturgical practice of 'lament'. In particular, in Jer. 4.5-8 and 9.16-20.[19] The second of these is the only instance in the Book of Jeremiah in which the verb קין appears, and it is the same conjugation as that used in describing Jeremiah's participation in the lament for Josiah in 2 Chron. 35.25, and in 4Q385a 18 ii. 4-5.[20] Jer. 9.16-18 reads:

> Thus says the LORD of hosts: Consider, and call for the mourning women (מקוננות) to come; send for the skilled women to come; let them quickly raise a dirge over us, so that our eyes may run down with tears, and our eyelids flow with water. For a sound of wailing is heard from Zion: 'How we are ruined! We are utterly shamed, because we have left the land, because they have cast down our dwellings' (Jer. 9.17-19, NRSV).

In the following stich, Yhwh instructs women directly to 'receive the words of his mouth; to teach a lament to your daughters, and each woman a dirge to her friend'. The lamenters in this passage are explicitly female—a distinction that seems to have been blurred in the time of the Chronicler, who includes men and women 'singers' (2 Chron. 35.25) in the performance of Jeremiah's lament for Josiah.[21] The existence of professional lamenting 'guilds' and their participation in funeral processions appears to have included both men and women throughout the ancient Near East. However, in the earliest recorded Sumerian and Akkadian laments it is abundantly clear

---

19. Cf. also Jer. 7.29; 34.9; 49.3. In the book of Jeremiah, expressions of lament are employed in the use of the hiphil form for ילל (masc. = Jer. 4.8; 25.34; 47.2; 48.20, 31 [= 1cs with reference to Yhwh], 39; 51.8; fem. = 48.20 [but cf. Q = Mss Syr Tg Vg]; 49.3), ספד (masc. = Jer. 4.8; 16.4-6; 22.18; 25.33; 34.5; fem. = 49.3), and קין (fem = Jer. 9.16). Jeremiah 9.9 records an expression of lament in the first person (אשא בכי ונהי), which was amended in LXX and Syr to read as a second-person plural imperative, אוש (Carroll 1986: 241). William L. Holladay believes that the reading should be retained according to the principle of *lectio difficilior praeferenda est*: that it should be retained for its difficulty. Where the disagreement occurs is in the understanding of who the speaker is: whether it is Jeremiah (as John Bright (1965) or perhaps Yhwh (Holladay 1986: 303-305).

20. The verbal form of קין appears only in the polel stem, and in only eight instances in the Hebrew Bible. The first two are singular and attributed to David in his laments for Saul in 2 Sam. 1.17, and for Abner in 2 Sam. 3.33. Five of the remaining six are plural, occurring in the above passage and in Ezek. 27.32 and 32.16; three of these are feminine. It is noteworthy that in no place in the book of Jeremiah is Jeremiah actually portrayed specifically as leading the people in their laments as he is in Chronicles.

21. Van Dijk-Hemmes notes that in the Hebrew Bible the practice of lament was most likely primarily the property of women. While laments are generally ascribed to men, women are most frequently mentioned in the context of dirge performance, cf. 2 Sam. 1.24; Ezek. 32.16, and possibly Judg. 11.40 (Brenner and van Dijk-Hemmes 1996: 83-84, 86-90).

that women played a major—if not primary—role in the communal lamenting practice (Ferris 1992: 27-28, 74-75).[22] As will be illustrated in more detail in the following section, the employment of women—or perhaps the absence of men?—for this professional dirge may have deliberate implications that accord with Jeremiah's attitude towards women more generally.

At present, we shall concern ourselves with the other relatively clear depiction of a communal lament in Jer. 4.5-8, which is situated at the beginning of a series of poems in 4.5–6.30,[23] and reads as follows:

> Declare in Judah, and proclaim in Jerusalem, and say: Blow the trumpet through the land; shout aloud and say, 'Gather together, and let us go into the fortified cities!' Raise a standard toward Zion, flee for safety, do not delay, for I am bringing evil from the north, and a great destruction. A lion has gone up from its thicket, a destroyer of nations has set out; he has gone out from his place to make your land a waste; your cities will be ruins without inhabitant. Because of this put on sackcloth, lament and wail: 'The fierce anger of the Lord has not turned away from us' (NRSV).

In Holladay's commentary on Jeremiah, he notes that in Jer. 4.8 the call issued by the prophet to corporate lamentation is one that is characteristically prophetic, and is 'a genre that is found elaborately in Joel 1.5-14'—as well as in Micah 1.8 (Holladay 1986: 150, 153). What is noteworthy about this particular instance is the employment of military/tactical imperatives in vv. 5-6 (תקעו שופר, 'blow the trumpet!'; האספו, 'assemble together!'; שאו־נס, 'raise the standard!').[24] The use of violence and aggression appear to have been cardinal traits—or perhaps even 'virtues'—in the ancient Near East whereby men were rightly established as men (Chapman 2004: 1-13; Brenner and van Dijk-Hemmes 1996: 12; Haddox 2006: 181, 196-98). In his study of

---

22. Ferris notes that in some Inanna and Dumuzi texts, there is some confusion created in the frequent interchange of speakers and performers between various lamenting women and the *gala*-priesthood, which was likely composed of both men and women. Also there are appearances of the 'lamenting man', 'him of tears', the 'lord of lament', and a 'wailing man'. Cf. also Olyan, who notes that the predominant occupation of women in liturgical lament is probably constructed from the gendered ideal that women are 'cast as most suited to weep' (Olyan 2004: 49-51).

23. Carroll comments on the poetic material of the section from Jer. 4.5-6 that 'dividing the cycle into individual poems and editorial comments is difficult and a scrutiny of the commentaries will reveal a degree of disagreement about where units may begin or end (esp. in chs. 4–5)' (Carroll 1986: 160). I maintain here with Carroll a loose division between 4.5-18 and 19-22.

24. But cf. LXX Jeremiah 4.6, which otherwise reads 'Those who raise themselves up, flee towards Zion!' This is not necessarily an alternate rendition, as it does provide for the sense of the whole clause; for example, Jack R. Lundbom, who translates the whole of the first colon in v. 6 as a unit: 'Set up a flag, to Zion take refuge! Don't just stand there!' (Lundbom, 1999: 332, 336).

masculinity in the Hebrew prophets, Clines has observed that the element of violence or aggression, unsurprisingly, is a strong component of prophetic masculinity. In particular, this violence is expressed in the context of war and fighting, against women, and is especially pronounced in its expression of 'divine violence' whereby Yhwh is favourably depicted as a warrior and a killer (Clines 2002: 314-16). When applied to the above call to lament, the prophet's conscription in these verses then, should be read in accordance with his engendered characteristics of aggression: the prophet's militarized presence is implicitly emphasized even in his call for assembly and mourning.

Furthermore, one may detect in this call to lament an effort made by the prophet to feminize his audience. Ovidiu Creangă has written recently of the effect of 'spaces' in the construction of Joshua's masculinity as it appears in Joshua 1–12. Working from Don Seeman's study of gender and nationhood, and the application of symbolic, 'centrifugal' and 'centripetal' vectors in the Genesis 18 narrative, Creangă has observed that the conquest narratives similarly employ 'movements across space to construct masculinity (in opposition to femininity)' (Creangă 2007: 118). Joshua and his army are regularly depicted throughout as moving out from the encampment (centrifugal) and into the field of battle (e.g. Josh. 5.10; 9.6; 10.6, 15, 43; 11.4), while in the Ai pericope, for example, the sons of Israel 'fled before the men of Ai' (7.14) back towards the camp at Gilgal. Creangă claims this motion is symbolic and illustrative of the representation of masculinity through physical movement in the contest of war (Creangă 2007: 118).[25] The use of interior space in the conquest narratives 'suggest that interiority and restricted mobility "unmans" men and womanizes them' (Creangă 2007: 118). Such feminization also occurs in Jeremiah's call to lament in Jer. 4.5-8. In vv. 4 and 5 the recipients of this summons are told to 'go into' (בוא) the cities, and to 'flee (עוז) for safety' before the advancing enemy forces. In addition to the military imperatives issued by Jeremiah, there is also in this passage a depiction of interior space and 'centripetal' movement that emasculates his audience, as part of the instructions to raise a lament.

Clines has drawn particular attention to the 'verbal violence' that is displayed in the Hebrew prophets, and argues for this as an indicator of 'masculine strength' (Clines 2002: 314).[26] He makes his point by comparing the

25. Cf. also the description of the men 'sitting down in the camp' (Josh. 5.8), after having been circumcised, and thus in a position of vulnerability; also Josh. 9.6-15 where the sons of Israel were deceived while encamped at Gilgal.

26. Chapman also notes a consistent correspondence between ancient Near Eastern presentations of masculinity and military dominance (Chapman 2004: 22-33). In particular, she draws attention to 'feminization' as a discrediting characteristic for vanquished foes in Assyrian symbolism and texts (Chapman 2004: 48-58).

prophets globally on their use of aggressive language with expressions of comfort, encouragement and dispassionate popular expressions. While the parameters of his list have been slightly modified in this study,[27] it is significant to note that (in the book of Jeremiah expressions of destruction and breaking are quite prevalent) Of the twenty lemmas that are translated as 'destroy' or 'break' only four do not appear in Jeremiah (ערף, פצח, פרץ and חבל), and of the remaining sixteen, the Jeremianic occurrences are among the most frequent in the Prophets for twelve of them. It is not surprising that Jeremiah—the largest of the books of the Hebrew Prophets—is so well represented in these terms. Nevertheless, it also serves to show the extent to which the prophet Jeremiah is illustrative of the engendered characteristic of aggressive language.

Similarly, there is an underlying element of illicit terminology and themes in Jeremiah's poetry in particular that has been well recognized by scholars for some time now. Robert Carroll drew considerable attention to the graphic sexual images and 'abusive language directed at women who failed to conform' that are prevalent in a few of Jeremiah's prophecies (Carroll 1986: 34). What Carroll labeled as 'religious pornography' was applied to the prophecies of Hosea by Fokkelien van Dijk-Hemmes (van Dijk-Hemmes 1989), and later by Susan E. Haddox (Haddox 2006: 183-189). These were expanded upon in Athalya Brenner's discussion of 'pornoprophetics in Jeremiah and beyond (Brenner and van Dijk-Hemmes 1996: 177-93; Brenner 1997: Chapter 7); her first short essay concerns Jerusalem's personification as a female and the legitimate spouse of Yhwh in Jer. 2.23-25. In Brenner's assessment: '…female sexuality is objectified in this passage. By contradistinction male sexuality, represented by God's behaviour, is praiseworthy both socially and morally: it conforms to the acceptable conventions of human sexuality' (Brenner and van Dijk-Hemmes 1996: 182). Elsewhere in the selection of prophecies from Jeremiah 2–5, Yhwh—while playing the part of the loyal husband—is called 'father' (Jer. 3.4), 'master (3.14) and depicted as the longsuffering lord (3.6-13) who provides for his wife and children (Jer. 3.19; 5.7). The wronged master of his household is said to have led his bride in

---

27. Clines draws six comparisons in the Prophets between occurrences of words for *destroy* and *break* (318) and *Jerusalem* (248); between *die* and *death* (158) and *spirit* (155); between *fire* (154) and *holy, holiness*, and *sanctify* (146); between *anger, angry*, and *wrath* (193) and *voice* (174), *soul* (158), or *prophet* (156); between *evil* (66) and *good* (40); between *woes* (50) or *cursing* (31) and *blessing* (29). Speculating upon the raw, statistical data for the first comparison, there are potentially 20 different Hebrew roots for 'destroy' or 'break': חרם, כלה, אבד, דמה, הרס, חבל, and כלה, the *hifil* form of כרת, שדד, חתת, and שבר; also חתת, שחת and משחית, פרץ, פפר, רעע, שמד רשש, חתת, נפץ, נתץ, ערף, פצח, and שבר; also חתת, ברש, שבר, רעע, פרר, פרץ, פצח, ערף, נתץ, נפץ. A search of these words in the Prophets yields 377 separate instances for words commonly translated as 'destroy' or 'destruction', and 197 occurrences for words translated 'to break' or 'shatter'.

purity 'in a land not sown' (2.2), but is just and resolved in his indignation because of her adulterous crimes (2.29-32; 3.1; 5.9). In his ire he destroys her vine rows, and will 'strip away her branches' (5.10). Israel—the promiscuous wife—is designated the rightful property of Yhwh, and the 'first-fruits of his harvest' (Jer. 2.3). She is blatant and well travelled in her pursuit of lovers (2.33), and has 'played the whore' (3.1), all the while insisting on her innocence (2.35; 3.4) despite the clear evidence for her 'pollutions' (2.34; 3.1-2). The function of illicit imagery that degrades women is in part to maintain male dominance and the aggressive and violent character of what is unmistakably 'male' when it is applied to Yhwh. Thus, a more accurate portrayal of Jeremiah—in tone with that of other Hebrew prophets—includes an emphasis upon aggression and military activity, but also the objectification of women as part of this aggression.

But how is one to understand the language of aggression within the lament in Jer. 4.5-8, the feminization of Jeremiah's audience, and the otherwise common association (rightly or wrongly) of what appears to be considered more 'passive' activities with music and song? Such a connection was apparently made by the Chronicler, who recounted that Josiah's lament—composed and uttered by Jeremiah—became part of a standardized corpus of laments for the 'singing men and singing women', as noted above.[28] For the modern reader there is a likely tendency to think of lament in terms of song. In the present case, Jeremiah calls for public lament to be performed by the men in his audience, as indicated by the masculine plural imperative construction ספדו והילילו. This call is preceded by the military imperatives to 'blow the trumpet', 'gather ourselves together', and to 'raise the standard!' This rare example of a community lament in the book of Jeremiah is itself characterized by

28. Clines has argued that musical abilities in the Hebrew Bible are engendered attributes: while both men and women are portrayed as makers of music, it is more predominant that women sing, and men are depicted as players of stringed instruments (Clines 1995b: 227-28). This is loosely affirmed by van Dijk-Hemmes, as several of the more prominent instances of song recorded in the text feature women, such as the 'Song of Miriam' in Exod. 15.21 and the 'Song of Deborah' in Judg. 5.1 (Brenner and van Dijk-Hemmes 1996: 32-48). However, the designation of 'singing' as feminine does seem questionable, as noted by Creangă, who argues that the public singing of women reflected in the Hebrew Bible was probably an activity through which Israelite women asserted power in a patriarchal and masculine culture (Creangă 2007: 107-13). According to Creangă, '[g]iven that it is a common feature of ideal men to deliver public orations and poems (Jacob, Moses, Joshua and David all do so), for women to do so means to aspire to a position of power similar to that of men' (Creangă 2007: 112). Women may have exhibited considerable cultural influence in the performance of public song, and this is seen in the attempts of biblical authors to silence singing women—as in the book of Joshua—or in the reconstruction of women song leaders in the presence of leading men, such as with Miriam and Moses, and Deborah and Baruch.

'loud shouting' (קראו מלאו) and 'wailing' that seems to incorporate battle cries as opposed to what one might now consider singing. The lament in Jer. 4.5-6 is not akin to the funeral dirge depicted in 2 Chronicles, and more appropriately is issued by the prophet in part to feminize his audience, through the employment of military imperatives, and the forceful instructions to flee and hide. Given his gravitation towards violent language and in the employment of military imperatives, Jeremiah's presentation is thus in keeping with the ancient Near Eastern perspective of the ideal man. However, his employment of lament appears as an assault on the masculinity of his hearers; his instructions to 'enter' (or retreat) into the city and to flee and hide exhibit a sense of symbolic feminization through the centripetal movement inwards, and away from conflict. If so, then Rembrandt's dejected and self-effacing, singing poet quite typically envisaged in the modern mind is probably well off the mark.

3. *Jeremiah and Women*

Clines has drawn two preliminary conclusions regarding the prophets generally, and both are applicable to Jeremiah: '(1) this central metaphor for the prophetic role is inescapably gendered, and (2) no one notices' (Clines 2002: 312). The second is true in large part because of the first: in that, no one notices because Jeremiah's audience is always male. The above citation serves to illustrate what is challenging in engaging in 'masculinity' studies in the Hebrew Bible; as some theorists argue, there is really only one gender, 'female', which is to be distinguished from the universal norm of 'man' or 'mankind' (Butler 1990: 11).[29] Or, as Daniel Boyarin so vividly wrote: 'The world was divided into the screwers—all male—and the screwed—both male and female' (Boyarin 1995: 333). So it is that in studying Jeremiah's reputation from a gendered perspective, there is clearly evidence to distinguish what sets his character apart as distinctly masculine, such as those rare

---

29. Brenner rather considers that the only 'gender' is male; female is otherwise defined in the Hebrew Bible as a 'sex': 'A "female" is sexed rather than gendered: she is an "orifice"; orifices and holes require that they be filled. A "male" is gendered: he is the carrier of memory, the only one "to be remembered", thus a social agent. A female is there to be penetrated and to be receptive... In the course of culture's taming of nature, males—as their linguistic designation testifies—are the superior gender. In fact, they are the only gender: women are a sex, definable by a decisive physical characteristic' (Brenner 1997: 12). Brenner and van Dijk-Hemmes provide a helpful discussion on how to distinguish engendered texts according to their 'voice' as opposed to the traditional conception of authorship (Brenner and van Dijk-Hemmes 1996: 1-13). Despite their conviction that women composed biblical literature, they maintain that a text's 'voice' is 'the sum of speech acts assigned to a fictive person or he narrator within a text' (Brenner and van Dijk-Hemmes 1996: 7).

instances in which one can see his perception of women. We have already touched on Jeremiah's reputation for denigrating women through much of the illicit and graphic sexual imagery that is employed in the Book of Jeremiah. In what follows I shall focus on two instances in particular where Jeremiah is pictured interacting with women: in the aforementioned Jer. 9.16-20, and also in Jer. 44.15-23.

As already noted, the dirge in Jer. 9.16-20 is distinct in that in accordance with tradition this lament is performed by a group of professional lamenting women. The practice of lament was common for women within the ancient Near East, and this is reflected in various places in the Hebrew Bible: Ezek. 8.14 makes reference to the women who 'wept for Tammuz', a passage that has been linked to the prophet Jeremiah's criticism of the cult of the Queen of Heaven in Jer. 7.16-20 (Brenner and van Dijk-Hemmes 1996: 86-90). While the specific identity of this goddess is uncertain, she seems to be most reasonably associated with one of—or perhaps as a syncretistic adaptation of both—the Mesopotamian goddess Ishtar or the Canaanite goddess Ashtoreth (Schmitz 1999: 586-88). The connection to Ishtar in particular is appealing, given that women were customarily involved in the ritual performance of dirges as part of this popular religion (Brenner and van Dijk-Hemmes 1996: 87). Jeremiah more directly condemns the worship of the Queen of Heaven, which has been transplanted with the Jewish survivors of the destruction of Jerusalem to Egypt in Jer. 44.15-19:

> Then all the men who were aware that their wives had been making offerings to other gods, and all the women who stood by, a great assembly, all the people who lived in Pathros in the land of Egypt, answered Jeremiah: 'As for the word that you have spoken to us in the name of the LORD, we are not going to listen to you. Instead, we will do everything that we have vowed, make offerings to the Queen of Heaven and pour out libations to her, just as we and our ancestors, our kings and our officials, used to do in the towns of Judah and in the streets of Jerusalem. We used to have plenty of food, and prospered, and saw no misfortune. But from the time we stopped making offerings to the Queen of Heaven and pouring out libations to her, we have lacked everything and have perished by the sword and by famine'. And the women said, 'Indeed we will go on making offerings to the Queen of Heaven and pouring out libations to her; do you think that we made cakes for her, marked with her image, and poured out libations to her without our husbands' being involved?' (NRSV).

At first glance, the above passage does not appear related to the pericope from Jer. 9.16-20, in that it contains no lamenting activity, nor is it explicit that the two groups of women—the professional lamenters and the women of Pathros—are connected. Nevertheless, both passages are pertinent for this study in that they appear to be the only explicit points of contact that the prophet Jeremiah has directly with women. One should take note from Jer. 44.15-19 that while the worship practices envisaged appear to be familial, it is the women who are primarily involved and then censured in what follows for their patronage of the Queen of Heaven. Philip C. Schmitz has drawn attention to this and suggests that the cult perhaps provided some economic advantage for women, and was possibly reflective of the marginalized status of women in the 'Yhwh alone' movement that dominated the Deuteronomistic redaction of the Hebrew Bible (Schmitz 1999: 588). In the passage in Jeremiah 44, after he has issued Yhwh's judgment upon the Egyptian Jewish community in Tahpanes, it is the women who are singled out as those who 'had been making offerings to other gods' (v. 15). Their husbands are implicated, but it is clearly the women who have committed a great offense: 'Indeed we will go on making offerings to the Queen of Heaven and pouring out libations to her; do you think that we made cakes for her, marked with her image, and poured out libations to her without our husbands' being involved?' (v. 19, NRSV). Women are indicted and their husbands endure the blame for their actions of cultic infidelity (Carroll 1986: 735-36).[30] It is noteworthy, especially given the placement of this episode in the Book of Jeremiah,[31] that the pagan cult activity directed by women is offered as the 'last straw', so to speak, in Yhwh's long list of grievances. Given this disparaging view of women and their activities in this portion of the text, how then does this affect one's understanding of the presence of professional lamenting women in Jer. 9.17-19 above?

The appearance of the women in Jer. 9.17-19 has generated some interesting hypotheses over the past several decades. Elmer A. Leslie suggested that their employment was intended as a mockery of the women who lament the dead Baal (Leslie 1936: 212).[32] In his discussion of Jer. 9.17-19, Holladay has drawn attention to what may be an interesting parody on the covenant instructions of Deut. 11.19, and if this is the case, then the presence of women in Jeremiah 9 provides a twist. Deut. 11.18-19 reads: 'You shall put these words of mine in your heart and soul, and you shall bind them as a sign on your hand, and fix them as an emblem on your forehead. Teach them to your children (ולמדתם אתם את־בניכם), talking about them when you are at home and when you are away, when you lie down and when you rise' (NRSV). The NRSV translation is a little misleading in its much more inclusive rendering of what is clearly 'your sons' in v. 19. It is quite plausible that the

---

30. Cf. also Jer. 44.9 where the 'wicked women' from Judah's history are singled out as part of the reason for the downfall of the nation.

31 The LXX edition of the Book of Jeremiah ends with the abduction of the prophet to the land of Egypt, and with the condemnation of the women who worship the Queen of Heaven and their husbands (LXX Jer. 51.24-29). This is followed by a brief oracle delivered to the scribe Baruch (LXX 51.31-35) and an abbreviated account of the siege and fall of Jerusalem (LXX 52.1-33).

32. Cf. Ezek. 8.14 (Holladay 1986: 310).

opening lines of the lament in Jer. 9.19—a call to 'Listen, O women!' (שמענה נשים)—were intentionally reminiscent of the recurring Deuteronomic phrase to 'Listen, O Israel!' (שמע ישראל).[33] This is further reinforced by what follows, where the women are to 'teach' (ולמדנה) their 'daughters' (בנותיכם; cf. Deut. 11.19; also 6.7).[34] Holladay comments, 'How ironic that the masculine address is so frequently a summons to hear an appeal to repentance (e.g., 2.4), while the only feminine address is to help bury the covenant people; how horrible that those who are supporters of life are asked to deal with wholesale death!' (Holladay 1986: 314).[35]

If there is in the lament a parody on the status of the covenant community, then it is significant that the reversal of fortune from Deuteronomy is set in the words and actions of women as opposed to men, and delivered unto the peoples' daughters as opposed to their sons. This would be reminiscent of Clines's point regarding women in his study of masculinity in the Hebrew Prophets: that 'if in any text women are despised, or feared, or threatened, or blamed, or abused, or trivialized, or stereotyped, or marginalized, or humiliated, or ignored, it is *prima facie* evidence that it is a male text' (Clines 2002: 318). But even if there is no clear covenant reversal, nor any explicit mockery of the women who lament the dead Baal, it is likely that the appearance of women as the facilitators for the lament in Jer. 9.16-18 was no accident, and it may be that their employment is related to the same techniques used by Hebrew Bible editors to promote predominantly 'male' ideological and hegemonic interests. Saul Olyan argues, in discussing the social dimension of lament for this passage, that the 'centrality of humiliation' is a feature of this particular lament (Olyan 2004: 103), and this may also exhibit a poor reflection upon the presence women. Contrary to the omission of female singing from the conquest narratives in the Book of Joshua, which serves as masculinized propaganda (Creangă 2007: 109-13), the explicit appearance of women in Jer. 9.16-18 and 44.15-19 is a means to depict the shaming and death of the covenant community. On separate occasions, the skilled dirge-women announce its impending arrival, and the women of Pathros bear the blame for it. Such is certainly in keeping with the portrait constructed of Jeremiah thus far with all of its militarized aggressiveness and contempt for women left intact.

---

33. Deut. 5.1; 6.4; 9.1; 20.3; 27.9.

34. Only Holladay has commented on the occurrence of the masc. pl. pronominal suffix כם–, noting that it is 'curious' (Holladay 1986: 313-14). It may be that the presence of this masculine possessive is illustrative the gender distinction whereby there is a 'social bias for presenting males as active subjects/agents and females as receptive/objectified agents...' (Brenner 1987: 13).

35. Holladay remarks that this suggestion is owed to a former student of his, Rev. Ms Suzanne Burris.

4. *Shifting Perceptions: Softening the Edges of Jeremiah's Perceived Manhood*

Anything that might be said of the links that exist between the aggressive and androcentric prophet from the Book of Jeremiah and the emasculated figure from Rembrandt's 'Jeremiah' is far from definitive. Jeremiah was unabashedly masculine; the language and imagery attributed to him is typical of his era when men asserted their masculinity in terms of domination of women. His disdain for women—while not overt—was nevertheless pronounced through those rare instances of interaction with women, and formed the content of his explicit and graphic pronouncements of judgment. What then is to be made of the relationship between Jeremiah's Jeremiah and that of Rembrandt?

First, the 'Lamenting Prophet' is most likely a construction of the Book of Lamentations and not of Jeremiah. Van Dijk-Hemmes speaks of the character of Lamentations as particularly feminine (Brenner and van Dijk-Hemmes 1996: 85-86). Its imagery, the themes employed, and the content of the language reflect the nation in personified female terms. This is in keeping with frequent tendency in the Hebrew Prophets to speak of Israel, the אשה of Yhwh. She cites S.D. Goitein for suggesting that Lamentations contains 'reminiscences' of 'women's texts',[36] particularly where Jerusalem is featured and personified as a woman in chaps. 1, 2, and 4:

> She is addressed as if she were a mother or a virgin girl, or she speaks to herself. What is more, the atmosphere is feminine and women are spoken of a great deal—mothers with their babies, maidens, an abandoned woman and so forth. The environment is that of the inner city, not the field of battle (Goitein 1988: 26-27).[37]

Van Dijk-Hemmes shows how the dominant feature through these laments was the subject of Jerusalem as a menstruating woman. In Lamentations 1, she is pictured 'as one who is unclean' (v. 8) and whose 'uncleanness sticks to the hem of her garment' (v. 9). In vv. 11-16 the plundered city is then first compared to a widow, and then personified as a woman who has suffered mistreatment by her husband, who is in this pericope Yhwh (Brenner and van Dijk-Hemmes 1996: 85-86).[38] Van Dijk-Hemmes carries forward Goitein's

---

36. Cf. n. 29 above.

37. Cited by van Dijk-Hemmes (Brenner and van Dijk-Hemmes 1996: 85).

38. It is interesting to note that if some of the dirges in Lamentations indeed are products of an 'F voice'—as suggested by Goitein—then Yhwh's personification as the abusive husband makes better sense in the same context argued by Schmitz (cf. above). The women who participate in the cult of the Queen of Heaven are likely prompted to do so in large part because of their marginal status in Deuteronomic Yahwism. Does the poor (but non-explicit) depiction of the husband in this text reflect such a situation?

proposition that the content of Lamentations was produced in large part from
the repertoire of the same 'schools' of professional lamenting women as those
depicted in Jeremiah 9.17:

> [I]t is quite possible that Goitein is right in his assumption that "words like
> these were traditional on the lips of the professional lamenting 'wise women'"
> (Goitein 1988: 27); and that these words echo the amen of women whose
> individual situation was comparable to that of "Lady Jerusalem" (Brenner and
> van Dijk-Hemmes 1996: 86).

What took place then, in the history of the composition and the redaction
of the Book of Lamentations was that Jeremiah *assumed* those characteristics
already a part of the 'F-voice' when the collection was ascribed to him. We
have already seen that in those instances from the Book of Jeremiah where
Jeremiah is involved in ritual lament, the characterization of this activity is
hardly positive. In Jer. 4.5-8 the prophet's call to lament is issued in part in
an effort to feminize his audience. When he employed the professional dirge
women in Jer. 9.16-20, it was to commemorate the death of the covenant
community. It is then quite unlikely that any direct connection can be made
between the presentation of the prophet Jeremiah's lack of receptivity to the
activity of lament and his association with the Lamentations themselves,
particularly given the early entry of this literature into the religious language
and liturgical life of postexilic Judaism (Hillers 1972: xvii-xxiii).

Second—and this is a product of the previous point—if the prophet
Jeremiah had a 'feminine side' it was most likely not projected from his own
persona, but was rather a reflection—or more properly a *refraction*—of the
situation of the Jewish people. Jeremiah became associated with traditions of
lament and ritual mourning indirectly through his own personal expressions
of angst and anguish—as illustrated in the so-called 'confessions'—and the
personification of these feelings for a nation in exile (Moberly 1997: 878).
Timothy Polk speaks of the transformation from the centrality of the prophet's
message in the Book of Jeremiah to the prophet himself, as a paradigmatic
symbol of his message (Polk 1984: 125).[39] To that end, Jeremiah becomes a
figure upon which the future nation constructs its own cultic and political
hopes, as well as its own sense of remorse and martyrdom. The prophet who
was 'crying all the time' was really the exilic people who could not overcome

---

39. According to Timothy Polk (1984) this development is already prevalent in the
redaction of the Book of Jeremiah, whereby 'Jeremiah's life becomes his message'. Cf.
also Geoffrey H. Parke-Taylor, who has suggested that one purpose of the Jeremianic
Deuteronomists in preserving the prose traditions of Jeremiah was to create 'a reapplica-
tion and reinterpretation of Jeremiah's preaching (in Deuteronomistic language) to address
a post-Jeremianic situation' (Parke-Taylor 2000: 299).

the horrific memories of the destruction of Jerusalem and its intended, Deuteronomistically informed, outcome. It remains uncertain whether the construction of the 'Lamenting Prophet' was an attack on the masculinity of the prophet Jeremiah himself, or whether it was employed in part in an effort to humanize the hardened visage of his projection from the Book of Jeremiah. I am inclined to think that the latter is most likely; however, his association with lament also helped to draw the strongly feministic lamenting traditions into the mainstream of Jewish religious literature, which in the Second Temple period remained a man's enterprise.

Conclusion

The purpose of this paper has been to explore the relationship of the prophet Jeremiah to his reputation for lament through the perspective of his masculinity as it is presented in the Book of Jeremiah. I have briefly discussed the historical connection between Jeremiah and his characterization as the 'Lamenting Prophet' in Second Temple Jewish literature through examples in Chronicles, Lamentations, Ben Sira and in the recently discovered *Apocryphon of Jeremiah* C from the Qumran Scrolls. These texts show that such a connection was early and prevalent, and that Jeremiah's association with the activity of lament was a fairly positive one. I have also considered the engendered presentation of Jeremiah via the explicit examples of ritual lament that are present in the Book of Jeremiah, and have explored the treatment of women in Jeremiah with regard to how this reflects the male aggressive tendencies that are prevalent throughout the book. Furthermore, I have shown that in the Book of Jeremiah the occurrences of ritual lament are employed for the purpose of feminizing the prophet's audience, as well as to mark the end of the covenant community. While the specific roots of Jeremiah's reputation for lament remain obscure and speculative, this paper has shown that this aspect of the prophet's persona is most plausibly informed by the feminine imagery supplied from the Book of Lamentations, and is ascribed to Jeremiah through personification of the nation of Judah and its reflection on the destruction of Jerusalem. Rather contrary to how the ritual laments function in the Book of Jeremiah, the Lamentations retain a 'softer' and more ruminative voice that is in closer keeping with how Jeremiah the 'Lamenting Prophet' is otherwise imagined. Such an image is provided by virtue of the feminization of Israel in the Book of Lamentations as the abandoned and violated bride of Yhwh. Rembrandt's Jeremiah may faithfully represent the common (mis)conception that the prophet was one who was closely connected with his 'feminine side', in keeping with my colleague's belief that Jeremiah was 'crying all the time'. However, as this study has sought to show, this depiction is probably only true of Jeremiah's constructed persona only after it had been shaped by the painful memories of later Jewish writers, readers and performers of Scripture.

Bibliography

Alexander, Philip S.
 2008 *The Targum of Lamentations: Translated, with a Critical Introduction, Apparatus, and Notes* (Aramaic Bible, 17B; Collegeville, MN: Michael Glazier Book, Liturgical Press).
Boccaccini, Gabriele
 2008 'Where Does Ben Sira Belong? The Canon, Literary Genre, Intellectual Movement, and Social Group of a Zadokite Document', in G.G. Xeravits and J. Zsengellér (eds.), *Studies in the Book of Ben Sira: Papers of the Third International Conference on the Deutero-canonical Books, Shim'eon Centre, Pápa, Hungary, 18–20 May, 2006* (JSJSup,127; Leiden: Brill): 21-41.
Boyarin, Daniel
 1995 'Are There Any Jews in "The History of Sexuality"?', *JHistSex* 5: 333-55.
Bracke, John M.
 2000 *Jeremiah 30–52 and Lamentations* (Westminster Bible Companion; Louisville, KY: Westminster John Knox Press).
Brenner, Athalya
 1997 *The Intercourse of Knowledge: On Gendering Desire and 'Sexuality' in the Hebrew Bible* (BIS, 26; Leiden: Brill).
Brenner, Athalya, and Fokkelien van Dijk-Hemmes
 1996 *On Gendering Texts: Female and Male Voices in the Hebrew Bible* (BIS, 1; Leiden: Brill).
Bright, John
 1965 *Jeremiah: A New Translation with Introduction and Commentary* (AB, 21; Garden City, NY: Doubleday).
Budick, Sanford
 1988 'Rembrandt's Jeremiah', *Journal of the Warburg and Courtauld Institutes* 51: 260-64.
Butler, Judith
 1990 *Gender Trouble: Feminism and the Subversion of Identity* (New York: Routledge).
Carroll, Robert P.
 1986 *The Book of Jeremiah: A Commentary* (OTL; Philadelphia: Westminster Press).
Chapman, Cynthia R.
 2004 *Gendered Language of Warfare in the Israelite–Assyrian Encounter* (HSM, 62; Winona Lake, IN: Eisenbrauns).
Clines, David J.A.
 1995a *Interested Parties: The Ideology of Writers and Readers of the Hebrew Bible* (JSOTSup, 205; GCT, 1; Sheffield: Sheffield Academic Press).
 1995b "David the Man: The Construction of Masculinity in the Hebrew Bible," in Clines (1995a): 212-41.

2002   'He-Prophets: Masculinity as a Problem for the Hebrew Prophets and their Interpreters', in Alastair G. and Philip R. Davies (eds.), *Sense and Sensitivity: Essays on Reading the Bible in Memory of Robert Carroll* (JSOTSup, 348; Sheffield: Sheffield Academic Press, 2002): 311-30.

Creangă, Ovidiu
2007   'The Silenced Songs of Victory: Power, Gender and Memory in the Conquest Narrative of Joshua (Joshua 1–12)', in Deborah W. Rooke (ed.), *A Question of Sex? Gender and Difference in the Hebrew Bible and Beyond* (HBM, 1; Sheffield: Sheffield Phoenix Press): 106-23.

Denninger, David
1997   'שדר', in *NIDOTTE*, 1: 993-99.

van Dijk-Hemmes, Fokkelien
1989   'The Imagination of Power and the Power of Imagination: An Intertextual Analysis of Two Biblical Love Songs: The Song of Songs and Hosea 2', *JSOT* 44: 75-88.

Dimant, Devorah
2001   *Qumran Cave 4, Volume 21: Parabiblical Texts, Part 4: Pseudo-prophetic Texts* (DJD, 30; Oxford: Clarendon Press).

Doering, Lutz
2003   'Jeremia in Babylonien und Ägypten: Mündliche und schriftliche Toraparänese für Exil und Diaspora nach 4QApocryphon of Jeremiah C', in Wolfgang Kraus, Karl-Wilhelm Niebuhr and Lutz Doering (eds.), *Frühjudentum und Neues Testament im Horizont biblischer Theologie* (Tübingen: Mohr Siebeck): 50-79.

Driver, S.R.
1956   *An Introduction to the Old Testament* (6th edn; repr. New York: Meridian).

Ferris, Paul Wayne, Jr
1992   *The Genre of Communal Lament in the Bible and the Ancient Near East* (SBLDS, 127; Atlanta: Scholars Press).

Goitein, S.D.
1988   'Women as Creators of Biblical Genres', *Prooftexts* 8: 1-33.

Haddox, Susan E.
2006   '(E)Masculinity in Hosea's Political Rhetoric', in Brad E. Kelle and Megan Bishop Moore (eds.), *Israel's Prophets and Israel's Past: Essays on the Relationship of Prophetic Texts and Israelite History in Honor of John H. Hayes* (LHB/OTS, 446; New York, London: T. & T. Clark): 174-200.

Hillers, Delbert
1972   *Lamentations: Introduction, Translation, and Notes* (AB, 7A; Garden City, NY: Doubleday).

Holladay, William L.
1986   *Jeremiah 1: A Commentary on the Book of the Prophet Jeremiah, Chapters 1–25* (Hermeneia; Minneapolis: Fortress Press).

1989   *Jeremiah 2: A Commentary on the Book of the Prophet Jeremiah, Chapters 26–52* (Hermeneia; Minneapolis: Fortress Press).

Holm-Nielsen, Svend
1960   *Hodayot: Psalms from Qumran* (Leiden: Brill).

Japhet, Sara
1993   *I and II Chronicles: A Commentary* (OTL; Louisville, KY: Westminster John Knox Press).
Klein, Ralph W.
2006   *1 Chronicles: A Commentary* (Hermeneia; Minneapolis: Fortress Press).
Knoppers, Gary
2003   *1 Chronicles 1–9: A New Translation with Introduction and Commentary* (AB, 12A; New York: Doubleday).
Kraus, Hans-Joachim
1960   *Threni* (BKAT, 20; Neukirchen: Neukirchener Verlag).
Leslie, Elmer A.
1936   *Old Testament Religion in Light of its Canaanite Background* (New York: Abingdon).
Löhr, Max
1894   'Der Sprachgebrauch des Buches der Klagelieder', *ZAW* 14: 31-50.
Lundbom, Jack R.
1999   *Jeremiah 1–20: A New Translation with Commentary* (AB, 21A; New York: Doubleday).
McConville, J.G.
1993   *Judgment and Promise: An Interpretation of the Book of Jeremiah* (Winona Lake, IN: Eisenbrauns).
Moberly, R.W.L.
1997   'Lament', in *NIDOTTE*, 4: 866-84.
Moore, Michael S.
2007   'The Laments in Jeremiah and 1QH: Mapping the Metaphorical Trajectories', in John Goldingay (ed.), *Uprooting and Planting: Essays on Jeremiah for Leslie Allen* (LBH/OTS, 459; New York; London: T. & T. Clark): 228-52.
Olyan, Saul M.
2004   *Biblical Mourning: Ritual and Social Dimensions* (Oxford: Oxford University Press).
Parke-Taylor, Geoffrey H.
2000   *The Formation of the Book of Jeremiah: Doublets and Recurring Phrases* (SBLMS, 51; Atlanta: Society of Biblical Literature).
Polk, Timothy
1984   *The Prophetic Persona: Jeremiah and the Language of the Self* (JSOTSup, 32; Sheffield: JSOT Press).
Schmitz, Philip C.
1999   'Queen of Heaven', in *ABD*, 5: 586-88.
Skehan, Patrick W., and Alexander A. Di Lella
1987   *The Wisdom of Ben Sira: A New Translation with Notes, Introduction, and Commentary* (AB, 39; New York: Doubleday).
Tang, Alex
2006   'A Meditation on Rembrandt's Jeremiah'. Online: http.//draltang01.blogspot.com/2006/12/meditation-on-rembrandts-jeremiah.html.
White, R.E.O.
1992   *The Indomitable Prophet, A Biographical Commentary on Jeremiah: The Man, the Time, the Book, the Tasks* (Grand Rapids, MI: Eerdmans).

Wise, Michael O., Martin G. Abegg, Jr, and Edward M. Cook
     2005   *The Dead Sea Scrolls: A New English Translation* (2nd edn; New York: HarperCollins Publishers).
Wolff, Christian
     1976   *Jeremia im Frühjudentum und Urchristentum* (TUGAL, 118; Berlin: Akademie-Verlag).

Part IV

BIBLICAL MEN GENDERING BIBLE READERS TODAY

Negotiating Daniel's Masculinity: The Appropriation of Daniel's Dreams by Actual (Rather Than Ideal[1]) Readers

Andrew Todd

This paper is concerned with empirical research into the way in which Bible-study groups engage with the biblical text, and especially how gender informs, and is shaped in, that engagement. In other words, the paper focuses not on ideal readers of the text, but actual ones. At the heart of the paper is the examination of a particular group's gendered consideration of Daniel 7.

The paper draws on a wider study of three Bible study groups (Group 1, Group 2 and Group 3) located in rural churches in East Anglia (Todd 2009). That study considered how meaning and interpretation were achieved in the social interaction of these groups, and in the negotiation with the Bible that formed the focus of that interaction. This paper examines especially the gender dimensions of that interaction and negotiation. The original research was carried out through participation in meetings of the groups and recording, transcription and analysis of audio-recordings of proceedings. Close attention was paid both to the organization of conversation,[2] and to the linguistic resources that group members deployed in their engagement with biblical passages.[3] A particular interest, with parallels in the world of healthcare, was in the notion of 'voices' (Atkinson 1992; 1995; 1999; Mishler 1984; Sarangi 2004). This acted as a useful heuristic device, which elucidated 'the interaction of different interpretative approaches in the conversation of Bible-study groups; and how the different "voices" of Bible-study interrupt each other, or participate in dialogue, offering alternative contextualizations of the biblical

---

1.   The term 'ideal' is used here to denote the 'implied' reader envisaged by narrative criticism—the reader projected by the narrative itself, who responds in an ideal way both to the story and its characters, and to the way the story is narrated (Culpepper 1983: Chapters 1 and 7).

2.   For example, consideration was given to the role of group leaders and the extent to which they behaved like tutors leading a tutorial group (Mehan 1979).

3.   Thus attention was given to the way in which contemporary discourse, for example relating to inclusivity, provided a resource for discussion alongside more expected confessional approaches.

text and its interpretations' (Todd 2009: 14-15). A key concern of this paper is the way in which such interpretative 'voices' are employed and developed differently by women and men.

The paper will introduce the question of the groups' general attitude to gender, showing that two of the groups were alive to the question of 'gendered' texts. Worked examples will demonstrate a suspicion of particular authoritarian masculine readings, and a desire to uncover readings inclusive of women.

This will set the scene for a consideration of Group 1's approach to Daniel 7. Working from detailed consideration of the group's conversation about the biblical text, this main section of the paper will first show how the group established an inclusive approach to its interpretation. It will then offer a detailed analysis of the ways in which women and men in the group, taking advantage of the inclusivity, responded differently to Daniel's dreams. This analysis will then form the basis for a discussion of the multi-faceted part played by gender in this Bible-study discussion.

The Potential of Daniel 7

Before turning to that exploration, however, it would be helpful to consider what in theory Daniel 7 might offer to such a group, not least in relation to readings supportive of masculine identity. A clue to such a contribution lies in the treatment of dreams in the Hebrew Bible by Noegel (2001). In this chapter he establishes some clear parallels (as well as differences of emphasis) between dreams in Mesopotamia and in the Hebrew Bible, drawing on the earlier work of Oppenheim (1956). He identifies a number of dream passages in the latter text. These include dreams in which God spoke to, or about, key figures such as Abimelech (Gen. 20.3-7); Jacob (Gen. 28.10-16; 31.10-13); Joseph (Gen. 37.5-11); a soldier in the camp of Midian overheard by Gideon (Judg. 7.13-15); Samuel (1 Sam. 3.4-14); Solomon (1 Kgs 3.5-15; 1 Chron. 1.7-13); Daniel (Dan. 7). But they also include the dreams of others, interpreted by key figures: Joseph interpreting the dreams of Pharaoh (Gen. 40.1–41.36) and Daniel interpreting the dreams of Nebuchadnezzar (Dan. 2.1-45; 4). Noegel examines the dreams for their ideological and literary significance, concluding that they serve to legitimate key figures in Israel's history, frequently enhancing their character in contrast with that of non-Israelites (who also dream but have no understanding of the meaning of their dreams). This is so, even in the case of Abimelech, whose story enhances Abraham's standing as a prophet; and in the case of the soldier of Midian, whose dream reinforces Gideon's authority (Noegel 2001: 55-59).

Dreams would appear to contribute, therefore, to a number of narratives which set forth the character of some of Israel's heroic figures. God speaking to them in dreams; or speaking about them to others; or their ability to interpret dreams as indicators of God's purpose serve as key aspects of character development. In narrative terms, a number of questions arise. Do dreaming and/or interpreting dreams contribute to possibilities for identification with these characters? Do such possibilities extend beyond the ideal (or implied) reader of the text into the lives of actual readers? In the contemporary world, therefore, can these traits enhance the ability of Israel's heroes to stand as role models within and beyond communities of faith? The discussion that follows examines what happened in practice on one particular occasion, rooting one group's response to Daniel's dreams in a wider understanding of their approach to issues of gender in interpretation.

Attitudes to Gender in Bible-Study Groups

Turning, therefore, to consideration of the attitudes of particular Bible-study groups to gender, part of the background is supplied by Group 1 (Todd 2009: Chapter 5). In a first meeting with me they discussed how they interpreted the Bible (Todd 2009: 92-100; cf. Todd 2005: 223-29). It quickly became apparent that the group exercised both a critical, deconstructive hermeneutic of suspicion and a positive hermeneutic of inclusion. The former approach involved a critique of the authority of the text and of its received interpretations. This included an understanding that the text of the Bible was gendered.

> Further examination of this meeting made clear that the group's desired freedom of interpretation is from the views and agendas not only of commentators on the Bible, but also of churches, of different translations from the original language and of the writers of the texts themselves (particularly as, to quote [F1.2][4], 'quite a lot of [the Bible]'s written by men'). No stage of the composition, transmission or interpretation of the Bible is free from the hermeneutic of suspicion which handles authority claims with some caution (Todd 2005: 226).

The picture of suspicion directed towards men, as part of a critical negotiation with authoritative viewpoints, was reinforced by discussion at a number of other points in meetings with Group 1 of male figures in contemporary church life. These discussions, evoked by reading passages from the Bible, were critical of those who imposed their authority on church members. Group 1, therefore, exhibited an aversion to a construction of masculinity in which male authority is a taken-for-granted norm. As will be seen, this

---

4.   Throughout quotations from Groups 1, 2 and 3, and in the transcriptions of their conversations, members' names have been replaced by a code consisting of a letter and numbers, in order to safeguard their anonymity. F indicates a woman participant, M a man. The first number indicates the group, the second the participant. So F1.2 indicates the second woman participant to contribute to discussion in Group 1.

aversion is rooted both in negative personal experience of cultures in which such a construction operated (particularly conservative Christian traditions), and a sense that readings of the Bible in such settings were, and are, unproductive.

The positive hermeneutic had evolved, as the group's discussion revealed, as an alternative to being held to a particular authoritative interpretation. The key question members asked of a text was, 'What does that say to me/us now today?' This 'voice' was inclusive of different points of view and interpretation, which were held in tension with received understandings of what a passage meant (see e.g. Todd 2009: 97-98). The inclusion of members' different understandings of how a text spoke to them will be seen to be important in understanding their later engagement with Daniel. It created an arena in which different 'voices' could be articulated by men and women.

Group 2 (Todd 2009: Chapter 6) provides an example of another Bible-study group wrestling with issues of gender and inclusivity. In one meeting the group was discussing John 6, including the Johannine account of the feeding of the five thousand. A reference to that number being specifically men in Jn 6.10 provoked a question from one of the participants. In the following transcription of the conversation (adapted from Todd 2009: 143-44), F2.7 is the questioner; M2.1 is the group leader on that occasion; other participants are likewise indicated as F and a number if they are women, M and a number if they are men (as explained in footnote 4 above). As in other transcriptions in this paper, double brackets enclose an editorial comment; square brackets on adjacent lines indicate where two people's talk overlapped; longer pauses are noted with the length of the pause in seconds.[5]

Extract 1

```
1 F2.7.   then why just changing tack slightly
2 M2.1.   yeh
3 F2.7.   why was it just men that count
4 M2.1.   interesting point interesting point only men count er that's a general
5         phrase ((laughter)) er which
6 F2.1.   not to be taken literally ((more laughter))
7 M2.2.   you've [been playing too much golf
8 F2.1.          [had a hard married life
```

5. It should be noted that, while not portraying all the detail possible in transcription of conversation, the intention behind transcriptions in this paper is to give a good impression of the conversation as it happened. This is the reason, not only for showing overlapping speech, but also for including such features as repeated and incomplete words, and incomplete sentences. Further, punctuation has not been imposed on the conversation, although spellings follow the norms of written English, rather than the actual sounds of the words used ('was', rather than 'wus', for example). The extracts do therefore read in a rather different way to dialogue in a novel or a play.

9 M2.1.   been playing too much golf yes er I think we come back to the sort to
10   the patriarchal um spirit of the times really and do feel free to chip
11   in anybody
12 F2.7.   well it's just I thought other times men a- women listened as well to
13   [to Jesus
14 M2.1.   [well that's why there is a suggestion for instance amongst some
15   of the commentaries that that feeding the five thousand was only the
16   men were counted there could have been you know
17 F2.7.   [oh I see
18 M2.1.   [fifteen thousand there could have been women and children as well
19   well er there clearly was a little kid there
20 F2.7.   so they were counting the men
21 M2.1.   so it's
22 F2.7.   right
23 M2.1.   perhaps you know I don't know whether it was a bit like the Masai as
24   well I mean who actually counts these er is it one two three many
25   that's the way the Masai work isn't it when they're they're
26   counting so it I think we can take it to mean a large number and
27   there's also which we said in previous sessions that that this is erm
28   John and it it it's we believe that that this is written some time
29   afterwards you know several tens of years afterwards so it's sort of
30   reflecting back on er er on on the position ((3s pause)) interesting
31   ((change of tone)) yes but sadly we haven't been able to er keep
32   that to perpetuate that that only men count bit
33 F?.   mmmm[mm ((with rising and falling pitch))
34 F?.   [haah ((high pitch))
35 F2.4.   shall I just push him off his chair
36 F?.   yes ((general laughter))
37 M2.3.   I'm going to move away I think ((laughter))

The question asked by F2.7 works on at least two levels (see further Todd 2009: 144-45). There is an apparently straightforward question about what kind of counting the Gospel portrays. This is tackled in lines 9 to 22; and in the comparison with how the Masai count today in lines 23 to 27. This is a question about other cultures. And the discrimination that is being explored is excused as belonging to a more 'patriarchal' setting than is the case today. However, there is also an implicit question about who counts today in group members' own culture; and in particular whether women count today. This is indicated by the exchanges involving M2.1 in lines 4 to 11, and 31 to 37.

In these exchanges the laughter suggests strongly that M2.1 is behaving in an inappropriate way—that is not 'politically correct'. In lines 4 to 5 and 31 to 32 (note the ironic 'sadly'), M2.1 introduces an impropriety (Jefferson, Sacks and Schegloff 1987). He implies in a 'humorous' way that only men count today, provoking a significant reaction, especially in lines 33 to 37. As with Group 1, Group 2 is alive to gender questions as they read the Bible. Despite M2.1's somewhat clown-like interventions, the group as a whole are suspicious of texts and readings that exclude women. This is a parallel to Group 1's aversion to traditional gendered constructions of authority. Group 2 are reacting against constructions of humanity where maleness is the norm and women are invisible. In other meetings there were also traces of a positive inclusive reading. Texts which spoke of judgement were brought into dialogue with concepts of inclusion and fairness, for example.

Both groups exhibit, therefore, a sensitivity to issues of gender that can generate a critique of dominant ways of handling the text, particularly those that are noticeably male-oriented (including those in which women are invisible). Further, the groups have at least begun to explore inclusive readings, in which diverse interpretations may co-exist. This would appear to be an example of what Fowl describes (1998: Chapter 2)—'determinate' readings are deconstructed through the development of anti-determinant readings, which lay bare some of the assumptions of 'canonical' understandings.[6] However, the outcome of this deconstruction, in terms of gendered readings, is not yet apparent. Further discussion of groups reconstructive work is necessary, in order to examine what manner of arena is constructed by their suspicion of traditional masculine constructions and their desire to include different perspectives and experiences. If men and women speak differently in this space, do they generate readings which speak positively of, and to, women, or alternative masculine readings, or both? This question sets the scene for a closer examination of Group 1's engagement with the book of Daniel.

Reading the Book of Daniel

Group 1's reading of Daniel 7 provides a fascinating window onto contemporary practical hermeneutics—the interpretation of the Bible by members of a local church group (see Todd 2005: 229-33; 2009: 100-107). Mapping this interpretative conversation, however, is not only worth doing for its own sake; it is also preliminary to the consideration of a gendered conversation about Daniel's dreams which follows it.

The starting point for the discussion of Daniel 7 was an all too familiar stand-off between two well-worn interpretative stances. In response to a question from one of the group members, I responded to the invitation to talk about the historical origins of Daniel. I drew attention to the theory that the book might have come from two different historical contexts; chapters 1 to 6 from an historical period in which a figure such as Daniel might have existed; the remaining chapters from four centuries later.[7] One member of the group, F1.3, reacted strongly against such a notion. She advocated an approach

---

6. On 'canonical' readings, see further (Todd 2005).
7. See, for example, Davies (1985: Chapter 2)

which worked from the literal truth of the text—which should be taken 'at its face value'. And therefore the book was all by Daniel. As the group discussed this approach, not without some caution, key aspects of the lexicality of such a hermeneutical 'voice' were apparent.[8] As well as being taken at its 'face value', the text was 'the word of God' and 'God-inspired'.

However, the conversation did not remain in either of these hermeneutical tracks. Nor did the stand-off between a literal approach and a critical historical one determine the path of the discussion. For, while these two 'voices' successfully interrupted each other, by providing alternative, and competing, contextualizations of the text, no useful dialogue developed. The first bid to escape from this territory, and to discover a third 'voice', came from M1.1, and is to be seen in the following transcript (adapted from Todd 2005: 231; 2009: 102-103). As elsewhere, R in the transcript stands for researcher, i.e. the author.

Extract 2

```
1 M1.1.    but if it's the word of God does it have to be taken at face value can you
2          can you trust it as being the word of God ((2s pause))
3          [and not necessarily take it at face value
4 F1.3.    [can you what what trust it
(Lines 5 to 14 involved clarifying what M1.1 had said for F1.3's benefit).
15 M1.1.   which involves ((3s pause)) having the confidence to handle it in a
16         different way ((3s pause)) it was interesting to begin with you know we
17         were talking about well you F1.3 were talking in particular about a
18         particular way of handling Daniel in terms of I don't know well
19         yes in terms of relating to Christ and yet we seem to have gone round
20         and we've encouraged each other to look at it in a different way and we
21         said this is in fact a different sort of writing and as R has said it's
22         spread out in time and things so I think well I'm I'm just intrigued
23         it it gives us a sort of a if if we can still believe it and trust it
24         being the inspired word of God we don't have to take it at face
25         value but we still get something out of it which is *in*spired is that
```

While seeking a trajectory which escapes from the literalist approach that takes the text 'at face value', M1.1 continues to draw on other aspects of the lexicality of this kind of reading—'word of God', 'inspired'. In a way that is not uncharacteristic of the group's overall approach, he wishes to retain a confessional approach to the Bible, in which it is still very much 'scripture'; but he also wishes to have a greater freedom of interpretation than he perceives to be offered by the literalist hermeneutic. However, the response to this bid was a restatement of her position by F1.3, which indicated that, at this

---

8.   On lexical choice in relation to particular kinds of conversation, see, for example, Drew and Heritage (1992: 29-45).

stage of the conversation, taking the text at face value was non-negotiable. None of the conversation described thus far was antagonistic; but nor did it stimulate a creative engagement with Daniel 7. Further, the conversation took place at a 'meta-' level of interpretation. The discussion had much to do with how group members might interpret Daniel and much less to do with what interpretation they might draw.[9]

A second bid to change the direction of conversation, this time from M1.2, was rather more successful. It is revealed in the following transcript, adapted from (Todd 2005: 340; 2009: 103-104). Immediately preceding conversation had compared the understanding of their being three 'Isaiahs' responsible for the Book of Isaiah, with the possibility of their being more than one 'Daniel'.

Extract 3

1	M1.2.	…it doesn't *actually* matter
2	F1.3.	[no no
3	M1.2.	[because what- what I think I've- my responsibility is to look at this
4		passage and say what what does that say to me *now*
5	F1.3.	yes
6	M1.2.	and how can that help and encourage me and how can that perhaps can I
7		use that to encourage other people mm and I I I and knowing that it
8		that this is a word from God to to us and and and to each generation and
9		and and actually trying to say what is the word what is God's word what
10		is God saying and how how are we to respond to it that for me is the
11		important thing now no I can't have a conversation with my family at
12		home as I I tried last week on a couple of occasions and it almost ended
13		up in in in in in tears again because they just they can't they can't
14		come at anything that's not the literal absolute literal truth every verse is
15		is is is true and their faith is wonderful their their their commitment to
16		God is wonderful and and that's fine I've no problem with that I can't
17		I can't go there now mm and I don't particularly I didn't ask to not
18		go there I didn't ask to end up seeing things in a different way but it's
19		happened it's part of the journey
20	F1.3.	((breath)) nn but we will all see if we read the chapter because it's the
21		living word of God and we're all different and no two of us is the same
22		if we want to seek the truth as the prayer said at the beginning then
23		God will speak to us possibly in different ways varying ways to
24		each of us we haven't it's unity in diversity we haven't necessarily
25		got to all see it exactly the same have we
26	F1.2.	no
27	F1.3.	to to grasp the truth that's *in* it mm because otherwise you get into

---

9. Group 1 were unusual in the context of the overall research, in being able and willing to conduct this kind of conversation. Their ability to reflect on their own hermeneutic probably grew from their long experience of Bible-study, both as individuals and as a group.

28	terrible trouble if for example R said now you've all got to believe
29	A B C and D about this passage we'd all go home distressed because
30	we we mightn't heh we mightn't all feel the same

There are several facets of this discussion which ought to be noted (cf. Todd 2005: 340-41; Todd 2009: 104-105). First, M1.2 changes the temporal location of the conversation—from one which was concerned with the origins of the text in the past, to one concerned with its present significance for him (lines 3 and 4). Secondly, M1.2 establishes a clear distinction between this approach, which is about what God says in the present through the text, and a literal approach to the Bible. He does this in lines 6 to 11, presenting the new approach as offering the possibility of encouragement. And M1.2 reinforces the distinction between approaches through the use of personal narrative in lines 11 to 19, which constructs that distinction as a difference between him and the rest of his family. 'Home' in line 11 is Northern Ireland (as other conversations made clear). This also underlines the difference between his new-found inclusive approach and authoritarian readings, given that critical discussion of overly authoritarian interpretation of the Bible by Group 1 on other occasions included reference to specific (male) church leaders in Northern Ireland. This extract contributes to a picture of M1.2's hermeneutical journey being from a strict male-dominated Protestantism, to a more inclusive approach to Christianity which gives rise to a more encouraging way of reading the Bible.

This has the somewhat surprising effect of drawing out the response from F1.3 found in lines 20 to 30. Having previously defended a literal approach to the text in a forthright and adversarial manner, she now orientates strongly to the direction M1.2 offers the group. In her lexical choice—'living word of God'—there is both a shift of interpretative approach, and an acknowledgement of the temporal shift proposed by M1.2. The phrase offers some continuity with F1.3's previous use of 'word of God', but also stands in contrast to it. Both the emphasis on the present, and on God's word being alive, are further emphasized by her view that God will speak to group members in line 23. Most surprising, however, is her acceptance in lines 23 to 25 and 30 of plural interpretative positions—which offer 'unity in diversity'. Lines 20 to 30 offer something of a 'formulation' (Garfinkel and Sacks 1970; Heritage and Watson 1979) that summarizes key points of the hermeneutic into which the group's conversation now shifts. As I concluded elsewhere:

> The tenor of this part of the meeting recalled things espoused by group members in our first meeting. They had suggested that they held a variety of views about how to interpret the Bible; and worked with different views as facets of God. It was important for them that different views were valued; that there was freedom to doubt. This was in keeping with the weight they placed on fellowship and supporting each other (Todd 2009: 105).

What followed next is discussed below. Of particular interest will be group members' response to Daniel's dreams. To anticipate that discussion a little, it is worth noting here that the exchange between M1.2 and F1.3 did unlock the group conversation. Many more of the members participated than had been the case up to this point. And they did begin to talk about how the text spoke to them. This marked a shift from talk about how to interpret, to conversation about what their interpretation might be. It also marked the arrival of a genuine third 'voice', of particular significance to the women present, which offered a distinctive re-contextualization of the interpretation of Daniel 7.

Responding to Daniel's Dreams

Following the transition discussed above, I asked the group to expand on what it was that was in the text for them today. This prompted a number of different responses, including a very specific response on the question of dreams.

Extract 4

1 F1.5.	I was just thinking when you when you first asked your question and
2	before you put the second part on the question that one of the things it
3	*does* tell us is that God *does* speak to us in dreams and I believe that he
4	still does do that now and sometimes the dreams can be perhaps not quite
5	as obscure as Daniels's dream but just because they seem you know
6	strange and incomprehensible it doesn't mean that God's not trying to tell
7	us something [so that's one thought I had
8 M1.3.	[I have one problem with that
9 F1.5.	yes
10 M1.3.	I never remember anything I dream
11 F1.5.	no
12 M1.3.	it's a complete blank the following [morning
13 F1.3.	[you would if God wanted
14	[if he he spoke to you in a dream
15 F1.1.	[absolutely yes
16 F1.3.	you [would never forget it
17 M1.3.	[ah well that that tells me something
18 F1.3.	he's not said anything yet in a dream ((laughter))
19 M1.1.	just keep dreaming
20 F1.1.	I used to I I I used to say that
21 M1.3.	day dreaming
22 F1.1.	because um I never remember what I dream either um I believe that I
23	dream because people tell you that you do and never remember anything
24	and I went on a on a course that included something about you know
25	dreams and how might God speak through how might God and there were
26	these people who had you know they could remember they had these

27	wonderful technicolour dreams they could remember all of them all these
28	things God had said to them through the dreams and how I was kind of
29	sitting there thinking ummm ((rising pitch)) but then I think F1.3's
30	absolutely right there is one occasion when I had an extraordinarily vivid
31	dream and I remembered everything about it and a couple of days later
32	God explained it to me and it's but it's only happened once ((4s pause))
33 M1.3.	my time is yet to come then
34 F1.1.	possibly

A number of significant points emerge from this transcript, supported by evidence from subsequent conversation. First F1.5 displays a very positive orientation to the concept of God speaking to people in dreams. F1.3 in her comments to her husband (M1.3) also clearly believes that God speaks in dreams. This is supported by her contribution to discussion immediately following this extract. F1.1 has shared the experience of God speaking, but only once. And F1.2 subsequently shared that she dreamed and believed that God was speaking to her, but found it difficult to get at what God's message was. The women present, therefore, share openness to God speaking to them in dreams.

For the men present this idea is much more problematic. M1.3 owns to never remembering his dreams. He does not share the women's experience. A little later in the conversation than the extract he appealed to other men in the group as to whether they remembered their dreams. Some said that they did. But they did not go on to talk about God speaking to them in dreams. Indeed M1.2, while remembering at least some dreams, indicated that he 'wouldn't say [he'd] ever considered them particularly significant'.

The interaction between women and men in this extract is also interesting. What F1.3 says to her husband M1.3 in lines 13 to 18 is ambiguous. She appears to keep alive the possibility that God may speak to M1.3 at some point in the future, but is also quite clear that this has not happened yet (see line 18 and the laughter that follows). However, when M1.3 suggests later (in line 33) that his time 'is yet to come then', in relation to God speaking to him in dreams, F1.3's response of 'possibly' does not appear to hold out much hope for her spouse. One might be given to wonder how open the women of the group really are to men sharing their experience of dreaming.

The difference in the way women and men in Group 1 relate to dreams in the above extract is in keeping with research into dreams in the European context, for example at the Central Institute of Mental Health, Mannheim, Germany.[10] Thus, Schredl and Reinhard, of the Institute, in reviewing the literature on dream recall, and drawing on 175 independent studies (Schredl and Reinhard 2008), concluded that differences in recalling dreams between women and men, and the greater likelihood of women recalling their dreams,

10. http.//www.ziumfragen.de/schlaf0.html; http.//www.dreamresearch.de/.

could be explained by processes of gender-specific socialization. The argument is that because gender differences in dream recall only emerge at adolescence, rather than in childhood, and continue in adulthood, then those differences are the result of the different experiences of men and women as they grow up. Schredl and Reinhard (2008: 129) speculate that this could be because girls receive greater encouragement to talk about dreams, either in the family setting or amongst peers. This in turn might increase the focus on dreams and therefore recall of them.

Certainly in Group 1, unlike the men, the women members did appear to be used to talking about their dreams, and to have a ready language for discussing them. Further, their ambivalence to the men in the group seeking to enter the dream conversation does suggest a sense of previously-developed female solidarity around dream recall. The experience of F1.1 (lines 22-32) fits interestingly here. She appears to have received a late socialisation into this culture of discussing and interpreting dreams, which is her point of entry into the shared conversation of the women group members, and their shared identity. When the experience of the men and women of Group 1 is placed in this wider context of different gender experiences which have shaped adult engagement with dreams, albeit tentatively given the small size of the group, this locates it as a cultural phenomenon, rather than a biological one. However, this background of women being more likely, by virtue of their socialisation as they grew up, to be attuned to dreams, is but one factor in the interaction within Group 1. Further investigation is necessary to integrate this within a more complex picture of their social interaction.

Two questions are pertinent at this point. One has to do with the way in which the women are interpreting Daniel—what kind of gender hermeneutic is operating? The second has to do with exploring further why the men in the group are not engaging with the idea of dreams as messages from God. This question demands some more evidence from the discussion, which will be offered below.

Reading Inclusively

It would seem that the gender inclusive hermeneutic at work in this part of the meeting has created space for the women present to identify a connection between the text and their own experience of dreaming. An important part of that experience is God speaking to them directly, as well as via the text of the Bible. In this sense, a biblical narrative of God speaking to Daniel independently of any text, stimulates a discussion of similar revelation today. That this is a significant line of discussion is emphasized by a later section of the conversation involving principally F1.2.

> She followed…with an anecdote about a Gypsy she had known who could not
> read. This woman would visit the Christian Bookshop where F1.2 worked, and
> say that God had said something to her, and would ask F1.2 to find it in the
> Bible. The implication seemed to be that the Bible was only one channel by
> which people received God's word today… (Todd 2009: 106).

It is perhaps not insignificant that the women in the group value direct communication from God, albeit communication which is nonetheless consistent with their understanding of the Bible. This has the potential to stand against the dominant interpretations of the Bible by male leaders, which is part of members' past experience. It reinforces the women's independence as interpreters. The irony is that a biblical passage, which locates the authority of one of Israel's male hero figures in his ability to hear God speaking through dreams, appears to stand as a contribution to the authority of women members of the group, as those who can interpret the Bible in their own right; where that authority stands over against the authority of contemporary male leaders who have previously determined the interpretation of the Bible for the women.

But what kind of reading does the gender inclusive hermeneutic enable for the men in the group? There is already evidence that they do not enter this interpretative space in the same way as the women (they enter the conversation about dreams only with some difficulty). But do they develop their own 'voice'? Answers to these questions lie in an episode of conversation that took place after extracts 3 and 4 above.

The broad, gendered hermeneutical context for this conversation emerges by focusing first on M1.2, who spoke at some length during the conversation, in interaction with his wife, F1.2 (although she spoke more briefly). His interventions were triggered initially by remarks from his wife about the limits of her interest in the detail of the passage:

> [she] had made it clear that she was content to stick with the odd 'gold nugget'
> that she could extract from the 'big lump of stone' that was the passage. In her
> case this was the picture of God as 'ancient of days' (Daniel 7.13) (Todd
> 2009: 107).

M1.2 appeared not quite as ready to let go of his interpretative heritage as his wife was. He specifically recalled what he had been taught in conservative Christian settings about every verse offering 'meaning', and having a 'purpose'; and their being 'benefit' in trying to understand each verse. He referred to a particular group, the Brethren, and the detailed way in which they would explore a passage such as Daniel 7. The thrust of his questioning was whether such attention to detail was a distraction 'from the job we're here to do'[11]; or whether in avoiding the detail, and going for the 'nuggets', something important about the text was lost.

That this was a gendered conversation is shown by the way in which M1.1 joined M1.2 in considering whether the detail of Daniel 7 might offer something to readers today.

This was a conversation about the politics of Daniel and its contemporary application, which included consideration of the four kingdoms represented by the four beasts of Daniel's dream. Earlier in the meeting there had been limited discussion about the ancient kingdoms originally envisaged by the author, or redactor, of the text. At this later stage there was conversation about how other groups of readers today would expect to identify contemporary political situations that paralleled that of the ancient four kingdoms. M1.1 spoke, for example about those he had met in Transylvania interpreting Daniel 7 in relation to the history of Romania and Hungary, and the successive regimes which had controlled the lives of the Transylvanians[12].

The interaction between M1.2 and M1.1 dominated some seven minutes of conversation. In contrast, in shorter turns, F1.2 consistently maintained that such attention to detail was not worth the effort. And she was joined from time to time by other women in the group (F1.1 and F1.3) in holding to the idea that what was important was how God spoke to each person in the present. While all members of the group reacted against the authoritarian interpretations of their past experience, the men seemed to be more reluctant to move into new interpretative territory, more likely to hark back to what might be lost, than the women. While on other occasions (see extracts 2 and 3) both M1.1 and M1.2 shared the commitment to explore diverse understandings of how God spoke to group members through the text; here they appear to want to keep a foot in interpretation which involves more detailed exegesis of the text.

Men and Dreams

This leads us to the question of why the men of Group 1 engaged with Daniel's dreams in the way indicated above, rather than in the way the women did. Some light is thrown on this question by a section of conversation that took place towards the end of the meeting at which Group 1 and I discussed Daniel 7. This was prompted by me, asking participants to reflect on what important questions had been asked in the meeting, and on what aspects of the conversation had stood out for them. This led to the following exchanges.

---

11. The context indicates that this means getting on with being a Christian in practice.

12. M1.1 made mention of Ceauşescu, the Hungarian Empire, the German Empire and the Magyars (in that order).

Extract 5

1 F1.3.	I think F1.5's remark is very stands out for me that God speaks to us in
2	dreams and um God's the same yesterday today and tomorrow and
3	therefore he it can still be done
4 M1.1.	I think I would I would say yes to that as well but to me dreams are much
5	more than what happens in the night um I love day dreaming
6 F1.3.	I'm sorry
7 M1.1.	I love day dreaming because I can remember the dreams better
8 F1.3.	that's quite different
9 M1.1.	but I think God speaks to us that way as well
10 F1.2.	yes he [does
11 M1.1.	[seriously I really do
12 F1.2.	he does
13 M1.1.	I really do
14 F1.3.	right [I mean
15 M1.1.	[it's a calming down and a releasing and using both sides of the brain
16	and all that and I think I really do feel that the Lord speaks to me in that
17	way more than I think through the night ((2s pause))
18 M1.3.	You don't feel that it's a Walter Mitty side of your character ((3s pause))
19 M1.1.	might be ((3s pause)) but it works well it works for me and if it works for
20	me then its something which I give value to ((2s pause)) because I can't
21	remember what I've dreamt at night very often
22 M1.3.	no
23 M1.2.	I think
24 M1.3.	but even [sorry
25 M1.2.	[it's alright go on
26 M1.3.	day dreaming you've got all sorts of ideas floating through your head
27	largely they're inconclusive you don't look for hidden interpretations of
28	what you're dreaming about

In this extract, following F1.3's highlighting of the conversation about dreams initiated by F1.5, M1.1 bids for a distinctive approach to the question of God speaking in dreams. He connects this with his love of day dreaming. This provides a connection for him with the conversation, because he can remember day dreams better than the ones that happen at night (lines 4, 5 and 7). This suggestion, despite the inclusive atmosphere within the group, is not received without comment. F1.3 (line 8) doesn't think that the connection is there. And M1.3 (line 18) wonders about whether what M1.1 is talking about lies in the realm of Walter Mitty-type fantasy. Interestingly, M1.3 also questions this new direction on the basis of whether there is really any close parallel with Daniel 7—with day dreams 'you don't look for hidden interpretations of what you're dreaming about' (lines 26-28).

On the other hand, F1.2 supports M1.1 in lines 10 and 12. And M1.1 defends his viewpoint fairly vigorously both within this extract and in subsequent conversation. In particular, he justifies his suggestion in confessional language in line 16: 'I really do feel that the Lord speaks to me in that way…' He also justifies himself in terms which fit very well with an inclusive approach to individual interpretations, in lines 19-20: '…it works well for me and if it works well for me then it's something which I give value to.' M1.1 goes on, a few turns of conversation after the extract, to address M1.3's criticism. The response to M1.3 is that, for M1.1 day dreaming is not necessarily 'unstructured' and that for him it connects with particular schools of meditation, such as that represented by Anthony de Mello. And at the end of this section, M1.1 restates his bid to be included in the conversation about people dreaming today: 'But we all agree that God speaks to us through dreams whatever they are'.

In much the same way as he did in extract 2 above, M1.1 is exploring how far the group's interpretation can be stretched. There is a characteristic playfulness about his contribution, although this need not imply that his bid for day dreams to be included in the conversation is not important to him. In many ways his contribution is a half-way house between the women's conversation hitherto about dreams, and the men's different engagement. M1.1 talks about dreams, but they are day dreams; they involve 'both sides of the brain', implicitly bridging gender divides; they are 'releasing' but also not entirely without structure. There is an apparent openness to God speaking in dream-like ways, but M1.1 remains an active participant in that process.

However, while drawing out engagement with *his* viewpoint from other members of the group, what M1.1 does not accomplish is a shift in conversation whereby others (including men in the group) engage with the central issue. They do not follow him in exploring how their day dreams might provide an interpretative connection with Daniel 7. And, as already noted, M1.3 is somewhat sceptical that such a connection is possible. M1.1 is not successful, therefore, in establishing a bridgehead between the different perspectives on Daniel's dreams to be found amongst women and men in Group 1.

Gendered Readings of Daniel 7

The argument thus far allows us to draw together the threads of an interaction between members of Group 1 and Daniel 7, which shows a number of signs of being shaped by factors related to gender. A significant catalyst for the Group's approach is shared experience of authoritarian approaches to the interpretation of the Bible, dominated by male figures and characterised by paying considerable, even exhaustive, attention to the textual detail of a passage such as Daniel 7, matched by similar detail in the application of the passage to contemporary Christian life. All members of the group exhibit a desire to move on from such a hermeneutic, which they have found to be oppressive, un-productive and unhelpfully masculine.

As can be seen from extracts 2 and 3, together with the accompanying discussion, group members negotiate their way beyond the hermeneutic as they
read Daniel 7, as they did on other occasions in relation to other texts. The
way forward involves focusing on what the text says to members in the present, and on including and honouring diverse views and interpretations. This
may come at some personal cost, as it did in the case of M1.2 who experienced being divided from his family 'back home' by differences in biblical
interpretation. But it also generates a strong alignment to the principle of
inclusiveness, not least from F1.3 (extract 3, lines 20-30), who had previously advocated a strong literalist line on the interpretation of Daniel.

However, as the group engage with Daniel's dreams, the way in which
their new hermeneutic works out in practice is noticeably gendered. Women
in the group orientate strongly to the idea of God speaking to them in dreams.
There is some indication that this is accompanied by a wider sense that God
speaks to people directly, independently of biblical texts, although what is
received will be in keeping with the Bible. As already suggested, it would
seem reasonable to infer that God speaking directly to women, through
dreams and in other ways, acts as a powerful alternative to the voices of
powerful male church leaders.

The men in the group find it difficult to engage with the women's approach
to Daniel 7. Partly this has to do with their general difficulty with engaging
with dreams, to which they are markedly less attuned than the women. As
was discussed above, this may well be due to a contemporary culture in
which women are socialised, probably as part of their upbringing, in such a
way that they expect to recall and pay attention to their dreams, and men are
not. This manifests itself in group interaction in the women's greater famili-
arity with, and facility in, talk about dreams and their interpretation.

Sitting alongside that wider cultural picture is M1.1's bid to be included in
the conversation about dreams late on in the meeting, together with the social
interaction surrounding it (extract 5). The bid is constrained by elements not
present in the women's previous interaction: not least M1.1's remaining
attachment to structure and conscious involvement in the dreaming process.
He cannot quite enter into the world of God speaking through night dreams,
and his half-way house approach does not stimulate others to leave their
previous positions either.

Alongside the different reactions of women and men to God speaking in
dreams, the other significant factor is the evidence that the men's reaction to
the inherited authoritarian approach to biblical interpretation is different to
that of the women. Whereas the latter have embraced wholeheartedly the
concept of God speaking in different ways to each person in the present, the
former, on this occasion at least, show some reluctance to fully embrace this
principle (M1.2 in particular is concerned that, in moving on from detailed

exegesis of the text, characteristic of his past experience of conservative Christian groups, something of the importance in the biblical passage may be lost. With M1.1, he appears to be more tied to this aspect of the authoritarian framework and together they revisit inherited interpretations of Daniel's dreams which connect them with world politics. But then perhaps, as a man with some authority in the local church, M1.1 has more to lose, and less to gain in embracing inclusivism than the women, even in this enlightened group. Whether or not this is the case, the men's remaining attention to exegetical detail stands in contrast to the women's bolder (or riskier, depending on your perspective) leap into extra-textual sources of revelation.

The acceptance of plural readings in the groups allows both interpretations of Daniel 7 to co-exist: that God continues to speak to people in dreams; and that Daniel's dreams have significance for an understanding of how God acts in a political context. However, the gender differences explored above, while enabling women and men in Group 1 to explore those two different perspectives, also inhibit their bringing them together. The potential of Daniel 7 is only realised in two fragments, yet to be united in a hermeneutic whole.

Conclusion

Mapping the paths by which texts are interpreted by actual readers is a complex business. It involves holding an understanding of interpretative approaches voiced in settings such as the Bible-study groups discussed here, in tension with a picture of the social interaction within such groups. As can be seen from this brief study, a variety of factors are at work in the practical task of interpretation: personal and group histories; the interaction of confessional, critical and contemporary 'voices'; experience of conflict, or disagreement arising from the use of different interpretative approaches, together with the discovery of new 'voices' that offer a more creative alternative; and the influence of the wider cultural setting within which interpretation takes place. And in this particular instance of Bible-study gender plays a crucial, multi-layered role in the interpretative interaction; and in both enabling and limiting the creative possibilities that emerge from it.

Daniel 7 stimulated a differential response amongst the men and women of the Bible-study group. For the latter the text offered the opportunity of articulating the importance of their experience of God speaking also to them in dreams. For the former, this experiential engagement with the text was more problematic; and previous approaches to interpretation, which retained a closer connection with the detail of the text, remained attractive. In this practical exercise of interpretation both men and women were reacting against their shared past experience of more authoritarian, masculine hermeneutics, which they had found oppressive and not entirely rewarding. But the extent and nature of their reconstructive work is different. And for the reasons high-lighted above, the men in particular cannot quite make the leap to a new masculine interpretation in which contemporary dreams from God feed political engagement.

In this discussion, and the wider Bible-study interaction considered in this paper, gender appears with different degrees of clarity to both group members and those who observe them. Members of Group 1 (in common with Group 2) engage in explicit conversations about gender and biblical interpretation, about ways in which men may have dominated the field historically, and about the way in which this occludes the place and contribution of women. This in turn contributes to Group 1's skilful deconstruction of male leaders who have played a significant, but oppressive role in their faith histories; and to their espousal of an approach which is inclusive of interpretative diversity. Beyond this, Group 1 act out gendered responses to their explicit discussion of which they seem less aware. The women enter more boldly into the freedom from authority offered by the inclusive arena, and draw on their shared experience of dreams, and of God speaking directly to them, as new interpretative resources. The men are more constrained by structure, conscious thought and the detail of the text and appear to want to travel less far from the exegetical tradition than the women. The tension between these different responses is felt by members, reflected indirectly in their conversation, but not discussed explicitly by them.

And if this gendered interpretative interaction is clearer to the observer than to those who act it out, then there are other gender layers which even the observer can only see in part. Those aspects which appear in partial view include the suspected difference in approach to authority: that the women of Group 1 embrace the authority of direct revelation from God in dreams; while the men are less certain about letting go of traditional patterns of authority, guaranteed by their participation in the 'canonical' (and cognitive) interpretation of the Bible. This might in turn make the observer suspect that while the group has found freedom from one stereotypical pattern of gendered interaction (that of the dominant male leader), they partially reconstruct another such pattern. This latter is the stereotypical tension between the ordered, rational interpretation, authorized by historical continuity—seen as characteristically 'male'; and the intuitive, experiential, risk-taking (even dangerous) hermeneutic, rooted in personal authority, sometimes labelled 'female'. While this is rightly named as a stereotype, it nonetheless appears to identify one dimension of what was played out in group discussion of Daniel 7; but of which group members show little explicit awareness.

Bibliography

Atkinson, P.
1992   'The Ethnography of a Medical Setting: Reading, Writing and Rhetoric',
        QualHealthRes 2: 451-74.
1995   *Medical Talk and Medical Work: The Liturgy of the Clinic* (London/
        Thousand Oaks, CA/New Delhi: Sage).
1999   'Medical Discourse, Evidentiality and the Construction of Professional
        Responsibility', in S. Sarangi and C. Roberts (eds.), *Talk, Work and Insti-
        tutional Order: Discourse in Medical, Mediation and Management
        Settings* (Berlin/New York: Mouton de Gruyter): 75-107.
Culpepper, R.A.
1983   *Anatomy of the Fourth Gospel: A Study in Literary Design* (Philadelphia:
        Fortress Press).
Davies, P.R.
1985   *Daniel* (Sheffield: JSOT Press).
Drew, P., and J.C. Heritage
1992   *Talk at Work: Interaction in Institutional Settings* (Cambridge: Cambridge
        University Press).
Fowl, S.E.
1998   *Engaging Scripture: A Model of Theological Interpretation* (Malden,
        MA/Oxford: Blackwell).
Garfinkel, H., and H. Sacks
1970   'On Formal Structures of Practical Actions', in J.C. McKinney (ed.), *Theo-
        retical Sociology: Perspectives and Developments* (New York: Appleton–
        Century–Crofts): 339-66.
Heritage, J.C., and D.R. Watson
1979   'Formulations as Conversational Objects', in G. Psatha (ed.), *Everyday
        Language: Studies in Ethnomethodology* (New York: Irvington): 123-62.
Jefferson, G., H. Sacks and E. Schegloff
1987   'Notes on Laughter in the Pursuit of Intimacy', in G. Button and J.R.E.
        Lee (eds.), *Talk and Social Organisation* (Clevedon, Avon: Multilingual
        Matters): 152-205.
Mehan, H.
1979   *Learning Lessons: Social Organization in the Classroom* (Cambridge, MA/
        London: Harvard University Press).
Mishler, E.G.
1984   *The Discourse of Medicine: Dialectics of Medical Interviews* (Norwood,
        NJ: Ablex).
Noegel, S.
2001   'Dreams and Dream Interpreters in Mesopotamia and in the Hebrew Bible
        [Old Testament]', in K. Bulkeley (ed.), *Dreams: A Reader on the Reli-
        gious, Cultural and Psychological Dimensions of Dreaming* (New York/
        Basingstoke: Palgrave): 45-71.
Oppenheim, A.L.
1956   *The Interpretation of Dreams in the Ancient Near East: With a Translation
        of the Assyrian Dream Book* (TAPS, 46/3; Philadelphia: American Philoso-
        phical Society).

Sarangi, S.
    2004   'Towards a Communicative Mentality in Medical and Healthcare Practice',
                Communication and Medicine 1: 1-11.
Schredl, M., and I. Reinhard
    2008   'Gender Differences in Dream Recall: A Meta-analysis', *JSR* 17: 125-31.
Todd, A.J.
    2005   'Repertoires or Nodes? Constructing Meanings in Bible-Study Groups',
                JApL 2: 219-38.
    2009   *The Talk, Dynamics and Theological Practice of Bible-Study Groups: A
                Qualitative Empirical Investigation* (PhD dissertation, Cardiff University).

Part V

R EFLECTIONS

FINAL REFLECTIONS ON BIBLICAL MASCULINITY

David J.A. Clines

This volume, probably the first of its kind in being focussed on the construction and representation of masculinity in the Hebrew Bible, is demonstration enough that the study of masculinity in this sphere has come of age. It still has a long way to go to match the range and depth of feminist biblical criticism, but it has not been starting from scratch: it has been able to model itself on the progress of feminist criticism of the Bible.

This volume develops some important methodological frameworks. In the first paper Susan Haddox introduces the simple but important distinction between hegemonic and subordinate masculinities. The hegemonic construction of masculinity in a society is likely to be a single one, a recognized norm, a dominant factor in the power structures of the society; the subordinate masculinities will be many, more commonly attested than the hegemonic, and inevitably in conflict with them.

Looking at the depiction of the patriarchs in Genesis, Haddox arrives at the somewhat surprising conclusion that not one of them (Abraham, Isaac, Jacob) represents hegemonic masculinity; indeed, it is often their rivals (Ishmael, Esau) who do. The case seems undeniable. How then to explain the less than hegemonic-style masculinity of Israel's revered male ancestors? Here the proposed answer is less certain, that there is a theological reason. Haddox infers that according to Genesis 'God favors the less masculine' (p. 15). I am not so sure that we can move so readily from the observation that the favoured leaders are the less masculine to the claim that they are favoured *because* they are less masculine, that they 'model a proper relationship with God' (p. 15). Still less am I convinced that their less hegemonic masculinity reflects the comparatively subordinate position of Israel vis-à-vis other nations, and offers Israel strategies for survival in the world of conflicting powers. Nevertheless, Haddox has rightly raised an interesting question, to which others will have to attempt an answer of their own. The narratives would certainly be much less attractive if their heroes were uniformly exemplars of hegemonic masculinity, and one wonders if this aspect of the patriarchal narratives, that makes them such imperfect men, is much more than an ancient self-deprecating Jewish joke. And there still remains the headache whether we have done rightly in so defining hegemonic masculinity as to exclude the masculinities that are actually best attested in reality.

Roland Boer, who is always so sure-footed in the realms of theory, further refines the concept of hegemony, noting how in the social sphere it is 'inherently uncertain and shaky' and 'continually undermined from within and without' (p. 21). Chronicles is for him an example of the undermining of Israelite gender politics, in this case by the Levites, a sub-class secondary to the priests. Unreconciled to their subordinate status, they find a fulfilling outlet for their energies and ambition in the invention and maintenance of the minutiae of religious observance. This religious observance, we must note, takes place within an entirely male sphere, at the centre of which stands the 'phallic' temple—a figure for the books of Chronicles themselves (p. 24). This 'priapic' temple, with its tower 120 cubits high (as against the mere 30 in Kings) is 'the image par excellence of the overwhelming if desperate effort to assert a male-only world' (p. 25).

Yet there are strains of a subordinate masculinity in this Levite arrangement, the 'campy machismo' (p. 28) of 'foppish dandies' (p. 29) fixated on matters of interior design, household furnishings and musical performance. Chronicles 'consistently undermines the masculine hegemony it so desperately seeks to establish' (p. 30). I do wonder, however, whether this very interesting polarity rests upon a prior decision that 'interior design', for example, is definitionally non-masculine. Did any ancient Israelite think of Levites as defective males or camp or representative of an subordinate masculinity because they were into music and incense? From what materials was the concept of Israelite masculinity constructed that Chronicles is subverting?, I ask myself. I am equally puzzled to know whether all tall structures, like church steeples and spires, lamp-posts, skyscrapers and perhaps also trees, are also phallic, and what benefit would come to me from detecting such a proliferation of symbolic phalluses everywhere I go.

Brian DiPalma moves in the same area as the foregoing papers in proposing that the Pharaoh of Exodus 1–4 is depicted as 'a failed man' (p. 36). He is right that Pharaoh fails to act wisely even when making wisdom his explicit goal (in 1.10), that he fails to act independently of women by making his success hang upon the obedience of the midwives (1.15), and that he fails to exemplify masculinity as a persuasive speaker, a killer, and a womanless man (1.22–2.10). The Pharaoh is being depicted as less than a real man in his failure to achieve traditional expectations of masculinity.

However, in the narratives about Moses these traits of masculinity are by no means uncritically endorsed: while he is depicted as a killer, killing is shown to be an ineffective means of resolving conflict; being detached from women is not desirable, but actually dangerous for Moses; in functioning as a persuasive speaker, who can win an argument with God, he asserts his masculinity, but at the same time he negates the value of rhetoric by claiming that he is not 'a man of words'. These chapters therefore both reinscribe and undermine normative masculinity. Nevertheless, the worry lingers in the mind that the contrast between normative and non-normative masculinity may be in need of a rethink.

Mark George takes a different tack with Deuteronomy, offering some fresh analytic categories for masculinity. In Deuteronomy, he argues, key elements are the male body, a man's place in society, how time is categorized, the spaces and place a man passes through, and a man's religion. Taking as his starting point the fact that Deuteronomy is addressed to the Israelite male, he is able to relate everything said in Deuteronomy to the Israelite conception of masculinity. So, for example, food is brought within the sphere of masculinity. The organization of time is a regimen for men, space is classified in according with male norms, and in general the myriad of classificatory systems endemic to Deuteronomy are tokens of Israelite masculinity. This is a valuable challenge to how we profile masculinity in the Hebrew Bible, but I do wonder whether the classificatory drive of Deuteronomy is not an end in itself and only incidentally related to masculinity. But I will then ask myself, Can anything be related to masculinity 'only incidentally'?

Ovidiu Creangă sets himself the task of analysing the masculinity of Joshua in the Conquest Narrative of Joshua 1–12, distinguishing when necessary between the representations of masculinity in the pre-Deuteronomistic and in the Deuteronomistic strata. In general, in the earlier (pre-exilic) stratum Joshua is a warrior figure, in the later (exilic or postexilic) a religious leader in the mould of Moses. The two portraits are not necessarily at odds: the warrior Joshua commands and the Joshua who is a spokesman for Moses reasons, but they are both exemplars of efficacious speech (p. 94). Interestingly, Creangă does not label the latter portrait an example of subordinate masculinity, but regards both as representative of hegemonic masculinity (marginalized men, like the Gibeonites, however, are to be encountered in the narratives). He is intrigued by the absence of any reference to a wife or children of Joshua, which he is tempted to think 'cast[s] a shadow of doubt over the heterosexuality of the military-autocratic figure of Joshua' (p. 93), noting especially the possible homoerotic undertones in the nocturnal meeting of Joshua with the Captain of Yhwh's Hosts in 5.13-15. It might suggest that Israelite masculinity could accommodate sexuality outside heteronormativity.

On the theoretical front, Creangă introduces into the discussion a further refinement of the distinction between hegemonic and subordinate masculinities. Following Connell, he also identifies 'complicit masculinity' and 'marginalized masculinity' (p. 86), both of which can be observed in the Joshua narratives.

In their paper on the narrative of Naaman, Cheryl Strimple and Ovidiu Creangă introduce a significant new dimension into the discussion of masculinity by focussing on 'disability' as a means of reinforcing a version of normative Israelite masculinity. Disability in itself does not necessarily cast a man outside hegemony (p. 112): Naaman is a 'mighty warrior' as well as suffering from a virulent skin disease (2 Kgs 5.1). The narrative exhibits a subtle play between the differing male statuses of the two protagonists, Elisha and Naaman.

Maria Haralambakis takes up the figure of Job in the *Testament of Job*, identifying his roles as father, husband, a wealthy king, a wrestler in combat and a benefactor of the poor. Central in this portrait is the idea of Job as a man in charge—even on the dung heap, which does not represent a loss of his masculinity, but serves as an arena in which he wins his victories (p. 140). This paper helpfully introduces new material into the discussion of Israelite masculinity.

Sandra Jacobs advances the novel claim that the Priestly representation of masculinity bases itself on perceptions of fertility and virility; masculinity is above all the capacity to procreate (I had thought it was strength and violence, but I was not focussing on the Priestly writing). For the midrashic sages, ideal masculinity is defined quite differently, as the chosen object of divine desire, realized in the form of the circumcised male. It would be interesting to explore this further in relation to other strands of Hebrew Bible thought.

Ela Lazarewicz-Wyrzykowska turns to the Samson tales, bringing to the surface the concern of the narratives for honour. Such honour is constantly in danger, and the Samson narratives depict how his honour is first challenged and temporarily reasserted, then lost, and then finally regained (p. 184). The theme of masculinity at risk runs through the paper, and is an important reminder of how masculinity is constantly under negotiation.

Jeremiah's masculinity is the topic of Patrick Davis's paper. The question is raised whether his lamentations, so commonly regarded as characteristic of him, were perceived as threatening to his masculinity, since lament was typically a female activity. Davis notes by contrast the singularly aggressive language of Jeremiah and his 'disdain for women' (p. 204), arguing that the prophet's call to lamentation was at least sometimes an attempt to feminize his audience. The familiar image of the weeping prophet seems to have been transferred from the speaker of the Book of Lamentations to the prophet Jeremiah. The prophet of the Book of Jeremiah is a traditional male, who makes no concessions to any 'female side'.

The final paper, by Andrew Todd, takes an unusual but rewarding empirical turn in shifting the focus from texts to readers, and considering how masculinity influences the way the Bible is read by modern readers. Especially notable in the discussion groups he monitored were the differences between male and female readers of the Bible over authority in interpretation and the values of biblical teaching. He concludes that, although a traditional pattern of male dominance in interpretation may have been given up in the circles he studied, a parallel pattern has to some extent taken its place, 'the tension between the ordered, rational interpretation, authorized by historical continuity—seen as characteristically "male", and the intuitive, experiential, risk-taking (even dangerous) hermeneutic, rooted in personal authority, sometimes labelled "female"' (p. 230).

So much for the contents of this volume. A word finally about its omissions.

(1.) The theoretical basis of masculinity studies has yet to be broadened. It is not surprising, and even forgivable, that even if masculinity studies in the Hebrew Bible has come of age, it still lacks theoretical refinement. Until the range and scope and weight of expressions of masculinity in the Hebrew Bible are recognized and nailed down there is not a lot for theory to get its hands on. We need a hundred such studies as those in the present volume before we can begin to think we have an adequate supply of data to theorize. Of course, without any theory at all, we will hardly know what to call evidences of masculinity, and theory must inevitably develop along with the identification of data.

(2.) Especially by comparison with the beginnings of feminist biblical criticism, masculinity studies in the Hebrew Bible seem strangely lacking in passion. One gains no impression from the articles in this volume that masculinity studies is a *movement*, to which people have a commitment. Perhaps it is not. Perhaps there is no agenda in masculinity studies, other than intellectual curiosity.

If indeed that is so, I am disappointed. I regard the ubiquity of masculine thought and language in the Hebrew Bible as a problem, or rather an outrage. I regard its casting of the whole of the Hebrew Bible's contents, its poetry and its narratives, its ideas and its religious opinions, in the forms and dress of the masculine as a crime.

I want to urge that there is an injustice, damaging to women and men alike, in the Hebrew Bible's assumption of the normativity of masculinity. The people who should be noticing it, writing about it, and protesting against it, are biblical scholars. No one else in such a good position to speak with understanding and discernment about the situation. Our first task, as it was with the feminist movement, is consciousness raising. Our second task as I see it, is apology; we are doing a lot in our professional lives to keep the biblical books alive, and it is our duty as academics to distance ourselves from unlovely aspects of what we teach and research, and not to give the impression that because we are experts on these texts we subscribe to them warts and all. Our third task is to constantly refine what it is about masculinity that is objectionable. Masculinity is not a vice, and it is no part of a proper study of the subject to smear all expressions of masculinity with the wrongs and excesses of some of its manifestations.

I want to urge, in short, that it should not be possible to remain 'objective' about the issue of masculinity in the Hebrew Bible. It is a political matter, and a refusal to speak out about it is a dereliction of our moral duty. I want to urge a masculinity movement, not, as with feminism's project to assert the rights of women and to redress inequality, but to assess, critique and row back from the kinds of unthinking masculinity that are spread all over the Hebrew Bible.

3. Most conspicuous by its absence in this volume is the elephant in the room, the quintessence of masculinity, Yahweh. In one figure, the Hebrew deity incorporates the masculinity of Hebrew culture: he is strong (supremely so), a killer (from the Flood onwards), womanless (consort-free, and approachable only by holy men), beautiful ('glorious'), and persuasive (forever speechifying). If we once begin to seriously unpick the masculinity of Yahweh, we might well wonder what will remain. Yet this is a fundamental task for the history of religion, theology, Jewish self-identity, Christian worship, and everyday popular religious belief and practice. What language exists that can be used about Yahweh that is non-masculine, or at least not offensively masculine?

To repair the omissions of this volume will take a generation at least. Not every Hebrew Bible scholar in sympathy with the work of this volume is represented in its pages, no doubt, but it is noticeable how both the authors here and those they cite do not generally come from among the most senior and established scholars of the biblical guild. We shall have to wait and see what the landscape looks like when that is what they have become.

FINAL REFLECTIONS ON BIBLICAL MASCULINITY

Stephen D. Moore

How odd that this fine collection should have been so long arriving. The first study, after all, of biblical masculinity (if we may use the monolithic singular for the moment) appeared in 1994, and was not done in a corner.[1] On the contrary, *God's Phallus* (Eilberg-Schwartz 1994) was a major monograph. 'David the Man', the first of David J.A. Clines's many essays on biblical masculinity appeared the following year (Clines 1995). In certain neighboring fields, meanwhile, most conspicuously literary studies, frenetic publication was already in full swing on every imaginable facet and variant of masculinity—or masculini*ties*, as we soon learned to say: hegemonic masculinities, subordinate masculinities, marginal masculinities, imperial masculinities, subaltern masculinities, deessentialized masculinities, queer masculinities, female masculinities…. 'Masculinity' had achieved the dubious status of a critical fetish and *mana* word, and by the end of the 1990s masculinity studies would be seen as one of the four most significant critical trends of the decade, alongside cultural studies, postcolonial studies and queer studies.

Why Masculinity Studies Has, and Has Not, Succeeded

So why has masculinity studies not taken off in Hebrew Bible studies? Certainly it is not due to any shortage of men in or around the texts of the Hebrew Bible—texts filled mainly with men, probably written exclusively by men and for men, and until relatively recently studied almost exclusively by men. What Roland Boer has to say of 1 and 2 Chronicles in *The Queer Bible Commentary* could equally be said of most of the other writings of the Hebrew Bible: 'Chronicles reminds me a little of East Sydney: men as far as the eye can see. Men in couples, men in night-clubs and bars, men firmly muscled and flabby, moustached and clean-shaven…' (2006: 251). And so many of these Hebrew Bible men are *real* men, what is more—violent men, promiscuous

---

1. Nor was it a *creatio ex nihilo*. As Björn Krondorfer observes, '[a]n early interest in men and religion by religious studies scholars is already discernible in the 1980s, though it took about ten more years before these scholars began to identify themselves—albeit often tentatively and loosely—as belonging to a group working on common themes' (2009: xiv).

men, men who spit and swear. No queerly celibate Jesus to puzzle over (or so it might appear at first glance anyway), a multiply anomalous male who, although he did throw his weight around in the temple on one occasion, even employing an improvised whip according to one account (John 2.15; cf. Matt. 21.12; Mark 11:15-16; Luke 19.45), is better known for the more severe whipping, and worse, that he himself later had to endure. No army of male Jesus-emulators either, led by a queerly celibate Paul, who can't even boast of wielding a whip but only of the whippings he has received (2 Cor. 11.23-25; cf. Acts 16:22-23).

Celebrations of hypermasculine aggression, however, have not been a notable feature of biblical masculinity studies, which has tended, whether explicitly or implicitly, to be allied with feminist studies. The present collection is no exception. Any misguided reader eagerly ransacking this volume with the words 'Men', 'Masculinity' and 'Bible' in its title for reaffirmations of 'biblical manhood'[2] would be sorely disappointed. Everywhere she, or more likely he, would encounter studies of biblical masculinity that are allied with feminism, inflected by feminism, informed by feminism—or are themselves feminist studies outright—and as such are not affirmations, reclamations, or celebrations of traditional models of masculinity. Masculinity studies in biblical studies exists in a symbiotic relationship with feminist studies (which is not, however, to say an unproblematic relationship, more on which below). And feminist studies has, for several decades now, been an established, substantial and influential presence in biblical studies. Once again, then: why has masculinity studies not taken off in Hebrew Bible studies—or in New Testament studies, for that matter, which, if the number of books with a central focus on masculinity be taken as an crude index of success, has no more to show than Hebrew Bible studies, namely, one monograph (Conway 2008) and one edited collection (Moore and Anderson 2003)?

The answer, it seems to me, has to do with the disciplinary specificity of feminist biblical studies, which is markedly different from the disciplinary specificity of, say, feminist literary studies. Around the same time that feminism was beginning to establish roots in biblical studies, following field-constituting monographs by biblical feminist foremothers such as Phyllis Trible (1978; 1984) and Elisabeth Schüssler Fiorenza (1983), feminism in literary studies, already established if embattled, was beginning to change at a rapid pace due to the dissemination of deconstruction and other forms of poststructuralistm in the discipline, on the one hand, and increased disciplinary attunement to such issues as class, race/ethnicity, colonialism and imperialism, on the other hand. All of these elements combine, for instance,

2. A curious search quickly turned up more than a dozen books with that phrase in their titles (representative of the academic end of this evangelical spectrum is Piper and Grudem 2006), and even a Biblical Manhood series.

in two immensely influential articles from 1985, Gayatri Chakravorty Spivak's 'Can the Subaltern Speak?' (1985a) and her 'Three Women's Texts and a Critique of Imperialism' (1985b).

But 1985 also saw the appearance of Eve Kosofsky Sedgwick's *Between Men*, a book that, in retrospect, would be seen as signaling and catalyzing the expansion of 'second-wave' feminist studies into 'third-wave' gender studies. Implicit in Sedgwick's innovative version of feminist studies was not only what would eventually come to be termed 'masculinity studies',[3] but even what would eventually come to be termed 'queer theory', since her book was also a bravura exercise in queer criticism.[4] "I started work on the book at a moment when feminist scholarship seemed like a single project," Sedgwick recalls in her preface to the book's second edition (1992: vii). By the end of the 1980s, however, feminist literary studies had become what it has been ever since: an exceedingly diffuse, highly heterogenous, thoroughly theorized set of loosely related projects—poststructuralized to the nth degree, for the most part, and acutely attuned not so much to the unity of sisterhood in struggle as to the differences (class, racial, ethnic, national, sexual...) that complicate the notion of sisterhood itself.

Discontent with these developments came to highly visible expression as early as 1991 in Tania Modleski's *Feminism without Women: Culture and Criticism in a 'Postfeminist' Age*. What Modleski targeted especially, however, in the multifaceted field of third-wave gender studies, was the turn toward masculinity in the critical study of gender, coupled with the rise of 'male feminism' among academic men. This, above all, was the tide against which Modleski stood (and her voice and the others raised with hers did not, of course, succeed in turning it back). But it is a tide that, for better or worse, has yet to roll over biblical studies. In short, masculinity studies became a thriving enterprise in literary studies because of certain fundamental changes in feminist literary studies—or, more precisely, because of a fundamental shift in the general perception of what the critical study of gender should entail.[5] And masculinity studies has not caught on in biblical studies, I would

---

3. The term 'masculinity studies' did not come into common use until the late 1990s. It was not available to me when I was writing *God's Gym* (1996), but I seized on it gratefully in *God's Beauty Parlor* (2001) to describe a major facet of my project. The earlier term 'men's studies' was a squirm-inducing one for many of us with analytic interests in masculinity, as it seemed to shade over too easily into the anti-feminist backlash in extra-academic US culture evident in such prominent 1990s phenomena as the Promise Keepers and the mythopoetic men's movement.

4. For detailed discussion of the significance of Sedgwick's study, see Reeser 2010: 55-71.

5. Further on the relationship of masculinity studies and feminist studies, see Gardiner 2002; Murphy 2004; Edwards 2006: 22-38; Moore 2003: esp. 1-4.

argue, because those changes or that shift have not occurred, except at the fringes of the discipline.

'[W]hat's in these new developments *for feminism* and for women?" is the central question that animates Modleski's manifesto (1991: 5, her emphasis). None of the contributors to the present volume engage this question thoroughly, but several provide passing or oblique answers to it. The topic of 'women in the *Testament of Job*' has attracted much scholarly attention in recent years, notes Maria Haralambakis (130 in this volume), while the topic of men *as* men has not. 'Women are immediately visible as women (as "other")', she continues, 'but men remain invisible as men, because they are perceived as the norm, as the general human being' (130). To continue to treat masculinity as invisible, however, is to continue to reify its power, while the goal of Haralambakis's analysis of masculinity in her essay, as she explains, is precisely the opposite. A similar aim is articulated differently by Brian Charles DiPalma. He insists that his 'intentional focus on men and masculinity' in Exodus 1–4 is not designed 'to subvert the important work of feminist scholars' that has focused on 'the women in these chapters' (36 in this volume), and he goes on to explain that he will explore the construction of masculinity in the text only to demonstrate how it eventually deconstructs itself (37). Ela Lazarewicz-Wyrzykowska, while not explicating the relationship of her study to feminist scholarship, similarly claims that 'using the lens of masculinity reveals Samson's gender instability' (185 in this volume). Ovidiu Creangă is more explicit: 'In contrast to a homogenous picture of masculinity sometimes assumed by feminist studies, mapping Joshua's masculinity in the Conquest Narrative (Josh. 1-12) is a challenge' (Creangă in this volume: 83). This homogenized masculinity would be 'hegemonic' masculinity (to appeal to a term that recurs throughout the volume and is the object of frequent definition). Creangă later asserts that

> [w]hat needs further investigation—and this is just one area where feminist and masculinity scholars can join hands—are the ways in which a logocentric phallus discriminates against those without a symbolic or biological phallus (emasculated men and women, respectively), as well as against those who wish to be recognized as fully-fledged men through practices and attributes outside the current hegemonic trend. (Creangă: 88)

Relatedly, Cheryl Strimple and Creangă propose that 'more reflection is needed on how disabled men in the Bible perform masculinity, that is to say, how they negotiate between or contest established norms of masculinity' (112 in this volume). Roland Boer, for his part, engages in a thorough queering of the seemingly hegemonic masculinity everywhere in evidence in Chronicles. On the one hand, 'Women are few and far between in [Chronicles]' (21 in this volume). On the other hand, Chronicles presents us with 'a resistant masculinity...that makes mockery of the phallic rigidity of the temple' (28).

Put a little differently, 'Chronicles consistently undermines the masculine hegemony it so desperately seeks to establish' (30).

These and other such statements within the present collection amount to at least partial answers to the question of what masculinity studies might have to offer feminism and women—even if the license to obsess explicitly and constantly about masculinity that masculinity studies provides will continue to make some feminists wary or dismissive of it. Introducing their masculinity studies anthology, Rachel Adams and David Savran articulate the risk inherent to the field: 'Unlike many of the fields that are its models and precursors, masculinity studies analyzes a dominant and oppressive class that has, arguably, always been the primary focus of scholarly attention' (2002: 7). But if this is the risk of masculinity studies, it is also its rationale. Ultimately it may be more accurate to conceive of masculinity studies as more like Marxist studies than, say, African American studies or lesbian and gay studies. As it happens, Boer reframes masculinity studies along such lines in the present volume (see esp. 21-23), reminding us of the largely forgotten Marxist origins of the term 'hegemonic' and attempting to retool the stock masculinity studies concept of 'hegemonic masculinities' in light of that suppressed knowledge.

A Grammar of Biblical Masculinity

How is the topic of masculinity in the Hebrew Bible best approached? In the context of broader ancient Near Eastern concepts of masculinity, is the answer our biblical-scholarly programming predisposes us to venture. The problem, however, is that there does not yet appear to be a monograph or essay collection on ancient Near Eastern ideologies of masculinity per se. For the most part, contributors to the present volume make do with certain stretches of Cynthia R. Chapman's *The Gendered Language of Warfare in the Israelite–Assyrian Encounter* (2004), coupled with Harry A. Hoffner's now hoary 'Symbols for Masculinity and Femininity: Their Use in Ancient Near Eastern Sympathetic Magic Rituals' (1966). More often than not, it would seem, the best evidence for the ancient Near Eastern concepts of masculinity informing the Hebrew Bible is the Hebrew Bible itself. The mainly inductive methodology employed in the study of masculinity in the Hebrew Bible contrasts with the mainly deductive methodology employed in the study of masculinity in the New Testament and other early Christian literature. For the latter fields, the volume of relevant comparative literature available is enormous. Best of all, we don't have to sift it ourselves for the concepts, codes and conventions of masculinity that inform it. That labor has been underway for decades in the field of classics, much of it originally impelled by the second and third volumes of Michel Foucault's *History of Sexuality* (1985; 1986), which, while produced outside the field proper, prompted much reaction, refinement and extension within the field, including other catalytic volumes by such classicists as John Winkler (1990) and David Halperin (1990). All of this industry eventually yielded encyclopedic handbooks of ancient Mediterranean masculinity, such as Craig A. Williams's *Roman Homosexuality: Ideologies of Masculinity in Classical Antiquity* (1999), or of the ancient Mediterranean sex/gender system generally, such as Marilyn B. Skinner's *Sexuality in Greek and Roman Culture* (2005), handbooks that the student of early Christian masculinities can now lazily consult and use to parse out the gendered performances of Jesus, Paul and other early Christian or proto-Christian males. This is an oversimplification, of course, but not a huge one. This deductive way of proceeding essentially informs every essay in *New Testament Masculinities* (Moore and Anderson 2003)—with the telling exception of its one Hebrew Bible contributor (see Clines 2003)—as well as Colleen M. Conway's *Behold the Man: Jesus and Greco-Roman Masculinity* (2008).

Is there anything in the copious body of sex/gender work in classics for the study of masculinity and sexuality in the Hebrew Bible? In effect, Saul M. Olyan has addressed this question in his '"And with a male you shall not lie the lying down of a woman": On the Meaning and Significance of Leviticus 18:22 and 20:13' (1997), an article oddly missing from all the bibliographies in the present collection. Ultimately Olyan contends that a different logic informs the Levitical proscriptions of male–male sexual congress than anything found in classical Greek or Latin sources (1997: 413-14). In the process, however, he discovers that there are certain notable similarities between these sources and the corpus of ancient Near Eastern legislation known as the Middle Assyrian Laws on the topic of properly masculine sexual behavior (403-406). The further question his article prompts us to ask is whether there might not be other important continuities between ancient Near Eastern and classical ideologies of masculinity, the Hebrew Bible being fully included in the ancient Near Eastern sources, so that the classical sources might occasionally illuminate the Hebrew Bible on the topic of masculinity across the gulf that has traditionally separated them. This is a question to keep in mind as we turn to ponder the hulk of biblical masculinity that the contributors to the present volume have exhumed.

This collective effort of exhumation may be loosely characterized as a 'structuralist' endeavor, even though structuralism is nowhere explicitly invoked in the volume. The signature gesture of structuralism, it may be recalled, was an insistent movement from the particular to the general, from individual instance to underlying law. Literary structuralists, for instance, attempted to elaborate general narrative 'grammars' that would isolate and explicate the rules, codes and conventions that enabled and determined the production of individual narratives. Might we then speak of a 'grammar' of biblical masculinity? What are the rules, codes and conventions that enable and determine the production, the construction, the performance of biblical masculinity or masculinities?[6] Much in the way of a general grammar of this sort emerges from this volume.

Many of the contributors venture generalizations on ancient Israelite masculinity, which occasionally shade over into generalizations on ancient Near Eastern masculinity. Simplification vies with complication in certain of these formulations. 'It could be that I have let myself become locked into a grid of my own devising', muses Clines, 'or it could be that the image of masculinity in the biblical literature is really rather uniform' (62). 'There is a growing need to recognize the limitations of generalization', cautions Creangă (87). DiPalma demonstrates how counter-evidence can be adduced to argue the opposite of several of the generalizations (see also Creangă: 87-88), suggesting that all that may ultimately be claimed for commonly cited criteria of masculinity in the Hebrew Bible is that they 'are *some assumptions* about *some masculinities* in the Hebrew Bible' (DiPalma: 39, his emphasis).

And yet a kind of identikit profile of the ideal Israelite man does emerge nonetheless as one works through the essays. The fundamental logic of biblical masculinity, not surprisingly, turns out to be a binary logic: To be a man is not to be a woman. To state this prime negative directive a little differently, to be a man is to avoid feminization. In particular, this means not being identified *as* a woman. A man is a male who dresses as a man (Deut. 22.5; George: 72), and does not act like a woman (Haddox: 4). But neither should a man be identified *with* women. To be a man is to avoid unnecessary association with women, and even to avoid emotional attachment to women (Haddox: 4; cf. Clines 1995: 206; Clines in this volume: 57-59). Jacob's 'inordinate love of Rachel', on Haddox's reading, 'marks a diminishment of his masculinity' (11 in this volume). Conversely, David's apparent lack of emotional attachment to his many wives, on Clines's reading, is a mark of his masculinity (1995: 206). Related is Davis's argument that the 'objectification of women' in the prophetic literature, by means of imagery degrading to women, also plays a significant role in the construction of masculinity (165-66 in this volume). To be a man is to assert, or assume, the inferiority of women. Masculinity is disdain for femininity (cf. Clines 2002: 318, cited in Davis: 169). Davis writes of the 'militarized aggressiveness and contempt for women' characteristic of the construction of masculinity in Jeremiah (169).

For an ancient Near Eastern male to be a paragon of masculinity, however, militarized aggression also needed to be extended to fellow males. Violence and generalized aggression appear to have been 'cardinal traits' of ancient Near Eastern masculinity (Davis: 164; cf. Chapman 2004: 1-13; Brenner and

6. Cf. Clines in this volume: 46: 'masculinity *is* a performance, the performance of a learned script' (his emphasis).

van Dijk-Hemmes 1996: 12; Haddox 2006: 181). Not surprisingly, then, Clines finds that the 'fundamental characteristic' of a man in the Hebrew Bible 'is that he should be a fighter', which, being translated, means: 'capable of killing another man' (Clines: 46 in this volume; cf. Clines 1995: 216; Goldingay 1995: 39; Washington 1997: 326; DiPalma: 31 in this volume).[7] To be a consummate man, therefore, is to be a warrior, one skilled in weapons and warfare (Haddox: 5 in this volume; George: 60 in this volume; cf. Hoffner 1966: 337). To put this 'cardinal trait' in general terms, to be a man is to be capable of dominating others physically.

In elite Greco-Roman sources, domination of others and self-domination frequently go hand in hand—are, indeed, but two sides of the same coin.[8] What of the Hebrew Bible? The theme of masculine self-control does not appear to be a prominent one in the Hebrew Bible, but neither is it absent altogether. According to Deuteronomy, as George reads it, 'an Israelite male eats with self-control, both in terms of putting limits on what types of food he eats and drinks, as well as how much he consumes' (George in this volume: 58). George also writes of 'the self-control Israelite men are to show in battle.... Deuteronomy presents a code of conduct for Israelite men in battle, one in which self-control on the part of the army is required' (60). And it is not only in Deuteronomy that there are hints of the theme. Haddox argues that 'Jacob's control of himself and his family is impeded by his attachment to Rachel' (Haddox in this volume: 11). DiPalma, meanwhile, in the course of his account of Pharaoh's incremental emergence in Exod. 1.8-2.10 'as a thoroughly deconstructed and emasculated man' (DiPalma in this volume: 35), notes the hyperbolic rage implicitly attributed to Pharaoh (35). DiPalma does not construe this rage as one of the 'emasculating' traits, but he might have, as a failure in self-control.

More transparently bound up with the index of domination in the Hebrew Bible is a more prominent index of ancient Israelite masculinity than self-control—that of honor. 'It is all right to be violent and kill in defense of your masculine honour', as Lazarewicz-Wyrzykowska notes (152 in this volume, paraphrasing Exum 1993: 83). To be a man, then, is to possess honor and avoid shame (Haddox: 5 in this volume; cf. Stone 1996). And masculine honor in turn is defined by such traits as generosity, hospitality, honesty (being 'a man of one's word') and the ability to protect one's family, especially the chastity of one's women (Haddox: 5-6).

7.   Clines cites the example of Moses as illustrative of this principle (46-47), but DiPalma interestingly complicates that example (35-37).

8.   'Mastery—of others and/or of oneself—is the definitive masculine trait in most of the Greek and Latin literary and philosophical texts that survive from antiquity' (Moore and Anderson 1998: 249).

That Greco-Roman masculinity was a brittle, unstable quality, easily fractured or tarnished and hence in need of constant care and maintenance, is a recurrent theme in the work of classicists on masculinity (e.g., Winkler 1990: 49; Gleason 1995: 59, 81; Williams 1999: 141-42; Skinner 2005: 212, 248, 254). What of ancient Israelite masculinity? Lazarewicz-Wyrzykowska comes closest to sounding this theme: 'In this essay, I applied the anthropological understanding of masculine honour to engage with the model of masculinity represented by Samson. The sense of insecurity inherent in such a notion of honour is evidenced by the fact that the character's masculinity is constantly endangered...' (153 in this volume). One suspects that there is considerable potential in this concept of a constantly menaced masculinity for future studies of masculinity in the Hebrew Bible, as it is precisely the sort of masculinity that one would expect to find in an honor/shame society.

Also bound up with the masculine criterion of domination is the criterion of persuasion. '[P]ersuasive speech was in ancient Israel a typical mark of male behaviour' (Clines in this volume: 47; cf. Creangă in this volume: 78). More broadly, to be a man is to be wise and articulate and hence persuasive (cf. Haddox in this volume: 6; DiPalma in this volume: 31). But that is to put a benign spin on this mark of masculinity. Word and sword frequently change places. Creangă notes how '[i]n the portraits of Joshua...as well as within the Conquest Narrative more generally, domination through sword and/or word is the main feature of masculinity' (73 in this volume). But even when the words are not punctuated with the sword, the words can be expressions of the masculine imperative to dominate. Clines writes of 'the power of words...as instruments of control' and hence of 'the weapon of words' (48 in this volume; cf. Clines 2002: 314; Davis in this volume: 164).

The index of masculine honor is also bound up with a further index of manhood. 'Deuteronomy's representation of what it means to be a man in Israel is perhaps best encapsulated in the concern with having a name in Israel', argues George (56 in this volume). And having a name means having honor, 'living in the land with honor and living beyond death itself' by 'having sons who can carry on that name...'' (62). The case is similar for the Priestly material: 'the Priestly representation of masculinity is based largely upon perceptions of fertility and virility...' (Jacobs in this volume: 122). Intrinsic to this conception of masculinity is an 'ability to reproduce prolifically' (125). A man is a married male with offspring, then, most importantly sons (George in this volume: 61-62),[9] the role of husband being inseparable from that of father (cf. Creangă in this volume: 76). Joshua's and Samson's masculinities are anomalous in that neither of them are said to produce

---

9.   While a man is himself a legitimate son, and physically 'whole' (Deut. 23.1-2; George: 64, 67).

offspring (Creangă: 75-76; Lazarewicz-Wyrzykowska: 153). That we have not strayed far from the masculine criterion of domination is suggested by Creangă's phrasing of the problem: 'How can it be that Joshua could have a hard military phallus, but not a procreative penis?' (76). To be a man is to be sexually potent (Haddox in this volume: 5), but virility has its dark side. Potentially the Israelite man is a voracious, even predatory, sexual subject. George notes how in Deuteronomy captive women 'are deemed spoil to be plundered by Israelite males for their enjoyment (Deut. 20.14)' (George: 59).

   Talk of domination and predation puts one in mind of the active/passive antithesis beloved of analysts of Greco-Roman masculinities (e.g., Foucault 1985: 47; Halperin 1990: 33). Activity, in this sense, is but a synonym for the masculine imperative to dominate others—lesser males, all females, etc. Given that so many of the contributors to this volume link ancient Israelite masculinity with domination, it is surprising that Susan Haddox is the only one to invoke the active/passive antithesis. As emerges from her analysis of Abraham's, Isaac's and Jacob's masculinities, to be a man in Genesis is to be an active agent, to avoid being a passive pawn (Haddox: 7-9, 12; cf. Sawyer 2004: 169). The sexual ideology that such gender ideology yields is graphically expressed by Athalya Brenner: 'A "female" is sexed rather than gendered: she is an "orifice"; orifices and holes require that they be filled. A "male" is gendered:...a social agent. A female is there to be penetrated and to be receptive...' (Brenner 1997: 12, quoted in Davis in this volume: 167 n.29). In Greek and especially Roman antiquity, the hard/soft, dominant/submissive, penetrator/penetratee antithesis is a literary and philosophical commonplace, issuing in the masculine ideal that classicists have dubbed 'the impenetrable penetrator' (e.g., Walters 1997: 30-33; Williams 1999: 7). Is the true Israelite man also an impenetrable penetrator? Among the contributors to this volume, Creangă comes closest to suggesting as much. Of Joshua's defeat of the Canaanite kings he writes: 'In the end, the kings are unable to protect their bodies and their people, which is tantamount to being emasculated. Their failure illustrates the subordination of this type of men...and of this kind of body (penetrated by sword [Josh. 10.26], hanged and buried unceremoniously [Josh. 8.29; 10.27]) to the type of man and masculinity that rules successfully over others and maintains bodily integrity' (84).

   The more one brings the active/passive gender antithesis to bear on the Hebrew Bible, the more counterintuitive does Clines's isolation of beauty as a further important criterion of ancient Israelite masculinity seem to be. Clines's claim for this criterion is, indeed, broader than ancient Israel: 'Beauty is a masculine ideal in the ancient world', he writes; 'the evidence is unassailable' (50 in this volume). I would submit that the situation is more complex than that in Greek and Roman antiquity at least. In the philosophical and literary sources, male beauty tends to be the province of youths—youths who are looked at, desired, acted upon, mentored and formed by 'real' men who themselves are not ordinarily said to be beautiful.[10]

That being said, we should expect ancient Israelite models of masculinity to contain elements not found in Greco-Roman models of masculinity. A further criterion of masculinity suggested by Todd in this volume possibly falls into this category. 'Dreams would appear to contribute…to a number of narratives which set forth the character of some of Israel's heroic figures', writes Todd (178), later remarking on the 'positive masculine role model (of the dreaming leader)' (191). Furthermore, any grammar of ancient Israelite masculinity, as a structuralist or quasi-structuralist enterprise, can be expected to yield poststructuralist moments. To these we now turn, along with certain postcolonial moments in addition.

The Rise and Rise of the Non-Phallic Masculinities

'I suppose that study of masculinity in the Bible is to some extent still in the stage that feminist biblical criticism was at in the 1960s and 70s', remarks Clines, 'identifying and collecting the data, monitoring the language and the rhetoric of gendered discourse, and so on' (52 in this volume). I both agree and disagree. Certain researchers are certainly busy with such activities, not least in the present volume. Parallel with that positivist sensibility, however—and frequently intersecting with and complicating it—is what, for want of a better term, we might call a 'poststructuralist' sensibility, one also very much in evidence in the volume. It comes to expression, for instance, in the following assertion by DiPalma: 'While the text [Exod. 1–4] relies upon assumptions about masculinity to deconstruct the power of Pharaoh, it also deconstructs the masculine values themselves and subtly begins to construct a reconfig-ured, if not yet fully formed, gendered identity for Moses' (42). It also comes to expression in Creangă's acute attention to destabilizing complications: 'Joshua's hegemony is tightly woven around specific models of gender behav-ior and male sexual identity found throughout biblical and ancient Near East-ern literature, but, as I want to argue, these are destabilized by ambiguity and the absence of key masculine traits' (70).

Intriguingly, however, the principal source in the volume of deconstructive destabilization, complication and contradiction is none other than God. To begin with, 'Israelite males [in Deuteronomy] are the vassals of Yhwh. They

10. The chapter 'Beauty' in Johnson and Ryan's *Sexuality in Greek and Roman Society and Literature*, for instance, notes at the outset: 'In same-sex love scenarios, the adult male was aroused primarily by youthful beauty, revealed in the multiple references to smoothness of skin and beardlessness' (2005: 38). But they also note that male heroes in epic and martial poetry are regularly 'idealized as beautiful in accordance with their embodiment of an intense masculinity' (38).

once were slaves to Pharaoh in Egypt, but now they are slaves (servants) of Yhwh' (George: 66; cf. Creangă: 84). But Yhwh is a slave master who demands unequivocal worship, and the worship of whom is a mark of Israelite manhood, and not only in Deuteronomy. The essential trait of Deuteronomistic masculinity, as articulated by Strimple and Creangă (102), is worship of Yhwh alone. God is a spanner in the workings of hegemonic masculinity in the Hebrew Bible. Writing of the anomalous masculine performances encoded in Genesis, Haddox remarks: 'Submission to anyone, even a deity, is not part of the standard construction of masculinity...' (13). As such, she reads the 'subordinate masculinities' of Abraham and especially Isaac and Jacob as an implicit critique of 'hegemonic masculinity as the way to approach God' (13).

This leads in turn, however, to another significant theme that also runs through several of the essays. Haddox argues that 'the subordinate masculinities of the patriarchs in many ways reflect the position of Israel among the nations.... When the nation acted according to the norms of hegemonic masculinity, thinking it was powerful, it was crushed by nations in a position of real strength.... These subordinate masculinities offer the nation of Israel strategies for survival' (13-14). Eventually, I would add, such gendered survival strategies will yield a text such as *4 Maccabees*, in which the gruesomely tortured Jewish martyrs become icons of masculine power redefined as an affair of the will, which need have no recourse whatsoever to physical superiority. This redefinition happens to be consonant with the political circumstances of the subordinate, colonized community to which the book is addressed. As such, *4 Maccabees* presents us with a Hellenistic Jewish version of Greco-Roman masculinity thoroughly tailored to the experience of imperial oppression (Moore and Anderson 1998).

The theme of subordinate masculinities as strategies of national survival that Haddox insightfully identifies might be brought into sharper relief if focused through the lens of postcolonial theory and even of contemporary postcolonial literatures. A defining characteristic of such literatures, it has been argued (although not without controversy), is the presence within them of 'national allegories', in which literary representations of individual colonial subjects stand in allegorically for the histories and destinies of entire colonized peoples.[11] Compare Creangă on the shifting representations of Joshua: 'The fashioning of Joshua's body in each portrait (warrior, student of the Law) is a projection of, and for, the social body and the body politic of Israel in each...historical [period] (pre-exilic and exilic/postexilic)' (85 in this volume). Davis makes parallel claims for the construction of Jeremiah's complex masculinity:

11. For the beginnings of the debate on national allegories, see Jameson 1986; Ahmad 1987; Slemon 1987.

if the prophet Jeremiah had a 'feminine side' it was most likely not projected from his own persona, but was rather a reflection—or more properly a *refraction*—of the situation of the Jewish people.... Jeremiah becomes a figure upon which the future nation constructs its own cultic and political hopes, as well as its own sense of remorse and martyrdom (170-71 in this volume, his emphasis).

The construction of masculinity as national allegory also comes to expression in Jacobs's analysis of rabbinic masculinity—a masculinity now so thoroughly trodden under the weight of successive imperialisms as to acquire more extreme and more exquisite forms: 'the rabbinic sages—having faced the loss of the Second Temple and the failure of both the Hasmonean and Herodian dynasties, and also having experienced the reality of direct Roman rule in Judea—reconfigured their ultimate, ideal, representation of masculinity to include singularly more than the benefits of fertility and sexual virility, idealized in Priestly tradition' (136 in this volume). For the sages, ideal masculinity resides in 'being the chosen object of divine desire' (122), such desire, specifically, being for 'the circumcised Jewish male' who is 'the chosen human partner for the symbolic consummation of divine love' (137). The queered masculinity already implicit in the patriarchal narratives that Haddox analyzes has now fully flowered. Here, too, the beauty that Clines attributes to every true Israelite man unproblematically finds its place. The rabbinic sage passively and willingly adopts a 'feminine' subject position in relation to the infatuated gaze of the most dominant male in the universe, the hegemonically hypermasculine God of Israel.[12] Yet even hegemony is 'inherently uncertain and shaky', as Boer reminds us (19 in this volume). And so even the masculinity of Yhwh (curiously underexamined in this volume) can be expected to exhibit fractures and fissures if examined closely enough—not in response to yet more potent hegemonic forces, however, but rather in response to its own inevitable internal contradictions and incoherencies, which are those of ancient Near Eastern masculinity writ large.

Bibliography

Adams, Rachel, and David Savran (eds.)
    2002   *The Masculinity Studies Reader* (Oxford: Blackwell).
Ahmad, Aijaz
    1987   'Jameson's Rhetoric of Otherness and the "National Allegory"', *Social Text* 17: 3-25.
Boer, Roland
    2006   '1 and 2 Chronicles', in Deryn Guest, Robert E. Goss, Mona West and

---

12. I have examined this fascinating phenomenon at length elsewhere (Moore 2001: 29-39).

Thomas Bohache (eds.), *The Queer Bible Commentary* (London: SCM Press): 251-67.

Brenner, Athalya
1997   *The Intercourse of Knowledge: On Gendering Desire and 'Sexuality' in the Hebrew Bible* (BIS, 26; Leiden: Brill).

Brenner, Athalya, and Fokkelien van Dijk-Hemmes
1996   *On Gendering Texts: Female and Male Voices in the Hebrew Bible* (BIS, 1; Leiden: Brill).

Chapman, Cynthia R.
2004   *The Gendered Language of Warfare in the Israelite–Assyrian Encounter* (HSM, 62; Winona Lake, IN: Eisenbrauns).

Clines, David J. A.
1995   'David the Man: The Construction of Masculinity in the Hebrew Bible', in his *Interested Parties: The Ideology of Writers and Readers of the Hebrew Bible* (JSOTSup, 205; GCT, 1; Sheffield: Sheffield Academic Press): 212-43.
2002   'He-Prophets: Masculinity as a Problem for the Hebrew Prophets and their Interpreters', in Alastair G. Hunter and Philip R. Davies (eds.), *Sense and Sensitivity: Essays on Reading the Bible in Memory of Robert Carroll* (JSOTSup, 348; Sheffield: Sheffield Academic Press): 311-28.
2003   'Paul, the Invisible Man', in Moore and Anderson 2003: 181-92.

Conway, Colleen M.
2008   *Behold the Man: Jesus and Greco-Roman Masculinity* (Oxford: Oxford University Press).

Edwards, Tim
2006   *Cultures of Masculinity* (New York: Routledge).

Eilberg-Schwartz, Howard
1994   *God's Phallus and Other Problems for Men and Monotheism* (Boston: Beacon Press).

Exum, J. Cheryl
1993   *Fragmented Women: Feminist (Sub)versions of Biblical Narratives* (JSOTSup, 163; Sheffield: JSOT Press).

Foucault, Michel
1985   *The History of Sexuality*; Vol. 2: *The Use of Pleasure* (trans. Robert Hurley; New York: Random House).
1986   *The History of Sexuality*; Vol. 3: *The Care of the Self* (trans. Robert Hurley; New York: Random House).

Gardiner, Judith Kegan (ed.)
2002   *Masculinity Studies and Feminist Theory: New Directions* (New York: Columbia University Press).

Gleason, Maud W.
1995   *Making Men: Sophists and Self-Representation in Ancient Rome* (Princeton, NJ: Princeton University Press).

Goldingay, John
1995   'Hosea 1–3, Genesis 1–4, and Masculinist Interpretation', *HBT* 17: 37-44.

Haddox, Susan E.
2006   '(E)Masculinity in Hosea's Political Rhetoric', in Brad E. Kelle and Megan Bishop Moore (eds.), *Israel's Prophets and Israel's Past* (New York: T. & T. Clark International): 174-200.

Halperin, David M.
    1990   *One Hundred Years of Homosexuality: And Other Essays on Greek Love*
             (New Ancient World; New York: Routledge).
Hoffner, Harry A., Jr
    1966   'Symbols for Masculinity and Femininity: Their Use in Ancient Near
             Eastern Sympathetic Magic Rituals', *JBL* 85: 326-34.
Jameson, Fredric
    1986   'Third World Literature in the Era of Multinational Capitalism', *Social
             Text* 15: 65-88.
Johnson, Marguerite, and Terry Ryan
    2005   *Sexuality in Greek and Roman Society and Literature: A Sourcebook* (New
             York: Routledge).
Krondorfer, Björn
    2009   'Introduction', in Björn Krondorfer (ed.), *Men and Masculinities in
             Christianity and Judaism: A Critical Reader* (London: SCM Press): xi-xxi.
Modleski, Tania
    1991   *Feminism without Women: Culture and Criticism in a 'Postfeminist' Age*
             (New York: Routledge).
Moore, Stephen D.
    1996   *God's Gym: Divine Male Bodies of the Bible* (New York: Routledge).
    2001   *God's Beauty Parlor: And Other Queer Spaces in and around the Bible*
             (Contraversions: Jews and Other Differences; Stanford, CA: Stanford
             University Press).
    2003   '"O Man, Who Art Thou...?" Masculinity Studies and New Testament
             Studies', in Moore and Anderson 2003: 1-22.
Moore, Stephen D., and Janice Capel Anderson
    1998   'Taking It like a Man: Masculinity in 4 Maccabees', *JBL* 117: 249-73.
Moore, Stephen D., and Janice Capel Anderson (eds.)
    2003   *New Testament Masculinities* (SemeiaSt, 45; Atlanta: Society of Biblical
             Literature).
Murphy, Peter F. (ed.)
    2004   *Feminism and Masculinities* (Oxford Readings in Feminism; Oxford:
             Oxford University Press).
Olyan, Saul M.
    1997   '"And with a male you shall not lie the lying down of a woman": On the
             Meaning and Significance of Leviticus 18:22 and 20:13', in Gary David
             Comstock and Susan E. Henking (eds.), *Que(e)rying Religion: A Critical
             Anthology* (New York: Continuum): 398-414. Originally published in
             Journal of the History of Sexuality 5 (1994): 179-206.
Piper, John, and Wayne Grudem (eds.)
    2006   *Recovering Biblical Manhood and Womanhood: A Response to Evan-
             gelical Feminism* (2nd edn; Wheaton, IL: Crossway Books).
Reeser, Todd W.
    2010   *Masculinities in Theory: An Introduction* (Oxford: Wiley–Blackwell).
Sawyer, Deborah F.
    2004   'Biblical Gender Strategies: The Case of Abraham's Masculinity', in
             Ursula King and Tina Beattie (eds.), *Gender, Religion, and Diversity:
             Cross-Cultural Perspectives* (New York: Continuum): 162-71.

Schüssler Fiorenza, Elizabeth
   1983   *In Memory of Her: A Feminist Theological Reconstruction of Christian Origins* (New York: Crossroad).
Sedgwick, Eve Kosofsky
   1985   *Between Men: English Literature and Male Homosocial Desire* (New York: Columbia University Press; 2nd edn, 1992).
Skinner, Marilyn B.
   2005   *Sexuality in Greek and Roman Culture* (Ancient Cultures; Oxford: Blackwell).
Slemon, Stephen
   1987   'Monuments of Empire: Allegory/Counter-Discourse/Post-Colonial Writing', *Kunapipi* 9: 1-16.
Spivak, Gayatri Chakravorty
   1985a   'Can the Subaltern Speak? Speculations on Widow Sacrifice," *Wedge* 7/8: 120-130. Reprinted and expanded as 'Can the Subaltern Speak?', in Cary Nelson and Larry Grossberg (eds.), *Marxism and the Interpretation of Culture* (Urbana, IL: University of Illinois Press, 1988): 271-313.
   1985b   'Three Women's Texts and a Critique of Imperialism', *Critical Inquiry* 12: 243-61.
Stone, Ken
   1996   *Sex, Honor, and Power in the Deuteronomistic History* (JSOTSup, 234; Sheffield: Sheffield Academic Press).
Trible, Phyllis
   1978   *God and the Rhetoric of Sexuality* (Overtures to Biblical Theology; Philadelphia: Fortress Press).
   1984   *Texts of Terror: Literary-Feminist Readings of Biblical Narratives* (Overtures to Biblical Theology; Philadelphia: Fortress Press).
Walters, Jonathan
   1997   'Invading the Roman Body: Manliness and Impenetrability in Roman Thought', in Judith P. Hallett and Marilyn B. Skinner (eds.), *Roman Sexualities* (Princeton, NJ: Princeton University Press): 29-43.
Washington, Harold C.
   1997   'Violence and the Construction of Gender in the Hebrew Bible: A New Historicist Approach', *BibInt* 5: 324-63.
Williams, Craig A.
   1999   *Roman Homosexuality: Ideologies of Masculinity in Classical Antiquity* (Oxford University Press; 2nd edn, 2010).
Winkler, John J.
   1990   *The Constraints of Desire: The Anthropology of Sex and Gender in Ancient Greece* (New Ancient World; New York: Routledge).

INDEXES

INDEX OF ANCIENT SOURCES

OTHER ANCIENT SOURCES

INDEX OF SUBJECTS

INDEX OF AUTHORS

Gordon, R. 101
Gramsci, A. 20, 21, 22
Gray, J. 84, 92
Green, A. 160
Greenspahn, F.E. 8
Groneberg, B. 154
Grudem, W. 241
Gordis, R. 61

Haas, C. 135, 136
Haddox, S.E. 8, 16, 101, 113, 189, 196,
198, 234, 246, 247, 248, 249, 250
Hall, R.G. 164
Halperin, D.M. 98, 249
Hamilton, V. 150, 155
Hamlin, E.J. 96
Haralambakis, M. 139, 237, 243
Hardt, M. 22
Harrington, D.J. 92
Hayes, J.H. 13
Hawk, L.D. 89, 102
Hearn, J. 87, 95, 130
Hendriks, H.J. 5
Hentrich, T. 112
Heritage, J.C. 218, 220
Herzfeld, M. 5, 172
Hess, R.S. 100
Hillers, D.R. 147, 190, 191, 205
Hirsch, E.G. 90, 92
Hoffman, L. 150, 151, 153, 157
Hoffner, H.A. 36, 37, 92, 100, 146, 147, 184, 244, 247
Holladay, W.L. 190, 195, 196, 202, 203
Holm-Nielsen, S. 190
Hooper, C. 21
Horbury, W. 153
Horowitz, E. 91
Horst, P. van der 127, 128
Hutchings, K. 87
Hyatt, J.P. 56, 59

Jacobs, S. 148, 237, 248, 252
Jaffee, M.S. 98
Japhet, S. 20, 193

Jarick, J. 20
Jefferson, G. 216
Jameson, F. 251
Jennings, T.W., Jr 87, 98
Johnson, M. 250

Kaufman, M. 127
Kelle, B.E. 5
Kelso, J. 20, 24, 25
Kim, S.H. 171
Kimmel, M.S. 128, 130, 136
Kirkegaard, B.A. 137
Klawans, J. 69
Klein, L.R. 129
Klein, R.W. 192
Kline Silverman, E. 155
Knoppers, G.N. 20, 191, 192
Koehler, L. 71
Kohler, K. 138, 139
Kraft, R.A. 129
Kraus, H.-J. 190
Krondorfer, B. 240
Kuan, J.K. 6
Kugler, R.A. 131

Labahn, A. 24
Lake, K. 54
Landy, F. 15
Lapsley, J. 36, 37, 40, 44, 46, 47, 48, 50
Larson, J. 13
LaValley, A. 26
Laukewish, V.A. 91
Lazarewicz-Wyrzykowska, E. 177, 237, 243, 247, 248, 249
Lee, J. 3
Legaspi, M.C. 132
Leick, G. 147
Leslie, E.A. 202
Levinson, B.M. 65
Lindisfarne, N. 3, 13, 86
Lipton, D. 148, 179
Lohfink, N. 89
Löhr, M. 191
Long, B.O. 110
Lundbom, J.R. 196

Machinist, P. 130
Macwilliam, S. 88
Majors, R. 133
Malamat, A. 103
Mangan, C. 130
Matthews, V.H. 13
McConville, J.G. 194
McKenzie, S.L. 20, 115
Mehan, H. 212
Melamed, Z.E. 154
Melcher, S.J.
Messerschmidt, J.W. 86
Meyer, M. 26
Michasiw, K. 26
Milgrom, J. 69, 154, 159
Miller, A.S. 112
Miller, G.P. 4
Miller, J. M. 13, 115
Miller, P.D. 66
Miller, T. 88, 97
Mishler, E.G. 112
Mitchell, D. 122, 123
Mitchell, G. 102
Moberly, R.W.L. 57, 193, 194, 205
Mobley, G. 178, 184
Modleski, T. 242, 243
Monroe, L.A.S. 67
Moore, G.F. 175, 176
Moore, S.D. 23, 87, 99, 136, 162,
    171, 241, 242, 245, 247, 251, 252
Moore, M.S. 190
Morgan, D.H.J. 136
Murphy, P.F. 242

Najcevska, M. 43
Negri, A. 20, 22
Nelson, R.D. 67, 71, 73, 84, 89, 92,
    110
Nicholls, P.H. 129, 138
Niditch, S. 11, 12, 14 172, 174, 175,
    176, 177, 178, 179, 180, 182, 183
Noegel, S. 213
Noth, M. 59, 84, 91, 115, 116

Olson, D.T. 2, 36, 37, 43, 44, 47, 88,
    113

Olyan, S.M. 13, 69, 112, 113, 115,
    153, 194, 196, 203, 245
Ogden, G. 61
Oppenheim, A.L. 213
Otto, S. 115

Pardes, I. 36, 50
Parke-Taylor, G.H. 205
Parpola, S. 5, 6
Passamaneck, S.M. 160
Paul, S. 148
Peristiany, J.G. 172, 173
Pick, B. 90, 92
Pilch, J.J. 110
Piper, J. 241
Pitt-Rivers, J. 172, 173
Polaski, D. 87
Poliva, J. 143
Polk, T. 205
Porter, J.R. 89
Pritchard, J.B. 99
Provan, I.W. 110

Quisumbing, L.R. 43

Rabello, A.M. 164
Rad, G. von 10
Raphael, R. 114
Rashi 92
Reeser, T.W. 242
Reinhard, I. 222, 223
Robertson, P. 26
Rofé, A. 83
Rohrbaugh, R.L. 131
Römer, T. 83, 91
Rooke, D.W. 88
Rowlett, L.L. 89, 96, 102, 177, 183
Ryan, R.J. 175
Ryan, T. 250

Sacks, H. 216, 220
Saldarini, A.J. 92
Sarangi, S. 212
Sarna, N.M. 150, 153, 154
Satlow, M.L. 98, 158
Satterthwaite, P.E. 116

CPSIA information can be obtained at www.ICGtesting.com
Printed in the USA
235730LV00003B/69/P

9 781907 534096